Justice on the Job

Justice on the Job

RESOLVING GRIEVANCES IN THE NONUNION WORKPLACE

David W. Ewing

Harvard Business School Press
Boston, Massachusetts

The paper used in this publication meets the requirements
of the American National Standard for Permanence of Paper
for Printed Library Materials Z39.48–1984.

Harvard Business School Press, Boston 02163

93 92 91 90 89   5 4 3 2 1

Library of Congress Cataloging-in-Publication Data

Ewing, David W.
    Justice on the job : resolving grievances in nonunion workplace /
David W. Ewing.
      p.   cm.
    Includes index.
    ISBN 0-87584-217-8 (alk. paper)
      1. Grievance procedures—United States—Case studies.
    2. Grievance arbitration—United States—Case studies.   3. Grievance
procedures—United States.   4. Grievance arbitration—United States.
    I. Title.
HF5549.5.G7E95   1989
331.88'96—dc20   89-36083
                                                            CIP

CONTENTS

Preface

The research on which this book is based began in January 1986, ended in December 1988, and was funded by the Harvard Business School. I began by reading everything on the subject that seemed relevant, including a number of legal treatises and cases. Drawing on contacts and the many excellent directories at the School, I then began writing companies, telling them of my interest and requesting the opportunity to interview a selected number of their people if they had a nonunion grievance procedure meeting my tests. Altogether, I wrote and/or phoned several hundred companies. Most of the companies were "people-minded," yet the great majority indicated they did not have the kind of procedure I was interested in. It appears that very few companies in this country—possibly as few as thirty to fifty—have had effective grievance procedures in place for several years or more. A great many companies have what is called an "open door," meaning the right of an aggrieved employee to go up the line from one boss to another, but for reasons to be mentioned later, that sort of procedure does not pass the tests.

In selecting subjects for study, I excluded companies that had only a year or two of experience with their procedure. Certainly many of these corporate procedures will prove out; indeed, some were quite impressive as described. For the purposes of this study, however, it seemed wise to limit the purview to companies that had at least four years of experience with their system. This restriction allowed a focus on problems in operation as well as revisions made on the basis of experience.

In addition, I ruled out any company that could not assure me that decisions went against defending managers as well as for them, and any company that was unwilling to talk about management reversals as well as decisions sustaining management. However, I did not rule out a candidate simply because its procedure was informal or thinly staffed. Such a procedure leaves something to be desired in offering effective complaint resolution for all employees of an organization, but for this study it provides more variety and makes more comparisons possible.

The net result of applying these criteria was the selection of fourteen companies, from Bank of America in San Francisco to SmithKline Beckman in Philadelphia, as the subjects of personal interviews. Another company, TWA, was added on the basis of a fine write-up by a former executive and a brief correspondence with management.

All the companies chosen for interviews made schedules of people for me to see. In one case, the interviews were conducted over a period of a couple of months, but in most cases the interviews were scheduled tightly over a period of one or two days. All interviews were tape recorded, and most took close to an hour to complete. After transcribing the tapes from a visit and putting the material together, often with supplementary data from other sources, I sent the write-up to the company for corrections and approval. All write-ups were released for publication in this book. The only exception to this procedure was TWA, where I used secondary sources.

As for the plan of the book, Part I contains my analysis of the data; Part II, each company's write-ups as released by management. In Part I, Chapter 1 defines the subject and terms (for a more complete listing of definitions, see the Glossary), outlines briefly the benefits of what I shall call corporate due process, and then lists the reasons that this approach succeeds as it does. Chapter 1 also lists the assumptions that guided me in the study.

In Chapter 2 I examine the genesis and evolution of corporate due process—sixteen trends and forces that have pushed it up and into visibility on the corporate landscape, like an outcropping of rock. This is the only chapter in the volume that is not mostly clinical and is based only in part on observation and testing. The conclusion of this chapter is that the development of nonunion grievance procedures is no will-o'-the-wisp and will not go away; such procedures are going to spread through the economy and affect every organization.

Chapter 3 proposes some tests of a nonunion grievance procedure. What separates real corporate due process from sham procedures or unworkable approaches? About a dozen such tests are described, all based on the experience of the fifteen companies in the study. This chapter gives an idea of what an organization will be getting into if it decides to establish a good nonunion grievance procedure; the tests should also help interested readers to evaluate other companies' systems.

Chapter 4 is for corporate policymakers. What major issues arise when an organization sets up a nonunion grievance procedure? Top management's commitment to the idea, the strength of the human resources department as a kind of infrastructure for the procedure, the purpose in establishing a system—these and other questions are significant and will affect the outcome in many ways. My attempt in these pages is to epitomize the experience of other companies and save readers contemplating such a system from some of the wheel-spinning and turnabouts that might be necessary without such experience.

Chapter 5 poses a series of questions for administrators and planners—from the details of choosing an investigator or selecting board members to record keeping and drawing up provisions for company policy. Here, again, the experience of the fifteen companies can teach a lot about what and what not to do.

In Chapter 6, I look at some of the shortcomings, limitations, and drawbacks of corporate due process as well as various alternatives that managers often consider. The system is not a panacea, and it is as subject as any management system to foibles and human error. All in all, however, it represents a net gain for the organization that seeks to stay union-free, wishes to reduce litigation costs, seeks maximum compliance with personnel policy, and in general, wants to do the right thing by employees.

Chapter 7 presents some conclusions about corporate due process. I have tried to distill some of the "corporate common law" that appears to be emerging from the procedures observed. Here, too, is an attempt to put this approach in perspective and relate it to long-held American ideals concerning equity and fair play.

Part II consists of write-ups of companies studied. Investigator-adjudicator systems are set apart from board-type systems. Within each category the write-ups are arranged by alphabetical order of the companies. If you are considering incorporating a procedure and have some notion of what kind of system might be desirable for your organization, turn to one or more of these write-ups. The short introduction will give you a glimpse of the more detailed description that follows so you will not have to waste time finding a company with the kind of system you are interested in. In addition, you may find one or more company write-ups useful for purposes of planning and training.

I am grateful to the administration of the Harvard Business School for its unstinting support of this study. The word processing department speedily and efficiently typed all drafts of the manuscript as well as hundreds of letters. The conclusions, of course, are my own and do not necessarily reflect the views of the Harvard Business School faculty or the administration.

I am grateful to Mary P. Rowe, Eliza C. Collins, Christopher A. Barreca, and others for their very helpful and constructive comments on early drafts of the manuscript.

Winchester, Massachusetts   David W. Ewing
April 1989

PART

I

Analysis and Recommendations

I

The Promise of Corporate
Due Process

The job of the U.S. corporation is to produce and market goods and services efficiently and at a profit, not dispense justice. However, a company is a type of society, its management a type of government, and managements that manage justly, as employees see justness, gain potent advantages over managements that do not.

In this book I focus on a significant new trend in U.S. industry: the development of in-company mechanisms and procedures for resolving employee disputes fairly, promptly, and inexpensively without a union. As we shall see, such approaches are significantly different from grievance procedures under collective bargaining agreements. The nonunion approaches owe a lot to the arbitration experience, but in concept as well as execution they reflect a manner of thinking that is new on the American business scene.

Only a tiny minority of corporations have mechanisms for ensuring employee justice today. However, this minority is growing by leaps and bounds, and it seems safe to predict that the time is not far off when a majority of sizable corporations will have systems like those of the companies described in Part II. When that happens, many more millions of employees will be covered by nonunion grievance procedures than by union procedures. Notions of justice and equity will have taken a quantum leap forward, evolving, maturing, passing back and forth between businesses and the community as easily as people and goods do.

It is difficult to foretell what the effect on American productivity and competitiveness will be. We know that efficiency cannot be isolated and managed apart from the quality of life in an organization. The two affect each other in subtle ways, and so far as we know, there is no way of telling that such and such an improvement in the quality of life (itself an amorphous term) will lead to such and such an improvement in efficiency and

3

productivity. It can only be said that managers in companies with procedures to ensure employee justice have gut feelings that the work environment is better, and the organization more competitive, as a result.

Both visible and invisible effects were cited by the managers interviewed
for this book. The visible effects have mostly to do with the observation that
employees who use effective complaint resolution procedures leave with the
feeling that, win or lose, they had their day in court. That is a salubrious
result. The invisible effects concern far larger numbers of employees, both
supervisors and subordinates, who know that an effective grievance
procedure is available to be used *if necessary*. The effect of this belief is
extraordinary.

The Meaning of Corporate Due Process

I shall use the term *corporate due process* to describe effective mechanisms
and procedures for ensuring equity and justice among employees. For one
thing, the term is in use in some of the companies studied. For another, it is
a useful extension of the term we have come to know so well in legal and
community life.

In the Fifth and Fourteenth amendments to the Constitution, U.S. citi-
zens are protected against deprivation of life, liberty, and property without
due process of law. The Fifth Amendment applies to the federal government; the Fourteenth, to state governments. The nature of due process has
evolved continuously in the courts for more than two centuries, and it
refers, generally speaking, to all the acts from the beginning of a legal action
to its end that have to do with an individual's right to a fair legal proceeding. A fair arraignment, application of understandable and accessible laws,
rules of evidence, the right to confront one's accuser—all these and many
other notions are part of the meaning of the concept.

Although corporate due process is a far more primitive set of standards
than due process of law—and in fact involves no law at all, only corporate
policy—it springs from the same basic notion of equity. In effect, the
corporation says that no employee should be deprived of his or her job and
well-being in the company without a fair hearing. In a number of companies today, standards of corporate due process are being forged case by
case just as they were years ago in the legal arena. Later in this volume I will
look at these standards.

Corporate due process can take many forms. In some companies it takes
the form of a panel, board, committee, or other tribunal that considers both
sides of a complaint and renders a decision. In other companies, it takes the
form of objective investigators who look into both sides of a complaint and
resolve it. Whatever the form, corporate due process implies that the board
or investigators can (1) get the facts on both sides, (2) exercise independent
judgment and decide or recommend for or against the complaining em-

ployee depending on their evaluation of the evidence, and (3) get corrective action taken if necessary.

To illustrate, let me give a few brief examples of what due process is and is not:

> At a manufacturing company, an employee is given an official warning for violating a safety rule. Going before the company's nonunion grievance board, the employee claims that the warning was unfair. After hearing testimony from the employee, the manager, and any others it wishes to call, the board decides that the warning will or will not stand. This is an instance of corporate due process.

> At a bank, an employee finds that damaging criticisms have been put into his personnel file without his knowledge. Believing that the act runs counter to the bank's personnel policy, the employee calls on an objective investigator to remove the damaging criticisms. After studying both sides of the argument, the investigator makes a decision based on the merits. If necessary, the investigator will get the decision implemented by a senior executive. This, too, is an example of due process.

> If in the foregoing case the investigator can only mediate, hoping to get the parties to agree on a settlement but unable to use more than persuasion, the example is not an instance of due process because the investigator does not render an enforceable decision.

> At a retail store an employee is suspended for violating a dress code. The employee pleads unsuccessfully with her boss, then goes to the boss's boss, and so on up the line. No neutral, independent party is available to hear and decide on the complaint. This is not an example of due process, even if the employee gets her way, because the hearing parties are not neutral and independent.

> If the same employee calls a company hot line to complain of harassment, the example does not constitute due process. A hot line can inform the employee of her rights, and perhaps it can alert someone who does have power to correct wrongs, such as the company legal department, but by itself it cannot adjudicate. The same goes for group meetings at which employees let their hair down and sound off to managers about what is wrong. Though the senior manager can point to an assistant and say "Look into that," there is no guarantee that the assistant will do so impartially.

> If an employee can go to someone in the personnel department and scream about a wrong perpetrated but the personnel official has no authority to dig for the facts on both sides of the complaint and render a decision, the example does not constitute due process.

In short, the term *corporate due process* as used in this book means that which is due a complaining employee in the light of contemporary standards and ideas of fairness. "That which is due" includes a timely, accessible, and inexpensive process; the right to be represented by another employee of the complainant's choice (though rarely an outside attorney); the right to present evidence and rebut charges made by the other side; as much privacy

EXHIBIT 1-1

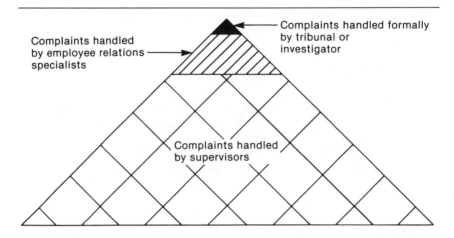

and confidentiality as is practicable; a fair and impartial fact-finding process and hearing; a decision that is objective and reasonable plus corrective action if such is called for; and freedom from retaliation for using the procedure. These and other elements are spelled out in Chapter 3.

In an organization with corporate due process, the great majority of complaints are handled informally by employee relations people, supervisors, and managers, not by the formal appeal procedure. The formal channel is very important, however. Its presence adds strength, credibility, and trust to the informal channels; moreover, cases that can't be handled informally are often significant. Thus, the term *corporate due process* refers to a *system* for complaint resolution. Exhibit 1-1 presents a conceptual scheme of such a system.

What Can Due Process Do for Management?

Here are the results most prominently mentioned by the managers and nonmanagers interviewed in this study:

First, if you want your management to develop a relationship of mutual trust and respect with employees, due process is a valuable and powerful means. It enables you to go beyond words and exhortations, demonstrate your willingness to listen objectively to complaints of unfair treatment, and act on the basis of facts and evidence. Due process won't turn the trick by itself, but in suitable combination with other measures, it can enable you to create the desired relationship.

Although evidence for this finding tends to be tricky and "soft," supporting facts appear in the company write-ups:

- Donnelly Corporation's due process system is one of many features giving the company the reputation of being a good place to work. Donnelly rarely

advertises openings for new employees. If word is let out to employees on Friday afternoon, it goes around town so fast that applicants for the opening can be found waiting in the parking lot early Monday morning.
- Several companies in this study periodically conduct attitude surveys of employees. They try to gauge changes in employees' feelings about the company, supervisors, trust or cynicism in relationships, power to take action about a grievance, and so on. Sometimes directly, sometimes indirectly, the survey results make a convincing case for the value of the complaint resolution procedures. Bank of America, Citicorp, and Federal Express are prominent examples.

Second, corporate due process is a good way to hold unions at bay. At every company where I interviewed, managers cited it as a valuable and proven defense. In fact, in some companies studied, the concept was not seriously supported until after a union scare. Said one executive, tipping back in his chair and folding his hands, "What can a union promise employees that we don't already have? Not more pay—we're competitive with other companies. Besides, we can't stay in business if we pay more. Not better working conditions and fringes—those are good here. What a union *used* to be able to promise was more equity. 'You can't stand up for your rights against management without a union.' But they can't promise that anymore, now that we have a good procedure in place."

Here is more evidence of the effects of corporate due process:

- General Electric's range plant in Columbia, Maryland, installed an effective hearing system during the height of union attempts to organize workers. After workers became convinced that the system was for real and that management was going all-out on their behalf, the union threat receded. Today, it is almost nonexistent.
- Several companies in this study have collective bargaining agreements for a portion of their work forces. Since installation of grievance procedures for nonunion employees, the union has been effectively contained and has not widened its control.
- Northrop actually decertified one union, partly because of the good word-of-mouth reputation of its nonunion grievance procedure. (The union had organized a company before Northrop bought the firm a few years ago.)

Third, corporate due process helps to reduce litigation and litigation expense from lawsuits filed by former employees. Although a good procedure does not eliminate lawsuits, it often cuts down many would-be suers at the knees. One reason is that many attorneys, some courts, and a number of state employment agencies give weight to the verdict of a corporate hearing procedure. For instance, one executive of a leading due process company told me: "In discrimination suits, our procedure is often recognized by the courts as a valid testing of complaints. If the employee used it, the court will subpoena our reports and use them. The procedure has been a plus much of the time."

Another reason why due process helps to reduce litigation is that it often takes the wind out of employee objectors' sails. No matter how wrong they think the judgments of the board or ombudspersons who considered their claims, they may stop imagining that their arguments are compelling and see their complaints realistically.

Factual evidence to support this inclusion is hard to come by. The yearly trend in lawsuits by employees and recent employees is a poor gauge because the trend reflects many things besides satisfaction or dissatisfaction with the in-house procedure. Comparisons of companies with and without due process are similarly tricky. To what extent is a company's grievance procedure rather than other factors responsible for a difference? However, one piece of evidence is suggestive. On the basis of confidential data from three pairs of companies with roughly similar work forces, one company in each pair having a nonunion procedure that qualifies as due process and the other having none, I find an enormous difference in number of lawsuits in favor of the former—an average differential of 11 : 1. The pairings were in the communications, financial services, and manufacturing industries.

Fourth, many managers find that due process ensures greater compliance with the company's personnel policies. Ann G. Liebowitz, senior legal counsel for Polaroid, made the following statement in an address to the New England Labor Council:

> A working grievance procedure is an effective means of assuring that decisions made by line supervisors meet company expectations of employee relations. The fact that they are held accountable by having their actions and decisions subject to open review and debate has an astonishingly strong tendency to keep them "honest" and prevent abuse of discretion.[1]

Gwen Lerner, an attorney for Control Data, spoke as follows about the values of the company's review board system:

> The review board system encourages management to think twice about arbitrary actions. Review boards help to ensure proper use of management discretion and fair treatment of employees. And they allow problems in policies and practices to be found and fixed quietly, without the cost and negative publicity of a prolonged legal battle.[2]

Fifth, a good complaint procedure puts pressure on managers and supervisors to deal constructively with their subordinates' complaints and solve them on the spot if possible. In every company studied, managers testified to this fact. At the end of one long day of interviews, I had a couple of drinks with a department head. He said:

---

[1] "Grievance and Arbitration in the Nonunion Employment Sector," address to the New England Labor Council, Boston, October 30, 1983.
[2] Quoted in Lucinda Lamont, "Control Data's Review Process," *Labor Relations Update,* February 1987, pp. 9–10.

You go before a bunch of managers to defend what you did. Hey, who needs that? It's embarrassing. Maybe you got the facts on your side, your ducks in a row, but it's awkward as hell. So you try your damnedest to make a hearing unnecessary. You try to work out that guy's complaint before he takes it any further.

Sixth, an effective hearing system is likely to give you valuable feedback on how various policies and practices affect employees. I was standing with one executive by his office window high in a steel-and-glass building. Pointing to the people on the street far below, who seemed to crawl back and forth like ants, he said, "We're always changing the way we do things, though we don't make changes arbitrarily, only after discussion. Still, they haven't all worked out like we thought they would. But from up here, it's as hard to see the effects down the line as it is to make out the people on that street down there. Our complaint system brings those people to us full size."

Perhaps the epitome is Federal Express. Its management believes it has made innumerable improvements in policies and practices as a result of information gained from its Guaranteed Fair Treatment Procedure. The Memphis-based concern is by no means the only one reporting such gains.

Seventh, a good due process system boosts morale. The amount of gain is difficult to quantify, but every management interviewed in this study believes in the relationship. For a subordinate to be able to go to an ombudsperson or hearing panel and have an unjust decision overturned is a bracing tonic. The word spreads like lightning. "Did you hear? Carol got reinstated!" It is also bracing when a chronic sorehead whose complaints have tired everyone uses the procedure and gets his or her come-uppance. "Harvey lost at the hearing. They finally got wise to him!"

Eighth, a reputation for due process helps a company to attract and hold able employees. In the next ten to fifteen years, such an advantage will be of great importance to many organizations. Because of falling birth rates in the latter 1960s and first half or so of the 1970s, the pool of new workers is growing more slowly than at any time since the 1930s. From now to the end of the century, authorities believe that labor markets may be tighter than at any time in recent history. In a job seeker's market instead of an employer's, the presence or absence of due process may spell the difference between getting the people you want and not getting them.

In sum, your organization doesn't need a due process procedure if there is already strong mutual trust between management and nonunion employees, if you have no fear of union success in an attempt to organize employees, if you are not worried about lawsuits by former employees, if all managers and supervisors down the line appear to understand and comply with personnel policy, if managers deal promptly and ably with subordinates' complaints, if you have plenty of feedback on the effects of personnel policy, and if employee morale appears to be about as high as it can be. If any of these conditions are lacking, however, due process can be helpful in overcoming the gap, and you should read on.

Why It Works

Why is a good due process procedure useful to an organization? Here are the most important reasons given by the people I interviewed.

1. It is needed. In almost any organization of more than, say, one hundred employees, bad decisions are made with the best of intentions. Executives sometimes say, "Oh, but our managers are so well trained that subordinates don't have complaints." Pure delusion! By almost any standard, the organizations covered in this study rank among the nation's first in progressive employee relations policies. Yet they have due process. They know that legitimate conflicts arise despite the best intentions and skills of managers.

Take discharge, for instance. Experts' estimates for the number of non-union employees who get pink slips unjustly every year range from seventy thousand to two hundred thousand. But the figures on the number of actual ousters are only the tip of the iceberg. In companies lacking due process, untold thousands of employees silently endure shame and humiliation because they are afraid to challenge an unfair or neurotic supervisor for fear of losing their livelihood.

In a position paper for management that led Control Data to adopt its peer review procedure, manager David G. Robinson wrote, "It is inherently difficult for the management power structure to concede to a system which allows review of its decision making." But it must be done, he concluded. "Any concept of employee justice is incomplete without the presence of some mechanism to challenge the power system." (For more about Robinson's paper, see Part II.)

2. Ethical conduct cannot always be legislated by management. Sometimes it must be forged in the resolution of conflicts over actual problems. Is it right to keep on a sales manager who, though able and productive, has falsified a few expense accounts? Is it ethical to fire an employee who failed to follow a procedure when the procedure wasn't completely clear? Questions like these arise in profusion when people work together. What due process does is allow such questions to be aired and debated in a neutral corner. It succeeds where a code or policy guidebook may fail because it allows situations that cannot be anticipated to become part of the webbing of rules and standards by which employees are bound.

If you want to judge the ethics of a corporate organization, do not look at its pronouncements and writings alone. Look also at its mechanisms for considering and judging behavior. In ethics, as in communication, the medium is often the message.

3. To get all managers to observe corporate policy, you need an independent board or person to hear complaints. One executive explained the weak-

nesses of the conventional "open door" that his company had prior to establishing due process. If subordinates believed they were being treated unfairly, he said, they were encouraged to go to their boss's boss, and then, if necessary, to that boss's boss. He pointed out why that didn't work:

> Unfortunately, this sequence emphasized procedure at the expense of resolution. An employee could be told again and again, "If you don't like my answer, you can go to the next level"—up as many as six administrative levels. Understandably, many grievances died along the way.
>
> Moreover, if I'm a middle manager and a grievance comes across my desk, I'm probably going to review it with my supervisor, explain how I plan to handle it, and solicit his or her support. If the affected employee is dissatisfied and tries to go over my head, there's little chance that my superior will rule differently.[3]

The presence of a board or investigator-adjudicator serves as a strong incentive to managers to deal thoughtfully with subordinates' complaints. Many executives whom I interviewed believe this to be one of the greatest benefits enjoyed by their organizations.

4. Complaints are heard, investigated, and resolved by people who know your organization firsthand. They are not resolved by outsiders who, however able, don't understand the ways of your organization. This can make a big difference. Employee conflict of interest does not mean the same thing at Company A as it does at Company B. Company C's warning system, though worded the same as Company D's, is not intended to be practiced in the same way. Outsiders cannot be expected to know this. Insiders do.

5. Corporate due process is prompt. In the companies in this study, it takes a couple of weeks to several months in most instances for a decision to be rendered. In court cases, by contrast, it may take a couple of years to complete the trial, and another year or more to complete the appeals. If you are the grievant or manager, that is a long time to hang by your thumbs. The speed of a corporate procedure saves employees a lot of anguish.

6. It is efficient. In the companies studied, management strives hard and usually with success to avoid the adversarial atmosphere of a courtroom. There are no lawyers, no rules of evidence, no bailiffs. However necessary and appropriate these things may be in a courtroom, the companies consider them unnecessary in a corporate hearing, and their absence makes it possible to proceed with dispatch to questions of what happened and why.

7. It is inexpensive. If your system is like IBM's Open Door, your costs are the salary and travel expenses of the investigators; if it is like Federal Express's Guaranteed Fair Treatment Procedure, you have travel costs to the hearing plus staff costs. Such costs are peanuts, as corporate costs go these days. In 1988, *The Wall Street Journal* reported that Federal Express

[3]Fred C. Olson, "How Peer Review Works at Control Data," *Harvard Business Review,* November–December 1984, pp. 58–68.

paid about $10,000 in travel costs for one hearing. This outlay was higher—in most cases, considerably higher—than any reported to me. Several companies' out-of-pocket costs for the whole *year* of 1986 or 1987 amounted to no more than a few thousand dollars. (Of course, when salaries and other overhead are allocated, the expense is greater.)

8. Employees feel comfortable with it. I don't mean that they feel comfortable at the hearing; as the write-ups suggest, a hearing is often fingernail-biting time. But they feel comfortable with a procedure that rights wrongs. All their lives they have been around such procedures—in civic organizations, sports, schools—and have come to think of them as part of the American way.

9. The form of due process can be tailored to the particular needs and style of your organization. You can choose an investigator approach, as at CIGNA, which is low-profile and informal, or you can choose a two-tier hearing system, as at Federal Express, which is high-profile and carefully structured. You can have "judges" who are picked on a case-by-case basis, as at General Electric's Columbia plant, or who serve indefinite terms of office, as at John Hancock. You can have "judges" who are managers, as at Honeywell, or who are elected from the employee-at-large ranks, as at Donnelly. You can have the group's decisions be final, as at SmithKline Beckman, or you can cast the group in an advisory role, as at Control Data. Or you can choose some combination of these forms or a form that is entirely new. One of the reasons corporate due process works so well is that its form is not cast in iron but can be adapted to the wishes of each organization. If it meets reasonable tests of performance (see Chapter 4), form does not matter.

10. Due process is not a bar to corporate profitability and efficiency. Federal Express, which instituted a very advanced form of due process a number of years ago, has grown dramatically. Northrop, whose system is more than forty years old, is considered by many close observers to have the lowest costs of any sizable company in its industry. Donnelly Corporation, which has also had a fair hearing system in place for a long time, has grown more than sevenfold during the past fifteen years and has such an enviable production record that it began selling parts to a leading automaker in Japan several years ago.

Why So Late?

If corporate due process is such a good thing, why is it so late in getting established in the U.S. economy?

Perhaps the most important reason is managerial tradition. In industry, if not in government, we have become accustomed to the notion that if top executives are decent people, the organization doesn't need checks and balances. In addition, American managers have traditionally been about as interested in mechanisms for curbing supervisory power as in the plague. The name of the game, as they see it, *is* power and control, not the need to limit them. Significantly, no business schools in this country, so far as I know, have given much attention to specific measures to ensure fairness and justice in the workplace. Even cases and classes devoted to participative decision making, job enrichment, employee morale, and related matters have been flavored heavily by managers' needs to control and direct effectively, not by perceptions that mistakes in handling subordinates should be corrected objectively.

Second, and closely related to the first reason, it has long been a management custom to think that good top executives are loyal to their lieutenants in return for demanding their loyalty to the executives, and that this means backing them up when they get in trouble. In the great majority of the cases I know of in which a board or investigator has reversed a manager, that manager made the initial decision with the explicit or tacit approval of his or her boss.

Loyalty down the line is a fine, noble, and very human tradition, and we don't want to hurt it. In my opinion, corporate due process doesn't do that, though managers who don't understand it may think it does. Corporate due process simply says, in effect, "If we want a committed and loyal work force in this organization, one that can compete with the best in the world, we have got to have a good system of complaint resolution."

Third, corporate due process is an imperfect alternative. Since its shortcomings and imperfections are spelled out later (see Chapter 6, in particular), it need only be said here that it is not unknown for investigators and tribunals to make mistakes. Also, they can be an extra irritant in the long day of managers who have plenty of irritants and pressures already. "I don't need that," the supervisor says—and who can blame him or her for feeling negative? It is quite fashionable, therefore, for managers to emphasize the liability side of corporate due process and minimize the asset side.

Assumptions and Biases Sometimes Swept Under the Rug

I do not pretend that the analysis and recommendations that follow are unbiased. The viewpoint is managerial, gained from long service with the *Harvard Business Review,* from 1949 to 1985. The managerial viewpoint does not imply, however, an uncritical acceptance of corporate statements. In this field of employee rights in particular there has been a lot of pretense and double-talk, not all of it insincere but misleading nonetheless. It began to show in a couple of surveys I conducted for *HBR* in 1971, and it became increasingly evident as whistleblowers, employee objectors, and others responded to articles I wrote on employee rights in newspapers and magazines in the 1970s. In 1983, I documented more than twenty cases of employee objectors in a book entitled *Do It My Way Or You're Fired!*[4] That

[4] New York: Wiley, 1983.

experience left no doubt in my mind that many of the things managements say they do for employees, and may in good faith believe they do, are simply not true. Accordingly, in conducting the interviews on which this book is based and in writing them up and generalizing from them, I have done my best to avoid the many pitfalls that may catch the unwary reporter.

To make the cautious reader's job a little easier, let me list some assumptions I have made:

> *Management must manage.* Somebody has to decide to allocate so much for this line of advertising and so much for that. Somebody has to choose whether to invest in renovating the present production line or building a new plant—or perhaps sourcing production to Korea. Maybe a subordinate has a better idea or understanding than the boss, but it is the boss's job to decide as he or she sees fit. The naivete of those who think that management decisions can somehow be democratized never ceases to amaze me.
>
> *Organizations are important.* They have lives of their own which must be protected and nourished if the American economy is to continue to function competitively.
>
> *Managers have a right to expect their subordinates to work loyally and with commitment.* They have a right to expect employees to be honest. They have a right to expect people down the line to put in a fair day's work. They cannot look the other way when a subordinate flaunts a rule or fluffs off.
>
> *Most managers and supervisors are good people.* So are most nonmanagers. In many ways, managers are a representative cross-section of Americans, and no better and no worse than the people you see at a basketball game or a concert, no better and no worse than the employees they direct. This means, however, that at least some are neurotic dingbats, shameless self-promoters, or wimps. This fact, combined with the indisputable fact that even the best-intentioned managers have bad days and make mistakes, necessitates checks and balances on management.
>
> *If a company has a strong personnel department and/or high employee morale, it doesn't need a union; its managers can manage better without a union to contend with.* But the *if* is crucial. The truth is, a great many companies don't have strong personnel organizations, don't usually care much about their employees (though they may give lip service to the principle), and are natural targets for organizers. When the organizers succeed, according to the maxim, "the companies get what they deserve." It is then the unions that set up due process for employees in the form of arbitration, and of course it is the unions who get the credit for advancing the ideal of fair play in the workplace.
>
> *Employees don't have property rights in their jobs.* This concept has been advanced by some thoughtful and prescient observers, including Peter Drucker, but it is not important to the thesis of this book, and in my view it is of questionable merit. The notion of property rights is a legal principle applying to land, buildings, automobiles, books, and so on. It is not necessary to apply it to the work performed by employees. If employees had true property rights in their jobs, they would be entitled to all sorts of treatment

they don't get even in the most progressive firms, and the law of employee relations would have to be rewritten.

For a great many industries and companies, competition has become global. It is not enough for a firm to have a climate of trust and productivity that is as good as any domestic competitor's; it must have an employee relations climate that is good by worldwide standards, too.

The Human Angle

In this book I focus on concepts, rules, trends, practices, and other features of corporate due process and employee rights. These abstractions are necessary, but the reader should never forget that the lives, feelings, and aspirations of people are involved. These people are as real as you and I, and what happens to them as a result of corporate due process, or the lack of it, is often as important to them as anything else in their work lives.

One employee I talked with was the subject of a case that could not be released for publication in Part II. To preserve his privacy, I shall call him "Wright" and describe his employer as a financial services company. Wright was an energetic, red-haired, somewhat flamboyant fellow in his mid-thirties. Although loud, he was liked by other employees; he often regaled them with his devastating mimicry of politicians. He was happy with his job and prospects in the company until he learned that he was not going to get a promotion he was counting on.

Wright had been moonlighting two evenings a week for a law firm in order to supplement his salary with extra savings that he could put into a down payment on a house. The house meant a great deal to him and his wife. Not only would it put them in a better neighborhood, but it would give them more room for their two children.

Wright's supervisor felt that the moonlighting, although not a technical violation of the company's rules about conflict of interest, was a violation in spirit. He said that twice he had spoken to his subordinate about this. Wright, on the other hand, had not taken the warnings seriously. Each time, he said, the boss had admitted that his moonlighting was not a conflict of interest, strictly speaking; and each time, as he recalled it, the boss had hastened to add that he wasn't going to "do anything to me because of it."

For several weeks, Wright fumed, fretted, and agonized over his failure to get promoted. He felt humiliated and disgraced. For a while, in his shame, he wouldn't even tell his wife that he had been turned down, and when friends and relatives asked him how things were going on the job, he gave evasive answers. He lost sleep. He began doing strange things at work that caused other employees to raise their eyebrows. He convinced himself that his boss was afraid of him because he was too good.

At length, he went to the employee relations office and confided in a specialist. With Wright's permission, the specialist went to the boss to get the other side of the story; the specialist then brought the two together in his office to see if the conflict could be ironed out. But the supervisor stuck to his guns, and Wright continued to think that he had been wronged.

After another talk with the specialist, Wright then took his case to the appeals board, the final step in the complaint resolution process. There, in a little conference room in front of three people, he presented his case. The three board members, who were picked at random from a list, sipped coffee and tea while he gave his side of the story, then they took twenty-five minutes to question him. When he was through they thanked him, and the chairman said that they would communicate their decision to him by letter within two weeks. They had already talked to his boss; now they wanted to talk with Wright's witnesses as well as witnesses offered by the superior.

In a week and a half Wright got a two-page letter saying that the board, after weighing the evidence, had decided not to overturn his boss's decision. In the letter the chairman mentioned the boss's talks with Wright, summarized the impressions given by the witnesses, and cited the wording of a provision in the company's personnel policy. The chairman acknowledged that perhaps the supervisor had not been as candid with Wright as he might have been, but the board believed that the warning was adequate. The chairman pointed to the testimony of Wright's own witnesses, one of whom said that Wright himself realized that he was "shading things pretty close," and another of whom recalled Wright's once saying that "I know Glen [the supervisor] would be in his rights if he shot me down."

Naturally, the supervisor was relieved. Judging from what I heard and saw, he had lost a lot of sleep over the case, too, and reportedly he had said that he hated the thought of being held to blame by Wright's friends. Now he felt exonerated.

As for Wright, he was shocked and infuriated. It had never occurred to him that he would lose the appeal. In his anger, he even went to see a lawyer to find out what kind of legal case he might have. The lawyer, after calling the appeals board chairman, told Wright he didn't think a court would support him. It began dawning on Wright that perhaps he wasn't as right as he had thought he was. His friends at work, although personally supportive, believed that the appeals board, which had a good reputation, had reached its decision honestly. "Even my wife," he told me, "thought that Erskine's [the board chairman's] letter was a good one."

When I talked with Wright, he had found a job in another company and was bullish about his prospects there—he was getting more pay, and he liked the people. His only regret was that the new company didn't have a grievance procedure like the old one had. He said that the old company's board had cleared the air and enabled him to forget his loss as "just one of those things." He told me, "I'll never admit that I was wrong, but I think they tried, you know. They gave me a fair shot, and you can't ask for more than that."

Experiences like this are duplicated thousands of times a year in companies with corporate due process.

2

Deep Roots and Growing

Corporate due process is not a fringe benefit, nor is it an invention of imaginative staff people looking for something to do. It is a response to a deep and heartfelt need of employees. This need is not ephemeral but growing and pervasive. It can be seen in almost every industry and part of America. Industries like electronics and chemical manufacturing are often called the handmaidens of modern personnel practices, but there appears to be no evidence that they are more or less prominent in the development of due process than are many other industries, such as banking, pharmaceuticals, insurance, or defense contracting. And in industries where, thus far, due process has not appeared, such as agribusiness, mining, and wholesaling, the need for it seems to be as great as in industries where it has appeared. In short, employees need due process because they are human, not because of peculiarities of the work situation.

What accounts for the greening of corporate due process in the United States? What trends, forces, and conditions have whetted employees' desire for due process and led corporate leaders to experiment with it? Let us look at a series of developments that lie behind this remarkable event, not attempting to document them (for others have done that) but simply to describe them enough to provide a sense of perspective. Although I shall categorize the trends, it should be borne in mind that in reality they are not separate but closely related and intertwined.

Crumbling of the Pillars

The heads of organizations used to be revered. They were considered wiser, more knowledgeable, more prescient. The less rank-and-file employees knew about them as human beings and personalities, the greater the halo of their authority. For at least a century, however, this reverence has been eroding. Whether one believes with economist J. Kenneth Galbraith that the erosion began with the stupidities of the trenches in World War I, with theologian Duncan Littlefair that it began with the modern rise of freedom of inquiry, or with writer Peter Drucker that it began with the proliferation of scientific thinking, or with someone else—makes no difference. The fact is that managers and executives today may be respected because of their power and position, but they are not revered as their predecessors were, no homage is paid to them, and they are not considered right because of their elevated status in the world.

Yesterday's employees did not demand hearing systems for the simple reason that they rarely, if ever, called "Foul!" If a supervisor's inhumanity ever did provoke such a reaction, the judgment of a department head or vice president as to the merits of the controversy was sufficient. "They know more than I do. They must be right." Lawsuits were rare. By contrast, today's employees view and read continually about the blunders of the corporate presidents, Wall Street titans, corporate wheelers and dealers, admirals and generals, union chiefs, university heads, and public leaders. Why aren't their supervisors, too, liable to go off the track? They readily accept the necessity for leadership and supervision when work is to be done, but they are quick to stand up to seniors when they feel wronged. "Rank has its privileges but it is not always right." They hunger for some forum or procedure in the organization that will enable them to be heard by impartial arbiters. They are litigious, sacrilegious, and prodigious.

At NBC a young employee got bawled out by a senior executive, went to the personnel officer, protested that the senior's language was too harsh, and demanded that something be done (see the write-up in Part II). A generation or two ago, few employees would have thought of doing such a thing, even though they might have been equally indignant. Today cases like this occur every day in U.S. business.

The Influence of Education

As the proportion of employees with college degrees has grown steadily, from a fraction of 1 percent in 1920 to about 3 percent in 1960 and more than 10 percent today, with one out of every four workers now entering the work force having a degree, the willingness to joust with supervisors has increased. Not only are college-degreed people better able to take on seniors orally and in writing, but their training tends to make them more interested in the weight of facts than in the prerogatives of rank. Something is right or wrong not because Mr. Manager says it is but because of the evidence. When, therefore, they feel that they have been the victims of unfair treatment, they are less willing than their predecessors were to swallow hard and be "good soldiers." They want a place where they can throw in the gauntlet.

At SmithKline Beckman, "Paul" is an example of such a person (see Part II). The formal reprimand that Paul received from his boss probably wouldn't have been contested by his father, if he had received such a warning, for the father was not as well educated and would have felt uncomfortable jousting verbally with an articulate senior. But Paul, a degreed person, saw no reason why he shouldn't take on the manager. In a battle of words and arguments, he felt equal to the senior, and his education told him to pitch in and assert himself. The Pauls are everywhere in corporations today, and they are not just the degree-holders from Rice, New York University, and so on, but smart computer programmers, market analysts, accountants, and many others without college degrees who have become proficient in a field of knowledge, acquired the confidence that comes with learning, and learned to think for themselves.

"Everybody Here Has an Accent"

As mobility, diversity, and homogeneity have increased in the work force, so have conflicts in expectations and values among well-meaning employees. In consequence, the need for good complaint resolution procedures has risen straight up like a space shuttle.

Let me mention two examples.

Not long ago, I visited a company in Houston. As we were finishing up at the end of one afternoon, I joshingly mentioned to an executive that I hadn't heard much Texicana in my interviews with his subordinates. "In fact," I said, "you're the only one who sounds like a Texan." He answered, "To me, everybody here has an accent." He went on to explain that his secretary came from Seattle, his chief assistant from Bangor, his chief metallurgist from India, his operations manager from Nashville, and so on.

For complaint resolution, this was significant. It said that the fellow's organization would be prone to cultural clashes and misunderstandings despite the fact that it was pulling together beautifully in work output. Much the same observation might be made of thousands of other organizations. In fact, the work force that doesn't have this tension is becoming an anomaly in the United States.

This is one of many reasons why U.S. corporations should move toward due process *in their own way* and *for their own reasons*. Many other countries do not have the diversity and mobility that we have.

In another company, a subordinate was contesting her supervisor's decision to let her go because she didn't feel that she had been adequately warned of poor performance. The more I saw of the case, the more I realized that both she and her boss were honest, hard-working, well-meaning people. However, what the boss thought of as warnings had not struck her as such; coming from a completely different background, she had interpreted them as mere "talk." She hadn't taken them seriously, and she had attached more significance to his pleasant manner with her, smiling gestures, and so forth. "If he had meant to warn me," she said at the hearing, "why didn't he get me aside and tell me?"

The View from the Top

Interviewing at companies with due process, one realizes that sometimes chief executive officers themselves are part of the trend. In recent decades we have seen people rise to the top who feel that loyalty is more of a two-way street than corporate heads used to think of it. The new CEOs want to back up their managers, yet they feel that it is not an imposition on line people to allow their decisions to be questioned. "It's a part of being tough-minded," said one senior person whom I interviewed. "You've got to accept the fact that it's no disgrace to be reversed. It's unpleasant, but it's not the end of your career."

Let there be no illusions about the number of such top executives. They are in the minority. Just the fact that they exist, however, is notable, for it was not long ago that practically *no* one in top management took such a heretical stance.

In the chronicles in Part II, three such CEOs are described—John Donnelly of Donnelly Corporation, Edwin Land of Polaroid, and Thomas Watson, Jr., of IBM. All three took a hand in setting up due process in their organizations, not so much because of pressure to do so as because of the conviction that *it was right*. With Donnelly and Land, the thought process appears to have been primarily intellectual, an effort to conceive of the employee-company relationship in contemporary terms. With Watson, the thought process may have been more visceral, relating to paternalistic feelings that he and his father had toward those who worked loyally and dutifully for IBM. In both cases, the actions taken were inner-directed, that is, not a response to trends and conditions outside the firm but an urging to do something that made sense in view of how they felt about themselves and their roles as business leaders.

In 1912–1913, Henry Ford approved the establishment of worker committees to review discharges. At that time, productivity and employee relations at Ford Motor Company were a model for the world. Unfortunately, the committees did not survive World War I, and Ford Motor later became infamous for its employee policies. Not until recent years did the company resume its innovative role in industrial relations.

Great Expectations

As former labor secretary Ray Marshall explains in *Unheard Voices: Labor and Economic Policy in a Competitive World*, employees want and expect to be able to participate in decisions affecting them.[1] This general desire leads naturally to the expectation that somewhere in the corporation an unhappy employee can have his or her day in court and, if found deserving, get restitution for unfair treatment. It is no answer to such persons to say "If

[1] New York: Basic Books, 1987.

you don't like it here, you're free to find a job elsewhere." They believe that a right to a fair hearing goes with their corporate citizenship, and that to banish employee objectors for contesting a superior's decision is treating them like traitors when they are not being disloyal at all. In terms of Abraham Maslow's well-known hierarchy of needs, due process satisfies an employee's social and ego needs.[2]

At Polaroid Corporation, "John Mortimer" felt that there was nothing wrong in challenging management's decision not to give him a promotion he had applied for (see Part II). He said he was a "nervous wreck" when he went to the hearing because he wasn't comfortable in challenging authority, yet he couldn't be true to himself without doing so. Justice was his due. When he got to the hearing, he found about twenty other employees protesting the same management decision! Welcome to the club, John Mortimer.

Creating a Sense of Belonging

In years past, companies motivated employees by paying them more, giving them advancement, and similar acts. The assumption was that money would buy satisfaction, productivity, and commitment. Very possibly that assumption was once valid; today, however, it is the exception rather than the rule. As George C. Lodge and others have pointed out, most employees today gain a sense of belonging to an organization only if they contribute to some of its policies and participate in parts of its management.[3] This does not mean so-called worker democracy, but it does mean exercising a voice in the direction of the operations that affect an employee's work.

As more and more managements try to respond to this fact of life, they find that employees' sense of justice is intertwined with it. The same need that makes employees want to participate in the administrative system also leads them to want a voice in the system of dispensing justice. Enter due process. Without due process they have no chance to defend themselves against supervisors' arbitrary actions; with due process they are able to speak out and have their day in court.

At Donnelly Corporation an employee named "Pete" got turned down for a promotion, arranged for one of the ad hoc hearings that the company is famous for, and at the hearing argued that he should get the job (see Part II). Now, Donnelly happens to be a corporate leader in participative management, and that is one of the reasons Pete liked to work there. His sense of belonging and commitment to the company would have been jolted rudely if there had been no due process procedure. In Pete's mind, one went with the other.

---

[2] *Toward a Psychology of Being* (New York: Van Nostrand Reinhold, 1982). See also David W. Ewing, *Freedom Inside the Organization* (New York: Dutton, 1977), pp. 47–48.
[3] *The New American Ideology* (New York: Knopf, 1975).

Do Loyal Employees Protest?

Another trend behind the desire for due process is the changing quality of loyalty. Employee loyalty today is not the simple one-dimensional, either-or type of loyalty that it was, say, fifty years ago. It is a more complex attitude. It says that an employee can be loyal to the corporation *and* to other groups, such as associations of engineers or scientists. It says that an employee can be loyal to various groups even though their interests may sometimes conflict, as when the code of an engineering group calls for disclosure of a safety problem whereas corporate management wishes to keep the problem secret. Most important, the loyalty that drives today's employees says that it is not disloyal to challenge authority provided that it is done in a proper way and in a proper place. What is frustrating to employees is that too many corporations are unwilling to provide such a place and medium.

If this more complex standard is viewed from the standpoint of yesterday's all-or-nothing norm, it is easy to see why so many business executives perceive a decline and deterioration in employee loyalty. In a survey of senior executives' concerns conducted in 1987 by Egon Zehnder International, Inc., three-quarters of the respondents reported that grave concern over declining employee loyalty had spurred discussions on the topic at their company during the past year. Other pollsters have found similar results. As loyalty would have been measured fifty years ago, there has indeed been a decline. It would be a mistake, however, to conclude that corporate loyalty is a thing of the past. It is not. Employees simply feel that their corporations are not the only fitting objects of their loyalty, that while they may feel intensely about the merits of their employer organizations, they may also possess strong concerns for family, the environment, scientific codes, environmental movements, or other causes. Call this a decline in loyalty if you want, but the reality is that, as *The Wall Street Journal* reported, a company like IBM can still be "widely regarded to have loyalty so intense that many observers liken it to a religious order or the military."[4] As noted earlier, IBM has a strong nonunion grievance procedure.

In the Zehnder survey, most of the senior executives polled felt that "American companies should do a great deal more to foster loyalty." One such way is due process. To some it may seem paradoxical to state that an organization maintaining a forum where employees can challenge management decisions can expect greater loyalty as a result, but that is exactly what appears to happen. Employees seem to say, "The fact that we can contest a supervisor's decision without prejudice makes this organization more important to us." It may be more than coincidence that some of the companies enjoying the greatest measures of employee commitment—IBM, Donnelly, Polaroid, and Northrop, to name just a few—are companies that also maintain nonunion grievance procedures.

At CIGNA, "Sarah" could scarcely have avoided being impressed by the

[4]July 11, 1985.

company's concern and interest in her gripe that tested employees were being overlooked for promotion in favor of college grads hired off the street (see Part II). If her story had ended with the nonchalant supervisor who shrugged her off, instead of with "Speak Easy," a hearing, and some management action, would she have felt more or less loyal to her employer?

The Aura of Participative Management

Another important trend that has awakened interest in due process is participative management. Quality circles, participative problem-solving groups as developed by Texas Instruments and described by M. Scott Myers,[5] the kinds of job enrichment elaborated by Frederick Herzberg and Robert Ford, the high-commitment work systems discussed by Michael Beer and his associates at the Harvard Business School,[6] so-called foreman-less plants—these and other approaches that attempt to enlist operators' help in job design, assembly, scheduling, quality control, and other functions have made managers and nonmanagers alike more receptive to the notion of due process. If an employee has a voice in operations management, why shouldn't he or she also have a right to protest a managerial decision seen as unjust? The very fact that there is a dialogue between managers and operators on questions of how best to get the work out strengthens the case for fair hearing systems to handle complaints.

Perhaps the best example of the congeniality between due process and participative management is Donnelly Corporation (see Part II). The people I interviewed at Donnelly felt that operators who often select their team leaders, set production goals, plan how best to meet them, and so forth don't divide work questions from those of equity, expecting to be treated as mature adults in one case but not in the other. If employees' involvement in operations is important to the development of employee commitment, so is their involvement in decisions affecting employee job status.

Personnel Departments with Clout

When the personnel or human resources department becomes influential in management, it usually wastes little time in working for a good complaint resolution system. It may not opt for due process, and if it does, it may not be able to persuade the rest of management to its way of thinking, but at least due process becomes a possibility. It is no accident that all companies in this study have strong personnel philosophies and employee relations people. Nor is it coincidence that no company without a personnel-minded top management boasts a due process system.

One of the reasons that due process is unusual in U.S. industry is that

[5] *Every Employee a Manager* (New York: McGraw-Hill, 1970).
[6] *Managing Human Assets* (New York: Free Press, 1984), pp. 152–176.

strong personnel departments have been unusual. However, this situation is changing. Though it is still the rare chief executive officer who comes up from personnel, vice presidents of personnel, employee relations, human resources, and industrial relations are becoming more common, and more important, they are gradually coming to exercise more influence in corporate policy. The situation that Fred Foulkes found in the mid-1970s, when only thirty-seven of the last fifteen hundred members of the Harvard Business School Advanced Management Program came from personnel or industrial relations,[7] is going out of date.

One of the first major American companies to give personnel a high rung on the managerial ladder was Sears, Roebuck in the 1930s. For many years the vice president for retail administration—one of the top jobs, under General Robert E. Wood—was in charge of personnel administration. Personnel's job was to deter unions and develop a progressive program for employees, from an employee-elected profit-sharing council to employee attitude surveys. The surveys showed that three things correlated strongly with high morale: a belief that the company dealt fairly with employee complaints, confidence in the future offered by the company, and the feeling that it provided interesting work.[8] Sears was the first American company to establish by survey evidence that complaint resolution plays a crucial role in employee morale.

During World War II personnel departments got a boost that they might never have gotten in peacetime. The government promoted a wide range of personnel practices—seniority provisions, exit interviews, turnover records, grievance handling, and others—that in turn led to the formation of numerous personnel departments. The trend continued after the war. The number of personnel and labor relations professionals grew from fewer than thirty thousand in 1946 to fifty-three thousand in 1950 and ninety-three thousand in 1960, a growth rate that far outstripped the growth rate of other professions in the U.S. labor force.[9]

The New Conscientious Objectors

As employees learn—often firsthand—of the potential hazards and dangers of modern industry, and as they become more sensitive to the complex interdependencies in society, conscience compels many to speak up when they see wrongdoing. Here are three statements by employee protestors that shed light on their motives:

[7] "The Expanding Role of the Personnel Function," *Harvard Business Review,* March–April 1975, p. 71.
[8] Sanford M. Jacoby, "Employee Attitude Testing at Sears, Roebuck and Company, 1938–1960," *Business History Review,* Winter 1986, p. 612.
[9] James N. Baron, Frank R. Dobbin, and P. Devereaux Jennings, "War and Peace: The Evolution of Modern Personnel Administration in U.S. Industry," *American Journal of Sociology,* September 1986, p. 375.

I cannot envision anything more important than the health and safety of the public in this generation. . . . —*Engineer sacked for protesting unsafe conditions in nuclear power plants*

I know it may sound hackneyed today but I believe it: the only thing necessary for evil to prevail is for good men to do nothing. —*Veterans Administration doctor fired for criticizing drugs used on patients*

A corrupt system can happen only if the individuals who make up that system are corrupt. You are either going to be part of the corruption or part of the forces working against it. —*U.S. Interior Department employee in trouble for protesting strip-mining policies*[10]

In the past we have thought of conscientious objection principally in terms of religion; that is, no one should be compelled to perform an act that violates his or her religious principles. Today's conscientious objectors are more likely to be found protesting corporate or governmental actions that violate their sense of being their brother's keeper than actions that violate their perceived religious rights. Many of these people will, if necessary, go to the wall for the sake of their beliefs—or, more accurately, go to the sidewalks and start ringing doorbells.

Marie Ragghianti, former head of the Tennessee Board of Pardons and Paroles who got fired for speaking out against graft in prison administration, once suggested to Frank Serpico, who got in trouble after blowing the whistle on police corruption in New York, that the two of them had been rewarded for their efforts, despite losing their jobs, by public acclaim and understanding. Serpico pooh-poohed her idea. People who buck the system get bucked back, he asserted. "The reward is one's own dignity." The remark characterizes many employee objectors. They are motivated more by self-image than such things as money, position, and power.

It is hard to say whether conscience and ethical convictions are becoming more or less important in the minds of employees, but it does seem safe to say that employees today are more willing to risk their job security when conscience stings. As a result, companies large and small feel a nagging pressure to do something so that objections can be voiced inside company walls rather than outside.

Let me stress that managers are prominent in this trend. There should be no illusion that corporate due process is a response only to the needs of operating people. In fact, some careful observers I know feel that in many organizations managers criticize, object to, and blow the whistle on company practices more often than nonmanagers do.

Jobs as a Species of Property

Jobs are gaining *some* of the characteristics of property. For instance, they are the primary source of income and retirement security for most people,

[10] Myron and Penina Glazer, "Whistleblowing," *Psychology Today*, August 1986, p. 38.

and employees invest in their job by taking courses. But, as indicated earlier, in my view it is dangerous to equate jobs with property—the two are different in many respects.

However, a good argument can be made that jobs should be protected up to a point. There is a growing sense that, just as a person cannot be deprived by government of, say, land or stocks without due process of law, so an employee should not be deprived of his or her job by management without some sort of review. The practical effect of this belief is to make it necessary for the employer to show just cause for dismissal (e.g., poor performance, immoral behavior) or economic necessity (e.g., the plant must be closed, a third of the workers must be laid off for lack of sales). No less an authority than Peter Drucker has lent his weight to this proposition:

> In every developed non-Communist country, jobs are rapidly turning into a kind of property. . . . Employing organizations will have to recognize that jobs have some of the characteristics of property rights and cannot therefore be diminished or taken away without due process. Hiring, firing, promotion, and demotion must be subject to pre-established, objective, public criteria. And there has to be a review, a pre-established right to appeal to a higher judge in all actions affecting rights in and to the job.[11]

This is not a new idea. U.S. Supreme Court Justice Swayne mentioned it prominently in a dissenting opinion in the *Slaughter House* cases in 1873. "Labor is property," he wrote, "and as such merits protection. The right to make it available is next in importance to the rights of life and liberty. It lies to a large extent at the foundation of most other forms of property. . . ."[12]

The rationale is simple. As Alan Westin has noted, jobs represent not only salaries but also health insurance, vacations, pensions, and other benefits. The courts, says Westin, are beginning to reflect the view "that companies can't just throw people out on the trash heap." Frank Tannenbaum puts it this way:

> We have become a nation of employees. We are dependent upon others for our means of livelihood, and most of our people have become completely dependent upon wages. If they lose their jobs they lose every resource, except for the relief supplied by the various forms of social security. Such dependence of the mass of the people upon others for *all* of their income is something new in the world. *For our generation, the substance of life is in another man's hands.*[13]

In almost all states, the doctrine of employment at will was espoused for about a century. This doctrine was the exact opposite of the jobs-as-property notion; it meant that an employer could fire or demote an employee for any reason or no reason. No due process was necessary.

[11] "The Job as Property Right," *The Wall Street Journal,* March 4, 1980.
[12] 83 U.S. 36 (1873).
[13] *A Philosophy of Labor* (New York: Knopf, 1951), p. 9.

Most businesspeople seem to think that the employment-at-will doctrine is a venerable notion that has existed since the Year One. This is wrong. Neither in the Middle Ages nor in most of the era of industrialization was employment at will accepted. For six centuries—from the fourteenth to the end of the nineteenth—the concept of master and servant controlled the law of employment. (In fact, in at least one famous law school library, cases of fired employees suing their employers are still to be found under the rubric of "Master and Servant.") Under this concept, the employee-employer relationship was *not* terminable at will. "The law," says Philip A. Selznik in a carefully researched volume, "visualized a relatively enduring relation and a commitment on both sides to honor the contract until the term of service was ended."[14] Unless agreed otherwise, the term was one year from the date of hiring. Employers were required to give notice—generally three months—and outright dismissal had to be for just cause.

Not until the latter part of the nineteenth century did the law begin to regard employment contracts as contracts at will—from a legal standpoint, says Selznik, as an encounter "as casual as the sale of a newspaper on a city street." This innovation was popular with employers because it strengthened their managerial hands and made it easy to lay off employees as economic fluctuations occurred. During the period that the doctrine dominated employer thinking, notions of due process appeared naive, irrelevant, and worse still, uneconomic.

Limitations of Professional Management

In recent decades corporate management has increased its skills, vision, and professionalism greatly. Some people ask, therefore, why it is necessary for companies to set up systems to dispense justice equitably. Don't the decisions of well-trained managers now make such systems unnecessary?

In years past, if this question had come up, the answer might have been yes. Today, however, it is a firm no, and the reason can be set forth simply. Employees have come to see justice as a *procedural* as well as a substantive matter. In particular, they don't believe that justice is accomplished unless both parties to an act have a voice in the resolution and either agree on the outcome or let a neutral party decide the outcome. This is another aspect of the desire for participation.

At Citicorp, a productive and hard-working middle manager named "Ed Evans" didn't want to work overtime in the occasional busy periods when everybody else had to work past 5:00 P.M. (see Part II). When his boss told him he was expected to do as the others did, Evans was so unhappy that he went to the ombudspersons in the human resources department. After investigating the situation, they told him that his boss was right. Although Evans was chagrined, he felt that justice had been done: fair-minded people

[14] *Law, Society, and Industrial Justice* (New York: Sage Foundation, 1969), p. 125.

had heard his side and the other side both. So he didn't take his case on up to the review board.

"The greatest benefit of the Problem Review Procedure," I was told by one Citicorp officer, referring to his bank's due process approach, "is the feeling it gives employees that there is another avenue than slugging it out with the boss. They don't have to duke it out with the boss to get a resolution."

Interestingly, managers have joined professionals as important complainers and whistleblowers, especially in connection with cost savings. Professor Mary P. Rowe of Massachusetts Institute of Technology tells me that managers go to employee relations specialists with concerns at least proportionate to their numbers in the organization—more than proportionate, many employee relations people think.

Filling the Void Left by Unions

In recent years union power has been declining in the United States. Many careful observers deem it unlikely that the decline will be reversed in the near future. One's first reaction to this trend might be something like, "Ah, now management can relax. Management is like the golfer with a chronic slice who can take a deep and happy breath when he gets past the woods holes." In fact, however, just the opposite is happening. With unions retreating from front stage, companies are feeling more pressure, not less, to do what union leaders might be doing in the area of employee rights. This event results partly from a changing sense of employee relations and partly from a "preventive unionization" attitude.

The lessening of union clout is well documented. In the dozen years before World War I, blue-collar workers broke out of their economic impotence in Western Europe and became a power for all to reckon with. Shortly after World War I, blue-collar workers in this country did the same thing, organizing in powerful unions and transforming the economy, society, and politics. Then, sometime in the late Vietnam War years, blue-collar employees began falling in importance, and their number has continued falling to the present. By the year 2010, predicts Peter Drucker, blue-collar workers will make up no larger a segment of the labor force than will farmers—about 5 percent. The decline in their numbers, he forecasts, will be greatest where the highest-paid jobs are.[15] While unions have organized many groups of teachers, office workers, nurses, and others, the drag of declining numbers of blue-collar employees has been difficult for union leaders to counteract, and their influence has slipped. The proportion of nonfarm workers unionized in the private sector is less than half of what it was thirty-five years ago—16.5 percent as opposed to 36 percent. Union leaders do not attempt to organize as often as they did then, either.

This trend has put management in a curious position. By improving

[15] *The Wall Street Journal*, April 22, 1987.

working conditions and instituting or increasing pensions, retirement income programs, child care programs, group insurance, medical insurance, educational assistance, vacation allowances, recreation programs, and other fringe benefits, management has taken the initiative in the welfare area in order to preempt would-be union organizers. It has done so much, in fact, that some economic historians have dubbed this effort "welfare capitalism."[16]

In the area of *employee rights,* however, corporations have been far less aggressive and imaginative. The number of companies establishing due process for employees is only a tiny fraction of the number that have forged ahead with progressive fringe benefits. The managerial assumption seems to have been that it can buy the loyalty and commitment of employees by offering bigger and better fringe benefits. In the past it could point to some stunning cases in point. For instance, says one business historian, "Diamond Alkali Company, a chemical firm near Houston, Texas, attributed its low absentee and turnover rates, shattered production records, and the union's loss, by large margins, of two certification votes, to its employee-run recreation program."[17]

Now, this assumption might have been valid a couple of generations ago. The quest for physical security and welfare was so keen that employees left it to the unions to hold the banner for due process. With the decline of unions and the stepped-up interest in rights, however, the assumption may have become questionable. In the final years of the twentieth century, can management satisfy employees by being progressive on one front alone? It seems doubtful. The unions are waiting in the wings if management fails, and many executives sense this fact.

Reviewing a book by three labor experts, David Warsh writes:

> There might be some reform of the labor laws, to make it easier for unions to organize workers. The diffusion of new labor-management techniques—consultation on the shop floor, first and foremost—might take hold. Or whole new organizing strategies might turn up. None of these will restore the glory days, the authors say, but a combination just might lead to a new and different kind of Golden Age of labor—one in which workers participate more than ever before in the choices that determine their fates.[18]

Judicial Jibes

As state and federal courts open their doors to employees suing their employers, a new form of pressure is growing on companies to install due process. As long as employment at will was the accepted doctrine in the

[16] See, for instance, Elizabeth Fones-Wolf, "Industrial Recreation, the Second World War, and the Revival of Welfare Capitalism," *Business History Review,* 60, Summer 1986, pp. 232–257.
[17] Ibid., p. 253.
[18] *The Boston Globe,* April 19, 1987, p. A5. The authors and book referred to are Thomas Kochran, Harry Katz, and Robert McKersie, *The Transformation of American Industrial Relations* (New York: Basic Books, 1987).

courts, companies had relatively little to fear from employee and ex-employee litigators. Now that the edges of the at-will doctrine are being nibbled away, however, companies have a great deal to fear. Every year, thousands of disgruntled employees turn to the courts to get damages and restitution, and they do not always leave empty-handed. Here are just a few items, picked more or less at random, that could make an executive's hair curl:

> Alan Westin estimated in 1987 that about twenty thousand cases alleging unjust discharge were pending in state courts (up from a handful in the late 1970s).[19]
>
> A recent study of unjust discharge cases in California showed that more than three-fourths of the jury verdicts went to the ex-employees prosecuting the cases. The latter received punitive damages in two cases out of five, with the average of $424,527. Some of the best-known American companies were the defendants in these cases.[20]
>
> In 1987, questioning by the law firm of Jackson, Lewis, Schnitzler & Krupman revealed that more than one-third of respondent firms had been hit by legal actions during the past year. Many of the firms reported having settled the cases for cash payments ranging from $1,001 to $50,000.[21]
>
> To the chagrin of numerous executives, not only are six-figure awards to disgruntled ex-employees common in suits that reach juries in some states, but attorney's fees for simply defending against a wrongful dismissal suit are likely to be at least $50,000. In Montana, a unique worker discharge law guarantees nonunion employees protection against arbitrary dismissal but puts a ceiling on the damages they can get; however, at this writing the Montana Supreme Court is reviewing that limit on the grounds that it violates the Montana Constitution's guarantee of "full legal redress for injury."

As noted earlier, the at-will doctrine sailed into legal waters in the latter part of the nineteenth century. It was stated in numerous court decisions, but perhaps the clearest declaration came in the case of *Payne* v. *Western & A.R.R.* in 1884, where the court proclaimed that employers "may dismiss their employees at will . . . for good cause, for no cause, or even for cause morally wrong, without thereby being guilty of legal wrong."[22] At the scholarly helm of the new doctrine was, in the words of Wayne C. Sander, "an Albany lawyer and prolific writer named Horace Gray Wood." Although Wood was renowned for his scholarship, he was off course in this case. Sander quotes Jay Feinman, a professor of law at the University of Miami, who finds various leaks in Wood's reasoning. The cases cited for

---

[19] Alan F. Westin and Alfred G. Feliu, *Resolving Employment Disputes Without Litigation* (Washington, D.C.: Bureau of National Affairs, 1988), p. 2.
[20] Ibid.
[21] *The Wall Street Journal,* November 3, 1987, p. 1.
[22] 81 Tenn. 507, 519–520.

authority were off the chart, Wood's interpretation of U.S. legal decisions was full of slack, and he offered no policy justification for the rule he proclaimed.[23] Interestingly enough, thinks Feinman, one reason management rushed to the support of the doctrine was the burgeoning group of middle managers in business; employers feared that they would become greedy for larger shares of the profits unless an at-will boom hung menacingly over their heads.[24]

The at-will doctrine continued on with practically no judicial challenge until 1959, when a California jury decided that a union officer could not be deep-sixed for testifying honestly in court.[25] About ten years later officials of public agencies were protected against firing for exercising the right to criticize their organizations' policies; this break with tradition came in the famous *Pickering* decision by the U.S. Supreme Court.[26] In the 1970s, numerous lower federal courts followed in its wake.

In 1975, a U.S. District Court in Connecticut jibed to favor a corporate employee, declaring that he had a limited right to free speech under certain conditions.[27] In 1977, a Massachusetts court decided in favor of a salesman who was fired in bad faith;[28] in 1978, a West Virginia court decided in favor of a bank officer who blew the whistle on illegal charges by his bank and was forced to walk the plank;[29] and in 1980, the California Supreme Court decided in favor of an employee who claimed he was fired for refusing to participate in an illegal pricing scheme.[30]

Then began a steady trickle of cases favoring employee objectors in industry, and the trickle swelled into a small stream. Today, an estimated forty states or more plus the federal courts recognize exceptions to the at-will doctrine.

From a management standpoint, the practical result of this trend is that if management doesn't watch out the company may see the aggrieved or fired employee in court. Like Captain Bligh, the dissident may return to haunt it. Management no longer has the luxury, which it had for many decades, of being able to rid itself of the sight of an employee it doesn't want hanging around. Despite the heavy costs and legal riptides that the aggrieved employee has to negotiate, he or she can haul the company into court and, with luck, end up with a sizable check from the treasurer. The possibility of such a pot of gold at the end of the legal rainbow, and the probability of warm and sympathetic coverage of the dissident by the media, have led thousands of employees to sue.

---

[23] "Toward a Theory of Freedom of Communication for Private Sector At Will Employees," Ph.D. diss., University of Pittsburgh, 1984, pp. 15–16.
[24] Ibid., p. 18.
[25] *Petermann* v. *International Brotherhood of Teamsters,* 174 Cal. App. 2d 184, 344 P. 2d 25.
[26] *Pickering* v. *Board of Education,* 391 U.S. 563 (1968).
[27] *Holodnak* v. *Avco Corp.,* 514 F. 2d 285.
[28] *Fortune* v *National Cash Register Co.,* 346 N.E. 1251.
[29] *Harless* v. *First National Bank in Fairmont,* 246 S.E. 2d 270.
[30] *Tameny* v. *Atlantic Richfield Co.,* 164 Cal. Rptr. 839, 610 P. 2d 1330.

The at-will doctrine is far from dead, but it has been crippled. It is like a ship with a broken mast—it can still move, but it can't tack and run before the wind. Employees, of course, are happy with the change; it gives them bargaining power that they never had before. Attorneys, naturally, are also happy; a whole new field of business has opened up for them. But corporate leaders are not so happy, and it occurs to many of them that the costs of corporate due process might be easier to take than the bad publicity and expenses of legal due process. Corporate due process is far from being an exact substitute for legal due process, but it has stopped many a would-be litigator in his or her tracks.

For instance, at Control Data, a fired and fired-up engineer fought his dismissal all the way to the company's "supreme court," the Review Board (see Part II). There he lost. But for the internal procedure, he probably would have sued. The reason he did not is that both he and his attorney realized from the Review Board hearing that the company was well prepared to beat him in court. Also, the company's procedure had opened his eyes to the fact that not all people were as moved by his predicament as he and his friends were.

State Solons Skew the Law

In more than half a dozen states, including Michigan and New Jersey, legislators have written statutory exceptions into the so-called law of master and servant. In many more state legislatures, bills have been introduced to protect certain kinds of employees from dismissal. One effect is to make companies more cautious in firing people and to consider checks and balances on the authority of managers to fire arbitrarily. A second effect is to encourage disgruntled employees to consider the possibilities of suing. Both effects strengthen the case for due process.

In Michigan, a 1983 bill requires companies to notify employees of the reasons for discharge, provides for mediation, if the employee wants it, by the Employment Relations Commission, and then creates a right to appeal to arbitration if the employee is dissatisfied with the results of mediation. The arbitration is binding on both parties. Employers with grievance procedures providing for arbitration (e.g., Northrop Corporation, as described in Part II) are one of the few groups excluded from the purview of the bill. In New Jersey, a 1986 bill prohibits employers from taking action against employees who disclose activities that they reasonably believe to be illegal, whether or not they are. The law carries stiff fines and punitive damages for employers who don't comply. Originally the New Jersey Chamber of Commerce fought the statute but changed its position after the bill was amended to require workers to complain first to management. In West Virginia and Illinois, the solons took a different approach, allowing common-law actions for employees who are fired for reporting illegal activities.

The numbers of employees who have sued under the umbrella of such statutes have not been reported yet, but judging from what lawyers and judges tell me, the early total must be in the thousands. For both the company and the dissident, many managers think, the cost would be far less if internal due process procedures were used.

Vibes from Abroad

As business has become more global, American managers are increasingly conscious of employee rights in other countries. In Scandinavia and Western Europe, procedures and forums of various sorts have been created to right the wrongs that employees can prove that they suffered or are about to suffer. Although many of these systems seem inappropriate for the United States—England's, for instance, suffers too much from a governmental presence to satisfy most managers on this side of the Atlantic—the principles behind them seem appropriate.

In Italy, nonmanagerial employees contest dismissals and other supervisory decisions in the regular court system. Usually they are assisted by union attorneys. Generally, several months go by before a legal decision is reached, but not a year or more as in this country. Managers, on the other hand, go to a standing arbitration board to contest dismissal. That board handles about one hundred cases a year. Interestingly, if it finds in favor of the complainant, the board never orders reinstatement, only special indemnities.

No End in Sight

The sixteen trends I have enumerated should leave no doubt about the future of due process. It is on a roll. This newcomer on the corporate scene is destined to become very familiar in the years ahead.

Looking back at the forces and conditions described, one is struck by their diversity, multiplicity, and combinativeness. The lessening of reverence for authority is combining with the effects of rising levels of education to whet the desire for due process. The initiative taken by a few CEOs is abetted by the rising expectations of the rank and file, and vice versa. Our perceptions of belonging, loyalty, and participative management are being broadened to include equity systems as well as work. Conscience is an inner motivator, but the concept of jobs as having certain characteristics of property works as an external motivator. General perceptions about the limitations of two great forces—professional management and unions—lead many to turn to due process. Zeroing in from different vantage points, judges and state legislators are giving due process a hand. A new development—the emergence of stronger personnel departments—is adding speed to the trend, but so is an old development, the creation years ago of due process procedures in Western Europe.

In the space of a few decades, equity and work are becoming opposite sides of the same coin. In this respect, Donnelly Corporation may be the bellwether of corporate governance, for the organization of the company is seen in terms of two structures—the work structure and the equity structure, each pertaining to the same employees, each independent of the other yet so tied in with the other that, from an employee standpoint, the two are inseparable.

For purposes of description and analysis, it is fine to use two separate terms for work procedures and equity procedures. Since they are like opposite sides of a coin, it is also appropriate to symbolize them in different ways. What is more, it is justifiable to put them in separate departments under the jurisdiction of separate top executives. It should never be forgotten, however, that in reality the two blend into one another and are not truly separate. They outline each other like the yin and the yang.

3

How to Tell Due Process
When You See It

Corporate due process is a dispute resolution procedure whereby a neutral agency or person has the power to investigate, adjudicate, and rectify. What kinds of systems meet these requirements? What do they look like, and what can they do? As you will see from a quick glance through the company descriptions in Part II, there are many and varied approaches, from the investigators at CIGNA in Philadelphia to Federal Express's dual board system in Memphis to Northrop's company board plus arbitration system in Los Angeles. However, all sound and workable due process systems possess certain characteristics in common. If you know these earmarks, you will be better able to plan for due process in your organization, establish it, and nurture it.

Let us look at a baker's dozen of tests. These tests cannot be ranked in importance because they are all essential; they are like links in a chain, all of which must hold if the chain is to do its job. The order in which they are described here, therefore, is only for convenience in exposition.

Does the Procedure Make a Difference?

If you can detect no change in the attitudes or behavior of employees, the procedure doesn't qualify as corporate due process, for due process *always* makes a difference. First of all, people use it. Regular use may not be apparent until, say, six months or a year after installation, but if by that time the procedure isn't in use, you can be sure that either it is not visible enough or, more likely, employees don't trust it. Second, the procedure changes employees' attitudes toward their jobs, management, and/or the company. These attitude changes may be latent in many cases, but they should show up in a good opinion survey or in managers' talks with subordinates.

Here are some examples of the kinds of difference a due process procedure makes and how those differences may be detected:

Use. Several to seventy-five cases a year before the final formal tribunal with board-type systems, and one or more complaints for every fifty or sixty employees with investigator-type systems should be processed. Check the personnel department's records.

Union threat. Organizing attempts should be fewer and farther between, and pro-unionization votes should be fewer (unless working conditions, pay, safety, etc. have deteriorated). At General Electric's Columbia, Maryland, plant, whose confrontation with the union has already been mentioned, the organizing threat, which had been rising dangerously, deteriorated to insignificance in the first four years after the grievance review panel was set up in 1982. The main competitors of Federal Express, Northrop, Polaroid, and Donnelly Corporation are unionized, but these four companies with corporate due process are not, nor do they face serious threats. At NBC, according to the Westin-Feliu study, several major union efforts to organize the clerical work force were thwarted, in part because of a counseling process that "is both confidential and perceived as interceding on behalf of employees."[1] The authors also reported that a division of E. R. Squibb and Sons won its "annual" National Labor Relations Board–supervised elections by greater margins as a result in part of the nonunion grievance procedure.[2] (Because of a corporate reorganization, the division no longer exists.)

Litigiousness. There should be fewer lawsuits from employees or exemployees than there would be with no procedure. Ask the legal department or the outside law firm retained by the company for data. Judging from what executives and attorneys told me, a decline of 5 percent or more per year should be expected for each year after establishment of a good hearing procedure and fairly widespread employee awareness of it. Of course, the before-and-after data should be comparable, with new kinds of suits (e.g., disease induced by work conditions), and suits due to other causes (e.g., layoff) eliminated from consideration.

Supervisory compliance with personnel rules. In all companies surveyed, managers and nonmanagers believed that supervisors and managers were complying better with corporate personnel policy as a result of due process. To get a reading on this, check with personnel about trends in the types of complaint received.

Employee trust. Companies like Federal Express which regularly canvas employees think it is clear that due process contributes to an atmosphere of trust and confidence in management. You may be able to glean evidence from talks with employees, but periodic employee surveys are more objective tools and also enable you to detect trends up or down.

Ability to hold and attract good employees. In the companies studied, managers . felt that their grievance procedures had improved the company's reputation

---

[1] Alan F. Westin and Alfred G. Feliu, *Resolving Employment Disputes Without Litigation* (Washington, D.C.: Bureau of National Affairs, 1988), p. 188.
[2] Ibid., p. 142.

as a place to work. The best sources of data are exit interviews, applications, and community opinion surveys. In the case of exit interviews, compare the losses of employees whom supervisors rate as above average. "Don't break the numbers down by reasons given, such as 'Need more pay,' " one manager told me. "Those reasons don't mean much compared to their feelings for the company." In the case of applications, look at the reasons applicants give for coming to the firm. In the case of community surveys, focus on respondents' perceptions of the company as an employer. In any or all of these categories, the results should be positive, and there should be at least some evidence that the grievance procedure is partly responsible for the good results.

Perhaps all this is another way of saying that due process is more than a "nice" approach to have, providing employees with more than a "warm feeling." It contributes in a positive way to employee relations, and though it is a link in a subtle chain, it contributes distinctly, not invisibly. Sometimes people say, in effect, "If you don't have unions or many lawsuits from employees, that must be because of your high pay or participative management, not your nonunion grievance procedure." It is true that one of the companies studied, Polaroid, is known for its generous pay levels, and that another, General Electric in Columbia, for its participative management. But several of the companies in the sample are *not* known for paying better than the competition, and around half are *not* known for participative management. In all of these cases, however, employee relations are good, union threats are not serious or are nonexistent, and legal actions from employees alleging unfair dismissal, discrimination, and related complaints appear to be low.

Is Access to the System a Right, Not a Privilege?

A good due process procedure is not like a London men's club whose membership is limited to gentlemen of certain social or familial standing. It is available, with only a few nominal restrictions, to *all* employees in the organization all the time. In his working paper for Control Data when that company's management was studying the problem, David Robinson said, "Policy must offer an explicit statement to the effect that access to the grievance system is a right, not a privilege." In short, the company promises the employee that when he or she feels the need, the doors will be open.

At Federal Express, Charlie Hartness put it this way:

> We call it the "Guaranteed Fair Treatment Procedure," but fairness and justice are perceptual. If you get yours and I get mine, I call that fair. If you get yours and I don't get mine, I call it unfair. *The only thing we can guarantee is that you get to go through the process according to the established guidelines.* [Emphasis added]

As we shall see in more detail later, all companies in this study limit their grievance systems in a few obvious ways. All require the complaints to be work-related; that is, employees cannot use the procedure to complain, say, about investments in South Africa or top management's decision to acquire the Soggy Hayseed Company or sexism in the cafeteria. A number of firms expressly limit grievances to violations of personnel policy; this spares investigators and boards from having to explain to grievants that a manager's judgment cannot be revoked if it is within bounds (much as an appellate court in the legal system won't substitute its judgment about witnesses for the trial court's). Most companies limit availability to employees who have worked a minimum period, such as ninety days, and many limit availability to full-time employees. At Northrop, the grievance procedure put in under Jack Northrop in 1946 has been restricted to nonmanagerial employees; in 1987, a separate procedure was instituted for managers.

If some employees in the company are organized by a union, they may be excluded, although it is worth noting that at NBC, where there is a strong and powerful union for part of the work force, union members are welcome, along with nonunion people, to use the company counselor. Indeed, union members have gone to him on various occasions.

In none of the companies studied did the limitations go beyond the foregoing. There were no gimmicks, no fine print containing exclusions, no unwritten practices limiting availability to employees in certain departments or buildings or at certain salary levels. Nor did employees have to be "in good standing." At one company I visited, a grievance was being won in the internal system by an employee who was busy suing the company in the courts.

Is the Procedure Simple and Easy To Use?

The grievance procedure must not be complicated and convoluted. It must not be full of pitfalls, subtleties, and booby traps, as procedure in our law courts is. If attorneys are excluded from representing grievants, as they are in all the companies I studied, this must be justifiable on the grounds that no employee needs an attorney to put his or her complaint in play. If the employee needs help (as when, let us say, he is not good at writing or she gets tongue-tied in the presence of managers), then that help must be available for the asking from the human resources or employee relations staff. Among the companies studied there is a division as to whether a staff specialist is an advocate for the complainer or a neutral, but in all cases the specialist gives the complainer as much help as he or she needs in presenting the complaint—in writing it out and/or summarizing the problem orally before a department head or the adjudicating board.

General Electric's form, shown in Part II, is a good example of simplicity. At the top the complainer puts his or her name, the supervisor's name, and such identifying items as shift and pay number. Under that comes a

2″ × 8″ space with the words "The Problem Is:" at the top. Under that space comes a 1½″ × 8″ space with the words "This is What Should Be Done." Under that is a line for the grievant's signature. That's all.

If the complainer wants more space to describe the problem, he or she simply appends an extra page. In most cases, the person elaborates orally at the hearings. If the problem statement is too short or cryptic, the employee relations specialist reframes it (with the employee's approval) and clarifies the issue.

At CIGNA, the employee who wants to lodge a complaint will find forms and envelopes for doing so in the company's Speak Easy program in holders located throughout the buildings. With the form comes a succinct, readable explanation of the procedure. The form provides space for the complaint, and a metered envelope is enclosed for the complainer to mail in the form. If the complainer can't describe the complaint in the space on the form, he or she attaches an extra sheet.

At Citibank, all the paperwork is prepared by the human resources generalist. When, for example, a branch teller contested his firing, generalist "Chuck Cummings" got the teller's side of it and the branch manager's, summarized them on paper, and at each stage of the appeal presented this written version to the adjudicators. All the teller had to do was sit down and tell Cummings why and how he thought he had been given the short end of the stick, and then review Cummings's written statement to attest to its accuracy. Both the teller and the branch manager saw what the other was claiming.

Is the Board or Investigator Independent of the Chain of Command?

This test, which more than any other separates the sheep from the goats in corporate due process systems, concerns the ability of the adjudicating agency to decide in favor of a subordinate complainer when it feels that that person is right. A quick version of this test is simply the question, How often do managers and supervisors get reversed? If the answer is never or 5 percent or even 10 percent, you can be pretty sure that the agency is not really independent because if it were, it would surely be deciding more cases in favor of grievants—at least, over a period of time. This is not a normative judgment but an opinion based on the experience of fifteen companies and the testimony of hundreds of managers.

Even in organizations with well-trained managers, many cases that get appealed to an advanced stage are candidates for reversal. There is one exception: fired employees who appeal their cases knowing that they don't have much of a leg to stand on, but figuring that they have nothing to lose by trying. When this happens, it weighs the percentages heavily in favor of the firing management. Even so, more than a small fraction of decisions will go in favor of the grievants, overall, if the procedure is objective.

For instance, in the first four years of Control Data's Review Board, as reported in Part II, about one-third of the decisions were reversals of management decisions; at Federal Express in 1986, a little more than one-quarter of the Appeals Board's decisions were management reversals, and of the 16 percent of cases that this board sent to the Board of Review for decision by the "jury system," about two-thirds ended up as management reversals, so that close to one-third of the cases heard by the two boards ended up as reversals; at Northrop in 1984, more than half of the Management Appeals Committee's decisions went against management.

I cite these data only to prove my point, which is that management reversals are substantial if the procedure is genuine. There appears to be no company where line managers are so enlightened and training is so effective that the reversal rate is insignificant.

In none of the three companies just cited, nor in any other company with due process that I know of, does a management reversal rate become a norm or an informal quota of some sort. This is due to a variety of factors, not the least of which is that the reversibility of decisions depends in part on what has been going on in the company. For instance, if the company has had to make layoffs, or if a tough new policy on performance appraisals is being introduced, there may be a large increase in the number of grievants, and the quality of their complaints will likely affect the reversal rate.

Perhaps the most dramatic instance of hearing committee independence that I came across happened in a division of Honeywell. A fairly senior manager was fired. Believing his discharge to be grossly unfair, he went to the tribunal. The tribunal members believed him, overturned the firing decision, and ordered his reinstatement in the company, but in another part. Their decision flew in the face of the division head, who had been informed about the intended discharge in advance and okayed it. *And it was he who had originated the tribunal in the first place!* In effect, therefore, his own creation was turning back on him. Much to this executive's credit, he accepted the tribunal's judgment.

Northrop is the only company studied in which a decision by the internal agency is, strictly speaking, in danger of being overturned. As explained in Part II, there the grievant can appeal to outside arbitration if dissatisfied with the decision of the company's "supreme court," the Management Appeals Committee. The arbitrator sometimes reverses the committee's ruling. Inside the company, however, the committee bows to no one. (Theoretically, the same thing could happen at Polaroid, which also provides for outside arbitration as a last step, but in practice this has not happened.)

How significant are reversal rates? For example, is it legitimate to compare the rates of different companies, drawing inferences that the rates in Company A are too high or too low because they are out of line with the rates in Companies B and C? I think the answer is clearly no. One reason is fluctuations like those mentioned earlier. A more important reason is that the character of cases decided by the court of last resort varies greatly from company to company. Company X may do a superb job of handling difficult cases *before* they go to the final stage of adjudication, whereas Company Y's human resources department may tend to back off from controversial cases. Company M may dispose of almost all performance appraisal complaints before they are appealed to the adjudication stage, whereas Company N may not, and since reversal rates vary with the substance of complaints, the figures from the two companies are not comparable.

Of course, the quality of managerial decisions may also vary greatly from firm to firm, with one company's managers so sensitively attuned to the decisions of the investigators and board that they nip grievances in the bud, while another's may not act that way at all. This difference, too, will affect the companies' reversal rates.

In companies where grievances are handled by investigators, it may be tricky to decide whether the officials are truly independent of the line. The test is, Do they have, or can they readily get, the authority to reverse a manager's decision when necessary? In one organization that I know of (not reported in this book), the investigator so clearly has this authority that supervisors, when she wishes to reverse them, rarely challenge her, but bite the bullet and agree to her finding. In many other companies, however, it is hard to tell. What is called mediation (i.e., voluntary agreement of the parties negotiated by an ombudsperson) may really be very close to adjudication. The company may like to call it mediation, because that suggests to managers that nobody is holding a club over them, but it may really be talking about a dispute resolution process that qualifies in every respect as due process.

In this book I include the latter variety of mediation as a form of due process and, to distinguish it from nonadjudicative forms, call it *power mediation*. For a comparison of power mediation with other forms of complaint resolution, see Exhibit 3-1.

Does the Ombudsperson or Board Have the Power to Get the Facts on Both Sides of the Case?

If the purpose of due process is to get at the heart of a problem and achieve justice while minimizing costs, complexity, and time, the adjudicators, whether they are tribunal members or investigators, must be free to question at will, investigate freely, and probe for facts without impediment. There must be no Bluebeard's chest of information that they open at their peril. There must be no file, no person who is above or beyond the range and scope of their inquiry. Thus, at SmithKline Beckman, grievance committee members are given a clear mandate to go wherever and talk to whomever they want, high or low. And at NBC, the ombudspersons can see

EXHIBIT 3-1

Forums for Resolving Employee Disputes

Minimal Power → Maximum Power

Outside Mediation	In-Company Mediation	In-Company Power Mediation	In-Company Objective Investigation	In-Company Adjudication	Outside Arbitration	Law Courts
State agencies in California, Connecticut, Massachusetts, Minnesota, New Jersey, New York, South Carolina	Many companies[a]	CIGNA NBC	Bank of America IBM	Citicorp Control Data Donnelly Corporation Federal Express General Electric (Columbia, Md.) Honeywell (D.S.D. and U.S.D.) John Hancock Northrop[b] Polaroid[b] SmithKline Beckman TWA[c]	Most unionized companies (non-managers only) Organizations contracting with American Arbitration Association	Open to all companies and employees

[a] Including all companies named to right.
[b] Outside arbitration may be used if grievant is dissatisfied with board's decision.
[c] Outside arbitrator chairs board in dismissal cases.

any personnel file in the company that they want to check and go to any person in any part of the company for information. Two dramatic examples come from IBM and John Hancock (each described in Part II):

> In the IBM example, the Open Door investigator has a sudden need to talk to an employee who now works in a facility a couple of thousand miles from Armonk. Without any rigmarole to comply with, the investigator calls the employee, makes an appointment, and hops a plane for the distant location.
>
> At John Hancock, the employee relations committee is petitioned by several troubled employees in a field office on the West Coast. The chairman and vice chairman pack their bags, fly there, and spend several days interviewing employees who know the situation firsthand.

In the examples just mentioned, the ombudspersons and tribunal members themselves do the investigating (if they want more information than the complainant and defending supervisor can furnish). However, not all companies with tribunals ask the adjudicators to go out and do their own fact-finding; they can only question the parties at the hearing. At some companies, in fact, the adjudicators do not even see the "plaintiff," "defendant," and witnesses, but rely on a written record. How are the requirements of due process met in situations like these?

First, let us take companies like Northrop, General Electric, and Donnelly, where the board hears the grievant and defending supervisor (plus any witnesses they choose to bring in). In this case, the requirements are met if the board members are free to ask any question and as many questions as they like. The theory is that the parties can and will produce every fact and argument in their favor. It is the same theory as that used in law courts, where judge and/or jury hear only the evidence that plaintiff and defendant bring to the courtroom. It is a perfectly good theory, even when it is borne in mind that as a practical matter the grievant or defending supervisor may stupidly fail to put him- or herself in the best possible light. Then, as one board chairman interviewed put it, the failure may be "costly indeed" to the party that makes it. In other words, like judges and juries, the committee members do not go out and find the facts that the party should have produced. They take the evidence as presented and make their judgment on that basis.

In none of the companies studied did I see any evidence that freedom of inquiry was curtailed, such as cautioning board members against asking embarrassing questions of a manager close to the chief executive, or a memo telling them that management's operations in a certain department or area are out of bounds in an inquiry. Any limitations of this sort would obstruct the purpose and raison d'être of the tribunal and mean that there is no corporate due process.

Next, let us consider companies where the tribunal members have only a written record to judge. Here Citicorp offers a good case in point. After being fired, a teller contests his supervisor's decision. A human resources generalist writes up the "book," as Citicorp people call it—a factual summary of the case. He sits down with the teller, then with the supervisor, then with others, then with the teller and supervisor again. No contention or issue raised by the teller goes unanswered, even if management feels it is ridiculous. The generalist can put any fact on record that he or she comes across, regardless of whom it favors. Any data that seem relevant are added in exhibit form, including photographs. What the generalist ends up producing is as complete a distillation of evidence as the two parties can give him or her, and it is this document that is given to the review board when it sits down to consider the case. The board is somewhat like an appeals court; that is, the written record that comes to it illuminates both sides of the case as well as the parties can state it with the generalist's help.

Suppose the generalist is incompetent or biased, or both? What is supposed to happen is that the review board discerns the weakness when it studies the write-up, asks questions, and debates the case. Although I saw no evidence of staff incompetence at Citicorp, Control Data, or Federal Express—quite to the contrary, these companies emphasize strong, able support groups—that is a potential hazard in this form of due process. The review board must be eternally watchful for any distortions or lacunae in the write-ups it receives.

Is Retaliation Kept to a Minimum?

If in the aftermath of using the company's due process procedure employees are harassed and punished by their supervisors, obviously they will think very hard before filing a complaint again. Retaliation can take many forms, some subtle and insidious. It can be so invisible, in fact, that it is probably impossible to stamp it out completely. However, in some companies it has been repeatedly and insistently frowned on by management for so long that the corporate culture disowns it. Managers and supervisors say, in effect, "We don't always like the decisions of the investigator or board— sometimes, in fact, they seem downright wrong to us. Nor do we like subordinates to question our decisions openly. But like it or not, we accept the idea, live with it, and don't retaliate against subordinates who use the procedure."

In Chapter 5 I will detail some concrete steps managers can take to minimize retaliation.

Is the Response of the Tribunal or Investigator Timely?

Company "courts" and ombudspersons have an enormous advantage over law courts: they can move faster because of fewer hindrances and requirements to meet. From the standpoint of equity and justice in the work force, this advantage is very important. Grievants and managers don't have to wait long for a hearing and decision, mountains are not made out of molehills, and if the grievance creates rifts and dissension while it is under way, the healing process can begin earlier. By contrast, in one law case with which I was involved, the legal procedures ate up more than eight *years,* causing endless turmoil and drains on employee time and energy. Corporate due process does not need to cause such havoc.

In the sample of companies studied, some succeeded better than others in coping with delays, but all succeeded better—far better—than courts of law. At IBM, strict deadlines are imposed on the investigators, and practically no excuses are acceptable. The investigator has twenty-four hours in which to contact the grievant, then fifteen working days to complete the investigation and recommendation. At General Electric–Columbia, the unit manager must meet with the complainant within three working days and render his or her decision in two; at the next level, a petition to the subsection manager, a meeting must be held within five working days and an answer given in five more; in the final stage, a hearing by the grievance review panel, ten days are allowed for organizing the meeting, and ten after that for a decision by the panel. At Northrop, a grievant may wait from two to eight weeks for a full-dress hearing by the Management Appeals Committee (the last stage in that company's internal procedure), and at Federal Express, a grievance may take seven or eight weeks to go through all five stages of the procedure.

These companies work hard to make their procedures swift and efficient. Obviously, a great deal depends on the complexity of organization, the difficulty of assembling a board, the corporate culture, and other factors. "In a sense," says the head of Federal Express's procedure, "we're driven by our own standards. If we can deliver a package from Boston to San Francisco by 10:30 A.M. the following day, why can't we process complaints faster?" This from an organization that already excels at speed of response to a complaint!

When I visited Northrop, the aircraft division was monitoring thirty-seven grievances. The employee relations group kept tabs constantly on all grievances, reviewing them every week or so on the basis of a computerized report that listed the name of the grievant, the number of the case, the issue (e.g., performance review, layoff), dates when appeals were made at different stages of the grievance procedure, the decisions rendered, and so forth. By virtue of this monitoring, management was able to keep grievances moving. But for such an effort, the whole process would have slowed down and the number of grievances outstanding would have become unmanageable.

Is Confidentiality Preserved?

When an employee goes to an ombudsperson or a personnel specialist, she wants to feel that she can talk freely without fear that her remarks will be bandied about afterward. If an employee lays his case out before a hearing board, he wants to know that his act won't become a black mark on his record and be put in a personnel file where inquisitive managers can see it. Every company in the study went to great pains to protect the privacy of grievants and the confidentiality of personal information divulged in the course of challenging a superior's decision. Some of the executives with whom I spoke felt that nothing could put the kibosh on due process more surely than management carelessness about confidential information.

Naturally, there are limits. As mentioned previously, for instance, an investigator can't take up a grievant's cause without communicating at least some of the facts to others in the company. "They come in and say, 'I want to talk to you, but I don't want you to talk to anybody,'" says Al Jackson, NBC's counselor at large. "I must then tell them, 'Okay, but if I can't talk to anybody, I can't do anything for you. In order to make a difference, even to verify what you've told me, I must do something.'" So there is some risk of breach of confidentiality simply by virtue of management action to correct a situation. Grievants can understand this. What they cannot and will not understand is unnecessary disclosures—too many or to the wrong people. Discretion is crucial. When so many employees complained to Jackson about one manager that he saw a pattern in that person's style, he went to the man and told him that he had received numerous complaints, had promised anonymity, and was taking the responsibility himself to get the problem corrected. The manager never found out who the complainants were. "You shouldn't even try to find out who they were," Jackson told him.

"If we are to do our job," says a key administrator for CIGNA's Speak Easy program, "the provision of confidentiality is very important. The employee who knows or suspects wrongdoing must trust us. He or she must have no doubt that confidences will be kept, that we will not discuss the problem with anyone without the reporter's permission." No matter how serious or urgent the problem, Speak Easy investigators don't break this rule.

At one large midwestern corporation, an employee can request that the record of his or her hearing go into the personnel file. If the request is not made, the record automatically goes into the confidential file of the human resources division, but into no personnel file where managers and others might see it.

At Federal Express, "Jim" went to the Appeals Board complaining that he had been unfairly denied a certain promotion. Along the way he wrote some nasty letters, including one to the chief executive. In the end, the board voted thumbs-down on his appeal. Later on he applied to become a manager and worried if the appeal would affect his prospects. He found that it didn't. Although a packet of information was put together about him, and although he had several long interviews with managers, there was no sign or word anywhere that his appeal was known to anyone outside the appeals channel. This time he got the promotion, and he has been in management ever since.

In this respect, corporate due process is preferable to legal proceedings, at least from the standpoint of grievants. In the courts, a plaintiff's conversations with his or her attorneys are, of course, privileged, but once the trial starts, every angry claim, every sordid detail, every embarrassing incident that comes out in the courtroom goes into the public record—and maybe to the press.

Is the System Visible?

Corporate due process does no one any good unless employees know about it. They must know of its existence; they must know—or be able to find out quickly—where to go and whom to see in order to use it.

This proposition is deceptively simple. One executive whom I interviewed felt that perhaps half the employees in his organization didn't know that a fine complaint resolution procedure was in place. But he feared the consequences of an aggressive publicity campaign. Every disgruntled employee in the company might be knocking on the doors with a written complaint in hand! So how much *should* the procedure be publicized? He didn't know. He wanted more exposure, but he didn't want the boat to be swamped.

At companies like Polaroid, Northrop, and IBM that have had their systems for decades, publicity is not such a problem; word of mouth has long since done the job. But for a company that has installed due process during the last half-dozen years, a thin line must be walked. In a later chapter we will look at some measures that have proved useful to management.

Are Cases Approached Rationally and Objectively?

Tribunals and investigators must be concerned primarily with the facts of a situation, not with the status of the parties or the political implications of a decision or recommendation. They must pay as little attention to the chemistry between them and the parties as possible. Chemistry may be important in a working relationship, but it should not affect fact-finding, deductions from facts, and attempts to judge situations equitably in the light of personnel policies. Philip Selznick writes:

> Whatever is arbitrary is offensive to legality [in a corporation]. Rule-making that is based on evident caprice or prejudice, or that presumes the contrary of clearly established knowledge, violates due process. Procedure cannot be "due" if it does not conform to the canons of rational discourse or if it is otherwise outside the pale of reasoned and dispassionate assessment.[3]

[3] *Law, Society, and Industrial Justice* (New York: Sage Foundation, 1969), p. 253.

In a more general discourse, the legendary Roscoe Pound states:

> If one will is to be subjected to the will of another through the force of politically organized society, it is not to be done arbitrarily, but it is to be done upon some rational basis, which the person coerced, if reasonable, could appreciate. It is to be done upon a reasoned weighing of the interests involved and a reasoned attempt to reconcile them or adjust them.[4]

Are the Processes and Decisions Predictable?

Managers and nonmanagers have to be pretty sure that, just as chronic complainers with flimsy cases of alleged mistreatment won't get anywhere, so supervisors who violate company policy will lose, and that if by chance a case comes up next month that is like the Joe Blow case last month, it will be approached in the same way. It must be predictable that the panel members, investigators, or other arbiters will, let us say, apply the company policy on job evaluation as stated in the rule book, or disallow a manager's warning to a poor performer if it isn't given in the required way, or reject an errant employee who attempts to smooth-talk his or her way to a decision that the facts don't justify. If the process is not predictable, it will soon become a mockery.

During my interviews at one company, I talked with the chief employee counselor. Her department is highly regarded, and usually distraught employees go to see her before they go up to the employee "supreme court" with a written complaint. She told me about an egregious case—an employee who had come to her with a story of terrible persecution by the supervisor. She went to the supervisor and found that the facts were true. But the supervisor gave her a smug smile and said, "Look, you're wasting your time. There's no way I'm gonna change that decision." She leaned toward him and said, "Okay, but if you don't, that employee is going to go to the hearing committee. And you know as well as I know that with these facts you'll be blown out of the water." The supervisor agreed to change the decision.

Of course, as employee relations people know, no two cases are identical, making it important for those involved to examine each one individually. A veteran of the Employees Committee at Polaroid told me:

> We try to take individual circumstances into account. This means that the same offenses may be treated differently. If, say, an employee violates a written policy on stealing, we don't look only at how the last employee who committed a similar offense was disciplined, but also at any unique circumstances that make this crime a little different. As a result, two employees committing the same offense may deserve different measures of discipline, in

[4]"A Survey of Social Interests," 57 *Harvard Law Review* 35 (1943); quoted by Selznick, *Law, Society, and Industrial Justice*, p. 255.

our view. We don't try so hard to be consistent as to be fair. Fair means not necessarily equal penalties.

This concern with facts, too, must be predictable. In short, the approach of the adjudicators must be consistent from one case to another. At Company A, they may interpret the no-fighting rule strictly, whereas at Company B they interpret it literally. This sort of difference is fine, allowing adjudicators to take into account individual corporate customs and employee traditions. But within Company A, as within Company B, there should be continuity and consistency of approach.

Are Staff People Ready to Help and Advise Employees with Complaints?

Supportive staff plays two crucial roles. First, it can monitor compliance with a decision on a case, as discussed previously. If the manager loses at the hearing, he or she may be sorely tempted to do what was originally intended but in a roundabout way, as when a subordinate who was reinstated after being fired is fired again, but for a different reason, or is encouraged to resign by assignment to miserable tasks. It is unrealistic to expect line management to watch for such tactics and go to bat for the grievant, if necessary. An adequate and capable staff is needed for the job. At some companies studied, a staff member sits at the board hearing and personally hears the discussion and decision so that there is no misunderstanding about the board's intent.

The second crucial role is assistance with complaints. In the majority of cases, grievants come up against managers who possess more experience than their subordinates, better training, superior communication skills, and useful connections with senior line managers. Staff people must be available to neutralize these advantages of managers, at least for the period of the complaint. Here are some examples from Part II of how grievants in a few leading companies get assistance:

> At Honeywell, a complainant about to present her case to the hearing board was advised by her doctor not to appear personally. She was too nervous and excitable. So a representative from the human resources staff took her case at the hearing (and won it).
>
> At Polaroid, Employees Committee representatives are available throughout the company to help grievants. Although they may guide the complaining employee about his or her complaint (e.g., by mentioning previous complaints that are comparable), they don't take it on themselves to judge whether the complainant is right or wrong. Their mandate is to represent that person as well as possible, procedurally as well as at the hearing.
>
> At Control Data, a representative from the company's Employees Advisory Resource sits down with the grievant and makes any necessary clarifications

in the complaint. What exactly did the manager tell the grievant on Thursday? How bad was the Friday snowstorm that made the grievant late, and what was said in the call from the toll booth? If the grievant can't seem to get started with a written report, the rep asks him or her to talk it, then the rep writes it out, shows it to the grievant, and makes any changes desired.

In one case at Control Data, says the manager of work problems counseling, the grievant needed the opposite kind of help; that is, he had a case of logorrhea and wrote ninety pages of description of his grievance. "We told him to cut the material down and focus it better. He wanted to write it himself so we let him. But we guided him. We told him that this point is critical to his case while that one isn't. We told him what parts seem to be too emotional rather than factual." He was urged to aim for a written report as close to ten pages as possible.

At the Columbia plant of General Electric, an employee relations specialist helps grievants. "When employees come to me with complaints, I coach them on how to present them. I may get them to practice what they're going to say and how they're going to say it." Sometimes the specialist will put the grievant on hold, go to the supervisor, and urge him or her to change position. "If the grievant goes to the panel," the specialist warns the supervisor, "they're going to beat your socks off." Feeling the heat, a wise supervisor will see the light.

Are the Rules Clear?

Company policies are the "law" that ombudspersons, investigators, and board members try to apply. They must be clear and understandable, and they must cover all important subjects in the employee-manager relationship, such as pay, promotion, job selection, performance appraisal, absenteeism, leaves of absence, vacations, paid time off, sick leave, maternity and paternity leave, layoffs, and, of course, discharge. Clear policies can do a great deal to take the pressure off board members, especially when they have a painful decision to make. One "judge" told me how difficult it was for her and several colleagues to affirm the dismissal of an employee whom they all liked. "But we said to ourselves," she explained, "that a rule is a rule, and maybe we liked him and didn't like the rule, but we had to apply it. It was very clear."

In the next chapter we will discuss this issue in more detail.

Summary

Although there are many possible forms of corporate due process, any and all must meet the same tests. Whether it uses an investigator or routes complaints through an appeal system culminating in a board, the procedure must be open to all employees. It must be simple and easy to use—with no lawyers necessary, no hidden expenses, no booby traps. It must be independent of the chain of command in the organization, free to decide disputes on their own merits, and as able to decide against a defending manager as against a grieving subordinate. It must have the power to get all the facts it wants—on its own, from the contending parties, or from investigators and presenters. Its decisions must not be negated by vindictive managers who are free to retaliate against grievants who win at the hearings or investigations. It must be able to respond in timely fashion to appeals from employees who believe they have been wronged. It must preserve the confidences and privacy of complainants and managers. It must be visible throughout the organization so that those in need will know where to go for help. It must approach cases rationally and objectively. Its processes and decision modes must be predictable. Employees who need it must be able to get whatever assistance they require in framing complaints and negotiating steps. And it must be bound by policies and rules that are clear to employees at all levels.

Exhibit 3-1 shows seven possible forums for resolving employee disputes with supervisors, ranging from the weakest to the strongest as measured on an adjudicative yardstick. The fifteen companies covered in this study are demarcated in the exhibit. All of these companies' systems qualify as due process, from power mediation systems to the left to the more formal adjudication systems near the right. It will be useful to keep this spectrum in mind when considering the policy and administrative questions raised in the next two chapters.

4

Questions for Policymakers

This study of the due process procedures of fifteen companies shows a wide range and variety of approaches, a veritable vending machine of different systems and concepts, each with an easy-to-take monetary price tag if not a low emotional price tag, each of proven worth and dependability. If time allowed us to add other companies' systems to the purview of the study, the variety would surely be even greater. What is more, there seems to be no pattern in the choice of procedure. Financial institutions do not opt for this type, manufacturing for that, smaller organizations for this, older organizations for that, and so on.

You might infer from all this that a due process system for nonunion employees can be chosen with a blindfold on. That is not the case. To get a good fit between system and company, managers need to look at a fairly wide range of questions, and to keep in mind how their organization thinks and operates. At Northrop Corporation, says the head of that company's grievance system, the procedure works "because we want it to work and take pains to see that it works." Obviously, the procedure meets perceived needs. What kind of procedure will so fit a company's needs that management will feel committed to it?

The purpose of this and the next chapter is to look at two sets of questions that people in a company should ask themselves when deciding, planning, and preparing to set up due process for employees. Although the sets are not exclusive, I will label one as policy-making questions and the other as administrative questions, for the first set has to do more with concerns that top executives are likely to have, whereas the second deals more with administrative and operating matters.

As you will see, these policy questions deal with many of the issues described in the previous chapter. In fact, with the previous chapter in mind you may be able to anticipate various questions that need to be discussed.

Commitment

Top executives should regard the commitment they are making as a long-term one. A due process procedure is not amortized and then, when paid off, considered for the junk heap. It becomes a part of the corporate body and grows with it, ultimately becoming an indistinguishable part of it. In none of the companies studied did top executives snatch a procedure off the shelf or borrow it lock, stock, and barrel from someone else. Instead, they adopted and adapted it carefully, making sure that it "felt" right, seeing to it that it meshed with organizational behavior, customs, and traditions as they understood them. As far as I can tell, this was never done by formula or numerical evaluation but by purely subjective judgment, in much the same manner as you might decide that a shoe fits. Bank of America is a case in point. When it revamped Let's Talk, management did so on the basis of numerous impressions of the strengths and weaknesses of the previous grievance procedure.

Once a company chooses a basic approach, it is difficult to uproot it. That can be done—in fact, two of the companies studied discarded the procedures that they started off with—but most companies have stuck with one system and let it evolve, cropping, pruning, and trimming it so that it looked and felt right. A good due process procedure has a lot of vitality. Once it takes root in the corporate culture, it grows robustly, and management can alter it over and over again without hurting its potential.

Professor Alan F. Westin of Columbia University uses the analogy of law courts to explain the long-term nature of the commitment: just as it is unthinkable that a Western nation today could abolish its courts, except under martial law, so no company could renege on its due process procedure once the organization has gotten used to it.

Ask, "Is this approach or system one that I think this organization can live with for a long time—much longer than my own tenure in management?" Don't choose an approach because of its prestige or track record with other companies.

Infrastructure

The infrastructure requirement is essential, crucial, indispensable. In every company studied, there was a strong personnel department (sometimes called employee relations or human resources). Without it, success with the due process procedure would have been impossible. Every top management considering due process seriously should ask itself, "Is our personnel department—the infrastructure—sufficiently strong to support the new procedure?"

How strong is strong? It is difficult to answer the question with data because so much depends on how and where personnel people are used. In the pharmaceuticals division of SmithKline Beckman, there is one employee relations staff person for every three hundred to three hundred fifty employees; in the aircraft division of Northrop, there is one employee relations rep for every one thousand employees. Yet both organizations have strong personnel departments—plenty strong to meet their needs.

Perhaps it is more useful to consider the task of personnel vis-à-vis the due process procedure: to handle and close out the great majority of complaints so that only a few have to get passed on to the board or investigator. At Federal Express, for instance, about two-thirds of complaints are closed out at one stage or another by the skillful work of employee relations and line management people; only the balance go to either of the two boards for a formal hearing. At Citicorp, something like seven hundred cases were handled by human resources people in 1986, all closed out successfully but for a dozen that went up to the Problem Review Board.

At John Hancock, employee counselors consider themselves the "gatekeepers" for the employee relations committee. In 1986, they were successfully heading off at least five complaints for every one that had to go up to the committee, and in one recent four-month period that I examined, nine complaints with substance were resolved for every one that had to be passed on to the committee. At Donnelly Corporation, employee representatives and personnel people are so successful in resolving disputes in the first three steps of that company's procedure that only a handful of disputes see the light of a formal equity committee hearing.

Ask yourself, "Is our personnel group capable of resolving most complaints informally so that only a few have to be passed on to the board or investigator?" As Exhibit 4-1 suggests, personnel should be able to handle the great majority of complaints that supervisors cannot handle. Mary Rowe, a wise and seasoned observer of complaint resolution, told me that although an estimate of the proportions of concerns that should be fielded by line and staff is exceedingly difficult to make, "Mine would be that supervisors should informally handle at least nine out of ten employee concerns, and employee relations, ombudspersons, and others should informally handle at least nine out of ten of the remainder of relatively serious concerns."

Normally, 2 to 20 percent of the work force can be expected to go annually to personnel specialists in companies with strong personnel staffs. Many of the people with concerns, by the way, are managers and professionals; gone is the day when only such as clerics, operators, and maintenance people complained. I am told by some employee relations specialists, in fact, that managers and professionals complain to personnel in greater proportion than others do, especially where matters of cost and expense are concerned.

But dispute resolution is not the only thing that an able personnel group must be good at doing. In most companies personnel officials are the ones who keep track of complaints and nudge any manager or committee who is taking inordinately long to process a complaint. It is also these people who instruct, advise, and if necessary, carry the ball for grievants so that the board or investigator won't be swamped with routine questions and pleas for advice. In this respect, General Electric's Columbia plant and Polaroid offer especially good examples.

In addition, personnel people are often a valuable resource for board members when a case is to be heard. For instance, employee relations people sit in on the Appeals Board at Federal Express when it considers cases every Tuesday. The three members of the board are liable to turn at any time to the personnel adviser with a question about the case or policy. In a session I attended, employee relations produced a photo of the accident damage that occurred in a case, saving the board from what might have been a lengthy postponement before its questions could be answered. At Northrop, employee relations people brief the members of the Management Appeals Committee before it holds its hearings.

In this study, no one could offer a recipe of talents and skills needed by a good personnel person. The consensus was that the best way to identify such a person is by looking at his or her day-to-day performance. One talent that separates the able from the not-so-able is willingness to stand up to line managers when necessary and blow the whistle on them. Another is the ability to confront a complainant with the facts of his or her poor performance when necessary—what the senior employee counselor at John Hancock calls "reality confrontation." For one expert's view of the skills needed, see Exhibit 4-1.

Andrew S. Grove, the president of Intel Corporation, was not thinking of due process in particular when he wrote about the job of human resources people in *The Wall Street Journal,* but his remarks are applicable to our subject.

> Simply put, human-resource people need to lay the track for ordinary, imperfect managers so they can easily discharge their people-oriented obligations. They need to prod managers when they are reluctant to act. And if the managers don't discharge these obligations even after prodding, human-resource people need to call this shortcoming to the attention of higher-ups.[1]

It is not easy for staff people to do this, Grove admits, and a great many of them fall short of doing their duty. They want to duck out when they see a shoot-out with a line manager coming. They want to oblige the line and avoid rocking the boat. He continues:

> Few human-resource people realize that when they avoid conflicts with a misbehaving manager, they may only be creating conflict somewhere else. Recently, I ran across a situation in which a human-resource manager stood by and watched while an operating manager undermined and devastated his subordinates. He never had the courage to intercede. His explanation was: "How could I possibly confront my manager, the one I support? After all, I

[1] "Is Anyone Minding the Monitors?" *The Wall Street Journal,* September 30, 1985.

EXHIBIT 4-1
Skills Needed by a Complaint Handler

—Dealing with feelings, especially rage, fear of retaliation and grief. Helping people get to the point of being able to make good decisions, and being able to deal effectively with their problem or complaint.

—Giving and receiving data on a one-to-one basis.

—Counseling with clients; inventing and exploring all the possible options, helping people choose responsible options; coaching on how clients may deal with problems directly if they choose to do so (i.e., helping people learn a method to help themselves); problem solving, role-playing, anticipating possible outcomes, etc.

—Shuttle diplomacy by a third party, back and forth among those involved in a problem, to resolve the problem at hand (sometimes called "conciliation" or "caucusing," or thought of as one form of "mediation").

—Having a third party bring together the people with the problem, so they can reach their own settlement (often called "mediation").

—Fact-finding or investigation. This may be done either informally or formally; results may be used, or reports made, either with or without recommendations from the fact-finder to a decision-maker.

—Decision-making, arbitration, or adjudication, where a single person (for example, a line manager), or a committee or board with formal authority, decides a dispute (this function may occur within line management channels as a normal part of management decision-making, or be structured as part of a formal complaint and appeals channel, or formal grievance procedure).

—Recommendations for systems change ("upward feedback"); designing a generic address to a problem or a complaint; actual change in policies or procedures or structures or plans, as a result of inquiry, suggestion, complaint or grievance.

Source: Professor Mary P. Rowe, Massachusetts Institute of Technology.

work for him." Does this operating manager, in fact, pay the human-resource manager's salary out of his own pocket? Of course not. The corporation does. The same corporation that pays the salaries of the underlings who were being trampled on."[2]

Purpose

What is your main purpose in installing a due process procedure? The answer affects your choices, actions, and priorities.

For example, if union organizers are breathing down your neck and your primary incentive is to hold them off, you want a procedure that has quick appeal and immediate visibility. Quick appeal means objectivity and neutrality—for instance, a board selected at random like Control Data's or a board chaired by an outside arbitrator, as at TWA, or perhaps simple arbitration under contract with an organization like the American Arbitration Association. (In 1987, according to George H. Friedman, vice president for case administration, the AAA administered three hundred forty-five dis-

[2] Ibid.

putes involving nonunion employment.) Immediate visibility means an open hearing with both sides presenting arguments. But if your main purpose is, say, to make all managers and supervisors more mindful of personnel rules, then a quiet, low-profile approach might be better; or, if your main purpose is to demonstrate top management caring and concern for employees, an approach stamped with the imprimatur of the chief executive might be best.

Choice of Procedure

Should you go the investigator route, as at IBM, CIGNA, NBC, and Bank of America, or the board route, as other companies have done?

The investigator approach tends to be more flexible, personal, and confidential. Its disadvantage is that it places an enormous burden on the investigators, and if they are not top-notch, the system gets very mushy. On the other hand, the board or "jury" approach probably ensures the maximum degree of fairness. Also, board members tend to support each other. They can test their perceptions of fact with each other, they can throw up ideas and see if they make any sense, they can share worries and concerns. "When you run into a tough case," I was told at General Electric by one employee who had served on a grievance review panel, "it sure helps to have four people to talk it over with."

But the board approach is formal, and because several or more people are involved, all of whom have other responsibilities to discharge, a board cannot move as nimbly as an investigator can. It cannot have that private tête-à-tête with manager and grievant and work out an ingenious solution that "fits the crime" precisely. Some boards, in fact, have rules that prohibit inventive compromises.

It is tempting to try to devise some kind of formula in which the degree of centralization, the strength of the personnel department, the proficiency of employees, and other factors could be combined to give management the right answer to this question. However, the inputs to such a formula are often difficult to generalize about, and it is also difficult to say that such and such a combination favors one approach whereas another combination favors the alternative. Federal Express and SmithKline Beckman are about as dissimilar in corporate culture as any two companies can be, yet both use a board approach with good results. IBM and Bank of America are extremely different, yet both use an investigator system. CIGNA and NBC, both using power mediation, are radically different businesses. Polaroid and Northrop are the only two companies in my study that make outside arbitration optional as a final step, and both companies devised that step in 1946 (without knowledge of the other's doing it); yet the two are as far apart culturally as they are geographically. About the only common denominator that the eight companies mentioned have is strong personnel departments and people-oriented managements. On the other hand, General Electric's

Maryland plant and Donnelly are culturally analogous in many ways, as are CIGNA and John Hancock, but each pair represents extremely different concepts of and approaches to dispute resolution.

In short, the choices of grievance procedure by the fifteen companies in the study support the notion that anything goes as long as top management supports it. However, judging from workaday experience with nonunion grievance procedures possessing different features, what managers have told me, and my own observations of the systems, you might think hard about the following matches of culture and system:

Employee skepticism. If you have a history in your company, not of outright distrust between managers and nonmanagers, but of skepticism and uncertainty in employee relations, consider installing a board procedure. An unbiased board that examines disputes objectively on their merits, and soon demonstrates that it will overturn managers when it finds them wrong, will gain credibility quickly and surely. If there is any question in your mind about the strength of your organization's personnel group, particularly its ability to stand up to line management when necessary, that, too, is an argument for a board or jury system, for the very presence of such a body does a great deal to strengthen personnel's hand in attempting to resolve disputes informally.

Top-down control mentality. If your management group feels deeply committed to the philosophy of detailed control over all operations, it will probably find the notion of autonomous boards and jury-style verdicts threatening. In this case, consider power mediation and the investigator approaches. An investigator can work quietly and supportively with the line manager involved in a case. The investigator approach also offers an option: later on, if management chooses, it can convert to a board system. (By contrast, it would be difficult to move vice versa, that is, from a board system to an investigator or power mediation system.)

Paternalism. If your company is paternalistic, with a long history of chief executive concern for managers and nonmanagers down the line, and with a desire to keep the chief executive highly visible in his or her concern for employees, then an investigator approach like IBM's is a good bet. In the IBM system, every Open Door coordinator represents the power, authority, and concern of the chief executive, and the "verdict" goes out on the CEO's stationery.

Strong employee family feeling. If managers and nonmanagers have a family or "we" feeling about the company, as told by surveys, low turnover, conversation, bulletin board notices, and other indicators, consider installing a board that is autonomous and more accountable to peers of the complainant than to top management. The company that goes farthest in this direction is Donnelly, where the deciding committee is elected. But companies that pick board members for each case by computer or random selection, such as Control Data, or by negotiations, such as Federal Express in its Review Board procedure, also say loudly and clearly to all employees, "See, this jury is not stacked against the complaining person. If you work here, you're qualified to serve."

"We're number one." If managers and nonmanagers in your company feel great pride in its products and services, are cocky about the organization's leadership in the industry, and have a durable faith in its capacity to stay out in front, don't hesitate to install a board whose members represent management and serve because of their official capacities in the corporation. Such officers represent part of the company's strength in the minds of managers and nonmanagers up and down the organization. Once they demonstrate their willingness to reverse management when they find it in error, employees will see the procedure as confirmation of what they knew all along about the company and its strengths.

Bureaucratic mentality. If your company is seen and felt by employees as a bureaucracy—a just and well-intentioned one but still an enormous, involved, complicated machinery of rules and procedures—you would do well to consider a fairly autonomous board with fixed terms of office (or possibly even indefinite terms). Members of such a board become fairly professional about their duties and skilled in the ins and outs of approaching cases. In this study, all such boards developed finesse, quickness, and sophistication about questioning witnesses, seeing issues, and unraveling case details.

Creativity, innovativeness, high competence. If the prevailing mood of your organization is one of proficiency and technical or professional competence, with a very visible measure of dual loyalty (i.e., to one's profession at large as well as to the employer), and probably with a lot of turnover, a good argument can be made for having a power mediator or investigator system. One reason is that a good investigator can talk in nuances with the two people in conflict, and much of the time nuances will be enough to get the desired action. It is not so much the decision that matters—the adjudicative aspect—as the attitudes and values expressed during dialogue. Another reason is that both superior and subordinate are more responsive to hints than in other companies, and still another is that in a company like, say, a broadcasting firm, accounting firm, or engineering institute, a good investigator, especially if he or she stays in the role for a while, lends stability and consistency to an organization that otherwise is mobile and constantly changing.

Admittedly, your company may possess two or more of the cultural attributes mentioned, and they may lead in different directions. That appears to be par for the course in this business. I also hasten to add that not all grievance procedures described in Part II are paired with the corporate cultures suggested above. I suppose you would say, for example, that the two insurance companies are office bureaucracies, yet only one of them has the kind of board membership described. This is because the field of non-union grievance procedures is young and, thus far, historical accident and other coincidences have played a large part in companies' selection of procedures.

Jurisdiction

How much of the corporation or organization should come under the umbrella of the investigator or board? At one large midwestern corporation, two divisions are subject to the hearing board. At General Electric, the Columbia, Maryland, plant has a certain grievance procedure, and reportedly several other GE plants have such procedures too—but not the whole company.

At SmithKline Beckman, on the other hand, corporate policy requires each division, old or new, to have an effective grievance procedure. The divisions can give their procedures different names, and the details can be different, but corporate wants every SmithKline Beckman employee to have access to a good procedure. At Bank of America, Let's Talk applies to the whole company, and the same goes for the grievance procedures of most of the other concerns studied.

If your company is a large one with many plants and divisions, especially divisions with varied cultures, you might want to start due process with one or two organizations and see how it works. When satisfied that it is feasible, you can begin extending it to the rest of the corporation, either putting the covered sectors under the umbrella of the same procedure or taking the SmithKline Beckman route and letting the divisions custom-tailor their approaches.

Standing to Complain

What employees are eligible to use the procedure, and what kinds of complaints will be heard?

As mentioned earlier, most companies say that only employees who have worked at the firm for some period like three, six, or nine months are eligible to use the grievance procedure. Beyond that requirement, most companies make no distinction between hourly and salaried employees, areas of work, or functions. Thus, salespeople, clerics, computer programmers, office workers, maintenance workers, accountants—these and all others are free to use the procedure. At Polaroid, however, the Employees Committee will assist only nonsupervisory employees, and at Northrop, managers are not eligible to use the forty-year-old procedure that is the subject of most of the write-up in Part II; since late 1987, a second procedure has been created for managers.

All companies in this study require the complaining employee to show that personnel policy was violated in his or her case. Thus, if policy says that sleeping on the premises is grounds for firing, the complainant fired for sleeping must allege either that he or she was not sleeping or was not doing so on the premises; and if policy says that posted job openings will be filled on the basis of merit and past performance, the complainant must allege that he or she had better credentials than anyone else who applied for the opening. At CIGNA, for instance, "Don" went to the Speak Easy program and complained about hiring practices in another part of the company. He was told that Speak Easy was not the right channel for such a complaint because he himself was not the victim of the disputed practice. At another company, an employee who went to the grievance procedure to challenge the merits of a corporate policy on drug testing was told that she could not use the procedure for that purpose; she must use another complaint system maintained by the company to challenge the substance of company policy.

Powers

Should your judgment-rendering group decide for one party or the other, or should it feel free, if it wishes, to devise an in-between solution—or to orchestrate a completely different outcome from that envisaged by either party?

Control Data stands for the first option. Control Data's Review Board is something like a law court in this respect; its architects wanted a board that could not compromise, cop out, or fudge its decisions but could render only "clean verdicts," that is, verdicts that give either the grievant or the defending supervisor the relief requested. The virtue of such a policy, of course, is that it forces the board members to choose and not try to be popular with both sides.

Federal Express stands for the second option. The company's Boards of Review or Appeals Board can decide for or against the grievant and give the relief requested, if it sees fit; or it can reduce a penalty and substitute a new one; or it can even refuse to apply a policy to the situation if it concludes that the policy isn't clear. IBM and John Hancock also stand for this option. The Open Door investigator at IBM can elect any solution that he or she wants, for the investigator represents the company chairman and his almost unlimited powers. At John Hancock, the employee relations committee can devise any solution it wishes, whether requested or not; it negotiates with the managers involved, to be sure, but it is not restricted by any terms set forth when the parties presented their arguments. In fact, one reason that only managers serve on the committee is that top management wants it to have considerable leeway and feels that managers are likely to possess greater skills in devising solutions than nonmanagers.

Accountability

To whom should the investigator or board report? At first blush, the answer is easy—top management. In actuality, however, the answer is more complex.

In the case of investigators, each company studied has a different type of accountability. At IBM, the investigator reports to an administrative assistant in the chairman's office. The investigator is seen as the chairman's representative (which is one reason that the program works as efficiently as it does), and the chairman signs the letters announcing the decision. At NBC, the counselor reports to a vice president. At CIGNA, the employee relations manager, who oversees Speak Easy, reports to the corporate director of employee relations.

In all of these cases, top management is involved, and that is probably the way it has to be. In the case of boards, however, there are more opportunities for variety.

In some companies—Citicorp and Control Data, for example—the board reports predictably to top management (the vice president for staff relations, in Citicorp's case, the vice president of human resources in Control Data's). However, at Federal Express and General Electric's Columbia, Maryland, plant, the chief executive sits on the board, and so the buck doesn't need to go further. (At Federal Express, to be concise, the chief executive sits only on the Appeals Board, but the second board, the Board of Review, takes many of its cases from the Appeals Board.)

At Federal Express, the chief executive knows how the other two board members vote, and that plus the fact that he appoints them means that he has effective control. At the GE plant, by contrast, the plant manager (whom I am calling the chief executive here) has one of the five votes, but since the other four ballots are secret, he has no control over the outcome. In effect, therefore, the grievance review panel at the plant is accountable to no one. Since the four panel members are picked by lot, the plant manager doesn't even have theoretical control.

At Donnelly Corporation, much the same situation exists. The equity committees are elected by nonmanagerial employees and report to no one in management. If you were to diagram the organizational structure at Donnelly, you would make two pyramids, one for operations management, one for equity. At the top of the equity pyramid there is no executive, only the Donnelly Committee, and right under the Donnelly Committee are the equity committees. The Donnelly Committee is so independent of management, in fact, that the late John Donnelly, the chief executive and principal owner, wasn't even allowed to sit at the meetings until the mid-1970s.

At Northrop, management accountability varies at different stages. When a grievant is pursuing his or her case through the first four stages, accountability to top management is very real—top management sits on the Management Appeals Committee, the highest in-company forum. However, if a grievant wishes to pursue the claim further, as many do, the case goes outside the company to an arbitrator—the fifth stage—and the arbitrator feels free to reverse MAC's decision.

Theoretically, the same holds for Polaroid. In reality, however, so few cases have gone beyond the Personnel Policy Committee, staffed on an ad hoc basis by top executives, that the situation is not comparable to Northrop's.

At TWA, the board is chaired, in termination cases, by an outsider, a professional arbitrator. That person is chosen individually for each case, and management has no control over him or her.

In effect, three of the eleven companies with boards say clearly, "The people who make the ultimate decisions about justice in the workplace do not report to top management. They are accountable only to themselves." In practice I think that at least three other companies—notably, Citicorp, Control Data, and TWA—say pretty much the same thing. The balloting is secret, the members are chosen on an ad hoc basis, and top executives have studiously refrained from interfering in the boards' decision making.

Thus, a majority of the companies with boards put the final judgments out of top management's control, which leads me to believe that the desire for control, more than any other one factor, decides a company's choice between an investigator- and jury-type system.

Personnel Policy

Don't consider having due process in your organization unless personnel policy is written clearly for all to see. As suggested earlier, this is a "must" for due process. Employees need to rely on the policy to bring complaints. Also, you don't want investigators and boards to be making the "law" of the company any more than the country wants courts to make the laws of the land. Decisions may be close and judgments fine, but always the investigator or board should be thinking of the meaning and intent of a provision in the written policy statement.

Ann G. Leibowitz, senior corporate attorney for Polaroid, delivered a paper in 1986 to the American Bar Association in Boston with some helpful suggestions for policywriters. For instance, she advises management to

> Provide broad policy statements that bind the company while including *nonbinding* suggestions for supervisors seeking to implement the policies.
>
> Avoid trying to define policies too precisely. For one thing, meticulously precise policies don't allow flexibility to react to changing circumstances. Although policy statements can always be revised, you must give employees adequate notice about changes in them, and that can be the subject of a grievance. "An employer who chooses to adopt rigid detailed policy language may find that he has, in essence, shot himself in the foot," writes Leibowitz.
>
> Make the language consistent. "If employee remuneration is 'wages' in one policy, it should not appear as 'pay' in another and 'salary' in another." Also, avoid expressions like *entitled* and *have a right to,* even in sections with nonbinding procedural suggestions headed by disclaimers.
>
> Pay particular attention to the clarity and understandability of conduct that can subject employees to discipline and discharge. "The surest way for an employer to lose an arbitration is to fire an employee for conduct the employee genuinely and reasonably did not recognize put his employment at risk." Don't try to list every kind of behavior that may lead to discipline, for the laundry list would go on forever, but such actions as stealing, insubordination, fighting on the premises, and drug use on the premises can be

specified. (For example, in its booklet *Working with Northrop,* an excerpt from which appears in that company's write-up in Part II, management lists one major offense in a way that is specific enough but also general enough to include all sorts of commissions. The offense is described simply as "immoral or indecent conduct on company premises.") Writes Leibowitz: "Collective bargaining agreements commonly refer to 'just cause' as being the appropriate catch-all standard for discharge. My personal preference is for 'conduct detrimental to the best interest of the company' which is almost—but not quite—the same."

Since personnel policies and rules may become important evidence for or against management in an employee lawsuit against the company, it is important that management believe in them. A case in point, which is especially apropos since the company in question is written up in Part II, is *Bratt* v. *International Business Machines Corporation.*[3] In this case the U.S. district court referred to the IBM Manager's Manual about the Open Door procedure and to internal company regulations about the disclosure of medical information. The U.S. circuit court, which received the appeal, also mentioned these sets of rules. Very briefly, the facts of the case are that Robert Bratt, an IBM employee in the Boston area, pursued several Open Doors when he thought that his work was not appreciated by his supervisors and when he believed management was holding against him the fact that he had resorted in the past to Open Door complaints. At one point he consulted with a physician who was under contract with IBM to examine employees. The doctor released her assessment of Bratt as "paranoid" both to the company medical department and to management. Learning this, Bratt was appalled. He had assumed his session with the doctor was confidential; personnel policy emphasized that confidentiality. When he sued IBM, most of his counts were thrown out, but the circuit court concluded that his privacy as guaranteed in company policy may indeed have been breached unfairly by the medical disclosures, and it remanded that part of the case for trial. Thus, part of the circuit court's reasoning was IBM's own personnel rules.

In short, IBM was, so to speak, hoisted by its own petard. Though it may have regretted losing the case, however, it had no regrets about the rules or its Open Door system. Management believed in them one hundred percent.

Management Support

Can managers and supervisors be convinced that due process does not undermine their authority? This is a problem—conceivably a chronic one—for every company that undertakes a complaint resolution system. In most companies covered by this study, it has been whittled down to only a minor problem, and in a few eliminated entirely, but in every case it has been a thorny issue at one time or another.

[3] U.S. Court of Appeals, First Circuit, No. 85-1545, March 6, 1986.

Due process could not have succeeded as it has in these companies but for consistent support for the approach from top management, communicated in many ways. In their study of dispute resolution systems, Alan Westin and Alfred G. Feliu come to a similar conclusion.[4]

Perhaps the most visible display of top management support occurs regularly at Federal Express, where the chief executive officer and the chief operating officer sit every Tuesday on the Appeals Board. At General Electric's Maryland plant, organization head Joe Carando sits on every session of the grievance review panel. At Donnelly Corporation, John Donnelly was a walking symbol of support for the equity procedure when he went about the plants.

Of course, not all chief executives and operating officers want to give such visible demonstrations of support, nor is it necessary in many cases. What is essential is that the head people communicate their support for the procedure over and over again, and demonstrate their support convincingly whenever suitable occasions arise. As noted earlier, for instance, one decision of the Management Appeals Committee at Honeywell impinged on a top management decision made prior to the hearing, but top management did not interfere with the decision. Many years ago, the appeals board of a large financial organization in Boston made a decision that horrified the chief executive. Rather than pull the carpet from under the board, however, the CEO swallowed his pride and went along with the decision.

Evaluation

How can you tell whether the due process procedure is doing what management wants it to do in the organization? There is no good reason not to subject the procedure to the same kind of scrutiny to which other activities are subjected. You do not have to let it fly on faith. As the old Pennsylvania proverb goes, "Faith saves, but it doesn't starch Grandma's nightcap."

Generally speaking, most companies with due process are looking for several broad accomplishments in employee relations: (1) justice and equity in work relationships; (2) companywide awareness of the procedure; and (3) employee confidence in the objectivity, fairness, and availability of the procedure. How are these purposes to be tested?

Progress toward the first goal has to be measured by reviewing the cases judged during the past year or half year, and that must be a qualitative judgment. Do the dispositions of the cases indicate that potential inequities were corrected? Only one number may be worth looking at, and that is the reversal rate. If the reversal rate is abnormally high or low, something is probably wrong. The industrial relations head of Northrop says:

[4] *Resolving Employment Disputes Without Litigation* (Washington, D.C.: Bureau of National Affairs, 1988), p. 221.

If we found that no reversals were happening, I would have to wonder whether employee relations is doing the job it should. Are we being tough enough on management? Are we seeing in depth the problems that exist on the floor? On the other hand, if management lost too many, I would begin to worry about the possible breakdown of our philosophy of management and whether we are really living up to the principles we espouse of being a good place to work and treating people fairly.

The employee relations administrator at Northrop finds former employees to be a good source of qualitative information:

All terminated employees are personally interviewed. Then about three months after the person leaves, he or she is sent a questionnaire. It includes questions about how the person felt about the grievance procedure—whether he or she knew about it, perceptions of how it worked, and so on. This information is a useful check for us.

The second and third purposes can be tested in a variety of ways, but perhaps the only truly objective approach is the survey. Every year Citicorp sends out questionnaires with thirty to forty questions on supervision—supervisors' skill in communication, their availability when a subordinate has questions, and so on. The response rate is close to 90 percent. Although no questions are asked specifically about the bank's Problem Review Procedure, respondents have ample opportunity to reveal their reactions to it pro or con.

Federal Express, on the other hand, asks employees directly about its Guaranteed Fair Treatment Procedure. In fact, Charlie Hartness, managing director of human resources analysis/employee relations, looks at the situation much as if it were a marketing problem, with GFTP as the "service" and employees who might use it as potential "customers." Every year Hartness's department surveys its customers to ascertain their reactions to GFTP, their understanding of how it works, and its credibility.

The beauty of surveys is that they reveal what employees are thinking—or not thinking—about grievance procedures. Reportedly, Wells Fargo began regular surveys of employees in 1986 because its complaint programs were used by fewer than 5 percent of employees and, in the words of Susan Palmer, the vice president overseeing the surveys, "We really didn't know what the silent majority felt."[5]

Surveys also enable you to see what effect, if any, organization and industry changes are having on employee attitudes. Thus, Hewlett-Packard surveyed its work force in 1986 for the first time in seven years because there had been a major organizational change in the company and business conditions had soured. "We were curious where we were, if this had impacted our

[5] *The Wall Street Journal,* October 27, 1986.

culture," said Robert Levy, a corporate personnel manager in Palo Alto. "Had we changed a great deal?"[6]

If you go to an outside firm to prepare and make your survey, costs are likely to vary widely. In 1986, companies reported quotations ranging from $50,000 to $125,000. Companies that used consulting firms to help prepare the questionnaires and analyze results reported to *The Wall Street Journal* that their charges ranged from $10 to $15 an employee.

Reporting

What, if anything, shall be reported to top management about the operation of a grievance procedure? What information, if any, should be released to managers in general? What data to employees in general?

In this sample, many more companies are interested in answering the first question generously than the second and third. Sometimes the reports are impressionistic, as in the annual statements by the chairman of John Hancock's procedure; sometimes they are terse and factual, as in Control Data's periodic reports; and sometimes they need be little more than a compilation of key numbers because of top management's close personal involvement with the procedure, as at General Electric–Columbia.

Reports to managers and supervisors in general are likely to be interpretative. Thus, IBM's chairman from time to time brings managers up to date on trends, opportunities, and questions about Open Door use. One time he talked about managerial fears about subordinates who resort to the Open Door; another time he talked about some subordinates' fears that using the Open Door would lead to retaliation by their bosses; another time he gave suggestions to managers whose decisions are challenged in Open Door cases.

Only a couple of companies in the sample tell the whole work force about use of the grievance procedure. One of these companies is Federal Express, which compiles data on the annual numbers of GFTP cases, subjects of the appeals, reversals, and other matters. In 1987, for instance, Federal Express's forty thousand employees were told in a newsletter about the numbers of appeals upheld and overturned in 1986. The top ten reasons for appeals were also disclosed in the bulletin.

Training

Should a company put on training sessions for supervisors in the handling of dissatisfied employees? Should it go even further, focusing on the workings of the grievance procedure itself?

Several years ago I studied a number of cases of employee malcontents who had "rocked the boat" in their organizations and made a lot of trouble

[6] Ibid.

for management, sometimes suing the company in the courts.[7] The study left no doubt in my mind that half or more of these egregious cases could have been nipped in the bud if supervisors had dealt with the complainers more skillfully at the outset. The potential payoff for good supervisor training is enormous.

In most of the companies studied, good on-the-job coaching comes from the personnel staff. Repeatedly I heard of cases where capable staff people had coached supervisors on how to handle dissidents, and more than one good manager confided in me that skillful coaching by staff people had given his or her career a big boost.

However, several companies are unwilling to put all their eggs in the coaching basket. They believe more is needed. For instance, Citicorp organizes courses for managers that focus on such subjects as discipline, supervising problem employees, and making performance appraisals. The courses are planned and run by human resources people, and the teaching technique includes role playing and staff-written cases. Managers do not have to take the course; participation is voluntary.

Again, Federal Express requires new managers to go through a program run by the Leadership Institute, an in-house operation staffed by company people. After going through the Leadership Institute program, new managers must take forty hours of course work during the year. One elective course is a one-day class on the Guaranteed Fair Treatment Procedure, and I am told that it is popular because managers learn early on that sooner or later they will have to handle an employee complaint, and the course will help them do that.

Two companies in the sample train tribunal members. General Electric's Columbia plant offers an eight-hour course in listening, interpreting evidence, and legal aspects. Only employees who take this course—it must be taken on their own time—qualify for the pool from which ad hoc board members are chosen. At Donnelly Corporation, those who are elected to equity committees attend workshops run by company people. There they learn how to manage their roles as elected representatives and how to handle grievances. The chairpersons of the committees get special training on how to run meetings, use witnesses, get the facts in a dispute on the table, and so forth.

Redundant Channels

Should there be different ways for employees to voice complaints? For instance, as an alternative to using the formal grievance procedure, should employees be able to turn to a hot line or "open door" office to raise questions or concerns?

Often worries or suspicions about pay, promotion, transfer, job posting,

[7]*Do It My Way Or You're Fired!* (New York: Wiley, 1983).

fraud, and other matters can be voiced simply—and confidentially—to a special office of the company. The troubled employee does not need to file a grievance. He or she can simply say, by note or call, "Hey, I think my boss isn't playing fair with me because . . ." The special office then gets the answer and calls or writes the employee.

Drawing on many years of intensive experience with complaint resolution, Mary P. Rowe of MIT writes that redundant channels and options are a "must" for an effective complaint system.[8] Employees must be able to choose between different avenues or they may not voice their concerns at all, preferring to seethe instead or look for another job. A. W. Clausen, chief executive of Bank of America, once explained to me why this is so. Some employees like to go directly up the line with a complaint whereas others don't; some employees like to stay anonymous whereas others don't; some prefer to write out their grievance or question whereas others prefer to present it orally, and of those who prefer the latter, some will choose the anonymity of a telephone call whereas others will go to someone's office and close the door.

One reason for these many preferences is personal style. Another is that employees using a complaint system often do so with different fears and reservations. Some fear retaliation from supervisors and co-workers; some are most concerned about losing their privacy; others are afraid they will be made to look silly; still others are afraid of appearing disloyal, though they are proud of their loyalty to the company. On and on the list goes. Because of an employee's particular fear, he or she may feel adamant against using this channel or that. In short, the employee voice, as Albert O. Hirschman calls it, requires different modes and options.[9]

Small Companies

Is corporate due process for large companies only? The answer is no. Any organization with, say, one hundred or more employees can make good use of this device.

Donnelly Corporation, included in Part II, employs about twelve hundred people in the United States. The General Electric plant in Columbia, Maryland, employs fewer than a thousand people. Clearly, these are not large companies as U.S. companies go. The approaches used by these organizations as well as those used by TWA, CIGNA, NBC, and certain other companies studied could serve many a small company well.

Alternatively, a small organization might combine with another company or companies to establish and operate a joint procedure. Indeed, this has been done successfully by two divisions of a well-known midwestern manu-

---

[8]"The Corporate Ombudsman: An Overview and Analysis," *Negotiation Journal*, April 1987, p 1.
[9]*Exit, Voice, and Loyalty* (Cambridge: Harvard University Press, 1970).

facturer. Another option is to turn to a group of professional arbitrators and contract with it on a case-by-case or year-by-year basis to hear and decide disputes. As pointed out earlier, the American Arbitration Association in New York City handles several hundred employee disputes a year for nonunion organizations. Its fees are reasonable and the procedure is straightforward.

In submitting the dispute to an outside arbitrator, management should make it clear what subject area is involved (e.g., whether an operator violated the company's rules about sleeping on the premises, or whether the assistant treasurer was guilty of falsifying her expense account). It should also send the arbitrator copies of the personnel policy and other relevant documents. Such material is helpful to the arbitrator in many ways, as indicated in the write-up on Northrop in Part II.

The term *arbitrator* does not have to be used, by the way. If it reminds management too much of collective bargaining or an unhappy experience, terms like *umpire* or *referee* can be used instead. Whatever the person is called, however, the company, defending manager, and complaining employee should understand that the outsider's job is to resolve the dispute in a final and binding manner.

Producing a Recommendation

If a management group is interested in setting up a company grievance procedure, how should it go about studying the possibilities and recommending a course of action?

No pattern emerges from my study. In some companies, a strong chief executive discussed the problem with lieutenants, got agreement on a few principles, and had one or more of them look into the matter. In others, someone at the second level, such as a personnel vice president, took the initiative, sold the CEO and other top executives on the idea, and produced a plan. No two companies followed the same course of action.

Unlike the situation a decade ago, a management group today can take advantage of the experience of other companies. From time to time during the course of my research I ran into people from other companies who were visiting the same organization I was visiting in order to report to their managements on due process procedures. In their report they could then say that so-and-so does this, so-and-so does that, and this course or that seems preferable and should work as well in their organization as it does in the other company's. Once I ran into a team of about six people from a Michigan company who were investigating one organization's grievance procedure. The team included third- and fourth-level managers as well as a first-line supervisor and a foreman, and it represented different functional areas, such as manufacturing, clerical, and industrial relations.

As noted in Part II, Control Data organized a formal task force in the late 1970s to study due process and produce recommendations for management action. At the time the company had a strong personnel department and a fairly conventional procedure for dispute resolution. The task force included a variety of managers, including the vice president of human resources. At the beginning, the group listed the six primary activities that needed to be done and plotted their time relationships on a simplified Gant-style chart (see Exhibit 4-2). In general, the activities were performed in the sequence planned, but the end result—the "internal arbitration system," which turned out to be the review board process now functioning—was achieved years ahead of time.

Summary

When thinking about setting up a nonunion grievance procedure, top management should consider a range of policy questions. It should pay particular attention to

Its willingness to make a long-term commitment to due process for all employees.

The depth and strength of the personnel department as a suitable infrastructure for an efficient and credible complaint resolution procedure.

Its main purposes in installing due process, and the effect of those purposes on priorities and actions.

The question of what system fits best into the corporate culture and management philosophy.

The scope or jurisdiction of the board or investigator.

Eligibility requirements for employees who want to file a grievance.

The judgment powers of the board or investigator, especially whether it must make either/or decisions or can orchestrate solutions in between or beyond what the parties have asked.

The accountability of the board or investigator.

The clarity and comprehensiveness of corporate personnel policy as the "law" of the company that investigators and board members will be bound by.

Its willingness to lend whatever visible or tacit support is necessary to give the board or investigator credibility and authority.

Means and measures for evaluating the success of the system after installation.

What information about its operations the board or investigator should release periodically to managers and nonmanagerial employees.

What formal or informal training, if any, should be given to supervisors who may come head-to-head with employees in the complaint resolution procedure.

Whether redundancy should be built into the employee relations system so that troubled employees can choose between different methods and forms of expressing their concerns, questions, and complaints.

EXHIBIT 4-2. Time/Activities Chart Produced by Control Data Task Force

Phased Proposals—Time Frame Chart

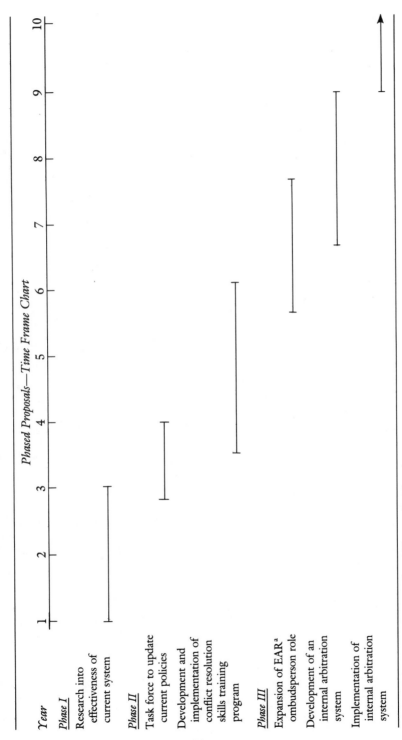

Year   1   2   3   4   5   6   7   8   9   10

Phase I

Research into
effectiveness of
current system

Phase II

Task force to update
current policies

Development and
implementation of
conflict resolution
skills training
program

Phase III

Expansion of EAR[a]
ombudsperson role

Development of an
internal arbitration
system

Implementation of
internal arbitration
system

[a]Employee Advisory Resource, the staff counseling function.

73

If an organization is small, whether it should employ an internal procedure, team up with other organizations, or perhaps contract outside for arbitration.

What kind of committee or task force, if any, should be formed to investigate the need and feasibility of due process and produce recommendations
for top management to consider.

If your management is interested in establishing due process, it enjoys
many luxuries not possessed by companies in the late 1970s and early 1980s.
Chief among these is empirical evidence about how and why due process
works. At the same time, the concept is still new enough to give the company installing it an innovative, out-in-front image. In the words of Alexan-
der Pope's famous couplet:

> *Be not the first by whom the new is tried,*
> *Nor yet the last to lay the old aside.*

5

Issues in Operations and Control

Because of great differences between investigator and board systems, this chapter will be divided into two parts, with investigator systems taken first. I shall devote a good deal more space to board systems, not because of pesonal preference but because more companies in the sample used them and because by their nature they give management a wider array of options.

As you consider the questions to be raised, bear in mind the comparisons made earlier. Investigator systems generally afford more flexibility in complaint resolution and more opportunity for close control by top management. Board systems, on the other hand, are likely to win more credibility. Also, their "jury" nature probably leads to a fairer weighing of the facts in difficult cases.

Investigator Systems

Who Should Do the Job?

This question is second to none in importance. Few people can be good investigators, and perhaps no more than one person in a thousand has the potential to serve as a good full-time investigator. The need is for someone who knows the company and its customs and idiosyncrasies, who relates well to many different kinds of employee, and who can wear two hats, that is, can go from the role of ascertaining the facts capably to making a fair judgment about the relative merits of a dispute. This is a tall order to fill, and companies that have good investigators should count their blessings.

Many will ask if there is a difference between *investigators,* as the term is used here, and *ombudspersons.* There is a great difference—not necessarily in ability but in role. Mary P. Rowe defines an ombudsperson as "a neutral or impartial manager within a corporation, who may provide confidential and informal assistance to managers and employees in resolving work-related concerns, who may serve as a counselor, go-between, mediator, fact-finder or upward-feedback mechanism, and whose office is located outside normal management structures."[1]

An important point in this definition is that ombudspersons do not decide on the equities of a situation. In a word, they do not arbitrate. But an investigator is often called on to do that. The Open Door investigator for IBM first ascertains the facts, then decides; the same goes for Bank of America investigators; the NBC counselor mediates as often and as much as possible but frequently must decide that such and such should happen; the same is true of the Speak Easy coordinator at CIGNA. Unlike ombudspersons, who traditionally do not change or set aside management decisions but rely instead on reason and persuasion, investigators may often find it necessary to reverse managers, or recommend reversal.

How Should Top Management Support Be Given?

The answer is twofold: (1) in words; (2) when necessary, in action.

At IBM, it is made clear to a manager from the beginning that Open Door investigators represent the chairman. Anything the chairman can do, the investigator can do. At NBC, the personnel vice president makes it clear to all managers that the counselor has authority to resolve disputes, that any problems that arise with the counselor will not be ignored, and that a wise manager will work the problem out with the counselor and not force top management to get into the act.

When action must be taken, IBM's chairman personally signs the letter affirming the investigator's decision. In short, the chairman's imprimatur goes on every decision reached by the investigators. The Open Door coordinator, who represents the head of the division where the dispute arose, sees to it that any necessary implementation is carried out. At Bank of America, the senior executive actually makes the decision.

A good example of top management action comes from an organization that must not be identified. The investigator found that a senior officer of the organization had made a practice over the years of requiring sexual favors from women in his office. Although the company had a clear commitment against sexism, the officer assumed that he was, so to speak, above the law; he scoffed at the investigator's concern. Bringing the proof of wrongdoing to the chief executive, the investigator said, in effect, "Our policy says this, he did that." After confirming the evidence, the chief executive got the offender out of the company within twenty-four hours.

What Format Seems Most Suitable?

At CIGNA, a troubled employee picks up a Speak Easy form from any of many locations throughout the company, fills it out, and sends it to the

[1] "The Corporate Ombudsman: An Overview and Analysis," *Negotiation Journal*, April 1987, p. 1.

coordinator or an executive. Depending on the nature of the complaint—whether, for instance, it concerns a policy, a question about some company practice, or an allegation of unfair treatment by a supervisor—the coordinator arranges a response. If unfair treatment is alleged, an administrator goes to the employee and begins an investigation. In other cases, a telephone conversation or written response may be enough.

This approach seems to work quite well. It is informal, flexible, and low-profile. As indicated in Part II, about 4.5 complaints per thousand employees are received annually at CIGNA. The corporate culture, primarily an office culture with traditionally strong employee relations staffs, a considerable amount of decentralization, and a kind of matrix organization where line and staff are concerned, supports the Speak Easy approach.

In an environment like IBM's, however, such an approach may be futile. IBM has a long tradition of enlightened paternalism, top-down management, and technological leadership. Its many plants and offices relate closely to each other. The Open Door not only fits into this scheme but actually strengthens it, for the procedure is centralized, tightly controlled, and minutely programmed, a continual reminder to all who come in contact with it of the power and authority of the chairman's office.

NBC's approach is like neither CIGNA's nor IBM's. It fits the need of an organization that is centered mostly in one place, even though it has outposts in other cities, and that by and large is staffed with a mobile, verbal, independent, fast-stepping cadre of people. Al Jackson, counselor for nine years, operates independently and with practically no supervision, reporting to a vice president.

Bank of America's approach is different still. It reflects the needs of an organization that was recently in crisis and whose top executives wish to support due process personally but must spend 110 percent of their time, as the saying goes, turning the organization around. Robert Beck, executive vice president, had personally seen and worked with IBM's Open Door while he was employed there. Coming to San Francisco a few years ago, he wanted a procedure that worked with the speed and efficiency of the Open Door yet was tailored to an organization whose main output was services, not products, and that was more loosely knit. Therefore he devised the two-stage approach now in use, with trained, neutral investigators in each stage reporting their findings to a senior executive who makes the final decision.

How Sacred Are Confidences Given the Investigator?

As emphasized earlier, every company I know of that operates an investigator system successfully—those covered in this study as well as some organizations not covered—believes that complete respect for confidentiality is absolutely essential. No ifs or buts. As one investigator told me, "I'm worthless if people don't trust me." In a great many instances, investigators do not pursue a case because, as they explain to the grievants, doing so would mean that they would have to divulge some of the facts to others, and the grievants are not willing to have that done.

Now, this ban on divulging confidential information applies to everyone in the company, including the highest executives. Rank has no privileges in this respect. Early in his career as company dispute resolver, NBC's counselor recounts this conversation with the executive vice president:

> I said, "Let me pose a question for you. Suppose you know about a problem, and I'm involved in it. You call me in to tell you what's happening. I say that I'm sorry but I can't tell you. Will you respect that? If you say yes, then this will work. But if you tell me I don't have the prerogative to safeguard a confidence, I can't do my job."

The agreement reached then, says the counselor, has been part of the foundation of his job.

How Can Management Make Sure That Agreements Are Carried Out?

Often managers aren't pleased with investigators' decisions and will be all too happy to sit on them if they think they can get away with it. Then, too, investigators are sometimes frustrated when the effort necessary to see that decisions are implemented is not made, especially if that means troubling managers who are already unhappy with a decision. Unless compliance is ensured, however, the system becomes a travesty.

At CIGNA, the administrator monitors the manager's action and gets periodic reports. Not until both manager *and complainant* agree that all necessary action has been taken does the administrator mark the case closed. At NBC, the counselor urges both manager and grievant to contact him or her when questions arise over the implementation of a plan, and is likely to call both parties up from time to time and ask them how things are going. At IBM, if the decision calls for the manager to take a certain action, the Open Door coordinator checks to see that this is done and then lets the administrative assistant in the chairman's office know. At Bank of America, assistant vice president Paula Elliott says:

> When I'm meeting with the manager and employee, I usually repeat what we have agreed on to be sure everyone understands the same thing. . . . I let both the manager and employee know that I'll be following up. I'll ask them to get back to me and tell me how it's going. If I don't hear, I'll call the employee or manager to find out.

What Records Should Be Kept in Cases?

In general, companies employing investigator systems are quite stingy about records. At NBC, the counselor makes personal notes only on cases; he puts no summary in a central file. At CIGNA, the administrator keeps confidential records—no manager is entitled to see them. At IBM, a confidential file on a case is kept in the chairman's office for three years, then it is destroyed. Nothing about an Open Door appeal is placed in the grievant's file. At Bank of America, correspondence and notes are kept exclusively by the personnel relations department.

Board Systems

Who Shall the Board Members Be, and for What Terms Shall They Serve?

Several companies want the majority of "judges" to be peers of the grievant. Others want them to be managers or supervisors, and a few want them to be members of top management. Top management people, of course, have the advantage of experience and control, whereas peers have the advantage of credibility.

It is interesting how different companies strive for checks and balances. For example, Northrop uses top management people for the board but, to ensure credibility, provides for outside arbitration as a last resort for grievants. On the other hand, companies like General Electric and Control Data, who have peers of the grievant on the board, limit the risk of bias by limiting board service to one case only, and General Electric minimizes the risk still more by training potential board members before qualifying them for a pool.

When it comes to length of service, there are also many options. John Hancock makes service more or less indefinite; Honeywell stipulates staggered three-year terms; SmithKline Beckman makes the terms ad hoc. These and other facts about boards are tallied in Exhibit 5-1. The data for this summary come from the company write-ups in Part II.

Your views on this question have a bearing on your answer to the next question.

How Many Members Do You Want on the Board, and How Do You Want to Choose Them?

The smallest board has three members; the largest, except for Donnelly Corporation, seven. (At Donnelly, the number varies but may exceed ten.) Three- and five-person memberships are the most common.

The advantage of a three-person board is ease of scheduling; of a seven-person board, credibility and weighing of the evidence.

As for methods of choice, Control Data uses a computer and random selection of two peers of the grievant and one executive for each case. Citicorp also uses random selection for each case, going to three peers of the grievant and one vice president, with the chairman, usually the staff relations head, breaking a 2–2 tie if necessary. General Electric picks its three ad hoc members out of a hat; Federal Express uses negotiation; TWA employs a combination of consultation and negotiation. John Hancock and Honey-

EXHIBIT 5-1
Data on Boards in Eleven Companies

Company	Citicorp	Control Data	Donnelly Corporation	Federal Express	General Electric (Columbia, Maryland, plant)
Name of board	Problem Review Board	Review Board	Equity Committee (5 in company)	a. Boards of Review b. Appeals Board	Grievance Review Panel
Years established	1977	1983	Late 1970s	1981	1982
Number of voting members	5	3	ca. 10–25 each	a. Boards of Review: 5 b. Appeals Board: 3	5
Terms	Ad hoc	Ad hoc	2 years	a. Boards of Review: ad hoc b. Appeals Board: ex officio	Ad hoc
Cases per year	ca. 12	ca. 8	3–4	a. Boards of Review: 37 (1986) b. Appeals Board: 209 (1986)	ca. 19
Number of cases per 1,000 employees	0.23	0.25	3	a. Boards of Review: 1 (1986) b. Appeals Board: 5 (1986)	20
Arbitration allowed as final step?	No	No	No	No	No
Reversal rate	n/a	22% (1985)	n/a	a. Boards of Review: 67% (1986) b. Appeals Board: 28% (1986)	n/a
Complaints processed by personnel staff	1982: 293 1984: 374 1986: 700	n/a	n/a	726 (1986) 62% of decisions appealed overturned	n/a

(continued)

EXHIBIT 5-1 *(continued)*

Data on Boards in Eleven Companies

Honeywell (DSD-USD)	John Hancock	Northrop	Polaroid	SmithKline Beckman (Pharmaceutical Division)	TWA
Management Appeal Committee	Employee Relations Committee	Management Appeal Committee	Personnel Policy Committee	Grievance Procedure	System Board of Adjust- ment
1981	1981	1946	1946	ca. 1971	Early 1950s
7	5	3	3	3	3
3 years	Indefinite	Ex officio	Ad hoc	Ad hoc	Ad hoc
ca. 2	15–20	15–20	ca. 20	ca. 8	50–75
0.33	1.5–2.0	0.33	2	1.3	7.1–10.7
No	No	Yes—1 case in 1984, 13 in 1986	Yes	No	No
n/a	n/a	60% (1984)	n/a	n/a	Over 50% in 1985; less than 25% in 1987–1988
n/a	ca. 120 (1985)	n/a	ca. 1,000– 2,000	n/a	n/a

well, with standing boards, depend on board members themselves to pick their successors.

When board members serve ad hoc, random selection is appropriate. It gives diversity and also provides credibility—no one can accuse management of stacking the board. If board members serve terms, however, hand picking is probably necessary, for the company wants to make sure it has interested, objective, and analytical people working together for extended periods.

At Donnelly, the company least interested in management control of due process, members of the equity committees are elected.

Who Should Chair the Meetings, and How?

For your chairperson, you want someone who is dependable, knowledgeable about the procedure and employee relations policy, and experienced. None of the companies studied pick the chairperson by chance; all appoint him or her (with the exception of Donnelly Corporation, where the chair is elected). For instance, during the period I interviewed at Control Data, all meetings were chaired by Beth Lewis because she was the Employee Advisory Resource ombudsperson. At Federal Express, Review Board meetings were chaired by a manager chosen by a senior vice president; at SmithKline Beckman, by a personnel official chosen by the personnel vice president; and at John Hancock, by a person chosen for an indefinite term by the president or executive vice president.

The main job of the chairperson is to see that the meeting runs in an informal but businesslike manner, that both the complaining employee and defending manager have their day in court, and that the two sides of the case are considered fairly by the "judges." Typically, chairpeople attach importance to getting the meeting started on the right foot. Thus at SmithKline Beckman the chair assures the grievant that an action will have no affect pro or con on his or her future at the company. The chairperson makes it clear that the company will tolerate no reprisals against the grievant for filing the complaint. With this simple stage setting, the chair then says to the grievant, "Tell us your side of the story."

If a good chairperson sees that the board is biased toward one side or the other, he or she may act as a gentle devil's advocate to make sure that the weak side isn't being swept under. If the chair sees that someone is talking too much, he or she will rein that person in so that others can participate.

At Control Data, Lewis prescribes no rigid format for a meeting, instead allowing each board to work out how it wants to proceed. But she does work from an agenda and does such things as

- Introduce the three board members to each other (since they are chosen at random, they may not know of one another's existence).
- Review the objectives of the meeting.
- Collect a pledge of confidentiality from each member.
- See to it that all relevant issues are discussed.
- Make sure that each board member participates.
- Guide the discussion, if necessary, to keep it from going off the track.

The only company that specifically trains the chairperson is Donnelly. It educates that employee in getting the facts out on the table quickly, controlling temper flare-ups, using data and witnesses efficiently, and matters of that sort.

What Steps Must a Grievant Take Before He or She Can Get a Full-Dress Hearing?

As noted, you want to protect your board against a deluge of cases. Something in the range of ten to seventy cases a year is manageable for most boards, but several hundred formal hearings would ordinarily be unmanageable.

The need is simply to make sure that your personnel department gets in the act and in effect has control over the complaint for as long as possible—right up to the last stage, when the board takes over. Thus, most companies want the grievant to try to work out the complaint first with the supervisor. That step failing, the grievant usually contacts the personnel group, and a person from that department either tries to thrash out the complaint in a session with the employee and supervisor or goes with them to a senior manager for a private office hearing. If the complaint cannot yet be resolved, still another step may be added before a board is convened to hear the dispute; for example, the grievance may go next to the senior vice president of the division, as at Federal Express, or to the division manager, as at Polaroid.

Neither John Hancock nor General Electric builds a long bridge between the original flare-up and the board. Each asks grievants to go to employee counselors if disputes cannot be resolved with supervisors. If the counselors cannot resolve the dispute, the board is the next and final step. Clearly, these companies place a lot of faith in their strong employee counseling arms.

Should the Decisions Be Binding or Advisory?

At Citicorp and Control Data, the tribunals' decisions are not final until a designated executive in top management approves them. However, all decisions to date in these two companies have been confirmed by the top executive, and the possibility of rejection by the senior man in no way seems to have dampened the ardor of tribunal members to get to the heart of a case and make the best decision they can, for or against management.

In a number of other companies, however, the investigator's or tribunal's decisions are final when rendered. At IBM, the Open Door investigator is the personal representative of the CEO; therefore, his or her decisions, as approved by the CEO, are by definition final. At Federal Express, the Appeals Board's decisions are, of course, final, since the chief executive and chief operating officer are members. But so are the decisions of the Review Board, to which the Appeals Board often sends cases for a jury-type hearing. At SmithKline Beckman, the grievance committee's decisions are final; occasionally division presidents have been infuriated by a decision and have protested to the CEO, but it did no good. Decisions are also final at the General Electric plant in Columbia, Maryland, even if Joe Carando, the plant manager, is at odds with the majority. At Donnelly, too, due process judgments cannot be overturned.

Making board decisions advisory instead of binding gives top management some measure of control. If a board goes wild and does some crazy thing, the senior executive who must okay its recommendation can cancel the advisory and reconvene the board or do whatever else is called for by the rules. But this advantage may come at a price. Employees may gain the impression that the system is rigged, much as if the decisions of the U.S. Supreme Court had to be approved by the president or vice president. Although you might point to a substantial rate of reversals that stick even after management review as evidence that the system is not rigged, skeptical employees may still not believe you. What should you do to counteract such reactions? One or more of these steps should help:

- Provide for arbitration as a final step, as Northrop and Polaroid have done.
- Pick members on a case-by-case basis, as described earlier.
- Have the board chaired by an outside arbitrator and let one of the two other members be chosen by the grievant, as TWA has done (though TWA board decisions are not advisory).

What Measures Should Be Taken to Protect Against Retaliation?

As indicated earlier, the possibility that supervisors will retaliate against a subordinate who wins at a hearing is troublesome. So far as I know, no company has found a fail-safe way of dealing with this problem. However, there are some concrete steps you can take.

First, you can add to personnel policy a clear statement that supervisory retaliation is a violation of policy.

Second, if you have training programs for managers, you can use them to show that retaliation is both unnecessary and dangerous to a supervisor's career.

Third, if the board or managers suspect retaliation, make it clear to them that they don't necessarily have to prove their suspicions. Proof or no proof, they can sit down with the suspect manager and counsel him or her. Says the corporate director of industrial relations at Northrop:

> It's human nature for a manager not to feel good about the guy that beat him or her before the person's bosses on the committee. The decision may reflect badly on the manager. I think you've got to worry about retaliation, however subtle, when the employee returns to work. Fortunately, we have a management climate here that says that you shouldn't retaliate. And if retaliation is suspected, employee relations has a face-to-face talk with the manager and says, "Look, this is not right. You got reversed, but we all make mistakes. It's not going to affect your career, so you shouldn't really be letting it affect the career of the guy who filed the grievance, either."

Fourth, make sure that employees realize that the appeal procedure can be used for claims of retaliation. If a subordinate feels that the boss is out to get him or her for winning at a hearing, that can be grounds for going to the appeal procedure again. I can't improve on the words of Michael O'Toole at John Hancock:

> If our recommendation favors the subordinate, we outline what management has agreed it will do and invite him or her to let us know if it doesn't seem to be complying. So the employee can always come back to us if that [retaliation] happens. The employee can always say, "They're not doing what they said they would" and open up the complaint again.

Among other things, you can make it clear to both manger and subordinate what work the latter will be doing in the period following the decision, what claims on equipment and facilities the subordinate will have, what travel and expense account privileges, and so on. These nitty-gritty are often where subtle retaliation takes place, as when suddenly the junior person finds his or her trips to conventions restricted or is assigned to miserable tasks.

Should the Board See and Hear the Parties to the Dispute or Should It Decide on the Basis of a Written Record?

The answer depends on whether you are more comfortable having the board act as a "trial court" or as an "appellate court." It is less time-consuming to have it act in the latter capacity. At Control Data, for instance, the board usually does not have to convene for more than a couple of hours, and at Federal Express, I saw the Appeals Board reach a decision on some cases in about half an hour (but it is not always so lucky). Also, deciding on the basis of a good written record tends to accentuate the issues in the case. Control Data, Citicorp, and the Federal Express boards obviously have a lot of faith in their employee relations staffs to provide a good written record, and experience shows their faith is not misplaced.

On the other hand, it is probably more fun and educational for board members to see, hear, and question the grievant, defending manager, and witnesses personally. Also, I gained the impression from interviews that many board members are very adept at this. The experience made a vivid impression on a number of "judges" with whom I talked; they could recall witnesses and lines of questioning in great detail.

If Grievants Appear Personally Before the Board, Should They Be Allowed to Have Spokespeople?

The universal answer seems to be yes. In almost all cases the reasoning is similar: some grievants get scared to death at the prospect of facing a group of employee "judges," others have language problems, others get so close to the case that they can't see the forest for the trees.

At the same time, all companies but one prohibit outside attorneys from appearing. They believe this might make the hearings controversial, and they don't want that.

The only question that some managers have is how freely and widely in the company grievants should be allowed to go when picking a representative. Should they be free to go to anyone, or should they be restricted to the employee relations advisers who know the case? Or should they perhaps be directed in some other way, as Polaroid has done by having the employee committee always represent a grievant? My own feeling is that the first option may be a little risky. I know of one case—not in any of the companies covered in this study—in which the grievant chose an eloquent friend who succeeded more in confusing the issues and costing the board a lot of time than clarifying the troubled employee's case. When grievants choose to go it alone, they may succeed in obfuscating the issues, too, but at least board members have the satisfaction of questioning the one who knows, and while doing so, gaining firsthand impressions of his or her character.

Should Outside Arbitration Be Provided if the Grievant Isn't Satisfied with the In-house Hearings?

This step is wonderful in adding credibility to corporate due process. Also, it counteracts any tendency for an in-company tribunal to get unduly conservative. There appear to be two reasons why only Northrop and Polaroid, of the fifteen firms examined in this study, use it: most executives are suspicious of arbitrators, and many managements feel that a good board of company people reflects the ways and customs of the organization better than any outsider can.

On both counts I urge readers to consider the opinions of Northrop's management in Part II. The company recognizes that some arbitrators are better than others, obviously, and uses a simple procedure to protect itself against a bad one being chosen. To bring the arbitrator in tune with company ways and customs, management has put together a fine booklet, which it gives the arbitrator as part of his or her homework for the case.

Arbitration does add time to the process of complaint resolution, and that may be a disadvantage. As for the out-of-pocket costs, they are quite reasonable.

How Much Time Should the Board Be Given to Reach a Decision?

A general answer is easy: As much time as the board needs to give a thoughtful, well-reasoned opinion. As Charlie Hartness emphasizes eloquently in the Federal Express write-up, the one thing management doesn't want to sacrifice is quality.

Subject to this qualification, the time allowances vary widely in the companies studied, from twenty working days at the Columbia, Maryland, plant of General Electric to the general proviso "in a timely manner" at Control Data. In practice, the range is from twenty days to several months. The latter may seem long, but it is shorter than union members often have to wait under arbitration clauses.

My impression is that a maximum of one or two months is usually enough time. I saw nothing gained, and often something lost, by decisions that dragged out longer. Assuming they are good, early decisions are helpful all around, and certainly their speed makes an impression on the rank and file.

Incidentally, one advantage of a good investigator system is that usually less time appears to be needed to reach a judgment. This is to be expected, of course, as investigator systems have less formality and a good deal more flexibility than board systems have.

Should the Grievant and Defending Manager See Each Other's Claims and Allegations?

At Citicorp, the generalist from human resources who prepares the "book" for the review board makes a point of showing the write-up for each side to the opposite side. The generalist not only shows the write-up to them but gets their inputs, that is, their additions or corrections. It is almost as if he were a judge holding a pretrial hearing. Control Data has a similar policy: both sides must see the allegations of the other in advance of the review board meeting. In fact, although Control Data goes to great lengths to preserve confidentiality—as shown in Part II, it even whites out names in documents reviewed by the board members—it will compromise privacy in this one instance, insisting that the grievant know what the defending manager's witnesses testify, and vice versa, even though that information may disclose who the witnesses are.

At the other companies in this study, there appears to be less importance attached to such a policy. Perhaps this is because those in charge of the procedure feel that the contending parties will learn of each other's allegations in the natural course of things. Having heard the people at Control Data and Citicorp talk about the policy, however, I think there is a lot to be said for it. Neither party can claim surprise at the hearing. Equally important, the issues tend to get focused better for the "judges" so that they can reach a swifter and fairer judgment.

What Rules Should Govern Voting?

Several questions may arise here. The first is whether a majority or unanimous vote is required for a decision. The pharmaceutical division of SmithKline Beckman requires a unanimous vote of all three board members, at least, at the first hearing on a case. If the first board cannot agree in this way, a second board is convened, and in its meeting a majority vote controls. In all the other companies, however, decisions are reached in all instances by majority vote.

The second question is whether the chairman should vote. Control Data's answer is no—the chairperson convenes the board and acts as a resource, as described earlier, but the only three members with votes are those randomly chosen. At Citicorp, on the other hand, the chairperson—the vice president for staff relations or a designate—is the fifth member of the board and votes if necessary to break a tie. At the Defense and Underseas Systems divisions of Honeywell, the chair always votes.

Generally, the power of the chairperson reflects the company's philosophy about board membership. If a company bends over backward to avoid any hint of prejudice and picks all or a majority of the board randomly, it is likely to want to give the chairperson a low profile. If, on the other hand, management is not so concerned about a random makeup of the board and appoints managers for terms, as is done at Honeywell, Northrop, and John Hancock, it will likely want to give the chairperson full voting power.

The third question is whether voting should be in secret. General Electric–Columbia has the five board members cast secret ballots; it virtually has to in order to keep the two management members from intimidating the nonmanagement members. At Control Data, on the other hand, the chairperson asks the members in advance how they want to vote; sometimes they opt for secrecy, sometimes not. On the Appeals Board at Federal Express, the three ex officio members register their opinions openly, but on the Boards of Review, whose members are selected by negotiation, voting is by secret ballot. Voting is open at Honeywell, John Hancock, and Northrop, whose board members serve for fixed or indefinite terms. Thus, not surprisingly, boards picked randomly or by negotiation tend to use secret balloting, whereas others do not.

What Records Should Be Kept?

None of the companies in this study tape meetings or have someone taking minutes. One reason given is free and open discussion—administrators fear that tapes or minutes will inhibit the parties. Another reason is the possibility that tapes or minutes will be seized in the discovery process if the grievant ends up suing the company. Remarks can be taken out of context, allegations and examples can be blown out of proportion and used as evidence. Citicorp goes so far as to say that board members can make as many notes for their own use as they want during a meeting, but after the meeting all such notes become the property of the employee relations division.

However, in all the companies somebody makes a note on the meeting afterward. It may be a four-line note or it may be a careful summary. For instance, Northrop keeps records of all key points and issues in a case and files them in the employee relations department. At Honeywell, the recording secretary of the Management Appeals Committee, who is appointed by the human resources department, writes a summary of the case that goes into the department's files; if grievants wish, they can have a copy of that summary for their own files.

Although Donnelly did not keep records in years past, it does now so that it can answer questions in case a disappointed grievant goes to a state labor board or the courts. However, its records are summaries, not tapes or minutes.

One prominent attorney goes much further than do most of the executives I interviewed in urging a careful record of the meeting. With the possibility of judicial review in mind, Alfred G. Feliu writes:

> An "adequate record" should be generated and preserved for judicial or administrative review if the internal decision is to receive any deference on review. An adequate record of the proceedings should include: transcripts, minutes, or summaries of meetings held at which evidence related to the dispute was elicited or arguments made; documents submitted by either party for consideration; copies or summaries of applications, motions, or requests made during the dispute-resolution process; and a written decision of the

decision maker or decision-making body setting forth factual findings and analysis supporting the ultimate decision.[2]

Should the Board Be Given Fact-Finding Powers?

At SmithKline Beckman, members of the grievance procedure board can go out and talk to whomever they want about a pending case—the "defendant," named witnesses, or others who may know something useful. This may mean going to other cities. The interviews may take a few hours or a few days, depending on the complexity of the case, and they may take place over a period of a day or a couple of months. The employee relations committee members at John Hancock do likewise. In one case cited in Part II, they flew three thousand miles to make their investigation. By contrast, at Honeywell, Donnelly, Federal Express, and the other companies with boards, members did not employ investigative powers, letting the parties to the dispute produce the facts.

From the standpoint of time management, it makes sense to do what the majority do, that is, put the burden on the complaining and defending employees to produce evidence. What explains the desire of John Hancock and SmithKline Beckman to send board members out to develop the facts, if they wish? Bear in mind that fact-finding is a power ordinarily reserved to investigator-type systems, which typically give top management a high measure of control. It may be that John Hancock and SmithKline Beckman want to ensure that their boards represent management as well as possible, but that they leave nothing to chance and no stones unturned in developing the evidence on both sides of a case. In a sense, therefore, their boards are an attempt to combine the fact-finding powers that investigator systems enjoy and the "jury" capacities that make board decisions credible.

Where Should Meetings Be Held?

If all or almost all employees under the jurisdiction of your board are in one place, the answer is simple: any convenient meeting room in the main buildings. This is the case at Donnelly Corporation, General Electric's Columbia plant, and others. If your board reviews only the written record of a case, as Control Data's Review Board does, the same answer holds. But if your company has major facilities in several locations and hears the parties in person, then it makes sense to do what Federal Express does; that is, go to the city where the complainant works and hold the hearings there. Not only is this approach less expensive (fewer air fares and hotel reservations), but more important, it is less intimidating to the grievant. "If you want to pursue your complaint, make an appointment to see me in my office in Metropolis" is a direction sure to scare off many potential grievants.

---

[2] "Legal Consequences of Nonunion Dispute-Resolution Systems," *Employee Relations Law Journal*, Summer 1987, p. 101.

How Should Management Publicize the Nonunion Grievance Procedure?

As noted earlier, this question is deceptive: the easy answer—by all reasonable means possible—is not always the right one, for the board does not want to be deluged with chronic complainers, which may happen if it publicizes too blatantly. Perhaps the first step is to find out how great the need for publicity is. This can be done by informal sampling in many cases, though nothing can take the place of a formal survey for nailing the facts down. If the grievance procedure is fairly widely known, then all that employees may need is reminders. But if there are fairly large black holes of ignorance about the procedure in the employee population, then more aggressive measures are needed.

Here are the main possibilities noted by managers with whom I talked.

Installations.   CIGNA has boxes in convenient and visible places throughout the buildings where troubled employees can obtain Speak Easy forms. At the Columbia, Maryland, plant of General Electric, there are receptacles about the plant for depositing grievance forms. Such facilities provide continuing evidence that the grievance procedure exists and is easily accessible.

Word of mouth.   This is a surefire way of publicizing a grievance procedure to some areas of the company. However, the grapevine has one important limitation: often it reaches only groups of employees, not the whole population. This is because (1) complaints may come mostly from one department or level, so that the word doesn't filter out to employees elsewhere, and (2) at least half of the parties to a dispute—the losers—can be counted on not to do much talking.

Employee relations staff.   These people can be extremely valuable in publicizing a complaint procedure; if they have a good reputation, they are the first people a grievant goes to talk to. My impression from the study is that management often doesn't get as much mileage from this resource as it might. For example, in only a few companies do personnel counselors *always* mention the board option if the grievant seems to have a good case; also, in only a few do counselors have some brief write-up of the procedure to hand to grievants who might want to know more about it. A more common practice is to refer the troubled employee to the page of the manual that describes the procedure—a helpful gesture, but often not helpful enough.

In a few companies, employee relations people do a fine job of publicizing the due process procedure when it is relevant to a grievant's case, and their words seem to go far in spreading employee understanding.

Media.   SmithKline Beckman publicizes its nonunion grievance system over closed-circuit television. IBM uses written channels effectively, and at one time Control Data even wrote up some cases in its company publication. Several firms run descriptive articles about their procedures from time to time in company newspapers.

What Kind of Form, If Any, Should Be Required for Making a Complaint?

The companies interviewed all seek to make it as easy as possible for the grievant. For instance, Bank of America requires no particular form at all (albeit, its investigator system by nature makes complaint filing informal). The Defense Systems and Underseas Systems divisions of Honeywell put most or all of the burden of writing up a complaint on the human resources staff. TWA and General Electric–Columbia require simple, one-page forms that ask for three main things: the grievant's name and position, the problem at hand, and the remedy sought. GE's form is reprinted in Part II.

Companies are able to require simple forms rather than fiendishly complicated forms because of the assistance their human resources staffs can render as well as the fact that their tribunals or investigators can get to the bottom of allegations in personal meetings.

How Should Grievance Activity Be Monitored?

The answer of Northrop's personnel group is to assign a representative to a complaint as soon as it is filed; the rep reports back whenever there is a new development. Every week or so meetings are held, with all reps attending and a printout showing the status of all grievances filed since the beginning of the year. Whether this meeting lasts half an hour or an hour and a half is not so important as that the reps fill each other in on problems they have encountered, impressions of morale, pluses or minuses of the grievance procedure, and so on. The reps exchange information regularly and help each other on problems experienced.

The printout should identify the grievant and his or her organization; give a number to the complaint; describe the complaint in two or three words (e.g., substandard work leading to discharge, producing discord leading to first warning, poor performance review leading to denial of promotion); identify the personnel department representative assigned to the case; and note the application dates, hearing dates, and decisions for hearings at the various stages. Exhibit 5-2 shows a portion of the "Grievance Activity Report" used by Northrop; I have changed grievants' names, identifying data, grievance case numbers, and year in order to protect the identities of the principals. This report, a computer printout, is issued weekly on the basis of data collected at staff meetings.

Should Grievants Be Required to Use the Internal Complaint System Before Going to Court?

In the personnel manual—and also in the employment contract, for the employee who gets one—the company can stipulate that no employee shall resort to the court or agency system until first exhausting his or her remedies via the in-house procedure. Although there are doubts that such provisions will be honored by the courts and agencies in all states, the idea is clearly a practical one.

EXHIBIT 5-2

Excerpt from Northrop Grievance Activity Report

GRIEVANCE ACTIVITY REPORT—ALL OPEN GRIEVANCES

AS REPORTED ON 06/03/88 AT 13.49 03 YEAR: 1988

GRIEVANT: NAME ORGN-SH- EMPNO SEX-MIN	GRIEV NUM	GRIEVANCE ISSUE	E REP STATS	DATE RECEIVED	ADMIN DEC	MAC APPL	MAC FOLD	MAC DEC	ARB APPL	DISPOSIT
AA ABLE 1111-2-22222 F/7	88888	INSUBORDINATION 3RD WARNING NOTICE	BJH OPEN	88/09/19 DUE HEARING DELVRD FINAL DEC.	10/30 10/16 11/04	11/11 — 11/10	12/09 —	01/05 12/15 01/20	01/27 AO DEC. MAC. DEC. ARB DEC.	11/04/ ADD 01/20 MDD
BB BAKER 3333-3-44444 F/9	99999	INSUBORDINATION DISCHARGED	BJH OPEN	88/09/19 DUE HEARING DELVRD FINAL DEC.	09/22 09/12 09/18	09/25 — 09/22	10/24 —	11/21 10/31 11/18	11/26 AO DEC. 05/18 MAC DEC. ARB DEC.	09/18 ADD 11/18 MDD
CC CHADWICK 5555-4-66666 F/6	12345	THEFT DISCHARGED	RMS OPEN	88/06/12 DUE HEARING DELVRD FINAL DEC.	07/09 06/25 07/29	08/06 — 08/06	08/29 — 08/29	09/29 09/08 10/03	10/09 AO DEC. 06/18 MAC DEC. ARB DEC.	07/29 ADD 10/03 MDD
DD DAVIS 7777-5-88888 M/7	67890	SUBSTANDARD WORK DISCHARGED	REO OPEN	88/04/29 DUE HEARING DELVRD FINAL DEC.	05/13 05/21 06/24	07/01 — 06/30	08/15 —	09/12 08/27 10/28	11/04 AO DEC. 05/29 MAC DEC. ARB DEC.	06/24 ADD 10/28 MDD

92

In fact, attorneys in Michigan and other states believe that management can go further, having the employee agree that the internal resolution of an employment dispute shall be final and binding. This means that grievants who lose in the company cannot turn around and go to court, at least on the same issues as those aired in the in-house procedure. Naturally, there are some qualifications to the rule—for instance, the in-house procedures must meet the tests of fairness, the employee must be seen as agreeing to the provision when employed, and the employee's suit must not be based on a statute.

When a court looks at a company's due process procedure and evaluates its fairness, what tests does it apply? Perhaps the bellwether case on this question is *Renny* v. *Port Huron Hospital,* decided by the Michigan Supreme Court in 1986.[3] The Michigan court cited five essential elements "necessary to fair adjudication in administrative and arbitration proceedings." These elements, says Alfred Feliu, are the same as those cited in section 83(2) of the *Restatement of Judgments.*[4] With some rephrasing in view of our interests here, the five tests are

1. Adequate notice to the employees who will be bound by the decision.
2. The right of employees to present evidence and arguments freely, and to rebut the evidence and arguments offered by the other side.
3. A formulation by the company tribunal at its hearing of the personnel rules in question and of the facts relevant to those rules.
4. Specification of the point at which the tribunal renders its final decision.
5. Other procedures as necessary to ensure a careful determination of the case (e.g., a special fact-finding effort, an extra hearing).

In the *Renny* case, the Michigan court decided that these tests of fairness were not met. Therefore it thought the case should be heard in a law court. The case involved a registered nurse at Port Huron Hospital who was fired; she went to the grievance board and did not get reinstatement or damages, as requested. When she went to court, her attorney was able to show that she was not notified prior to the hearing of management's defense or of the witnesses who would testify against her; nor did she have the right to present evidence and witnesses of her choice, or to be present during the hearing and hear the evidence mustered against her. But for these failures, presumably the Michigan court would have refused to hear the case.

For the majority of companies in this study, the *Renny* case rule is bad news; their due process procedures meet some but not all of the five tests described by the Michigan court. This does not necessarily mean that the companies should change their procedures, however, for they may still do the job that management most wants done.

[3] 427 Mich. 415, 198 N.W. 2d 327 (1986).
[4] "Legal Consequences of Nonunion Dispute-Resolution Systems," p. 86.

Summary

If a company chooses an investigator system, it is extremely important to fill the job or jobs with the right kind of people, a task that is often quite hard to carry out. Top executives should support the system in words and also, when appropriate, with swift and strong action. The manner in which the investigator operates should fit in with the style and personality of the company. Top executives should not expect to be made privy to confidential talks that the investigator has with grievants. Measures should be taken to ensure that agreements made between the investigator and managers are carried out. Records of grievance proceedings should be kept confidential.

If a company is willing to give up the closer control of proceedings offered by an investigator system in order to gain the greater credibility of a board or "jury" system, managers should ask these questions:

- Should board members be managers, peers of the grievant, or some other class of employee?
- Should board members serve for one case only, for a term of years, or indefinitely?
- Should they be appointed, chosen at random, or selected in some other way?
- How many people should serve on the board?
- Who should chair the meetings, and with how much power?
- Before qualifying to have his or her case heard by the board, what steps must the grievant take to make it possible to solve the problem at a lower level?
- Should the board's decisions be final, or should they be recommendations for a senior manager to finalize?
- Should grievants who appear personally before the board be allowed to have spokespeople?
- What steps and measures can be taken to reduce the threat of retaliation against a grievant?
- Should the "judges" hear the parties to the dispute personally, like a trial court, or rely on the written record, as an appellate court does?
- If grievants aren't satisfied by the decision of the board, should they be allowed to go to outside arbitration as a final step?
- How much time should the board have in arriving at a decision?
- Should the opposing parties to a dispute see each other's allegations before the hearing?
- Should a majority or unanimous vote of the board be required, and should the balloting be open or secret?
- Who should make a summary of the meeting for a confidential file?
- Should the "judges" investigate the situation personally or should they rely on the evidence offered by the parties?
- Where should the board's meetings be held?
- How much and how should management publicize the dispute-resolutions procedure?
- What kind of form, if any, should be required for a complaint?
- How should grievance activity be monitored?
- Should employees be required to use the in-house system for a complaint before going outside the company to court or to a government agency?

6

Shortcomings and Alternatives

Corporate due process is not a panacea for employee relations. Not only does it fall short of being a panacea, but it may fall short of what it aims at. In this chapter, I look at the shortcomings, limitations, costs, and dangers of due process. I also look at some alternative forms of coping with employee complaints and disputes.

What Nobody Ever Said It Can Do

First of all, due process will not by itself produce harmony in employee relations. It may improve morale and produce many gains, but the goal of harmony takes more than due process to achieve. Nor will due process lead directly to increases in productivity; no one that I know of has established a causal connection between the two, though many managers feel that such a connection exists.

However, these facts do not diminish the value of due process. It is like a spoke in a wheel. It is impossible to say which spoke is most important, or whether this spoke is more important than that one in making the wheel sound, but the value of all the spokes together is beyond question.

Second, due process procedures do not and intrinsically cannot operate in an error-free manner. The decisions are made by humans beings and, though not as far removed from the scene as a law court would be, they are still more removed than colleagues of the grievant and challenged supervisor are. As a result they can, and sometimes do, make decisions that the majority in the know see as wrong.

Example: At one of the companies studied, a con artist had gotten his way with the hearing board, and everybody in his department was furious. Not a soul who knew him liked him; not a soul wanted to work with him. He was a neurotic dingbat, undependable, quixotic, and manipulative. But for the same reasons that the man had been hired in the first place, he impressed the board. He was nice-looking, articulate, smooth, intelligent, and pleasant. He succeeded in pulling the wool over the board's eyes and explaining away the testimony against him. In the few hours of hearings, he was able to convince the board that he had been victimized.

To compound the potential for human error, boards and investigators may not deal with the substantive elements because the parties fail to present their cases well. The adjudicators are not God; they cannot always see what the supervisor or subordinate *should* be arguing. They have to make up their minds on the basis of the evidence given to them. "I tell them," says the head of one company's hearing committee, referring to the parties at a hearing, "that we have to decide on the basis of what you tell us. We can't read your mind."

In addition, error may be introduced because of the looseness of hearing procedures. In a law court, there are strict rules limiting hearsay testimony; in no corporate procedure that I know of is there such a rule. In a law court, there are opportunities for both defendant and plaintiff to cross-examine the other side; in some of the corporate procedures there is no such opportunity. All in all, I believe that corporate due process benefits from such informality, but there are occasions when the "judges" would profit from such rules.

The obvious rejoinder to this shortcoming is that no system depending on human judgment is error-free. Certainly "judges" and "juries" are not, and certainly, too, the chain of command is not when a grievant is forced to go up the line seeking redress from the boss's boss, the boss of the boss's boss, and so on.

Third, there appears to be no way that a corporate due process system can protect a grievant completely against retaliation. The personnel policy manual may strictly forbid retaliation by a supervisor who loses. The investigator or hearing group may encourage the subordinate to appear a second time if the supervisor retaliates. But the fact is, retaliation can be so subtle that it is practically impossible to prove. Like the engine knock that stops when you bring your car to the garage, often it cannot be seen or heard when you complain about it.

At one company, I talked to a woman who had won a major claim before the hearing committee. Stung by the defeat, her boss was getting back at her by not giving her enough to do; he was purposely withholding interesting work from her. An energetic, enthusiastic, ambitious woman, she found the taste of victory bitter. In the estimation of all members of the committee, her victory was well deserved, and she had presented her case brilliantly at the hearing. Yet I found her restless and unhappy, and I have no doubt that she was dusting off her résumé and preparing to send it to prospective employers. I asked her why she didn't approach the hearing committee again. "All he [my boss] has to say in defense is that in his *judgment* I have enough to do. No one is going to interfere with his normal business judgment." I then asked her why she didn't request a transfer to another part of the company. "In this particular company," she responded, "my talents are specialized, and there isn't another department where I will fit in."

There is no easy answer for this problem except developing an organizational culture where retaliation is frowned on. Some companies appear to have done that; others haven't. In any case, it takes a long time. Fortunately, many grievants are not in the sticky situation described in the example and are not easy prey for retributive supervisors.

Fourth, the new procedures usually don't allow employees to attack policies that are unfair or outdated. In the typical case studied, the written policies and rules are taken as a given by the hearing board or ombudsperson. They are the "law" of the organization. If a rule has not been followed by a manager or has been misinterpreted, a hearing system may be efficient and effective. But if employees' real complaint is against, say, nasty working conditions or an unfair promotion policy, the "judges" may be able to do nothing for them.

One conspicuous exception to this generality is Federal Express. As the write-up in Part II shows, when cases come to that company's Appeals Board, the three members may see inconsistencies, gaps, and unfairness in company rules. Since two of the members are the chief executive and chief operating officer, they have the power to direct changes in a company rule. On various occasions they have done just that.

In no other company studied, however, does the hearing board or investigator possess such clout. To cope with the limitation, the board or investigator can make an annual or semiannual report for top management setting forth impressions gained from hearings and recommendations for changes in policy. One of the companies where this has been done with good results is John Hancock.

Related to this limitation is the fifth: the corporate due process systems studied for this book rarely allow an employee to protest hazards or dangers to the public. A would-be whistleblower finds it difficult to use the company tribunal to, say, advance his or her claim that an ingredient the company is putting into a product should be banned. I ran into cases in which a fired employee claimed that such a belief was the real reason he or she was discharged or demoted. In no company, however, did I find that the tribunal or ombudspersons were forums for whistleblowers *before* some act was taken against them. It may be that the only good way to air such challenges is by means of scientific or technical investigations, such as the Federal Aviation Authority is now doing in the case of reported hazards in airplane traffic at airports.

Sixth, a good due process procedure doesn't make managers manage their subordinates fairly. It may provide a strong *incentive* for them to do that, but if they don't know how, the procedure won't teach them. Only training programs, counselors, and coaches can do that. Listening astutely, analyzing a situation objectively, responding capably—these are talents not easily learned except with instruction and coaching. In fact, a number of executives I have talked with regard the teaching arm of the company—the trainers and counselors—as a necessary infrastructure for due process; that is, these staff resources come first, and not until they are in place and working can management hope to set up a good due process procedure.

Seventh, such a procedure does not eliminate lawsuits. It may reduce their number greatly, and it may lead to great improvements in management's ability to defend its actions, but no tribunal or investigator system that I know of has reduced lawsuits by aggrieved employees to zero. Indeed, while I was interviewing at a company that has one of the most advanced due process procedures in the country, the legal department was worrying about a big lawsuit brought by a fired employee. Again, the Open Door program at IBM has surely saved that company from numerous legal actions and considerable legal expense, yet it was IBM that made *Newsweek* in 1986 when it lost a suit to an ex-employee.

Eighth, nor does a nonunion grievance procedure close the company's doors forever against a union. In the companies examined in this study, it appears to be doing that, but I see no guarantee that it will continue doing so, especially if firms allow their employee relations to deteriorate, let the procedure become a sham, or fail to keep employees aware of the presence of a grievance procedure for their use. It is worth noting here that nonexempt employees of Harvard University voted in a union during the spring of 1988, despite the fact that the university has a workable grievance procedure. In several large sectors of the university, however, there appeared to be little awareness of the procedure, and the union's appeal to nonexempt employees in these sectors was strong. It can be stated as a self-evident law that the less known, visible, open, and accessible a procedure is, the less good it can do.

Ninth, due process does not necessarily improve a company's earnings and profitability. The companies and divisions studied for this research and described in Part II tend to be above average by generally accepted economic measures. However, due process did not make them that way; their strategies, policies, and operating practices did. Due process may have helped—many company executives believe it has—but there is no reason in the world that a company with a good hearing system cannot fail because of poor strategy or mismanagement of operations, or that a company without due process cannot succeed because of other strengths.

Finally, corporate due process falls short of legal due process. For instance, in a corporate grievance procedure, complainants rarely have the opportunity to confront the other side's witnesses, as they would in court. They have no right to legal representation (though almost always to representation by a company spokesperson of their choice), as in court. They are not necessarily protected against hearsay, as in court. Nor can they always see and hear for themselves what the other side is claiming, as in court; that information is usually filtered through the personnel specialist. These court rights are well entrenched in the law as the result of countless decisions and hundreds of years of practice, but they are not part of the woodwork in corporate due process. Perhaps they shouldn't be. It may well be that in a grievance procedure one doesn't need all the rights and protections customarily afforded parties to a lawsuit.

Costs—From Peanuts to PITAs

With one exception, all companies in this study report that the out-of-pocket expenses of corporate due process are insignificant. On the high side, the expenses may consist of room, board, and travel for several people to the place where the hearing will be held—for one day—plus miscellaneous clerical costs. On the low side, out-of-pocket expenses may amount to practically zero, as in the case of General Electric's Columbia plant. Not surprisingly, therefore, due process procedures are rarely if ever budgeted, but rather are kept as an indistinguishable part of the employee relations or human resources budget.

On the other hand, the costs in terms of executive and employee time may bear looking into. At Northrop, 120 or 130 hours of vice-presidential time per year are required. As they say, "That ain't hay." And the time cost at Northrop is much less than at Federal Express. At the Memphis company, it is conceivable that the time costs for the company's number one and number two men alone, to say nothing of other managers regularly engaged in the process, may be several times the Northrop figure. At the other end of the range, NBC's cost is a good share of only one investigator's time, and a small share of one vice president's time.

Now, the highest of these costs may be the most reasonable in terms of what the company gets in return. Nevertheless, they are nothing to be sneezed at, and management should think about them seriously. Much depends on how important managers deem such objectives as good employee relations, a nonunion environment, and checks and balances on supervisory power.

A third possible cost is delay in production and operations changeovers. In at least one of the companies studied, some executives resent the slowdown in production change that they believe has been caused from time to time by disgruntled employees. The latter are seen to be using the grievance procedure to stall job transfers, layoffs, and new rules resulting from the introduction of new technologies, machines, and methods. For instance, the planned introduction of a computerized tracking system will displace a half dozen operators in this company, and under the company's rules, employees can block the change as long as their grievances are pending (even if the grievances don't have much chance of being sustained). Such tactics work only to delay change, not forestall it, and even so, the delay may not be long; nevertheless, for managers breathing hard in a highly competitive industry, the delay can be very irritating.

I did not run into evidence of this cost often. Some companies avoid it simply by insisting on early deadlines at each stage of the grievance procedure. Northrop and IBM are good examples.

A fairly common cost is abuse by chronic malcontents. In about half of the companies studied, managers worried about this problem. One executive I know phrases the problem in terms of the question, How much "due" is there in due process? That is, how open can the procedure be to perennial gripers, inveterate bitchers, and chronic soreheads? (One manager I know calls them PITAs, standing, he says wryly, for pains-in-the-neck.) The problem is real. In one company I visited, members of the hearing board were girding themselves to listen to the case of a malcontent who was appearing for the fourth time in a few years—this is an organization where only one employee in several thousand appears before the tribunal annually.

Although the problem is vexing, the cost is actually small. For one thing, a good many executives I talked to see the grievance procedure as a good way of shutting up malcontents. They see malcontents as the victims of the procedure, not the other way around. In their experience, malcontents tend to pull in their horns soon after getting zapped in a hearing. In the SmithKline Beckman write-up, for instance, one executive is quoted as saying that she actually urges chronic complainers to go to the procedure with their woes because she is so sure the wind will be taken out of their sails.

Another reason that the cost is small is peer pressure. Once employees gain confidence in the company's system, they find subtle ways to discourage co-workers who might be inclined to overuse it. As one operator told me, "You'd be surprised how many ways we have to check a guy who wants a lot of air time."

For some managers, the most threatening cost of due process is in supervisory morale. They fear the effects of having a supervisor's decision reversed publicly. The life of a supervisor is hard enough, they say, without adding the humiliation of a tribunal or investigator ordering a fired worker to be reinstated or a reprimand to be removed from a reprobate's personnel file. Without question, this cost is a reality. Even in organizations where due process has been working longest and most successfully, I found managers and supervisors who were stung by reversals and—at least for a few days, often more—resented the intrusion on their power and authority.

This cost should not be overestimated, however. For one thing, those supervisors who take reversals hardest often *should* be discouraged because they are not good managers. For another, in perhaps a majority of the companies where I interviewed, managers had come to accept the necessity of reversals from time to time. They no longer viewed them as a disgrace or ego-crushing disaster. "Nobody bats a thousand" was an expression I heard many times.

A sometimes troubling cost of due process is its constrictive effect on managerial volition. Superiors find themselves holding up on some act that they know in their minds and hearts is good and necessary for the organization, not because they are timid or indecisive, but because they don't know how to explain themselves in a manner that will satisfy a critical tribunal. Their antennae tell them things that are difficult to put in words. Or, more troubling still, they may seek a standard of initiative or excellence that is difficult to sell to people who are more interested in justice than in enterprise.

I think of an incident that came to my attention when I was interviewing in a leading manufacturing concern. An accounting manager had a history of so-so performance. Almost every performance appraisal ever given him showed it. Everyone knew that he was capable of doing better, but he realized that he could get by without giving his best, and so he did. Then a new boss came on board. The new boss was impatient with so-so performance. When the accounting manager didn't respond, the new boss fired him. "We don't need mediocrity in this company," the new boss said. The accounting manager took his case to the hearing committee and got reinstated.

What was the effect on the aggressive manager who demanded the best? Was the message he got "Mediocrity is institutionalized in this company and will be defended if necessary by the hearing committee?" I don't know. I hope not.

In practice, fortunately, this cost does not show its bland head very often. The company sample covered in this study is, in fact, studded with innovators and industry leaders, and often executives looked at me blankly when I raised the question of whether due process ever puts a brake on the search for improvement.

Another possible cost is an increase in bureaucracy. Especially in a large corporation with an active grievance procedure, the staff people who keep the process working may become so absorbed with the rules, gamesmanship, and departmental politics that they lose perspective. "There is a tendency for our people to forget that what they are trying to do is resolve issues equitably," laments a key executive in one large corporation with due process. Although management should always be on the alert to this danger, it is not helpless: ways of coping with bureaucratic growth have been well known for a long time.

Last but not least, due process may exact a toll on the emotions of the grievants who have been suspended. Especially in the case of employees who contest discharge, every day of waiting for a tribunal to decide is a day when it is difficult to think of anything else. The firing supervisor, too, may wait in anguish. If the decision takes weeks or even months to come, the people closely involved in it may end up fit to be tied. The boss may think, "The old way was very arbitrary, but at least the at-will rule meant you could get it over with."

Two things can be said about this cost. First, the lag time may be shortened. Several companies studied are working on the question of how to consume less time at various stages of the grievance process without losing decision-making quality. Second, the emotional cost of waiting for a company "court" is much less than waiting one to three years for a law court to render a decision.

What They Might Say It Can Do, but It Really Can't

The limitations and costs thus far discussed have been manageable. Most leaders and subordinates can live with them. There is, however, one weakness of corporate due process that may be fatal: top management can renege. In my study, I did not come across an instance of this happening, but there is no reason that it can't happen, and one of these days it surely will.

Every company studied has adopted due process voluntarily. No law, state or federal, stated that the company had to make the move. No such provision was enacted into the corporate bylaws. Nor was there even a stockholder or board resolution stating that nonunion employees with grievances would be entitled to a fair and neutral adjudication. A strong chief executive officer and/or top management group simply went ahead and instituted the change because they considered it desirable.

By the same token, a company that has had a nonunion grievance procedure for a number of years could cancel it, or just let it die for lack of support, like a vine withering for lack of water. There is no reason I know of why this couldn't happen in any of the companies studied. Changes of management, ownership, situation—all could conceivably provoke cancellation. Or the company could be taken over by raiders who have no interest in such woolly-, and soft-headed ideas as corporate due process, or a new generation of managers might take over who are interested in managing exclusively by the numbers.

When I raised this question with some respondents, they shook their heads. "It can't happen here. Now that employees have come to expect a fair hearing, the company wouldn't consider dropping it." It is true that a due process procedure tends to become part of the corporate culture after a few years, and that management could deep-six it only at the cost of some perturbation in the work force. However, much stranger and wilder things have happened in our business history than dropping a grievance procedure. If the time horizons of an unsympathetic new management are short enough, due process could easily become a victim of change.

In a large sense, of course, all of our civil liberties in this country are subject to change. The decisions of the courts can reshape them. Statutes can restrict and constrict them. Yet in public life there is a kind of semipermanence about civil liberties like free speech and freedom of religion, due as much to the practical difficulty of getting laws and court rulings changed as to the constitutional source of the freedoms. In the corporate world, where management is not bound by legislation and legal decisions, executives have great freedom to ditch the old, wipe the slate clean, and initiate new programs.

What Might You Do Instead?

Now let us suppose that you and your company are opposed for some reason to establishing internal hearing procedures. What alternative routes might you take? There are various possibilities.

Sit on your hands. The scenario foreseen by some executives in their fantasies goes about as follows: in the mid-1990s, a company that has not done a thing for or against due process finds that it has become a kind of hero in the business community. Its CEO is pictured in *BusinessWeek;* its reasoning is praised by *The Wall Street Journal.* While Northrop, Bank of America, Federal Express, SmithKline Beckman, Polaroid, and scores of other corporate leaders were wasting precious hours on grievance procedures, proclaim the media, our do-nothing corporation improved its employee relations in the simple time-honored ways, such as speeches by the CEO and press releases issued by the publicity department. "I knew all along that corporate due process was an illusion and mirage," the CEO tells a journalist. Fondling his gold cuff links, he adds, "I like to look before I leap."

End of fairy tale.

Fight for the return of the at-will doctrine. If you believe that the courts and state legislatures have made a big mistake in compromising the venerable at-will doctrine, you can lobby and crusade for laws that will return the status quo of 1959. If written strongly enough, such laws would allow the courts no leeway in deciding suits brought by employee objectors. Corporations would be free to fire, demote, transfer, and in general handle employees as they please, with ombudspersons and tribunals becoming as atavistic as the human appendix. Due process might be kept alive by a few companies more for reasons of conscience than anything else.

If you opt for this route, perhaps your best arguments before legislators are such as these:

> The at-will doctrine benefits both employer and employee because it permits them freedom to contract to suit their needs. Increased mobility and flexibility result. (Don't say anything about your increased vulnerability to unionization.)
>
> Decisions and evaluations about employees are best left exclusively to management. The courts have no business nosing into this area. An example of how far off the track a state court can go is the California decision of *Roulon-Miller* v. *IBM* in 1986, in which substantial damages were awarded to a sales manager who was transferred to another area after management found that she was dating her counterpart in a competitor company. (Don't mention hundreds of cases where the court was on firmer ground, though.)
>
> The managements of American companies need to concentrate all of their efforts, with no distractions, on making their companies competitive in the

world economy. Nothing in at-will legislation prohibits them from maintaining grievance procedures for nonunion employees if they believe the system will help. (Don't mention the importance of employee relations in productivity, however.)

If the legislators are polite, they will stifle their yawns. In almost all states, this argument is déjà vu.

In company communications with employees, make it clear that employment is at will and terminable at the option of the employer. Numerous business magazines have published one or more articles on this subject, and consultants have had a field day warning managements of the need to change their employee handbooks, employment manuals, and employment applications. Efforts in this direction have not been in vain. As noted by two authors in a recent issue of the *Employee Relations Law Journal,* some courts have upheld employee dismissals when they felt that the person had a clear contract with the company and that his or her employment was to be at will.[1] The statements must be carefully worded, of course, and they should appear in the handbook in sections on discharge, discipline, rules of conduct, and benefits. The authors of the article mentioned believe that such statements are especially effective if made in a document that the employee signs when beginning a job.

Although affirmations of employment at will are an alternative to due process, they are not always a good one. For one thing, top management often objects to them because they invite unions to come in. For another, employee relations managers often object to them because they leave a lousy taste in the mouths of employees. It's as if the handbook, employment manual, and/or employment application said, "Forget all the baloney we may have given you about how great it is to work at XYZ, Inc. The reality is that you can get sacked at any time for any reason." Finally, it seems safe to say that many state and federal courts will balk at such provisions if they conflict with the public interest or statutes prescribing the duties of employers and employees.

Remember that when King Canute bade the tide to recede he got his feet wet.

Encourage a union to come in and run a grievance procedure for your nonmanagement employees. Beginning in the 1930s, collective bargaining agreements introduced the notion of fair and impartial arbitration of differences between employees and management. In succeeding years, a nationwide cadre of professional arbitrators developed; they have done a great job. For many millions of employees, the union grievance procedure has been the shining symbol of justice in the workplace.

The main difficulty with this approach is that you may find it unpalatable and uneconomic. Although you may not quarrel with the professionalism of

[1] Reidy Witt and Sandra R. Goldman, "Avoiding Liability in Employee Handbooks," *Employee Relations Law Journal,* Summer 1988, p. 5.

arbitrators, you may indeed quarrel with other effects and implications of having your employees organized. In addition, the union approach leaves unresolved the question of equity for those many employees who are not usually organized—supervisors, salespeople, staff specialists, engineers, and many others.

The adoption of union grievance procedures is the approach that a growing number of companies are encouraging, albeit unwittingly, by their inaction. Like Grandma rocking away on the front porch while the house burns down.

Beef up the counseling staff. This is an excellent step to take for many reasons, among which is the fact that good counselors are able to solve many problems—often a great majority of them—before they come to a head before an investigator or tribunal. In every company I visited, I found that a strong counseling staff was part of the infrastructure of the non-union complaint system. The staff might operate under different rubrics— "employee relations specialists," "human resources advisers," "personnel," and so on. In action, however, they were more alike: their people sat down with angry or beleaguered employees early on, helped them see their difficulties in perspective, and often met next with their supervisors to get the other side of the story and, if necessary, urge a change. In every company that kept and revealed statistics on employee grievances, I found not only that counselors and advisers did most of the work in maintaining equity in the workplace, but that often they were people who had beautiful talents of listening, unraveling, understanding, mediating, and advising, as well as a strong and sure knowledge of company policy.

But although a strong counseling staff appears to be a crucial part of a good grievance system, it is not an alternative to effective investigators and tribunals. One reason for this is explained by an executive at John Hancock who is quoted in Part II. She explains that the very presence of a formal hearing as a possible ultimate step strengthens the hand of counselors and gives them needed leverage. It makes it possible for them to tell errant supervisors and managers, "Look, if you don't correct this problem, you are going to be dragged into a hearing where several people will see what a mess you made of things. Better to patch it up now than be made a fool of in front of peers and superiors."

A crude analogy is the good attorney who, seeing that a client is only partially in the right, helps to arrange a constructive out-of-court settlement with the other side. The attorney tells the client, in effect, "Look, if you don't compromise, you run a serious risk of losing everything when a judge or jury hears the case." But the attorney can get nowhere without the prospect of a hearing.

Open a hot line. Some companies enable employees to call or write to headquarters about complaints, troubling rumors, or problems. The calls or letters can be anonymous. At the other end of the line, someone in a central staff unit hunts up an answer and/or starts corrective action. Hot lines go under many names, such as "Speak Up" and "Open Lines," and they have rung up many successes. In 1983, a caller used the Pentagon's hot line to alert investigators to fraudulent practices by Rausch Manufacturing, a missile contractor. At one well-known bank, an anonymous call tipped off the control staff to some sleight-of-hand going on in one of the branches. Mary P. Rowe and Michael Baker report that one corporate hot line "defused potentially damaging rumors about the closing of branch offices," and that another corrected a misunderstanding that had troubled many employees who thought that one of their fringe benefits was being erased by an obscure change in the program.[2]

Despite their obvious strengths, hot lines are not a satisfactory alternative to due process. They are communication devices, not adjudication devices. Not surprisingly, Bank of America and other companies use them profitably in conjunction with the hearing arm, not as a substitute for it. In sum, a tack hammer is a wonderful tool, but you can't drive a spike with it.

Turn to a state mediation agency. California, Connecticut, Massachusetts, Minnesota, New Jersey, New York, and other states have set up agencies to mediate labor disputes in industry. For instance, in South Carolina a warehouse stocker complained to the Labor Management Services division of the state Department of Labor that he had been unfairly fired. The stocker had a good record—too good, apparently, for his boss seemed threatened by it. A mediator from the division helped the warehouse owner and the fired worker to work out a compromise in which the employee was rehired but put to work in a different location. According to the authors of the article from which this example is taken, "A big reason for the success of the South Carolina LMS approach is employers' preference for voluntary mediation over a system such as arbitration that overrides their authority to make the final decision."[3] Mediation is great when it works, but it's not always available when you need it, and it has chronic limitations.

Use outside arbitrators. University of Pennsylvania law professor Clyde W. Summers argues that it is unconscionable for the unionized minority of the work force to be protected against unjust dismissal and discipline while the nonunion majority remain unprotected. He urges a law giving nonunion employees a right to go to outside arbitration when they believe that they have been unfairly disciplined. Arbitrators would decide cases on the basis of just cause standards just as they do in the case of unionized employees.

A half dozen or more U.S. companies reportedly use arbitrators to settle the claims of nonunion employees. (Two of these companies—Polaroid and Northrop—are written up in Part II.) As under collective bargaining, they make arbitration the last of many steps in the grievance procedure. For instance, at Polaroid a disgruntled employee goes to arbitration only after

---

[2] "Are You Hearing Enough Employee Concerns?" *Harvard Business Review*, May–June 1984, p. 133.
[3] Leonard Bierman, Joseph C. Ullman, and Stuart A. Youngblood, "Making Disputes over Dismissals 'Win-Win' Situations," *Harvard Business Review*, January–February 1985, p. 162.

he or she has exhausted the in-company procedure with the help of the Employees Committee. Northrop also employs arbitration as the ultimate step for recalcitrant employees who exhaust the company's procedures. As I understand it, Summers's proposal does not conflict with such approaches. It does not put in-company procedures out of business by allowing employees to skip past them. It only guarantees that employees can go to arbitration when nothing else is available.

If only companies would buy this idea!

Employ minitrials, private adjudication, or other forms of what is called "alternative dispute resolution." These alternatives have much merit, and a positive trend in the employee relations landscape is growing discussion of them and corporate experiments with them. Thus, at the American Bar Association meeting in August 1989, the focus was on them. Again, a model procedure for employment dispute adjudication out of court has been drawn up by a committee of prominent lawyers. The results I am acquainted with have been very successful, and the future of alternative dispute resolution looks bright. It is quite possible, in fact, that companies like those covered in this study will add it to their arsenal, encouraging employees to use it as a final step or as an option. Indeed, as the concept evolves the day may come when some form or forms of private adjudication will be an element of corporate due process.

Don't hold your breath waiting for this development, however, as it won't come in force until the twenty-first century. Also, because of its expense and formality, the need for attorneys, and other characteristics, it cannot be a substitute for in-company hearing systems.

In Sum . . .

Nobody ever said (I hope) that due process will single-handedly produce harmony in employee relations, operate with zero defects, protect grievants completely against retaliation, make managers manage fairly, or eliminate lawsuits by disgruntled employees. In most companies, moreover, due process does not offer a way for employees to question corporate policies or technical hazards to the public. Although its dollars-and-cents costs are negligible, due process may upset some supervisors and managers, test the patience of those who have to listen to chronic malcontents, and in some cases, exact high tolls of a few executives' time. In addition, it may inhibit a certain kind of decision making, encourage bureaucracy, create anguish, and possibly even slow down the introduction of needed change and innovation.

Added to this litany of weaknesses is the fact that in the corporate world, due process may be transient; though it may seem firmly established under one management, a new management may take over someday and cut the procedure, or let it wither on the vine, almost as ruthlessly and autocratically as it may cut a product line or service or sell a factory.

But real as the failings, frailties, and foibles of due process may be, they are not fatal. Grievance procedures are alive and well in many nonunion companies, and spreading rapidly. What is more, the alternatives are questionable or inadequate. Inaction, trying to turn the clock back, hot lines, state mediators, letting a union come in and handle the job, beefing up the counseling staff, universal arbitration, private adjudication—these and other options either can't work, don't work, work in too limited a way, or aren't ready to work yet. In short, the pitfalls of no due process are greater than those of such a system.

A farmer listened to his neighbor complain about tractors—their cost, vibration, gas consumption, the difficulty of getting spare parts, and so on. "Yes, that's all true," said the farmer, "but they're still the best product of their kind on the market." The weaknesses of corporate due process may be many, but, as one manager told me, "It beats having nothing at all."

7

What Will Due Process Do to Us?

To begin this final chapter in Part I, let me look briefly at the ground already covered.

First, there is the promise of corporate due process. It aims to help management develop an atmosphere of trust and respect in the workplace, to reduce employees' need for unions, to cut down on lawsuits from employees, and to offer many other advantages. It is simple, inexpensive, and much needed; the main requirement to make it work is simply the will to make it work.

In the second chapter I reviewed the trends and conditions that give due process vitality and stamina on the corporate scene. The circumstances that impel forward-looking organizations to consider it are not going to go away. This phenomenon is not a will-o'-the-wisp.

I looked next at the distinctive features of corporate due process. Can all employees use it readily? Is the investigator or board free to decide cases on their merits? Are cases approached in a predictable way? A series of such tests enables due process to be placed on a spectrum with such other remedies as mediation, arbitration, and legal proceedings.

Then I considered the questions that policymakers should ponder when planning to adopt a nonunion grievance procedure. These questions range from the sufficiency of depth and strength of the personnel department to means of appraising the success and effectiveness of the procedure chosen after it goes into operation.

In the fifth chapter I posed a series of questions that managers and administrators should keep in mind when they look seriously at a nonunion grievance procedure. How should the investigator or board members be chosen? How should decisions be made? How much time should decision makers be given to render their judgments? and so on. I also summarized facts about the procedures used by the eleven board-type systems covered in this study—cases per year, number of voting members, reversal rates, and so forth.

Next I examined the limitations of nonunion grievance procedures. They are no panacea, nor are they error-free. Furthermore, they exist at top management's discretion and can be taken away by top executive decision—in theory, at least, their existence is more precarious than, say, our civil liberties laws. Still, they are the best thing of their kind that exists.

With this material in hand, I offer a final series of questions about due process. How does it affect efficiency, productivity, and the quality of work life? Looking at the experience of fifteen companies with nonunion grievance systems, what kinds of guidelines are emerging about the powers and restraints of investigators and tribunals? What are some implications of due process for our philosophy of the corporation?

A Two-Edged Sword

Some executives, when first hearing about due process, throw their hands up. Another disruption of the command system! Another monkey wrench in the machinery for producing high work standards! It is no wonder that such negative reactions occur, for U.S. management has been baptized by fire in recent generations, what with the difficulties of working with unions, obstacles presented by government, and intense, damaging competition from West Germany and Asian countries.

What are the everyday effects of due process on the work of an organization? Although it takes some prerogatives away from managers, it does not impair their ability to manage. In none of the fifteen companies observed, where grievance procedures have been operating for five years at a minimum and sometimes up to more than four decades, has an investigator or board system put managers in anything resembling a straitjacket. The operating results of the company bear this out clearly. In all but a few of the fifteen companies, in fact, growth and profits have been well above the national average since the procedures were installed.

To be sure, due process means that managers and supervisors can't act arbitrarily when they penalize subordinates for something they did or didn't do. Sometimes this is all that managers see when considering the subject. What they don't see is just as important—sometimes more important. This is that due process subjects subordinates to a discipline, just as it does their bosses. It subjects everyone to the discipline of productivity, profitability, and loyalty to the firm. In other words, a nonunion grievance procedure is a two-edged sword, limiting the subordinate as well as his or her boss, empowering the manager as well as his or her subordinate.

How does the procedure do this? In almost all cases that the boards and investigators in this study have considered, a fair hearing has served to remind complainants that they have obligations as well as rights. For instance, they must show up on time. They must use their brains. They must show the proper respect for authority, in particular, the managers to whom they report. They must cooperate with other employees. In short, although they don't have to be abused or kicked around, they must contribute to the success of the organization.

When employees are unwilling to give, they are likely to get little sympathy from boards and investigators. Evidence of this was ample. I saw cases in which firings were upheld without hesitation because subordinates refused to carry out orders or gave their superiors a hard time about the orders they were given. I saw cases in which boards or investigators sided quickly with managers who penalized subordinates for negative attitudes. I saw cases in which complainants got nowhere when they tried to overturn low performance appraisals reflecting their inability or unwillingness to perform well. I saw managers get plenty of support when they acted on sufficient evidence in demoting, "boondocking," or dismissing an assistant for lying, stealing, or bad-mouthing the employer.

I saw *no* cases in which boards or investigators showed the blatant disregard of corporate needs and goals that some state courts have exhibited in decisions that seemed hopelessly naive about economic realities.

I saw many cases in which corporate due process, in addition to enhancing fairness and the quality of work life, became a means of economic education. For example, board members and investigators would use the occasion of a complaint to educate disgruntled individuals on their obligations to the organization. To mention three everyday instances:

> At John Hancock, the employee relations committee saved a secretary from being sacked unfairly but put her on probation and told her, orally and in writing, what she must accomplish if she wished to be reinstated permanently. For instance, she mustn't talk excessively with co-workers, she must produce letters with few or no errors, she must follow instructions to a T.
>
> At NBC, the investigator (his title is employee counselor but he often acts as arbitrator) sat down with an assistant to the purchasing manager and helped him find new ways of working productively with his boss, instead of the often obstructionist ways that had gotten him in trouble.
>
> At Honeywell's Defense Systems Division, an employee who was denied promotion was instructed in writing as to what standards he must meet to get promoted later. When he improved, he was promoted.

My impression was that board members and investigators were mindful of the realities of competition, including global competition, and of the corporation's need to make a profit. There appeared to be no exceptions to this attitude. Of course, this recognition might be expected of boards composed of senior managers, but I saw no difference in the case of boards composed of middle managers and nonmanagers. In fact, when it comes to things like chronic tardiness, absenteeism, and shirking job duties, lower-level employees are likely to judge grievants more harshly than senior managers do. Clerics, office workers, staff analysts, machine operators, and other such employees are likely to have little sympathy with job-shirkers because they know all too well how difficult it is to work next to such people. "I was always picking up the pieces," said one blue-collar "judge" to me, recalling his bitterness about fellow employees who hadn't done their share of work. This person was not easy on a grievant who was known to be a slacker.

Far from being a hindrance to corporate economic goals, therefore, due process systems appear to be a support. To the extent that they make collective bargaining unnecessary, reduce lawsuits, and improve discipline, they lower corporate costs and boost productivity even more.

Subtle and Not-So-Subtle Effects

One of the most notable effects of corporate due process is on employee relations. Boards, investigators, and power mediators try to relate disciplinary measures in a reasonable way to the gravity of the offense. They look at such mitigating factors that may be brought up as an employee's long service or understandable confusion over a rule. In addition, they try to make their decisions corrective, if possible.

Now, there is nothing new in concept about either effort. In the past many managers and supervisors took it on themselves to make the punishment fit the crime and, where possible, make punishment corrective rather than punitive. In many thousands of arbitrations under collective bargaining contracts, arbitrators did the same thing. However, not all managers followed suit, and those who didn't wreaked havoc. What due process does is apply the principles of fair treatment across the board to all departments and to all manager-subordinate relationships in a nonunion company. In short, fair treatment becomes an enforceable companywide policy. This is a major change.

In somewhere between a fifth and half or more of the cases brought to an in-company tribunal or to an investigator, judging from this study of fifteen companies, supervisors and managers get reversed. Arbitrary or capricious actions, failure to follow personnel procedure, words or actions that mislead subordinates—these and other failures are common grounds for reversal.

In all instances studied, however, tribunals and investigators have been influenced heavily by the company's or department's norms, standards, traditions, and customs. Sometimes, in fact, they know no other. As a result, what is insubordination in one organization is not necessarily insubordination in another, and a supervisor's shading of the procedural rules in one firm might not be considered objectionable in another. In short, the decisions of boards and investigators in other companies and areas, if known, do not have precedential value.

Thus, corporate due process develops in a different way from arbitration and law. Arbitrators are often influenced by the decisions of other arbitrators, which are available through publication, even though they respect the subject organization's customs and culture. As for the people in black robes, they are supposed to and do pay a lot of attention to state precedent, if they sit on state courts, and to federal court precedent, if they sit on U.S. district or circuit courts or the Supreme Court.

Another effect is on standards of accusation and proof. Before corporate due process came along in the huge nonunion sector and at the nonunion levels of organized companies (as at TWA, NBC, and other firms), managers could penalize employees arbitrarily, without evidence of any sort that their demotion, firing, or other such act was justified. Not so now. In a nonunion company with a grievance procedure, a subordinate who has been disciplined can challenge his or her boss before the hearing board or investigator. The latter will ask, What evidence did the boss have that the subordinate was cheating on expense accounts, or flaunting safety rules, or upsetting morale? Not until the board or investigator is satisfied does the decision stand.

A subtler and longer-range effect of due process is on the quality of work life. Although it has no effect on working hours, compensation, fringe benefits, or other quantifiable aspects of work life, it does affect the atmosphere in which employees work. No longer are subordinates as defenseless as a patient lying on an operating table; in hearings and investigations, at least, they possess a sort of equality. Like a poor person suing a rich one in court, for a moment their disadvantaged status does not matter; what the investigator or board is most concerned with is the merits of the argument.

In turn, this means a shifting of the manner and burden of employee security. George C. Lodge, professor of business administration at the Harvard Business School, puts it this way:

> Implicit in the new premise is the notion that security of employment, carrying with it a reciprocal commitment to hard work, is a more competitive way in which to provide people with economic security than is security of income, where there is no such reciprocal commitment to work. Our Asian competitors have shown this. Until recently, we in the United States have assumed that managers had little responsibility for employment security, that they were empowered to hire and fire workers as market conditions and the satisfaction of shareholders might require, and that it was the responsibility of government to assure economic security. As in the other, older industrial democracies in the West, the U.S. government has met this responsibility by providing income security, typically requiring no work in return. Such an approach maintains consumption but does little for production, and it imposes the "overhead cost" of economic security on society as a whole. It follows, therefore, that both productivity and the national economy will be better served if business takes greater responsibility for employment security, and government correspondingly less.[1]

---

[1] "Opinion," *Harvard Business School Bulletin,* December 1986, pp. 40–41.

A Corporate "Common Law"?

In England centuries ago, the early courts began making law case by case. Over a period of time jurists could discern certain principles and attitudes that the judges had, and these became the beginnings of the common law.

Is there a "common law" emerging in the rooms where corporate tribunals sit and investigators make judgments on the merits of superior-subordinate conflicts? On the basis of my observations, I think there is—despite the strong tendency of investigators and tribunal members to be guided by local customs. In some ways these principles are those observed by arbitrators; in other ways they are not. Here are my impressions:

- Employees have standing in the grievance procedure only when they complain that corporate personnel policy has not been followed. (For an example, see the SmithKline Beckman write-up in Part II.)
- Written personnel policies and rules are the "law" of the company governing the case (e.g., Northrop).
- Superiors can fire or demote subordinates but must follow the rules in corporate personnel policy—so many oral and/or written warnings, deadlines for improvement, and so on (e.g., Citicorp).
- Subordinates who are disciplined are entitled to know why they are disciplined (e.g., IBM).
- Companies must erect no geographical or time barriers that make it difficult for employees to use due process procedures (e.g., TWA).
- Grieving employees must first try to work out their complaints informally, using the personnel resources made available by the company and following any prescribed steps for complaint resolution (e.g., Honeywell).
- In the case of a tribunal or board, the "judges" may be managers, peers of the grievant, or a combination of the two, but they must always be people who can approach the case fairly and objectively (e.g., the General Electric–Columbia plant).
- A grieving employee has a right to guidance on company time by the personnel group in the organization. At a minimum, guidance covers the merits of his or her case and use of appeal procedures (e.g., CIGNA).
- Differences in rank and status among parties and witnesses are irrelevant in the tribunal's or investigator's decision. Only the merits of the arguments count (e.g., NBC).
- A tribunal, investigator, or power mediator will not second-guess the judgment of a superior who disciplines a subordinate so long as the boss did not act capriciously and without reason (e.g., John Hancock).
- As a general rule, outside attorneys cannot represent either side at a hearing. If the grievant or defending manager needs a spokesperson, a fellow employee can be chosen. The one exception to the rule found in this study is TWA, which allows attorneys in certain cases.
- Although a penalized employee is entitled to know the charges against him or her and to rebut the superior's evidence, the employee is not necessarily entitled to confront the witnesses personally. For example, the testimony can be summarized in written form for the tribunal after individual interrogation

of witnesses by an employee relations specialist (e.g., Federal Express's Appeals Board).

- A penalized subordinate and his or her witnesses have a right to be heard—to have their "day in court" or testimony taken for the record—no matter how obnoxious they may be as personalities (e.g., SmithKline Beckman).
- Hearsay evidence is admissible but the board members or investigators can discount it as much as they want (e.g., Polaroid).
- If witnesses appear at a hearing or their testimony is taken for a record, the board members or investigator must be free to cross-examine them in any way they deem necessary, though the parties in the case may not be able to cross-examine them (e.g., Donnelly).
- As a practical matter, corporate due process is for employees below top management. The highest-level manager I encountered who used the procedure was a third-level manager at Honeywell. Subjective factors like compatibility, congeniality, and "chemistry" are generally so important at the top levels that executives leave the organization when the chief executive asks them to, relying only on their contracts to obtain severance compensation—their golden parachutes.

Governance and Accountability

In principle, corporate due process makes sense because the skills, energy, and dedication of employees are an asset of great importance, and due process enhances this asset. In an economy in which global competition, technological innovation, and product or service quality are crucial factors in a company's ability to survive, the level of employee commitment to the enterprise makes an enormous difference. As more and more thoughtful executives and business observers are saying, therefore, top management has become accountable to employees in much the same measure that it has long been accountable to stockholders. Accountable in what ways? To make work safe and stimulating, to make the quality of life in the office building or plant rewarding and fulfilling.

Professor and long-time corporate attorney Joseph Auerbach approaches the subject from a different angle but arrives at a similar conclusion:

> The business corporation will have to become, in concept, an economic institution, with its governance lodged in those interests concerned with its successful economic welfare. These principal interests are those who provide the capital and those who are employed by the enterprise. No other interest is of sufficient financial or social weight to be accorded a fixed participation in governance.
>
> In order for these two governing interests to be represented fairly, the electoral rights for the providers of capital should be essentially equal to those accorded to employees. The concept of "ownership" of the business corporation by its shareholders would become extinct, but the capital providers would have rights regarding the success, liquidation, or dissolution of the enterprise. The providers of capital are essential to the welfare of the corpora-

tion, not because they are "owners," but because of their having provided one of the two essential elements to the success of the enterprise. This entitles them to rents and rewards, and participation in the governance system.

As the providers of the other essential elements to success, the employees are entitled to responsible employment conditions, with security, rewards, and participation in the governance system.

Eliminating the concept of shareholder "ownership" is less radical than would initially appear. In lieu of their previous status, the corporate shareholders would, in analogy, become "partners" of the employee force with a common interest in achieving economic success. In the limited partnership form of business enterprise, the general partners are vested with full, discretionary management functions. They must carry out their responsibilities with integrity and due care and are assured of their reward when successful.

The employees would be, in effect, limited partners making a day-to-day, long-term investment in kind rather than money. That investment would be recognized conceptually as real, although remaining undefined on the balance sheet. Unlike the customary limited partnership, the general partners would also thus be responsible to "limited partners" of a different kind. This conceptual approach would constitute a fundamental change in the existing corporate system. But, management would remain the key to business success.[2]

For more than a century in the United States, economic theory has made management accountable exclusively to owners. There are good reasons that this was so. Owners took an interest in the company. They knew what was going on. They could evaluate management. But since World War II, this has changed. Today countless owners can't tell you anything about the companies they are invested in. A great many, in fact, can't even tell you for sure what companies they own shares in. As for those few stockholders who do turn up at annual meetings, they are likely to be regarded by top executives as nuisances, gadflies, and social deviates. More often than not, as Auerbach points out, the nominee owners of a company's shares are agents for brokerage firms and banks (nominee owners are commonly known as "street names" because they are the people listed as owners). Also, many owners are money managers; their interest in a corporation is not proprietary but monetary, which is to say, its ability or inability to generate income. Professional traders and arbitrageurs could hardly care less about corporate governance; they treat their shares like chips in a gambling game.

None of this is to belittle the role of investors. Their contribution is and always has been indispensable. But their role isn't exclusive, as it used to be in economic theory. The daily investment made by employees is equally important. In the words of the title of a popular *Harvard Business Review* article written a couple of decades ago by Curtis Jones, now a business executive, and James S. Hekimian, now a business school dean, "Put People on Your Balance Sheet."[3]

[2] "The Now and Future Business Corporation," working paper no. 9-783-054, Harvard Business School, February 1983, pp. 36–38.
[3] January–February 1967, p. 105.

The Founding Fathers Ride Again

Corporate due process works. It introduces justice to the workplace swiftly and effectively. It reduces lawsuits. It makes all employees, managers and subordinates alike, equal before the "law" of personnel policy. If working conditions, pay, and the material benefits in the organization are good, it makes collective bargaining unnecessary.

That due process works so well, and with such low costs, is one of the best-kept secrets in American business. Why has it been so long developing?

Perhaps the main reason is a value clash. In U.S. business, the management ideal has been perfect control. The aim of every chief executive, group vice president, division head, department manager, and project head has been to have perfect control over all that goes on under him or her. This ideal has rarely been reached, of course, but executives never cease to strive for it. It is no accident that they are perennially interested in new and better management information and reporting systems.

But corporate due process jars with this ideal. Corporate due process means that for a short time—the hours that it takes an investigator to determine the facts on a case, the days that it takes a tribunal to conduct a hearing—the manager is *not* in control. The facts are in control. The facts may go against him or her.

Therefore, due process represents a frustration of the ancient striving of managers for perfect control. By definition it means imperfect control, and that prospect displeases managers. The dilemma is between imperfect and perfect control. The trouble with imperfect control is that things may happen which go against the manager's wishes or even cross him or her up. The trouble with perfect control is that it is inhuman. Perfect control is good for machines, but it runs against the grain of the American psyche.

Only when a management comes to terms with this dilemma and decides that, yes, it can live with imperfect control, that insofar as due process is concerned, at least, perfect control is out of the question, can it open itself to the possibilities of due process and seriously consider a nonunion grievance procedure. But then, strangely, in the very act of doing this, it makes possible a greater degree of control than it could ever have achieved otherwise. It is the old case of the sharing, committed, bottom-up, enterprising organization versus the autocratic, bureaucratic, highly disciplined, military-type organization. The latter may get off to a faster start and make straighter leaps, but the former almost always wins in the end.

Corporate due process was invented by the unions in the decades between World War I and World War II. The concept of arbitration of employee-supervisor disputes by an objective, fair outsider was an innovation in industrial relations that remains largely unchanged to this day. But since World War II, top management in nonunion companies has taken the concept, altered and adapted it, and made it work in ways that the originators did not dream of. For a great many companies, and especially for the skilled employees, managers as well as nonmanagers, who sit at computer consoles, analyze data, keep accounts, coordinate production markets, supervise, and carry out all the other tasks that are increasingly becoming what we label work, work that determines the competitive fate of the corporation—for all these companies and all these people the mechanisms of corporate due process studied here work better than the union concept can. They are swifter, more knowing, nonadversarial, and non-litigational.

The new procedures will not make U.S. companies number one in global competition. Only enlightened policies for manufacturing, marketing, finance, and human resources can ensure that. But the new mechanisms will help.

Moreover, they are tailored to American ideals of dignity, equity, and fair play. They have "Made in the U.S.A." stamped all over them. It seems to me that the Founding Fathers would be proud of this noble effort. They would say, "Yes, that's what we'd do if we were still around." More than any other procedure or device on the business scene, corporate due process brings to the workplace the humanitarian philosophy that lit up the American sky two centuries ago.

PART

II

Company Profiles

A

Investigator-Type Systems

Introduction

Four of the fifteen companies studied have investigator-type systems. The descriptions of these systems follow, with the write-ups arranged in alphabetical order by company.

In terms of the conceptual scheme shown in Exhibit 3-1, two of these systems rank to the left and are close to the qualifying line for due process. In fact, some observers may question whether the systems meet the requirements of due process as described in this book. It is true that the systems employ investigators who are not officially considered to have arbitrative power. However, it seemed to me that the investigators were so firmly backed by top management that, even though they were known as mediators, their findings and decisions carried arbitrative weight. Using the definition discussed earlier, these investigators are power mediators. In addition, the two systems are useful for this book because they represent the border between corporate due process and what falls short of due process.

As the insets indicate, all four write-ups are based on interviews conducted by the author. The write-ups vary in depth and detail because of company information policies, time constraints, and other factors. Also, some companies have gathered and analyzed more data on their due process systems than have other companies.

Let's Talk at
Bank of America

For half a dozen years, Bank of America has operated an approach to employee complaint resolution called "Let's Talk." As with many corporate complaint resolution programs, Let's Talk begins with meetings with the manager, his or her manager if desired, and sometimes an expert from the personnel staff called a personnel relations specialist. The first stage is informal; nothing is put in writing. If the employee isn't satisfied with the results, he or she turns to one or both of two formal stages of Let's Talk. As will be explained in detail, these stages involve going to a senior manager in writing and frequently result in the appointment of a neutral investigator who collects the facts and summarizes his or her findings for the executive. After reviewing the findings, the executive makes a decision and reports it to the complainant.

Let's Talk is managed under the direction of Robert N. Beck, executive vice president of the bank's human resources division in San Francisco. Beck has worldwide responsibility for human resources matters for the bank and its subsidiaries. The corporate staff reports directly to him; human resources staffs in the divisions have a "dotted line" accountability to him. Beck modified Let's Talk in

Company: Bank of America		Products/Services: Full-service commercial banking
Headquarters: San Francisco, California		
		Date of Interview: March 31, 1988
Sales: $5.3 billion (1987)	Number of Employees: 57,000	

1982. The program supplants an earlier system that the bank had, and he and others feel that it does a better job of responding to employees' concerns in a more timely fashion. About fifty-seven thousand people now work for Bank of America (about forty-two thousand of them in retail operations), down from seventy-seven thousand in 1980. Management has merged about three hundred branch offices into existing offices and consolidated most back-room staffs. The process in the United States was done by way of redeployments, hiring, and attrition control rather than by layoffs. The surgery was drastic—it had to be—but good results are appearing. Beginning in the final quarter of 1987, Bank of America began reporting profits after several years of major losses, and there is a conviction in San Francisco and elsewhere that the good news is just beginning.

A member of the bank's managing committee, Beck reports directly to A. W. Clausen, the chief executive. Clausen has long been known for his staunch devotion to human resources.[1] "If the chief executive doesn't believe in human resources, nothing is likely to work," James J. Whaley, vice president and director of personnel relations, told me. "It all starts with him. If you don't have the CEO behind you, you are just paying lip service to the aims of human resources."

Visions, Vistas, and Vitality

Clausen believes that the bank's interest in equitable treatment of employees goes back to the founder, A. P. Giannini. "Giannini was a very human sort of person and wanted very much to foster a good working environment for all employees," Clausen says. "He could meet someone and not see him for several years but remember the name when he saw the person again."

Originally, Giannini served on the board of a savings and loan bank in the North Beach area of San Francisco. When he couldn't convince the board to open banking to Italian immigrants and others, he resigned and started his own bank, the "Bank of the Little People." Beck writes:

> His was a unique spirit in that he conducted many firsts as a risk-taking organization. One of the first in banking to consider the idea of sales and marketing, Giannini introduced advertising. Other banks at the time considered it a breach of professional ethics for banks to advertise. His was also the first bank to focus on accessibility. He did away with the private offices and the smoky backrooms, and had all officers sit in the open. His desk was placed near the front door. Giannini began a new tone in banking, which the whole nation finally adopted.[2]

Beck also points out in his article that Giannini was the banker who financed Walt Disney in producing *Snow White and the Seven Dwarfs*. Director Frank Capra has said that without Giannini, Hollywood would not be the center of the film industry. "As a result of the close relationship with Disney and Bank of America," said Beck, "we remain the only bank allowed to do business in Disneyland."

---

[1] See, for example, "Listening and Responding to Employees' Concerns," an interview with A. W. Clausen by David W. Ewing and Pamela M. Banks, *Harvard Business Review*, January–February 1980, pp. 101–114.
[2] "Visions, Values, and Strategies: Changing Attitudes and Culture," *Executive* (Academy of Management), February 1987, p. 33.

In the first month of Clausen's presidency in 1970, the bank decided to disclose to all U.S. employees what their grades were, what the minimum and maximum salaries of those grade levels were, and what kind of pay increase could be expected for good performance. Clausen also decided to let employees see their own personnel files—this years before the California labor code required it. In 1978, the employee assistance department was formed from what formerly had been two separate departments. Its efforts to work out employee complaints informally were bolstered by the existence of a "Let's Talk It Over" program that allowed an unhappy employee to appeal in writing to a top management review committee.

Because of Clausen's belief in the need for not one but several avenues of complaint, the bank also created "Open Line," a successful procedure for answering questions and complaints anonymously. Open Line continues in operation; in fact, reports Whaley, close to five hundred written queries come to Open Line in a typical year, each of which is answered. Many questions come by phone. In addition the bank reserves a section in its magazine *BankAmerican* and newsletter *On Your Behalf* for employees to print general interest questions and answers.

In 1982, during Clausen's absence from the bank to serve as head of the World Bank, Beck became executive vice president. (Formerly he had been with IBM as its director of benefits and personnel.) Beck quickly saw the need to make changes in the appeal procedure and in the relations between personnel experts and other employees. He says:

> The two problems that bothered me most when I came in and looked at the processes were (1) the appeal procedure was so structured and formal that you couldn't move fast through the system; and (2) the emphasis of the employee assistance officers, as they were called then, seemed wrong.
>
> As for the first, it was taking sometimes three, four, or five months to settle personnel problems. That's just too long. The procedure was too bureaucratic, and I wanted to streamline it. Everybody in the system seemed to be waiting for an outcome. When the files on the complaint came in, they'd be inches thick—just too much. In California you have to document everything if you don't want to end up losing in court—that problem is changing now, I'm glad to say—but the process still was too slow.
>
> As for the second problem, the work of the employee assistance officers bothered me. They kept track of their phone calls and meetings and gave me a report on how they spent their time. When I read it, I was shocked. As I recall, it turned out that about 75 percent was going into counseling employees and about 25 percent into counseling managers. I said, "Wait a minute, isn't this closing the barn door after the horse gets out? Wouldn't it be better to have managers manage better so that we don't even have the problems?"
>
> In one year's time we turned that around, so that the personnel specialists spent 75 percent of their time coaching managers on how to do it right and 25 percent on employees with complaints.
>
> It bothered me, too, that when I came, managers perceived the personnel department as against them and for the employees. As many managers saw it, it was the employee against management, and personnel was there to help him or her win over management. We've changed that perception, too.
>
> One of the things we did was set up a formal management development program for all managers. Our managers had not been taught how to manage people, so we started a program and said that every new manager must go to our corporate management school and learn how to manage within thirty days of appointment. We put ten thousand managers through in eighteen months. It was an incredible work load, all in-house, everywhere from bottom to top. Everybody had to go back to the fundamen-

tals—I call them "blocking and tackling." How do you write a performance appraisal? What's the complaint process like? What's merit pay all about? And so on.

Then I had the titles of the personnel people changed—from employee assistance officers to personnel relations specialists. It was a cosmetic change but important in that it sent signals. Actually the people are generalists, but we call them specialists when talking with line managers and employees.

I said, "I want to see bridges built to management so that when managers feel that they have got into tough situations, they'll pick up the phone, call a PRS, and say, "Hey, I've got a tough one. I've never fired anybody, never had a bad performer, but now I have one and have to act. What do I do?" I wanted a personnel specialist to be a consultant so that the manager wouldn't goof up, rather than wait for the manager to goof up and then play the part of the white knight running in and saving the employee.

Management credits personnel relations, Let's Talk, and related efforts with many important gains. Fewer lawsuits are brought by employees, and state agencies are bringing fewer complaints against the bank. "Because problems are being taken care of inside," says Whaley, "people don't have to go to an outside agency or to court." Another benefit is substantial gains in morale. For instance, during the three years after the new program began in 1982, employee opinion surveys produced far more positive answers from subordinates about how they worked together with their managers and about opportunities given them to express their ideas in meetings with managers to discuss their performance evaluations.[3]

Anatomy of an Appeal

As mentioned, the first stage of Let's Talk is a meeting with management and/or a personnel relations specialist. This stage is informal and oral. The second and third stages are formal. If you are the unhappy employee, you put your concern in writing and send it to the executive officer for your division. Within five days your letter will be acknowledged. The executive officer may meet with you personally, but more likely he or she will appoint an investigator to look into the problem. The investigator will meet with you, talk to other people involved in the matter, and make a recommendation to the executive officer. Where practical, the investigator will advise you of the findings to see if he or she missed anything. The decision may be on your side, your manager's, or somewhere in between. After studying the recommendation, the executive officer will tell you what his or her decision is.

Suppose you're not satisfied with the executive's decision. Then you may write the bank's vice chairman or the equivalent officer for your division. This is the third stage. The executive acknowledges your letter and appoints a different investigator who works in the same manner as in the second stage. When the investigation and recommendation are completed, the vice chairman tells you what his or her decision is.

An important feature of this problem is what Beck calls "line management ownership," that is, control by line managers even though personnel may play a strong advisory role:

We want employees to go up the line with their complaints—that's another change from what used to be. There was a big emphasis on going up to the personnel commit-

---

[3] Ibid., p. 38.

tee. But I wanted line management ownership, so I changed the approach. Now, if you are, say, in the retail bank, you go to the vice chairman of the organization. He doesn't have to investigate personally but can assign an investigator. The investigators are trained. The investigating isn't all done by personnel people. We have shifted that so that half of the investigators are line managers.

There are likely to be around fifty formal appeals per year at the bank. Whaley emphasizes that the overwhelming majority of complaints are taken care of informally, however; management counts heavily on both line and staff to solve as many problems as possible before they become formal. Beck says:

> We encourage the employee to go to the immediate manager first. We say, "If it doesn't work, you can always appeal." But maybe there's already a breakdown in communications, or a chemistry problem, and the employee says, "I'm just not going to see that jerk." Then we say, "Try the second line manager." A lot of problems get solved that way. Hundreds do. And if that doesn't work, we encourage the person to go to a higher manager, anywhere up to the senior vice president.

In the informal stage, says Whaley, resolutions are most readily reached. Frequently, at this stage, the manager and employee find some compromise solution. In the informal stage it may become clear quickly to the manager that he or she was wrong or misunderstood, in which case the decision will be changed. In the formal stages, by contrast, the manager and subordinate are more likely to be at an impasse, with the manager convinced that the right thing was done and the employee convinced that it wasn't. Gary Woodson, personnel relations manager, feels that close to one-third of managers' decisions are changed in the informal stage, and perhaps one-fifth or more changed in the formal stage.

Beck emphasizes that these changes are not always reversals of managers' decisions; more likely they are partial reversals. As an example of a full reversal, Beck gives inappropriate firing followed by reinstatement; as an example of partial reversal, adjustment of a performance appraisal. (For instance, the employee complains of getting a lower rating than deserved. Discussion or investigation shows that the supervisor didn't make it clear to the subordinate what was expected, so there is room for reasonable doubt. A compromise is reached, or the appraisal is allowed to stand and the subordinate is transferred to another work area, or some other accommodation is made.)

If a manager is reversed, that is not held against him or her if the action taken was reasonable. In Beck's words: "We tell the manager, 'Look, if you did it right, if you made the decision in good conscience and for good business reasons, you're not going to get penalized even if you got reversed. But if you were arbitrary or capricious, then you're going to get your helmet dinged.' "

Whether reversals and partial reversals are high or low, credibility is the crucial thing. "If employees went through Let's Talk and found it was weighted toward management, despite their evidence showing that mistakes were in fact made—once this got out, the credibility of the whole program would be shot," says Whaley.

No formal requirements are made for a written complaint. No particular form must be used, no minimum or maximum number of pages is suggested, no particular format is required. In fact, the written message does not even have to be typed; it can be handwritten. "We wanted to make it easy for all levels of employees," says Beck.

In most cases, it is likely to take only a couple of weeks to get a complaint resolved. Woodson elaborates:

> Management makes the commitment to give the employee's concern a high priority. Executive investigators want to get it resolved so that the investigator can be freed up and returned to his or her unit. They want to get back to their normal business as quickly as possible. Where resolution takes longer—months or so—it usually comes when there is a complicated and serious problem like termination, where all kinds of legal issues and people are involved. A number of people have to be interviewed, and maybe documents have to be researched. It gets to be a long-drawn-out deal. And more times than not, what also happens is that when the investigator goes back to the complaining employee and says, "Here are the facts I've found," the employee says, "Well, wait a minute, let me tell you about another thing. . . . " So then the investigator has to go back and start looking at other questions. Fortunately, there aren't many cases that are dragged out like that.

The privacy of the employee is paramount, says Paula Elliott, assistant vice president and personnel relations consultant. Nothing is placed in the employee's personnel file in either the formal or informal process. Since the formal process does have a file, upon conclusion of the investigation, the executive to whom the employee wrote forwards the correspondence to the personnel relations department for safekeeping. Personnel relations stresses this to employees so that they will know that records of their appeal cannot be seen by other line managers now or at a later time.

Investigators and Investigations

As mentioned, half of the investigators are line people; the rest come from personnel. Each investigator is selected by the senior vice president or executive vice president. The selection is based on knowledge and experience in the area of expertise required. However, the investigator cannot have been involved in the case in any way. Beck describes the process as follows:

> The investigator gets the facts and reports to the senior vice president. Depending on the complexity of the case, it may be an oral report or a written report. Then the SVP sits down with you, if you are the complaining employee, or writes you with his or her decision. Then you have the option of accepting the decision or appealing again. If you think you didn't get a fair shake, you will probably make a third-stage appeal. This means going to the executive vice president, vice chairman, or equivalent officer at that level. That officer does not have to be in your management chain. You can go to someone in another division. For example, suppose you don't know the vice chairman of the retail bank but for years you've known the chief credit officer, who is a vice chairman in another division. You could write or call him and say, "I think I got a bad deal here. It wasn't my fault on those loans, and I'd like you to investigate." You could do it this way, whatever way makes you feel most comfortable.

Woodson elaborates:

> When investigators are appointed, we take them from some unit other than the one you are in. They talk with you, talk with your manager, look at all the facts, then summarize what they've learned for the senior executive who appointed them. Some

investigations are very quick, some take considerable time. The senior executive can do the investigation personally, but from a practical standpoint it's difficult to do that, so normally he appoints an investigator. More likely than not, he gets the report orally.

But before the investigators report to the senior vice president, they normally confirm with you what they've found. This is for affirmation that, yes, they've got the facts of the picture, got the details right, haven't distorted the situation, and have talked to the right people. This step may stimulate more investigation. For instance, you say, "That's not really the way it happened. What my supervisor said was this." Or, "Did you look at this? Did you talk to so-and-so?" So the investigator goes back and talks to more people, depending on the circumstances. But they check with you before they summarize for the senior executive.

The investigators don't go to you and say, "Here's what I have decided." That's not for them. Final decisions are for the senior executive to make.

Woodson explains that the bank is creating a pool of trained investigators. They would not stay in the pool indefinitely but for a limited period like two years. They would not be asked to investigate more than, say, two complaints a year. The bank doesn't want to overload these people, Woodson says. A pool of qualified investigators makes it easier for the executive officer or senior vice president to appoint a person to look into a complaint. It saves time in getting the investigation started, especially since the investigator is already selected and trained. Woodson says:

> Candidate pools have been created by the executive officers for each of the divisions, and investigators are available to take cases across any division. Personnel relations maintains the list of qualified investigators, ensures their training, and keeps track of their investigation work load. When an executive officer needs an investigator, we can give him two or three different names to choose from.

PRSes—Advisers with Influence

Personnel relations specialists play an advisory role, leaving it up to line managers to make the actual decisions on complaints, but their work is crucial to the success of Let's Talk. Without them, the formal complaint procedures would be swamped with cases—or, worse, the system would lack credibility and not be used much at all. Beck says:

> I think that 50 percent of our personnel problems are breakdowns in or the absence of good communication. One thing the personnel specialists do is help get both sides talking. That's why we call it Let's Talk. I tell the specialists and others in human resources, "Your job is to help managers be effective and run the business in a positive upbeat way. It is to attract, motivate, and retain good employees.
>
> "Regardless of whom you report to, there are two things to keep in mind. One is the business side—your job and relationships at the bank. The other is that I'm responsible for your career. I expect you to have enough confidence and trust in the system so that you'll be willing if necessary to lay down in front of the train—fight for what you believe in."
>
> Originally personnel relations had very strong power—they could veto managers' decisions to fire. They were worried that our present system wouldn't work. I said, "No, you're going to be respected for your experience, your expertise, your advice and counsel. But you've also got to have confidence so that when there's a tough manager out there who says, "I'm going to do it" and you say no, you'll escalate up the manage-

ment chain quickly to protect the principle. You won't be sacrificing your career, you'll be protecting it.

Personnel relations sees itself as being an advocate neither for management nor employees, but for the organization as a whole. It is concerned with the merits of the situation, not taking sides. It wants no we-they attitude on the part of either managers or their subordinates. This calls for a lot of discipline on the part of a PRS. Says Woodson:

> It's very difficult to walk that line sometimes. People on both sides tug at you, trying to get you on their side. That's a problem that all of us have to be conscious of every day. We want to maintain our neutrality. We don't want to be perceived as an advocate for line managers or employees. We try to concentrate on the facts, the merits of each case we deal with. Justice and fair play in the workplace—that's the goal.

According to Whaley, the bank employs twenty-eight personnel relations specialists in California—eighteen in the northern part of the state, ten in the south. Another specialist is employed in New York City. Assuming around fifty-seven thousand employees, this means there is one specialist for about two thousand people. The specialists do not have territories; rather, personnel management assigns them where and as they are most needed. However, to build trust and confidence, a specialist is usually assigned to a group for a considerable period of time. Elliott says that much of a specialist's time is usually spent listening to employees talk about their problems and helping them to find answers. A specialist is also likely to spend a lot of time with managers and subordinates negotiating solutions to their difficulties. "We try to resolve conflicts so that both sides win," she explains.

A lot of this time is spent on the phone. Elliott herself is likely to be on the phone twenty-five or thirty times a day—five to six hundred phone calls per month. Other personnel relations people may spend more or less time on the phone, depending on their situations. In addition, she guesses that a specialist is likely to run two training classes per month, attend four to ten staff meetings per month in her clients' organizations, and meet about ten times per week with employees.

I asked Elliott to describe a few of the calls she had handled earlier in the morning the day I interviewed her. She answered:

> One call this morning was from an employee who had been given a low rating on her performance report. She was upset and wanted to talk about it with me. She asked me to call her tonight at her home, as it was hard for her to talk freely on the office phone.
> Another call was from a manager of an employee who is planning to resign in several weeks. The manager wants to accelerate that resignation.
> I was called by another manager who had a problem with an applicant. He wanted to hire the applicant but was told that the person's fingerprint record indicated that she had been charged with a petty theft that would rule her out under the Federal Deposit Insurance Corporation rules. What should he do? I told the manager that we must first find out what happened. He should sit down with the applicant, tell her about the fingerprint record, and ask her how the charge was resolved.

One of personnel relations' most important jobs, Woodson points out, is informing senior managers about trouble spots in the organization, potential problems, and dips in morale. Often personnel relations will learn about such problems because of the number of calls that come in from a particular area. When personnel relations talks with a senior manager about such volatile problems, it may suggest how the difficulties might be dealt with and the situations defused, but it never forgets that its role is advisory. Elliott explains:

> If problems keep arising with a certain manager, I have a responsibility to let his or her manager know about the trouble. I may also inform my own manager. I'll tell them that I've got some concerns based on this, this, and this. I'll lay out the facts as I see them. A lot depends on the seriousness of the trouble, but in any case it's up to them to take whatever action they think is necessary.

Qualities and Training

What skills and aptitudes make a good personnel relations specialist? Whaley answers:

> A good PRS doesn't feel intimidated by a high-level manager. While the specialist will be tactful, he or she won't be afraid to say what needs saying. For instance, specialists often need to talk to line managers about their people skills, and they often need to point out mistakes that were made in dealing with subordinates. They need to be able to do this without antagonizing management.
>
> Personnel specialists have to work long hours. They don't turn the meter off at five o'clock. Often they need to talk with employees in the evening because of the sensitivity of problems.
>
> I don't think you can tell good PRSes from their résumés and other documents. You have to watch them in operation. You have to get the feel of their approach to a problem; you have to make a judgment call.

What training do personnel specialists receive? Beck answers:

> First of all, they get one-on-one training through Jim Whaley's organization when they start. Second, we have personnel development seminars—PDS classes, we call them. We bring in personnel professionals for three days and put the specialists through a training program on all aspects of human resources management. Next, we try to rotate these people so that they become broad generalists (even though they are called specialists). They should know staffing, compensation, employee relations, and so on. Then, every six weeks or so in the auditorium we have a personnel forum that is open to all personnel people. There are two or three hours of presentations on what's going on in human resources, and we usually have one line manager come in—usually he or she is at the executive vice president level—to talk about his or her area of the business, what role they're trying to play, what role they expect personnel to play, and so on. So personnel specialists learn about the business and our customers as well as the dos and don'ts of going about their job. Despite all this training, the two most important key success factors are interpersonal skills and ability to see things in a broad objective way.

Working with Managers

After managers' informal talks with a personnel relations specialist, Whaley stresses they frequently change the actions and decisions originally made. Probably many hundreds of such changes are made during the course of an average year. Many problems are routine, but not all are. What really tests a personnel relations specialist is the unusual situation that prompts a manager to call. Woodson elaborates:

> The situation may be so unique that many managers will never see it, but all of a sudden the manager runs up against it. He or she picks up the manager's guide and finds nothing about it there, so a call is made to personnel relations. We're kind of the catcher of everything that's unique and extraordinary and not covered by some easily accessible policy. Part of what we do is common sense, part is based on what we've seen or done elsewhere in similar circumstances. There's very little that we can get hit with that we haven't seen someplace.

Elliott adds:

> A lot of situations we help managers with are gray. You can't look anywhere for the answer. There's no guide that tells you exactly what to do in *every* situation.
>
> So part of the challenge of our job is to look at a situation, look at the guidelines, and interpret the *intent* of guidelines. Then—based on the circumstances as a whole, the merit of the situation, how the bank has handled similar cases, and common sense—we ask: what's the bottom line? What makes sense for both the employee and the bank? Can we find a compromise that will make everybody feel comfortable with the solution? Striking that balance is one of the most challenging aspects of my job.[4]

Despite its eagerness to help managers who are at sixes and sevens, personnel relations scrupulously observes its confidential relationships with employees. For instance, says Elliott, suppose a boss who has been having trouble with a certain employee calls and asks her if the subordinate has contacted her yet. She won't tell him yes or no, only "I can't share that information with you"—unless the employee has specifically given her permission to disclose that fact to the boss. "Confidentiality is the backbone of our department," she says.

Early in the discussion with a manager, personnel relations seeks to define the problem, for often the problem is fairly fuzzy in the manager's mind. Woodson explains:

> We get a lot of calls for managers saying, "I've got this employee, I've got a real problem with him. He's moody, his attitude is bad." Our first question is: What behavior is it that you're talking about? What do you mean by attitude? What's he doing that gives you this perception? An arbitrary comment that a subordinate is "moody" isn't explicit enough. Sometimes what the manager means is that customers have complained about the employee snapping at them; sometimes it's that it is taking the person four times as long to walk from the coffee room to his work station as it does for everybody else; sometimes it's that the person is disruptive in staff meetings, making snide comments about management and undermining authority.
>
> So we try to zero in on the behavior that's causing the bad perception by the manager. If the manager says, "We-e-el, I don't know, I really can't pinpoint it," he or she has no business writing up the complaint. And he or she will have a tough time conveying to the employee what is wrong, or explaining it to someone else if the comment ever has to be justified.

Sometimes, as Elliott points out, the personnel relations specialist and the manager can't agree on what should be done. She adds:

[4] Robin Welling, "We're Here for Everyone," *On Your Behalf* (Bank of America), December 1987, p. 5.

I may feel the subordinate is right, but no matter what my feelings, I'll negotiate with the manager and not try to strong-arm him or her. The goal is to have everybody feel good about the solution. If after talks I still disagree strongly with what the manager is doing, I will escalate—that is, go to his or her boss. I'll tell the manager first what I'm doing. "We're not agreeing, I'd like to get so-and-so involved," I'll tell him.

Woodson elaborates:

While we want to be perceived as helping managers stay out of trouble, there are occasions when we'll make a recommendation and line management will say, "No, absolutely not. We're going to do it our way." When it comes to that—it doesn't often—we want them to know that we're not afraid to go up to the next higher level of line management, that we'll run it up the flagpole as high as we have to. We're not just going to roll over and play dead.

Under the bank's policy, managers who want to terminate employees, or remove them from their positions or downgrade them, must review their proposed actions with higher management *and* with personnel relations. Accordingly, personnel relations looks at every proposed termination, asking about the circumstances, number of times the problem employee has been counseled, and so on. The personnel relations officer may urge another counseling or some other preliminary step, or perhaps agree quickly that the manager has done more than he or she needed to do. "We try to look at all aspects of the situation," says Woodson. "Since we don't know the problem individual personally and haven't had him or her as a thorn in our side, like the manager has, we can look at the problem without pent-up emotions."

Often managers call personnel relations and say, in effect, "Here's what I've done—progressive counseling. But the guy's performance is still lousy. Now I want to put him on probation. Can you give me some insight as to how I need to document his work? What do I need to write, and where?" When this happens, the specialist advises the manager on how to document the person's work with the aim of being fair to the employee but also covering the manager if the decision is challenged. Also, the specialist wants to make sure that the employee has been told what the difficulty is and what must be done to correct it.

Sometimes the manager goes to personnel relations for help after blundering down the wrong path. In an interview, one manager confided:

I had a situation where I had messed up, to tell you the truth. And without beating me up about it, my PRS said: "Well, here's what you have to do. You should have done this earlier. You didn't. But let's talk about moving forward." And he gave me the steps to follow to rescue what had become a bad situation.[5]

After the personnel relations specialist and the manager agree on a course of action, the specialist keeps track of what is done. Elliott says:

When I'm meeting with the manager and employee, I usually repeat what we have agreed on to be sure everyone understands the same thing. Although I do this orally in most cases, sometimes I'll put down the understanding we arrived at in a letter to the manager. I let both the manager and employee know that I'll be following up. I'll ask them to get back to me and tell me how it's going. If I don't hear, I'll call the employee or manager to find out.

[5] Ibid., p. 4.

Responding to Employees

Often employees contact a personnel relations specialist when they are confused as to what to do. For example, a person has gotten a poor performance report, and he or she doesn't know what can be done. Where should the employee go? Maybe the person has heard about the Let's Talk program, but isn't sure of the details. The specialist listens, ask questions for clarification, and then advises—"Here's where you want to go next," or "You have a couple of alternatives. You could do such-and-such, or you could do this-or-that." One advantage the personnel specialist has is knowing many managers—their personalities, what makes them tick, and so on. This means that often the specialist can suggest that the employee approach a particular manager on the issue. Much of the time the specialist can achieve a win-win outcome in which both management and the subordinate profit. That is not always possible, but it is always the goal.

Often, too, as Woodson says, what the employee really needs is to put a picture in focus:

> They want to kick something around with somebody who doesn't have any impact on their performance reviews or careers. They're angry at their manager, let's say. If they went up to the manager and started screaming, they're not likely to get anywhere, so they go to a neutral corner and let it out. "I don't want you to tell anybody about this," they'll say. "I'm very angry, and I just want to talk first." Personnel relations is a kind of pressure release valve, a chance to vent.

Personnel relations specialists can help concretely in many ways. For instance:

- They may accompany the employee to talk with a line manager. If the manager is several levels higher, the employee may feel uncomfortable going to him or her alone. Even in the case of managers they know, employees often like the support given them by the personnel relations specialist. The latter makes a point at the meeting of letting both parties know that he or she is not representing either side but simply wishes to make sure that the issues are understood, offer any suggestions that might help, and help the employee express his or her thoughts.
- Often the specialist can guide the complainant to a step that the person at first balks at taking. Woodson says:

> For instance, they may not want to see a certain manager up the line whom they really should see. We encourage them to at least give the manager an opportunity to help. "If he or she says what you think they're going to say, okay. You've wasted a little bit of time, but you create fewer hard feelings if you don't skip over people, if you don't assume they're going to be uncooperative without testing them."
>
> We don't make them do anything, of course, but usually the vast majority take the suggestion. If they don't, that's fine; we'll assist them in going to the level they want to go to.

- If the complaint goes to the second or third stages of Let's Talk, the specialist may help the employee draft a letter, if desired, and offer any other support requested.
- Personnel relations specialists are candid with employees. If the employee's complaint is a familiar one that personnel people have listened to frequently before, and they know that there is little chance of the employee getting anywhere because the manager appears to have been acting appropriately, then they will tell the complainant that. "We have seen this in other cases, and your manager was acting within his authority." However, they won't close the door on the employee. If the person wants to take his or her complaint to the next level, the specialists say that they will be happy to help.

Sometimes it is the personnel relations specialists who would like to take the case to a higher level for testing, and the employee who doesn't want to. In all but one kind of case, the specialists feel bound by the employee's wishes. If the latter doesn't want to pursue the case but prefers to let it drop, the specialists don't try to push him or her or force an appeal that the employee isn't interested in making. Even if the specialists say that they would like to take the case to the next level themselves, they won't do so if the employee objects.

The exception is when the case has legal tones such as sexual harassment. Then the specialists say that the case *must* go to a higher level. Woodson explains:

> Even if the employee says, "Absolutely not, I want you to drop it," we'll insist. This is because the corporation has legal objections and can't let them slip. We explain that to the person. "I'm sorry but I can't drop this. It's in your best interest as well as ours to make sure that the practice stops."

Maintaining Visibility

How does Bank of America ensure that its employees everywhere know about personnel relations specialists and Let's Talk?

First, the department's cards are posted in almost every staff room around the bank, so that any employee can pick up the phone and call a specialist.

Second, personnel relations specialists often walk into various units and go around introducing themselves to people, shaking hands, asking how things are going, and so forth. Woodson elaborates:

> Lots of times a person says, "Can I talk to you a few minutes in private?" Or, "Can you call me at home tonight? Here's my telephone number. I really can't talk here but I'd like to talk to you tonight."
>
> Because we're perceived as people who can resolve problems, it is seldom that a PRS walks through a unit without people in the unit knowing who the PRS is. Always someone knows, and everybody else gets to know quickly. They notice who talks to you; they wonder what that person is saying. So we make an effort to talk not to one person but several or many. We never walk up to the manager of the unit, say "Hi, how are you?" and have a fifteen-minute conversation and walk out. I may talk with the manager but it's very important that I go around and talk to other employees. "Hi, I'm Gary Woodson in personnel relations. I figured I'd take a few minutes to stop by and say hello and see how things are going." Also I want to remind people that if they have any concerns or anything they want to talk about, I'm available.

Third, personnel relations puts out a monthly bulletin for banking employees called *On Your Behalf.* This bulletin contains articles on many subjects, including, of course, the efforts and activities of personnel relations specialists.

Fourth, in the management training sessions that each new manager attends, the role of personnel relations is mentioned many times as well as the operation of Let's Talk.

Fifth, Beck's position in the bank gives visibility to personnel relations and Let's Talk. Employees know that the department has a spokesman in top management and on the management committee. Whaley told me, "The fact that Bob works directly for Tom Clausen makes my job a lot better. I don't think that things here would be the same if he reported to a vice president or someone at a lower level."

CIGNA's Speak Easy Program

At CIGNA, the giant financial services and insurance organization formed in 1982 by the merger of Connecticut General and INA Corporations, due process takes the form of the "Speak Easy" program. Basically, Speak Easy provides a channel for employees to make written complaints about their treatment at work or about specific problems affecting their attitudes and performance. After reading a complaint and investigating it, an employee relations official arranges for corrective action to be taken if necessary. In up to two-fifths of the Speak Easys something in the work situation—an employee-supervisor relationship, a procedure, a decision, or a practice of some sort—gets changed. The Speak Easy program appears to be as valuable to the corporation as it is to individual employees. For instance, in 1985 no employee who was disappointed by the action taken in response to his or her Speak Easy complaint hired an attorney and sued the company in court. However, if the program had not been operating effectively, it seems fair to surmise that quite a few

Company: CIGNA	Products/Services: Insurance, financial services, investment management
Headquarters: Philadelphia, Pennsylvania	
	Date of Interview: May 14, 1986

Sales: $17.06 billion (1987)	Number of Employees: 50,000	

employee complaints might have ended up in the courts that year instead of in Speak Easy.

How the Program Works

An important advantage of Speak Easy, says Phillip E. Hyde, manager of the employee relations program, is that it has been operating for several years in CIGNA and has become part of the corporate framework. Employees are used to hearing about it, and they hear that it works. Although CIGNA and Speak Easy are only a few years old, each of the organizations that merged to create CIGNA was experimenting with due process before 1982. For eight years prior to the merger, INA had a program (also called Speak Easy) that invited unhappy employees to send written complaints to the personnel department. For several years, Connecticut General had another version of a nonunion grievance procedure called Open Line. Both approaches were superseded and "CIGNA-tized" in 1984 by Speak Easy, but they were a useful legacy. They gave the new system roots and made credibility easier to gain.

Speak Easy consists of three phases. The first phase is somewhat routine in that it urges the troubled employee to attempt first to talk things out with the supervisor or manager. The second phase is the crucial one: if the employee isn't satisfied with the boss's reaction or feels he or she can't speak with the supervisor about the matter, he or she can get a Speak Easy form, fill it out, and send it to the coordinator. The coordinator follows up with whatever talks or steps seem necessary to resolve the problem. If the employee still isn't satisfied, he or she may go to the third phase and send a Speak Easy form to the head of the operating group or staff organization. This process is closely monitored by the coordinator.

Confidentiality, of course, is crucial. Speak Easy has a reputation for maintaining confidences when requested to do so. If the coordinator can't proceed without disclosing details of the case to others, however, significant change is much less likely to occur.

Fran Young is Speak Easy's administrator for the property and casualty group. (Before the 1982 merger, Philadelphia-based INA Corporations included health management organizations, life insurance companies, and other firms, but were known best for their property and casualty business. Hartford-based Connecticut General included some property casualty business, but was primarily known for group insurance, pension businesses, and financial services.) Some cases she handles herself; others she hands over to the local manager of employee relations for the complainant's facility.

In the cases she personally handles, some are quite easy, involving one or two talks with the employee, and consisting mostly of clarification of policy (e.g., the timing of pay raises) or status (e.g., the privileges of an employee on probation) or some other matter. Other cases may be quite difficult and require many talks with a variety of people. For instance, an employee wrote out a Speak Easy form complaining that he had been unfairly placed on probation. Young spent considerable time over many weeks on the case reviewing records, interviewing employees, and getting the boss's side. The boss had been unhappy with the complainant for several reasons, including a habit of making personal telephone calls at company expense. In the end, Young concluded that the supervisor was right and, in a sit-down meeting with the complainant, told him why and how she had come to that conclusion. But the investigation took considerable time and effort.

As for cases that she turns over to the local employee relations manager, she talks with the person about the case and discusses what must be done. After the manager goes to work, she monitors what is being done and gets periodic reports. Not until everything is resolved, meaning that both the boss *and the complainant* agree that all action that needs to and can be taken has in fact been taken, does she mark the case "closed."

During an average month, Young is likely to get nine or ten second-stage cases. She gets far fewer third-stage complaints—perhaps only five to ten per year.

One of the strengths of Speak Easy is its visibility, handiness, and simplicity. Holders containing forms and envelopes are located throughout the company. The explanation and directions given users are readable and straightforward. Exhibit 1 shows part of the brochure explaining the program. Exhibit 2 shows the form that the employee fills out and sends to the coordinator. (If the employee needs more space than the form provides, he or she attaches additional sheets.) Included in the packet with the brochure and the form are two other things—a metered envelope for sending the completed form, and a brief letter of support for the program from the executive vice president.

Patterns of Use

Hyde's organization keeps a variety of records for Speak Easy. Here are a few important relationships that have been found:

- It is estimated that some 300 to 400 complaints per year are lodged in the first phase, that is, meetings between complaining employees and their bosses. With about forty-nine thousand employees altogether in CIGNA, this works out to about one complaint for every 120 to 160 employees, or six to eight complaints per thousand. Management very much wants employees to use Phase 1 before Phase 2. For one thing, it strengthens the position of line managers. For another, it saves Speak Easy administrators from a lot of investigation and counseling that can be done better by the supervisor or manager immediately concerned.
- In the second phase—that is, written complaints to Speak Easy officials—there were 134 complaints in 1985 and about 200 in 1984. The current average, says Hyde, is about 4.5 complaints per thousand employees.
- For the property casualty side of the company, the lowest annual number of Speak Easy complaints was over 90, the highest was about 140.

EXHIBIT 1

Excerpt from CIGNA's Speak Easy Brochure

Speak Easy

Speak Easy is a special program which gives you the opportunity to talk to management about work-related concerns. Speak Easy, with the support of CIGNA Corporation management, ensures an open line of communication and guarantees a timely response.

(*continued*)

EXHIBIT 1 *(continued)*

Through the Speak Easy Program, you may want to:

· Comment on your treatment as an employee;
· Describe a specific situation that is affecting your performance or the way you feel about your job.

Management wants to hear what you have to say . . . so Speak Easy.

Here's how the program works:

Phase I.   This is the first and most direct way to raise issues about your job or work situation. Go to your supervisor or manager and ask to talk over problems or questions. He or she is committed to listen and give you a fair and honest answer.

But if your supervisor or manager disagrees, cannot correct the situation, or is unwilling to change an earlier decision, Phase I offers you another step.

At your request, your supervisor will arrange interview(s) with additional levels of your management, including the top company official of your department or location. You will be invited to present your concerns, and every effort will be made to resolve your issue.

Phase II.   Phase II has been designed for privately raising matters not resolved in Phase I. You may be unhappy with the course of action taken or feel the matter is too touchy to go through your supervisor. Phase II will give you another audience—someone not directly involved in the situation. But it's important to note that this phase is normally **not a replacement for Phase I employee/management discussions.**

In Phase II of the program, your issue will be kept strictly confidential and reviewed impartially by the Speak Easy Coordinator. Only the coordinator will know your identity if you choose.

All you do is pick up a Speak Easy envelope located in holders throughout your office and fill in the pertinent information. (We have included a sample in this brochure.) Then, drop the completed form and envelope in the mail. You can expect a prompt response from the coordinator, so long as your signature, home address and phone number are on the form. Otherwise, you cannot be contacted and advised of the results of the coordinator's review.

If, for some reason, the review cannot be continued without revealing your name, the coordinator will tell you. It will be your decision whether or not to continue.

Please remember that the sole responsibility of the Speak Easy Coordinator is to make sure that your situation is dealt with fairly and equitably.

Phase III.   This is the final step if you still aren't completely satisfied with the decision. This phase gives you direct access to the Head of your Operating Group or Staff Organization.

If after using Phases I and II, you are still not satisfied with the decision about your situation, you may send a Speak Easy form or a letter fully stating the issue to the Head of your Operating Group or Staff Organization with a copy to your Speak Easy Coordinator.

The situation will be immediately reviewed and you will be informed promptly of the final resolution of your appeal. If the review supports the previous opinions or decisions, these will be upheld; if not, the prior decision will be modified.

EXHIBIT 2
Complainant's Speak Easy Form

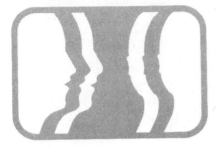

Before mailing, fill in your Group/ Division and location in the box on the envelope which accompanies this form. Although you are not required to sign your name, you can't receive an answer unless you identify yourself.

Only one person should use this form. If you wish, your name will be kept strictly confidential by the Speak Easy Coordinator.

Remember: If you want to submit a suggestion that will save money for the company, or improve the way we do business, contact the Employee Suggestion Plan Coordinator.

Date: _____

_____

_____

_____

_____

_____

_____

_____

_____

_____

_____

_____

_____

(continued)

EXHIBIT 2 *(continued)*

_____

_____

_____

_____

_____

_____

_____

_____

_____

_____

_____

(Please Print)

_____

Name   S.S.#

_____

Home Address

_____

City   State   Zip Code

_____

Home Telephone Number

_____

Office Location   Business Phone & Extension

_____

Please contact me at ☐ home   ☐ work

I have ☐ have not ☐ used Speak Easy Phase I concerning the issue discussed above.

Please keep my name confidential ☐

- On the property casualty side of the company, Speak Easy activity was highest immediately following the 1982 merger. CIGNA-wide Speak Easy activity has declined since its introduction in 1984. One reason for the decline is that many of the pains and trials of adjustment were worked out. Another is that CIGNA put more employee relations specialists in the field after 1984. These specialists are skilled at conflict resolution.
- As for the third phase of Speak Easy, wherein the complainant writes to top management, the chief group executives of the company got five Speak Easys in 1985. As might be expected, Speak Easy managers became involved in many of these cases, too.

What kinds of cases go to Speak Easy? Hyde divides the action into eight categories. The most common types of complaint, he finds, involve conflicts with management, disciplinary actions by supervisors, including termination and low performance appraisals, and problems over promotions or transfers. Three types of complaint that come with average frequency concern compensation, benefits, and problems classified as "miscellaneous," which may range from office conditions to training opportunities. The categories with the fewest numbers of complaints probably are working conditions and work load difficulties. Allegations of discrimination are included in the above list, but employees can go to the company's office on equal employment opportunity when they have these concerns.

Hyde emphasizes that the patterns of use change. The reasons that employees use Speak Easy vary with a number of things, from changes in expectations to changes in corporate policy and structure. The pattern just described could change significantly in years to come.

Do chronic complainers and soreheads tend to use Speak Easy disproportionately? This question troubles some executives in companies contemplating due process. The executives worry that a system will become clogged with hasslers and litigious types. Hyde says the answer is no. Speak Easy does not see the same employees over and over, he states. In fact, he believes that since 1984, fewer than five CIGNA employees have resorted to Speak Easy two or more times. Says Hyde:

> When you're talking about chronic complainers, you're really talking about dispute resolution skills. If supervisors have these skills, they explain decisions and situations to the complainer. They explain it the first time the person protests, and they explain it clearly. But if supervisors aren't skilled in dispute resolution, then, yes, chronic complainers might be a problem for your grievance process.

Resistance and Reversal

Any due process system is likely to have opponents in the managerial ranks, but Speak Easy appears to have a minimum of opposition. While supervisors here and there may be upset over the attention created when their subordinates complain to the Speak Easy coordinator, there seems to be little fear or anger about the procedure in management. It is accepted as part of the corporate culture despite the occasional discomforts it may cause.

And it may indeed cause occasional discomfort. As mentioned earlier, management reversals are far from uncommon. Looked at from the standpoint of the supervisor immediately concerned, a reversal may be cause for squirming and lip-biting—"too many checks and balances," the manager complains. Looked at from the standpoint of employees in general and the corporation, however, it may simply be an instance of good management. Here are some everyday illustrations:

A man whom I shall call "Cal" was hired to do data entry work and invoicing. After a while, he was assigned temporarily to do customer service work, which he liked very much because it meant talking with customers and working on a greater variety of problems. However, he was paid at the data entry rate, which was lower than what a regular customer service representative would get.

After several months had gone by, Cal asked his boss about a permanent assignment to customer service. "I've got to wait for an evaluation," the manager replied. A few more months went by with still no action, so Cal went in to see the boss again. He got the same answer as before.

After this had gone on for some time, with continuing inaction, Cal took a Speak Easy form from a wall holder, filled it out, and attached a three-page letter explaining his situation (he didn't think the space on the form gave him enough room). After reading this material, a Speak Easy official contacted Cal's boss, who happened to be a new man who had just come in. Both the official and the new boss agreed that Cal was in the right. His formal job assignment was changed to customer service, with the temporary status removed, and he was given a pay increase retroactive to the beginning of the year.

A woman whom I shall call "Sarah" noticed that fewer and fewer jobs were being posted for the information of employees who might want to consider transfers or advancement. Yet Sarah knew that the company was advertising new job openings in the newspapers, and that new people were being hired. Sarah had worked for the company for five years.

At a staff meeting, Sarah mentioned this fact to the manager. She thought it was inconsistent with other corporate pronouncements. She reminded him that the company had long talked about opportunities for advancement for employees. When you took a job in the organization, you weren't supposed to be stuck in it; you were supposed to be able to move on and up, if you wanted to. However, the manager shrugged her off. There were reasons, he maintained vaguely, why the new openings weren't being posted.

At a second meeting, Sarah raised the question again. Again the manager made excuses for inaction. Sarah and a number of others in the department got upset.

Wondering what to do, Sarah happened to talk about the situation with a friend. "Why don't you send a Speak Easy to the president?" the friend asked. Sarah wrote a one-and-a-half-page letter, attached it to the form that she took from a wall holder, and sent the letter to the president.

Soon the director of personnel contacted her. A Speak Easy officer would get in touch with her, the director promised. A few days later Young telephoned and asked a number of questions for clarification of the problem. Young then told her that she would like to talk with her personally in Philadelphia (Sarah lived and worked about forty miles from Philadelphia); but as an alternative, Sarah could discuss the situation personally with her local personnel director. She chose the latter course. Meeting with him, she described several ways in which she thought communications about job openings could be improved. She also thought it would help if the company would clarify what it expected in certain new positions, especially supervisory positions. One of the things that agitated Sarah and her friends was that college graduates and others without company experience were being hired as supervisors. "We know a lot more about our jobs than they do. Yet they have to ask us what we're doing!" That didn't make sense to Sarah.

The company responded promptly. It improved its communications about job openings. Of special value, in Sarah's opinion, it put on a new program about supervisors. In this program, she and others learned that it isn't necessary for supervisors to know a great deal about the *technical* skills of people at the terminals and computers. What is more important is that they have skills at coordinating, guiding, and directing the people with technical skills. "It was a revelation to me and many others," Sarah says. "We didn't know that."

An employee whom I shall call "Don" became upset that CIGNA was hiring temporary people from outside for jobs that, in his opinion, CIGNA employees would like. An employee in a financial office for many years, Don himself didn't seek one of these openings, nor had he ever applied for one of them. Knowing about Speak Easy as a result of notices and stories in company publications, he got a form from a holder and mailed it in. Don didn't go to his supervisor first, because there was nothing the supervisor could do about it.

In several weeks, Don got a call from the personnel representative familiar with the company's financial functions. They agreed to meet and, at the meeting, Don described his complaint in detail. The personnel representative said she was unable to help him directly in this case. "Speak Easy is primarily for employees who are affected personally by a situation," she said. "Since you and your job are not directly affected by this hiring practice, I can only notify the appropriate personnel officer of your concern." She also reminded him of CIGNA's job-posting program and employee suggestion plan.

Nasty Surprises

Any program with the power and credibility to get employees to report serious problems is likely to produce unpleasant revelations from time to time. My friend Joseph T. Nolan, who headed public relations for both Chase Manhattan Bank and Monsanto for many years, refers to these revelations as "Love Canals," an allusion to the public relations debacle that plagued Hooker Chemical Company for a decade. Does Speak Easy have the capacity to reveal "Love Canals"? Should it be expected to turn them up?

The answer to the first question is yes. Speak Easy has indeed brought to light a few practices and decisions that, if unchecked, might in time have grown to serious proportions. However, this prospect does not worry management. As one manager in the program put it, "We worry more about *not* finding nasty surprises than finding them." For if Speak Easy does not encourage whistleblowers to come in, and especially to come in early, the danger of a major debacle developing far outweighs the unpleasantness of learning about it and coping with it at an early stage. Furthermore, if a major debacle develops, news about it may go outside the company.

When Speak Easy turns up a nasty surprise, how much does it try to accomplish by itself? Only as much as it is comfortable doing. Given strong top management support, it can disclose the problem to those seniors in the company who have the power and latitude to take action.

In one sense, therefore, Speak Easy is a kind of early warning system that makes it possible for management to manage quicker and more effectively, and with less risk of outside publicity.

"If we are to do this job," says Young, "the provision of confidentiality is very important. The employee who knows or suspects wrongdoing must trust us. He or she must have no doubt that confidences will be kept, that we will not discuss the problem with anyone without the reporter's permission." No matter how serious the problem is seen by Speak Easy officials, no matter how urgent the need for action seems to them to be, they will talk about it with others if, and only if, the reporting employee consents.

Organization and Support

Hyde, who oversees other employee relations programs as well as Speak Easy, reports to the corporate director of employee relations. Hyde estimates that Speak Easy takes 25 to 30 percent of his time. Young, the administrator for the Philadelphia-based property and casualty group, spends from 25 to 75 percent of her time on Speak Easy problems. She reports to the employee relations director for the Philadelphia-based group. That executive, in turn, reports indirectly to the division head. Young has served with Speak Easy for seven years.

The organization of CIGNA is significant from the standpoint of a strong employee relations department. As one might expect, a company with forty-nine thousand employees has many divisions, areas, and offices. In a given office, say, Boston or Hartford (there are fifteen offices in the northeast area), the employee relations manager reports not to the vice president for the office, but to the employee relations director for the division. This means that the local employee relations managers are independent of the line managers at the places where they work. They work *with* those managers, but they are not subject to their authority. This type of organization makes it possible for Speak Easy to collaborate productively with personnel specialists in the field, reach independent judgments, and be a vital force in the company.

Speak Easy should be seen as part of a supportive corporate environment. For instance, the company runs comprehensive supervisory training programs, which provide supervisors with solid basic skills and means that Speak Easy does not have to begin at scratch when it confronts an errant supervisor—remedial support is available. There is also, as noted, an equal employment opportunity office that conducts a variety of affirmative action outreach programs. In addition, CIGNA sponsors a strong employee assistance program. When employees feel that alcoholism, marital difficulties, drugs, problem children, or other such problems are interfering with their job performance, they are invited to consult with the professionals on the staff of this program.

CIGNA also has a clear policy of employee privacy or, more accurately, protection of personal information. Employees can see their personnel folders at any time and, if they desire, contest the appropriateness of data in it.

These and other programs and policies in the employee surround have an important bearing on the potential of Speak Easy. Without them, Speak Easy might have as much trouble as a baseball team playing with only a first baseman.

What about the costs of Speak Easy? "Our biggest out-of-pocket cost," laughs Hyde, "is printing. The bill for that is about $5,000 a year. While the program takes a substantial part of several executives' time—those parts might add up to the full time of one executive—the return on this investment from an employee relations standpoint is immeasurable!"

The Open Door at IBM

IBM's "Open Door" procedure began with Thomas Watson, Sr., who was the company's first chairman. Watson frequently visited the plants and branch offices and would talk to employees about anything on their minds, including complaints. "If you can't solve your problems with your manager, go to your plant or branch manager. If you're still not satisfied, my door is always open," he would say, and that attitude became his policy. Many employees took him up on his offer, going to his office and describing their problems. If he would not settle the difficulty there, he would talk to their managers and work it out or informally ask an assistant to look into the problem and get it resolved.

Sometime in the early 1950s, as IBM's work force expanded to more than forty thousand, the procedure became more formalized, with Watson's administrative assistants—IBM calls them AAs—taking over the administrative duties. The AA would write up the complaint when it came to the office and set the wheels in motion for a thorough investigation. When the evidence was in, Watson would make the final decision.

Company: IBM		Products/Services: Information-processing products and systems
Headquarters: Armonk, New York		
		Dates of Interviews: March 13, October 27,
Sales: $51.25 billion (1987)	Number of Employees: 405,500	1986; February 5, October 9, 1987

In the three decades since then, with the work force growing to about four hundred thousand, the Open Door has become institutionalized. Basically, however, the philosophy is the same: any employee at any level is entitled to a review from any level of management up to the chief executive if he or she isn't satisfied with a decision made at a lower level. Dismissals, transfers, pay raises, performance evaluations—all these and many other issues are possible subjects for an Open Door complaint.

The Open Door is an important part of IBM's employee relations philosophy, practice, and culture. It has had the wholehearted backing of the five men who have succeeded Watson—Thomas Watson, Jr., T. V. Learson, Frank Cary, John Opel, and John Akers. It is brought to the attention of a new employee the first week on the job. It is talked about in meetings and written about in company publications. Every operating unit has an Open Door coordinator, that is, a person ready at a moment's notice to get an investigation of a complaint started for the CEO or operating unit executive, and make sure it is completed properly. In any part of the corporation, in the United States or abroad, a high priority is given to the resolution of Open Door cases. No excuse is acceptable from any level of management for failure to cooperate in an Open Door investigation.

At times the Open Door is expensive. It will take the time of highly paid managers. It may require costly airline tickets. But the return on this investment, in top management's opinion, is considerable:

1. Employees who feel that their grievances are important enough to receive fair and timely action are more likely to feel a strong sense of commitment to the company than employees who feel that they "only work here."

2. Management gets a chance to correct its mistakes. As Cary once said, "The Open Door allows the company to be 'flexible and big enough' to cope with errors. Human problems come in endless variety, and the system hasn't been invented that can anticipate them all."

3. The procedure often proves to be a valuable learning device, bringing to management's attention problems previousy overlooked. The Open Door gives top executives a kind of window on what is going on at lower levels that may cause trouble— such as policies and practices that are not being followed or should be changed (e.g., appraisals, attendance, etc.).

In a book written a couple of decades ago, Thomas Watson, Jr., had this to say about the Open Door:

Our management also recognized that the individual has his own problems, ambitions, abilities, frustrations, and goals. We wanted to be certain that no one got lost in the organization and, most of all, that no individual became a victim of any manager's unfairness or personal whim. In this regard, we developed what we call our "Open Door" policy. This is a key element in our employee relations.

The Open Door grew out of T. J. Watson's close and frequent association with individuals in the plant and field offices. It became a natural thing for them to bring their problems to him and in time [this] was established as a regular procedure. My father encouraged this in his visits. He spoke of it in his telephone broadcasts to offices and plants. If a man was not getting along, or if he thought he was being treated unfairly by his manager, he was told to go to the plant or branch manager. If that did not work, he was then invited to come and lay his case before my father.

Hundreds of employees literally did just that. Many would take the day off from our plants in Endicott, N.Y., and come to his office in New York City to talk about their problems. More often than not, he favored the complaining employee—sometimes, I'm sure, more than he should have. But he built up a lasting relationship with a great many employees and they helped him to keep in touch with what was going on in the company. At the time of his death in 1956, most of our then 57,000 employees thought of T. J. Watson as a friend they could count on.

The Open Door exists today as it did then. I'm sure that a policy of this kind makes many a traditional manager's blood run cold. He probably sees it as a challenge to his authority, or worse yet, as a sharp sword hanging over his head. But the fact remains that in IBM it has been remarkably effective, primarily because—by its mere existence—it exercises a moderating influence on management. Whenever a manager makes a decision affecting one of his people, he knows that he may be held accountable to higher management for the fairness of that decision.

From time to time we have had second thoughts on the practicality of this policy, especially now that IBM has grown to a company of over 80,000 people in the United States alone. Obviously, if everyone with a problem insisted on seeing the president or me, we would have run out of time long ago.

The answer, in the future, may have to come in a shift downward in this court of appeal, possibly to the level of division president or general manager. But whatever the difficulties, we certainly have no intention of denying anyone the opportunity to talk to whomever he wishes to in this business. Whether they exercise it or not, our people are reassured by the fact that they have this right. And by its existence, I believe, it acts as a deterrent to the possible abuse of managerial power.[1]

The corporate setting is very important to understanding the Open Door. IBM has long been a pioneer in employee relations. Although it is one of the world's largest corporations (its 1985 revenue of more than $50 billion was larger than the gross domestic product of Greece, Ireland, Turkey, and a number of other countries), it seeks a very special relationship with its employees. Some highlights of its employee relations policies are listed in Exhibit 1.

How It Works

An Open Door case may start, proceed, and end in so many different ways that all the possibilities cannot be described in this space. Let me describe the way in which it is likely to work in a typical case.

Let us assume that an employee named "Stone" feels that his manager has given him an unfair performance appraisal. Unable to convince his manager to upgrade the latest appraisal, he decides to "go Open Door," in IBM parlance. He may go to his manager's manager, the plant or branch office manager, the division president, or directly to the chairman. In a substantial majority of cases, Open Doors are handled and resolved at a lower level. Sometimes after the first decision they are appealed to the next higher level, and sometimes an appeal goes up many levels, landing finally in the chairman's office.

Stone decides to contact the chairman's office. An AA handles the initial contact. If the complaint is not clear, the AA tries to understand what the issues are and what the employee wants. Next he or she decides what organization should investigate it. He or she makes that decision on the basis of Stone's organization, his work, and the

[1] Thomas Watson, Jr., *A Business and Its Beliefs* (New York: McGraw-Hill, 1963), p. 21.

EXHIBIT 1
Some Highlights of Employee Relations at IBM

- In 1931, IBM built the first IBM employee-only country club, in Endicott, New York.
- In 1937, IBM began offering paid holidays and vacations to employees.
- In 1958, all employees, including production workers, were placed on salary.
- Most IBMers spend their entire careers at the company, and more than 70 percent of its professionals come straight from college.
- In the United States the employee turnover rate was only 2.8 percent in 1985.
- IBM spends more than $6 billion annually on employee benefits (about $15,000 per employee, nearly twice the average outlay of $7,800 cited in a 1984 U.S. Chamber of Commerce survey of 1,154 companies).
- As an example of how managers try to motivate employees, the general manager of one of IBM's largest manufacturing and development sites uses as many forms of reward as he can conjure up. Several dozen bulletin boards are littered with snapshots of workers getting a handshake or bonus check for excellence. One bulletin praises a group for 97 percent participation in the site's cost-effectiveness program; 278 workers submitted ideas that saved $1,784,552.
- The same manager writes about six hundred letters a year responding to questions or complaints dropped into slotted boxes. A full-time Speak Up coordinator retypes them without names and forwards them to him.
- In 1984, IBM spent an average of $2,278 per employee to educate its work force (more than several U.S. states spent on education per student).
- In 1984, IBM contributed $145 million to charity (about $23 million more than the Ford Foundation contributed).

Source: Data taken from *The Wall Street Journal,* April 7, 1986.

nature of his complaint. Normally the operating unit Stone is employed in will conduct the investigation.

The AA turns the complaint over to the executive of the operating unit chosen. Each division and major operating unit in IBM has an Open Door coordinator who assists the division president or operating unit executive in administering the Open Door program. Picked carefully on the basis of experience, aptitude, and ability, the coordinator assigns investigators to cases, and provides advice and counsel to the investigators before, during, and after their investigation. The investigator reviews the findings and his or her recommendations with the executives directly concerned and makes sure that any necessary follow-up action is taken.

In the case of the fictitious employee, Stone, the coordinator decides to ask an executive named "Rock" to investigate. Rock agrees. Like everyone else, she is busy, but she can delegate her normal work to subordinates and thus make herself free to concentrate on the case; also, she does not know Stone or his manager, and so she can be objective. Normally, an investigator of an appeal to the chairman must be at the level of director or above.

The coordinator and Rock review the issues revealed in the initial contact, and then she goes to work. She has twenty-four hours in which to contact Stone. She has fifteen working days to get the investigation completed and make her recommendations, and her clock starts running when she takes the case. Immediately she calls

Stone and makes an early appointment to talk with him in person. She will discuss the case with no one prior to her first interview with him. She tells him who she is and what her role is. She advises him that she will conduct an independent investigation and will make a recommendation; but the final decision is up to the chairman, and it will be the chairman who writes him about that decision. She makes it clear that she will treat the case as confidential, instruct whomever she talks with to keep the case confidential, and talk only to those directly involved, but naturally she cannot guarantee anonymity.

Meeting Stone in his office or location of his choice, she brings a note pad, asks a lot of questions, and listens. She makes no attempt to judge; she resists all temptations to advise Stone what to do. Listening sympathetically, she makes sure that he covers all the major questions or issues relevant to his situation—the existence of a performance plan, ongoing discussions with his manager about his performance, and the availability of resources to do his job. With Stone's help she builds a chronology of events. Although she listens attentively to his feelings, she emphasizes the facts of what happened. She gets Stone's ideas about what should be done to resolve the problem.

Although Stone had thought he could wrap it up in an hour, they are nowhere near done in that time—the meeting stretches well into the evening. At the end of their talk, Rock summarizes the main points to be sure she has them right. "Do you agree with that?" she asks. He agrees. She tells Stone what her next step will be, and she finds where she can reach him by phone in case she has further questions. In two or three weeks, she tells him, she will meet with him to review what she is recommending to the chairman and her rationale.

During her talk with Stone, Rock looks at the case only from his side. When she talks with his manager and others directly concerned, she continues to act as his advocate. Before each consultation, she emphasizes the need for confidentiality. She asks them not to discuss the case with anyone at any time.

One of the people she must talk to has left the area and is two thousand miles away. She calls for an appointment and hops a plane even though her talk with the man won't take more than a couple of hours.

Everyone she talks to, no matter how busy, is cooperative. This isn't due to altruism but to the simple fact that she is the CEO's representative.

Cataloging the information people give her, she separates facts from opinion and opinion from hearsay. She gives no inkling of the opinions she is forming to the people she talks with. Nor does she tell them any more about the case than is absolutely necessary. She may find it necessary to review some specifics with other staffs (e.g., personnel, medical, or legal) to get expert advice.

Eight workdays after starting, Rock is ready to write up her report. Now she must turn from advocate to judge, and—emotionally at least—this is not easy. Although she wishes she could help Stone because she liked his earnestness and brilliance, she believes that the lowered appraisal is justified. In privacy, she composes a report on her personal computer. She does this very carefully. "How many times will my work product end up on the chairman's desk?" she asks herself. Taking her write-up to the coordinator, she goes over it with him. He thinks the substance is fine but he makes several suggestions to improve clarity.

It will be hard for her to tell Stone that the appraisal will stand. She will not do this by letter or phone; she calls him and makes an appointment to sit down with him. When she discusses her conclusion with him, naturally he is disappointed.

Nevertheless, he has to admit that she got all the important facts, weighed them carefully, and tried to be fair.

Next she phones Stone's manager and tells him what she plans to recommend. Although she thinks his appraisal should stand, she believes that he should have been more candid with Stone in discussing the reasons for his low ratings. Stone was given most of the reasons but deserved to hear all of them. (If she were recommending that the appraisal be set aside, she would go to see the manager personally. I cannot reveal here the percentage of management reversals or the "reversal rate," as IBM calls it, but it is substantial enough to relieve any doubt about the fairness of the system.)

Back in her office, Rock writes up her final report for the CEO. In this she follows a precise format prescribed by the company. She summarizes the facts, lists the persons she interviewed, gives the chronology of events leading up to the appeal, ending with the first interview she had with Stone, discusses the key issues and indicates whether they are valid or invalid, presents her rationale, and recommends that Stone's appraisal be left as it is but that the manager be counseled so that he can improve his future evaluations. (One section of the form specifically asks for any comments on management errors. The criticisms may be blunt. Investigators' comments are not always negative, however—they may commend the managers for handling a tough job well.)

Rock then reviews her entire report with the executive of her operating unit. She must obtain the executive's agreement on the recommendation before it is sent to the chairman's office. (All this is in keeping with the philosophy that the Open Door is a management tool. The coordinator and investigator are there to help management.)

After receiving her report, the AA studies it to ensure that all issues are addressed and to test the rationale for fairness and clarity. He or she may request review by other corporate staffs. It is then summarized for the CEO. After a thorough review, the chief executive writes a short letter to Stone telling him that the evaluation stands, the coordinator makes sure that Stone's manager is counseled appropriately by his manager, and finally, the investigator sends all documentation to the chairman's office for confidential filing. In three years the file will be destroyed.

None of the documentation or any reference to an Open Door is placed in any employee's file.

Making the Open Door Effective

Every year, the division coordinators meet to review questions, problems, or trends that have concerned them. The meetings are opened by the chief executive. One of many purposes of these meetings is to ensure consistency in Open Door decisions and recommendations.

The Open Door coordinator who represents the division executive is responsible for overseeing the implementation of the Open Door decision in cases where a manager or managers are instructed to take certain actions. For example, if a manager is instructed to transfer a certain employee to a new job within sixty days, the coordinator checks to see that it is done and verifies this to the AA.

Despite its prestige and "track record," the Open Door creates managerial anxiety from time to time. The chairman himself may answer questions that arise, as was done in 1965 when Thomas Watson, Jr., discussed an employee's question in a company publication (see Exhibit 2).

In addition, the chairman frequently writes managers with his impressions, gained from Open Door cases and discussions of them, of their actions right and wrong. He may praise, criticize, or offer suggestions in these memos (see Exhibit 3).

Through surveys, it is estimated that approximately 10 percent of IBM's U.S. employees appeal annually to higher levels of management. Most appeals are resolved by the employee's second-line manager.

An Outsider's View

Looking at IBM's Open Door as an outside critic, I believe the following observations are in order.

First, it calls for a lot of work and top management support. The Open Door does not open automatically. It does not run by itself, and it does not run well unless many skillful executives put their hearts into it. If managers have "grown up with it," as they have at IBM, commitment comes easier.

Second, to make the Open Door work as it does, top management must make five crucial assumptions:

1. Managers know that their decisions are subject to review by higher management and that they will be held accountable.
2. Managers and others involved will do their best to keep Open Door complaints confidential. The few people who know about them will not gossip about them.
3. Most executives and managers in the company desire to handle complaints and superior-subordinate conflicts equitably. If this desire lags in one area at one level, it will be corrected quickly when brought to the attention of managers at a higher level.
4. An Open Door investigator can successfully wear two hats. That is, he or she can begin a case by taking the complainant's side and acting effectively as his or her advocate; but when the fact-digging and interviews are completed, the investigator can take off the advocate's hat, put on the judge's, and make a well-reasoned recommendation in light of IBM personnel policies and practices.
5. Managers are trained to avoid actions following an Open Door that could be perceived as retribution. If an employee feels that he or she has been treated unfairly because of a prior Open Door, that issue will also be investigated. Unfair actions against employees because they used the Open Door are not tolerated.

For many organizations in this country, one or more of these assumptions would be difficult to make. That IBM can make them is testimony to the extraordinary nature and personality of the company. IBMers may be the first to state that the Open Door does not work perfectly—what human system does? But its power and acceptance seem beyond question. A one-time IBM employee told me: "The Open Door has a mystique all its own. It's not sacred, but it comes as close to being sacred as anything in the company."

EXHIBIT 2

IBM's Chairman Answers a Manager's
Questions About the Open Door

Q: During my five years with IBM, entirely too many managers have negated what I assume is Mr. Watson's sincerity in maintaining the Open Door Policy. This negativism can only undermine the faith of the individual in his company, or at least, cause him to feel that his belief in the Open Door is naive. Here specifically, are the things I've heard about the Open Door—from Management—both in the Data Processing Division and in CHQ:

1. Only a fool or a nut would use the Open Door.
2. The Open Door leads to the street.
3. If an employee uses the Open Door and is sustained in his views by Mr. Watson he'll keep his job but he becomes a "marked man" in IBM and will never get ahead.
4. If a manager so bungles a man-manager relationship that an employee goes to see Mr. Watson, that manager has had it, too, in IBM. (I've heard it said that even if the manager is correct he's still had it because he wasn't skillful enough to keep the employee from going to Mr. Watson.)

I am certain that, judging by the frequency with which these points are made, virtually everyone in IBM has heard these descriptions of the Open Door in action. Do you suppose it would be foolish or nutty for us to ask for some definitive information about this much-maligned program?

A: In business, military, and other types of organizations, an individual who circumvents the normal chain of authority takes a certain amount of risk and we recognize that this is true when IBMers use the Open Door route. Remember, however, that through the Open Door Policy, an unhappy employee, who feels he is being treated unfairly, is guaranteed a fair hearing.

The Open Door Policy is an outgrowth of one of the basic beliefs upon which IBM is founded—respect for the dignity and rights of the individual. Although most problems should be settled in a frank discussion between the employee and his manager, a man occasionally can gain satisfaction only by going to a higher level. For the employee's protection, each investigation is based on the individual assumption that his complaint is valid.

If an employee is found to have a good case, he will be upheld in his complaint. One IBMer had proven in his own department a broadly applicable cost savings idea. In order to spread the benefits in other areas, he presented the idea to his division management and then to the corporate level without gaining acceptance. Recognizing that he stood to lose everything if he risked open conflict too often, he brought it to me. The concept is now being widely applied as a corporate practice and the employee has received an Outstanding Contribution Award.

If an employee's complaint is unfounded, he will usually gain a realistic view of the situation leading to it and return to the job with the air cleared. Regardless of whether he is upheld, an employee can continue to advance in the business.

Concerning managers, consequences are serious when we find evidence of mis-

(continued)

EXHIBIT 2 *(continued)*

management. One employee reported that a man who reviewed suggestions was offering to approve them if the suggester would "kick back" a portion of the award. When this was proven true, the man was dismissed from the company.

Managers who have handled Open Door situations well have gained recognition which has contributed to their advancement. A dismissed employee complained that his manager had persecuted him by demanding he perform a job that was impossible. Our investigation, however, proved that people in the area were doing similar tasks without difficulty. Also, the complainer had been carefully counseled over a six-month period prior to his dismissal. He was not reinstated and since then, the manager has made satisfactory progress in the company.

None of us like being scrutinized in the way necessary to clarify the issues in Open Door cases, but I feel the results of the policy justify the anxiety which is generated. Perhaps some of you who read this have suggestions on how to improve our procedures and, if so, I would appreciate hearing from you.

In summary, I am convinced the Open Door Policy is making a positive contribution to our people and I hope that future administration of the policy will add to the health of the company.

(signed) Tom Watson, Jr.

Source: "The Chairman Answers Speak Up!s," February 20, 1965.

EXHIBIT 3

Excerpts from Copies of Management
Briefings Sent to All IBM Managers

A. Number 4-67: July 19, 1967

To All IBM Managers: The Open Door Policy is one of our company's most valuable assets. It gives the IBMer who is having trouble on the job a chance to get at least two different people focusing on his problem. It lets the IBM company demonstrate, day in and day out, our belief in fair treatment and respect for the individual.

But you run the risk of turning this asset into a liability if you let the Open Door Policy intimidate you.

I stress this point because there is clearly a tendency among some managers to avoid action on difficult personnel problems if such action might lead to an Open Door case. I think this tendency will diminish if all of you understand what higher management looks for when it reviews such cases.

We try to find out whether the employee has received fair treatment. We want to know if he has been given every reasonable opportunity to know where he stands, to discuss his problems and to improve his performance. We also try to learn whether the manager has given the employee a consistent interpretation of company policy. However, on such matters as assessing the performance of an employee, we try not to second guess the manager. Those judgments are for the manager to make.

What we sometimes find in Open Door cases is that the problems come from the manager's inaction. Unwilling to make a difficult decision, fearful of creating an Open Door case no matter which move he makes, the manager may do nothing. That's the worst mistake he could make. It's usually better to make almost any decision than to make no decision.

Another mistake that some managers make is spending long, valuable hours putting everything about the case down on paper to protect themselves. That's a waste of time. Long memos to the file are not required. All that is needed is simple documentation of the essential points on which the case turns. Any manager who spends excessive amounts of time writing memos and building up a case just to protect himself lacks confidence not only in himself but also in IBM management. . . .

(signed) Thomas Watson, Jr.

B. Number 3-80: December 19, 1980

To All IBM Managers: Recently, I have reviewed a number of Open Door appeals from employees who have been demoted or dismissed. The managers involved had made big issues out of employment conditions, such as lateness, when the real issue was unsatisfactory job performance. Even worse, these managers had prepared a great deal of defensive documentation, apparently anticipating an Open Door investigation.

Where we find violations of working conditions, we should counsel employees and take whatever action is appropriate. But if poor job performance is the issue, then step up to it. Unsatisfactory performance has always been a valid reason for demotion or dismissal.

(continued)

EXHIBIT 3 *(continued)*

As for documentation, it should be simple and straightforward, covering the major points of commitment and action. The purpose is to help the employee improve performance, and not to create a record that condemns the employee and protects the manager.

The Open Door Policy, which guarantees every IBM employee the right to appeal an unfair management action, follows naturally from our basic belief in respect for the individual. It has been an effective deterrent to bad management because managers know their decisions may have to face the test of an Open Door investigation. Remember, however, that the test asks not what is the volume of documentation, but what are the issues, are they relevant, and has the manager treated the employee fairly.

(signed) Frank Cary

C.   *Number 2-82: September 21, 1982*

To All IBM Managers: A recent survey of IBMers in the U.S. reveals several findings about the Open Door program that I think are useful. First, a small but significant proportion of IBM employees used the Open Door program last year to appeal some action by their managers. Second, less than 5 percent of those IBMers appealed directly to my office, while about 70 percent appealed to their manager's manager. Most of the others went to division or personnel management. Similar studies of IBM employees in other countries suggest they respond the same way.

These are good signs. Most IBMers work out their concerns with their immediate managers. When they can't, they're not reluctant to use the Open Door program to appeal to higher levels—whether or not they label their appeal an "Open Door."

In addition, the survey reveals that the more managers and employees understand the program, the more positive their attitudes are about it, and the less likely they are to express concern about the impact an appeal might have on their careers. . . .

So there's room for improvement and there are several ways you can help strengthen the program:

—As managers, you can encourage confidence in the Open Door program by making sure your employees know what it is, how it works, and the confidential way we handle all appeals. The best time to do this is now. Certainly it should be done long before a problem arises, so that there's mutual trust in the program.
—Once you receive an employee appeal, act promptly. People who appeal a management decision are upset and, like any of us, they want the issue resolved quickly.
—When the appeal ends, forget about it. We will not hold a grudge, and there must be no retribution. That's the greatest fear people have about using the program. As managers, you have to reduce that concern by your example.

In far more cases than not, the Open Door program confirms that IBM managers have superb judgment. At the same time, the program shows that we respect an individual's right to appeal that judgment, and that's the most important point of all.

(signed) John Opel

NBC's Counselor System

At National Broadcasting Company, problems and injustices in the workplace are management's responsibility. However, to assist it, management has created a problem-solving process which centers on an employee counselor. The counselor, Alfred Jackson, is a personnel specialist who, with the support of a strong employee relations division, advises, mediates, and persuades, but has no formal power by himself to adjudicate, yet enjoys powerful enough support to right wrongs and make any other adjustments necessary, at practically any level of the organization, to solve personnel problems.

In a typical week, at least one employee is likely to seek Jackson out with a complaint. (Some complaints go directly to other offices in the company, such as personnel, equal employment opportunity, and the employee assistance program.) In dealing with that employee's problems, Jackson may have to contact supervisors, co-workers, and others who are involved in one way or another with the problem. A third of the people who come to him are managers; the rest are nonmanagers. Although the counselor system was set up to serve nonunion employees, union

Company: National Broadcasting Company		Products/Services: TV and radio broadcasting
Headquarters: New York, New York		Dates of Interviews: April 2, May 20, 1986; November 5, 1987
Sales: $3 billion (1987)	Number of Employees: 7,500	

members (about half of the work force) occasionally visit Jackson, sometimes because they think they may be interested in going into management someday, sometimes because they may perceive that there is more assurance of confidentiality in the counselor system than in the grievance procedure set up under the union contract.

Jackson works closely with other members of the employee relations staff. At their regular staff meetings, he and others discuss current problems and keep each other advised about what they are working on.

NBC employs about seven thousand five hundred people, the majority in its New York headquarters, the remainder in such cities as Burbank, Cleveland, Washington, and Chicago. Although counselor systems are not set up in the other cities, Jackson occasionally goes to them to work with managers on personnel problems. As a group, NBC employees are articulate, well educated, mobile, competitive, and interested in challenging work.

Problem-Solving with a Low Profile

The counselor reports to the vice president for personnel operations. Since the personnel department is a strong one at NBC, the vice president can give the counselor whatever backing is necessary to carry out his or her job. When the counselor system was created in 1977, management wanted a flexible, low-profile approach which would solve problems internally and reduce the need for employees to go to the outside to correct perceived injustices. In addition, the company intended to eliminate some of the issues which could fuel an interest in further unionization of its work force. The counselor system seems to have succeeded admirably in that purpose. "When I joined NBC in 1975," says Jackson, "the company was litigating so many lawsuits from employees and ex-employees that four or five company attorneys were kept busy with that job alone. Today there are not nearly so many lawsuits arising from work problems."

Generally speaking, the counselor doesn't go into action until an employee comes in with a problem. It can be any sort of problem, even including one that the employee isn't sure is a problem. In the words of one personnel executive, "We wanted to design something that people would use for a variety of purposes. We don't want them to feel they have to frame a complaint or grievance in any specific terms. We want them to feel free to come in and talk to the counselor about whatever it is that is bothering them."

Al Jackson, who came to NBC from the Grand Union Company and has served since 1979 as counselor (his predecessor served from 1977 to 1979), emphasizes that the employee may feel the trouble is acute but may be unable to define it clearly. Jackson helps the person to clarify it. Sometimes the employee is unsure of his or her rights. Sometimes he or she doesn't know whether the complaint is actionable. Sometimes the employee is angry over a poor performance review or a low raise and can't be rational until the anger is poured out. Sometimes the complainant can be very specific about this action or that of supervision but doesn't want to do much of anything—just wants to talk about it, at least, for the time being.

Confidentiality is the cornerstone of the counselor system, and it is important to a great many employees who come to see Jackson. If they didn't think they could trust him to honor their confidences, they wouldn't air their concerns. This may cause him problems, for until he is free to go out and talk to people about the issues there is little he can do except listen and clarify. "They come in and say, 'I want to talk to you, but I don't want you to talk to anybody,' " Jackson says. "I must then tell them, 'Okay, but if I can't talk to anybody, I can't do much for you. In order to make a difference, even to verify what you've told me, I must be free to act.' " The initial talk with the counselor is therefore a crucial first stage. Hopefully, the complaints that should go no further die in the counselor's office, but those that presage something wrong are pursued. In either case, the employee must feel able to be candid.

"One of the key conversations I've had, one that made all the difference in the world," says Jackson, "occurred when I sat down with the then executive vice president. I said, 'Let me pose a question for you. Suppose you know about a problem, and I'm involved in it. You call me in to tell you what's happening. I say that I'm sorry but I can't tell you. Will you respect that? If you say yes, then this will work. But if you tell me I don't have the prerogative to safeguard a confidence, I can't do my job. I need to be clear about that.' He agreed that we could work that way."

If the employee appears to have an actionable complaint and is also willing to have Jackson investigate, various things can happen. Promising only as much confidentiality as is possible, Jackson then goes to the boss, working associates, and/or others who may be involved in the situation described. He can see any personnel file in the company that he wants to. First, he finds out if the problem jibes with the complainant's description. If it doesn't, he goes back to the complainant and seeks to clarify what is really going on. If the facts verify the complaint, he decides what action to take. Such action may take the form simply of a tête-à-tête with the boss. In other cases, he may need to go further and urge that changes be made—staffing, a different practice, a new relationship. Although, as earlier mentioned, he has no formal power to insist on such a change, he has considerable influence to get the needed action taken.

The personnel vice president has made it clear that Jackson's authority is derived from his office. The vice president will intervene if he and Jackson agree that this is an appropriate strategy. He has made it clear, in other words, that he is not going to ignore the problem. He also points out that it is in a manager's interest to solve the problem with Jackson and not attract senior management attention to it.

If the supervisor balks at making a change Jackson recommends, Jackson speaks to him or her in words like these:

> "You can choose not to be cooperative. I'm not going to argue that point with you. If you don't cooperate, there are two things I can do. I can go to your boss and tell him the situation, or I can go to my boss and have him go to your boss. You have the option to decide whether to keep this problem under your control. It's in your best interest to do that. Why push it up to a level where it will hurt you? You don't need that. Why broaden the problem instead of fixing it?"

On only a few occasions, says the counselor, has it been necessary for him to go to a manager's superior. When that does happen, the superior is likely to ask Jackson for suggestions, then ask the supervisor to join the two of them to review the problem.

Knowing NBC as well as he does is very important to him, says Jackson. Also, he feels comfortable with the norms and policies of the company. When sitting down with a manager about whom subordinates have complained, Jackson tries not to threaten. "I'm here to help you," he says, "not punish you. I know what's going on. I've talked with the people. You need help right now. You've got a problem, and I can help you to solve it." Usually the manager sees the wisdom in this. "What can I do?" he asks the counselor. He recognizes that the counselor is an internal resource for him as well as the employee. "One of the worst things that can happen to an employee counselor," says Jackson, "is to get a reputation as a blow-hard or loudmouth."

He rarely writes up complaints. He makes notes on a problem but the notes are for his eyes only, and he produces no formal write-up for a central file or for another executive to see. When he and a supervisor agree on an action plan, he hardly ever produces a memorandum on that, either. He is a firm believer in putting such understandings only in conversation.

Putting Principles into Practice

How are notions of fairness and equitableness given meaning? The job is on the shoulders of all of management, but the counselor and other officials in the employee relations division have a particular responsibility. These people are catalysts, translators, and interpreters. However, they do not invent their own ideas of fairness. Rather, they try to apply the norms and standards that prevail in the organization. Sometimes these standards are spelled out in laws which have been embodied in company policy—equal employment opportunity, for instance. At other times the standards come out of NBC's own history and practices. In this case they are applied only after careful investigation and discussion. Let us look at three examples.

Case of paternalistic harassment. An employee whom we shall call "Elizabeth" told her boss that she was pregnant and would need to take maternity leave when the baby came. Almost immediately, it seemed to her, she was assigned to another job that struck her as a demotion, received salary increases that she believed to be less than her male counterparts received, and became a victim of harassment. The "demotion," she was convinced, made her more liable to layoff if staff cutbacks should become necessary.

Rather than complain to management or go to the personnel department, she went to an outside attorney and the Equal Employment Opportunity Commission. Following talks with her, the attorney wrote a letter to Jackson. This letter was the first information the counselor had received about her unhappiness.

Jackson met first with Elizabeth, then with her superiors. Were her claims valid? He questioned, probed, checked, and made notes. His investigation showed that the job she had been assigned to was not a demotion but a comparable job. Also, he found no likelihood of a staff cutback that would affect her there. As for the second claim, he gathered data on Elizabeth's salary and the salaries of males in similar positions. No inequities appeared, once the figures were laid out. These data he sent to her and the attorney.

Jackson's investigation did turn up evidence of a type of harassment, however. Elizabeth's managers were not *conscious* of harassing her for her pregnancy and planned maternity leave. Rather, they believed that anything they had said or done was for her benefit. "We don't want to subject her to unnecessary pressure. . . ." Such attitudes, Jackson believed, were "paternalistic, unwanted, and totally inappropriate from NBC's management perspective."

After talking with various executives, he went back to Elizabeth's superiors and got them to reverse her job assignment. In addition, he arranged for managers in the department to get extensive counseling on appropriate managerial behavior at NBC and on the company's expectations of them.

Jackson followed up to see that the understanding was carried out. "I asked the managers to call me whenever they had questions about what to say to her. I kept in touch with her, too. In cases like this it is up to me to check up and be sure that I remain a resource to the managers."

As for Elizabeth, she withdrew her charge of discrimination, did well at NBC, and received promotions.

Case of the office blowup.   Two employees got in a physical fight. They went at each other so furiously that it was difficult for cooler heads to separate them. When their supervisor demanded an explanation, they asked her to bring in the employee counselor. Each had gone to see him before and had come to trust him.

Calling and interrupting Jackson in the middle of a meeting, the supervisor asked him to come immediately. Arriving on the scene, he found that each of the brawlers had been taken to a separate office down the hall. He talked first with them, then with the supervisor. He found that the office was a tinderbox of tensions and dissatisfaction. For instance, five employees were crammed into a space about the size of an average executive office. They thought the work was dull and regarded the supervisor as weak, and in turn the supervisor felt that her own boss did not help much.

Jackson's next step was to call a meeting with the supervisor and her boss. The three of them worked out a program of action. Both fighters were put on progressive discipline; they could have been fired under the company rules, but it seemed to the three that the men deserved a second chance. The space that the five employees worked in was doubled by joining it with another office down the hall. The supervisor enrolled in the company's management training program, her boss was coached on ways to improve employee morale, and the two fighters themselves were counseled.

To make sure that the supervisor did as agreed, Jackson called her every so often afterward. "How're you getting along today?" He told her that he wanted to stay in touch with her. "I don't know whose fault this was, but I don't want to see it happen again," he told her. "I want you to stay close to me so that we can be sure it won't."

In a short time morale and performance improved. As for the supervisor and her boss, they were grateful to be able to handle the flare-up themselves without having to involve higher management.

Case of the unhappy purchasing agent.   When a new purchasing manager took over in one department, a subordinate whom we shall call "Ned" became petulant and dissatisfied. The new manager, a woman, didn't know the job very well, Ned thought, and he had to spend too much time "training and orienting" her. Not surprisingly, friction developed between the two. Soon Ned found himself placed on progressive discipline.

He went to the employee counselor and complained. After listening, questioning, and investigating, Jackson reached a different view of the situation from Ned's. "You dug a hole for yourself by the way you treated her," he told Ned. "You created a win-lose scenario with your boss, and when a subordinate does that, who is likely to lose?" Jackson also came to the conclusion that Ned had been losing interest in the job for some time—since long before the new boss came on the scene.

In this case, Jackson worked exclusively with the troubled employee. He helped him to devise new ways of working with the new boss—ways that were helpful instead of defensive and obstructionist. That guidance was for the short term. He also helped Ned to see that his best bet in the long run was to look for another kind of job. Ned did that and succeeded; his work record never showed how narrowly he had avoided being fired.

A Technique of Follow-Up

Suppose that a supervisor agrees with Jackson about the need for a change in personal style or behavior, promises to do it, but reverts after a while to former ways?

As indicated earlier, Jackson keeps monitoring the situation—with the supervisor and, if appropriate, with any affected subordinates. At the time of the agreement, he sits down with the supervisor and makes clear to him or her that he is going to stay in the picture for a while:

> I tell the supervisor that I'm going to follow up. I may suggest a meeting in a few days, and then another a week later. Also, I make it clear to the manager that his or her subordinates have a right to come to me whenever they want to. It's part of my job to keep my door open to them. Besides, I think it's appropriate. "In no way are they to be penalized," I tell the supervisor. "If they come to me and I learn something from them that may be helpful to you, I'll try to feed it back to you if I can do so without compromising confidentiality. So let's not play games with each other, because I'm going to know in one way or another what happens from this point on. My intention is to help you deal with these circumstances effectively."

Although a few supervisors may resent the counselor's role, most accept it, realizing that he is doing what he is doing in order to improve the situation.

Responding to the Situation

The counselor does not always work in the same way. Even with typical situations, he may have to devise a special way of handling the problem and personnel involved. The kind of problem that last week was solved in one way may, when brought to his attention from a different quarter next week, have to be approached in quite a different manner. The counselor has a lot of leeway at NBC, and he needs a great deal of tact and ingenuity to get results. This is in keeping with the way in which much of the rest of the organization operates.

For instance, five employees came to Jackson over a period of several months with almost exactly the same complaint about their manager. When each left his office, Jackson promised that he wouldn't tell the manager that the subordinate had come in to see him. Seeing a troublesome pattern in the manager's operations, however, he realized that there was a problem to be corrected. He went to the manager in question, told him that he had received a number of complaints but had promised anonymity, and stated that he was taking the responsibility himself to ask for corrective action. At first the manager resisted. The complaints were exaggerated, he told Jackson; the situation wasn't quite what the employees described, and so on. After Jackson talked with him for a while, however, it dawned on the manager that the problem might blow up in his face and damage his career. He promised to change his ways—and did. To this day, however, he doesn't know who the complainants were. "In fact," Jackson told him, "you shouldn't even try to find out who they were."

Another case involved one of Jackson's associates in the personnel department. A young man came to this official's office and said that a terrible thing had happened to him. He had left some papers in the photocopy machine, and a senior executive had bawled him out for that, using obscene language. The young man was offended and upset. "I don't care how big an executive he is, he shouldn't do that to me!" The personnel officer then went to the senior executive and described the situation as it had been told to her, adding how upset the young man was. The executive retorted, "But it was only two minutes until deadline and that blankety-blank left his papers in the machine!" "I know," said the personnel officer, "but you can't talk to employees like that." NBC's policy regarding professional behavior was clearly against the executive, and there had, in fact, been a workshop in which employees were told that they didn't have to be subjected to foul language if it offended them.

The executive nodded, agreed, and went to the young man to apologize.

On another occasion, a skilled secretary was assigned to a new boss, and almost immediately he annoyed her by calling her "sweetie," "dear," and so on. She went to the boss's manager and complained. "I don't like it," she said. "I don't want to put up with it." Going to the boss, the manager described the complaint, but the boss resisted. "Aw, I didn't mean it," he said, explaining that terms like those complained of were his "style" and shouldn't be taken seriously. So the manager asked the boss to come with him, and together they visited Jackson. The counselor reinforced the manager's opinion. They discussed the proper way to address subordinates, and Jackson made it clear that the company frowned on sexist terms. He persuaded the boss not to use such language again. "Your job is more than your job description," Jackson pointed out to the man. "It is more than the technical functions you perform. It is also your impact on people and on their personal productivity."

In still another case, an employee came to Jackson complaining about poor performance ratings and low raises. His work was good, he insisted. He had done everything and more than his job description called for. Gaining the employee's permission to investigate, Jackson checked first with his personnel records, then with the supervisor and others who knew the complainant. He found that in practically every situation the man had been in, associates considered him to be so interpersonally abrasive that he negatively affected their productivity. Because of his poor relationships, the supervisor had given him low ratings. Sitting down again with the aggrieved employee, Jackson told him what he had learned and said he thought the boss's decision was appropriate and should stand.

Seeing Through Smoke Screens

It is not always the subordinate who comes to the counselor for help, and the story given cannot always be taken at face value. Jackson recalls:

> I had a case some years ago. A department supervisor asked me to lunch. There he told me he wanted to make a move on a problem in his staff. A woman was making trouble, he said, and since she was volatile, he was sure she could continue to be a problem. He wanted me to advise him on how he should handle the situation with a minimum of bad publicity.
>
> He didn't know that I knew something about the situation already. The subordinate had questionable relationships with some of the men in the department, including the

director himself. Things were getting out of control. He wanted to get her out on another pretext. He didn't want to admit to me what was really going on.

I had to confront him with the real issue. I told him that I sympathized with his need to do something, but not with the way he was planning to do it. I learned that he was already locked into the strategy he was taking because he had talked to so many key associates and predisposed them to view the problem as he wanted them to. In fact, taking me to lunch was a way of trying to make me appear supportive of him.

He had boxed himself in, and I was sorry for that, but a matter of principle was involved. I told him, "The issue is bigger than you and involves your whole department. You can't bend the rules as you want to. This employee's actions do not warrant termination. You've made your bed, and now you've got to lie in it. If she complains about anything you do to her, it will be held against you." She did complain.

He threatened to get a lawyer but decided against it. We convinced him that he was bound to lose if he tried to fight. He didn't fire the woman as he had intended, but she did leave his department. She went to another part of the organization in order to get away from rumors and innuendos about her relationships. He was no longer considered promotable.

Getting Results

Although the counselor system works with a minimum of formality and a small staff, it appears to have brought fine results at NBC. When employees believe they have been wronged, they don't have to resign or turn to an outside attorney; they can give the counselor's office a ring and make an early appointment to talk. From the time of that appointment to the end of the investigation is rarely more than a few weeks. Jackson says:

> My role is to head off employees whose next step might be the state and federal agencies or law courts. It is to short-circuit potential litigation. If employees don't resolve their problems with my help and have to go outside the company instead, something is wrong. There's a direct correlation between doing my job well and reduced litigation. I get a report across my desk every month summarizing the number of employees in litigation, complaints, resolutions, lawsuits pending, and so on. Usually I know the people involved. Over the past five or six years, the number of litigations reported has taken a dive.

What conditions are necessary to effective operation of the counselor system? Here are six:

1. *The counselor must be willing to proceed without formal authority to adjudicate.* If necessary, he or she can bring the power of line management or the personnel department to bear to accomplish the change needed, but that mustn't be done too often. The counselor must be able to rely on ability to persuade and on managers' and nonmanagers' perceptions of him or her as a fair and rational problem-solver. "I don't use power plays if I can help it," says Jackson. "I won't say to the manager, 'You have to do what I say because I say so.'" Instead he relies on fact, reason, and company policy.
2. *The counselor must have unique personal skills.* He or she must be able to hear a series of often-conflicting reports, separate fact from fiction, and arrive at a true and workable solution—efficiently. Exceptional patience is important. As one personnel executive told me, "Even if you have heard the employee's story a hundred times before, you must listen, and listen attentively."

3. *The counselor must have a better perspective on the company than many employees do.* It will sometimes be necessary to let employees know that if they don't change their ways, they will be in real trouble. "I may have to tell them we just don't do that at NBC," Jackson says. "This may not be the place for them." Such a warning isn't credible unless it comes from a person who is seen generally as wise and knowledgeable. It also requires that the counselor's office not be a revolving door for aspiring personnel managers, with new people on the job every year or two. A good reputation, an established track record, and a convincing "image" can be very useful assets for the counselor.

4. *The counselor must have broad investigative powers.* At NBC he or she can look at any or all personnel records (including those that employees themselves cannot see, such as records of other employees' performance appraisals and data). He or she can go to any person in any part of the company for information and enlist help, if needed, from other members of the personnel department.

5. *The system must be visible.* If employees don't know that the function exists, they won't use it. At NBC, the employee handbook, given to every new employee, lists the counselor's telephone number. The system is mentioned in memoranda that go out from the personnel department, is listed in the employee telephone directory, and is referred to in training programs for managers and employees.

6. *The system can't do the job by itself.* It cannot by itself teach all employees in the company how their words and actions affect morale. It cannot by itself lead employees around the pitfalls of sexual harassment, racism, and intolerance. It relies on workshops and training sessions (often organized and taught by the present counselor). It assumes a strong, able personnel department. And it counts heavily on the positive examples set by top executives.

B

Board-Type Systems

Introduction

This section consists of the write-ups of eleven companies' board systems. All but one of these write-ups are based on interviews conducted by the author. Although the write-ups vary in depth of information, all begin with a brief preview of the procedure to be described so that readers can gain an overview of it before getting into the detail. The write-ups are arranged in alphabetical order by company.

In terms of the conceptual scheme in Exhibit 3-1, all eleven systems fall in the "adjudication" column. For a factual summary of some characteristics of the systems, see Exhibit 5-1.

Citicorp's Problem Review Procedure

Citibank, N.A. is the country's largest bank and, in the banking community, widely regarded as one of the best-run U.S. banks. It is wholly owned by Citicorp, a financial services organization employing approximately fifty-three thousand people in the United States and another forty thousand people in nearly one hundred countries abroad where it operates. In both organizations employee due process takes place under a system called the "Problem Review Procedure." The executive in charge is Joseph A. Fernandez, vice president for staff relations in the corporate human resources department of the bank. That department is headed by Pamela P. Flaherty, who reports to the chairman, John S. Reed.

The Problem Review Procedure is, in the words of one admiring Citicorp executive, "a dynamite procedure." The central mechanism is a review board that considers both sides of a grievant's case, reaches a decision, and recommends that decision to a senior line executive. The documents before the review board are prepared by human resources generalists and staff relations specialists who have investigated the case. Although the board functions differently from law courts in many important

Company: Citicorp		Products/Services: Full-service commercial banking
Headquarters: New York, New York		
		Dates of Interviews: April 3, December 9,
Sales: $23.5 billion (1987)	Number of Employees: 93,000	1986

aspects, it operates somewhat like an appellate court in that it bases its decisions on written statements of the facts and arguments. It may call in the "plaintiff" and "defendant" for oral questioning if it feels that desirable, but it relies principally on the record as marshaled by the staff relations specialists. The record is organized succinctly around claims, defenses, and the findings of the investigation.

The Problem Review Procedure has been operating for about ten years. It handles about a dozen cases per year, one for every forty-three hundred U.S. employees. To date, all its recommendations have been okayed by senior management. The great majority of employee complaints do not go to the review board; they are settled at earlier stages by the grievants and their supervisors or managers, often with the help of employee relations specialists. However, the presence and visibility of the Problem Review Procedure are very important to Citicorp employees, and people at almost all levels of the bank and holding company have used it.

Also, it has probably saved the bank from many lawsuits. "The Problem Review Procedure," said one close observer, "is a tremendous preventive mechanism. We have stopped a lot of cases right here. Many employees tell us, 'If I don't get this resolved here, I'm going to get a lawyer.' In fact, some already have an attorney ready and waiting if they can't get a hearing in the bank."

To show how the Problem Review Procedure works, I shall describe several recent cases from different viewpoints. We can then go on to consider some general questions about the operations of the system, its background, and its role in employee relations at Citicorp and Citibank.

A Busy Manager Serves on a Board

An executive whom I shall call "Chuck Cummings" was in charge of about five-hundred employees at the bank. They ranged from high-tech specialists to chauffeurs. An experienced manager, he had been at the bank for more than twenty-five years. He had always been a line manager.

Not long ago he received a call from one of Fernandez's assistants. "Have you ever served on a review board?" asked the assistant. Cummings answered that he hadn't. "Do you know what it is?" asked the assistant; Cummings said he did. "Would you be willing to serve on a case?" asked the assistant. Cummings answered that he would.

Shortly before the board met, Cummings received a "book" on the case, that is, a collection of documents summarizing the grievant's work record, his complaint, the supervisor's response, and other matters. Before the discussion started, he gained a fairly accurate notion of what the case was about and the arguments on both sides. The human resources generalist who had written the book had talked at length with the complaining employee and the supervisor, written up their views about what happened, showed the write-ups to them for approval, and combined these summaries with other documents that the parties wished to put in the record. This book was then presented to the staff relations specialist for final review.

The board met in a room near Fernandez's office. The room was about twenty-five feet by fifteen feet with a long table and about eight chairs. Six people attended. Cummings didn't know who the other members were, though he judged the chairperson to be the staff relations head or his designee. He knew that two of the "judges" had to be, like himself, officers or staff members of the same or higher grade as the grieving employee, because of the Problem Review Procedure's rules, and that at least one of them had to be a vice president. These four people were picked by the grievant from a random computer list. All of them would vote, with the chair voting only if necessary to break a tie. The human resources generalist who had prepared the book also sat in, answering any questions about the case that weren't clear from the record but having no vote. The generalist and chairperson also answered a few questions about Citicorp policy—the "law of the corporation"—as it applied to the case.

Opening the meeting, the chairperson walked the members through the main points of the case, asking for questions and discussion. To Cummings, the chair appeared very objective. "He tried to present it without swaying us in either direction. He kept his own opinion out of it so well through the meeting that I had to wonder how he really felt."

As the discussion went on, it appeared to Cummings that at least one member favored the grievant while at least one favored the senior manager. At one point a member wanted to ask the grievant to come in and answer a few questions. When the motion was first voted, two favored it, two opposed; seeing this, the two who were opposed agreed to ask the employee to appear in order to give him the benefit of a doubt. "It was clear to me that the board felt that if it had to err, it would err on the side of the complaining employee rather than the supervisor," said Cummings. "I agreed with that. You can never walk down the street exactly in the middle."

After the employee appeared and answered questions, he left. The board then resumed discussion, a vote was taken, and the supervisor's decision was upheld. About one and a half hours after the session started, the chairperson adjourned the board, and the case was over.

Cummings is a strong believer in Citicorp's due process system. He knows how easy it is for a good performer to become victimized by circumstances beyond his or her control, such as a personality conflict with the boss or an organizational change. "Suddenly a person who did everything right for a long time is at loggerheads with the supervisor and sometimes even getting documented," he says. (*Documented* is the organization's term for a type of disciplinary action during which absences or performance are monitored and the employee's promotability and transferability are put on hold.) If that happens, he adds, two results are likely. "The employee loses interest because he feels he can't win, and he takes days off to avoid a confrontation. To justify the situation, the boss documents endlessly."

Cummings encourages people in his department to go to the Problem Review Procedure when they are having trouble with their supervisors. "If they stew about it and wait, and finally bring the problem to me as department head—by the time that's happened, it's too late," he points out. "It's past the point when I'd like to get involved. I've got two people who are at loggerheads and no longer can agree on anything. Besides, I wonder if it's possible to provide a fair hearing to a boss or subordinate without turning it over to a group of people who have no ax to grind and who gain nothing no matter which way the decision goes. It's hard for me to be so fair. It's hard for me to pronounce guilty or not guilty, or yes or no."

Cummings sees no danger that the Problem Review Procedure will undermine the authority of managers. He finds no evidence of this in his talks with managers, and he believes that the low number of review board cases substantiates his opinion. The Problem Review Procedure has not become a way of second-guessing management, in his opinion.

A Personnel Executive Prepares a Book

A manager whom I shall call "Don Dudley" is the human resources generalist for a large area—let us call it the northwest area—in which Citibank operates with branch banks. He has many duties. He spends a lot of time coaching and training employees, during which period he emphasizes the company's goal of equitable and consistent treatment, among other things. He may become involved in numerous cases involving discipline or complaints, and this may mean laying down the company law to a boss as well as to a subordinate. For instance, when a supervisor gave a subordinate a warning about a serious error, but delivered the warning three weeks after the fact, Dudley told him that he must rescind the warning because he sent it out too late. He conducts employee attitude surveys, talking with the employees of a branch and summarizing their attitudes, likes, and dislikes in a talk with the branch manager. And he does many other things connected with training and morale.

As generalist for the northwest area, he also writes the book on any case in the area that goes to the review board. This takes quite a bit of time—a week just for the writing, to say nothing of the interviewing, is not uncommon—and so he may have to schedule himself for double duty when he sees an employee going to the Problem Review Procedure. However, he says, "Citicorp is known for long hours and hard work." Besides, he takes special pride in researching and presenting a case well.

A short time ago, a branch bank teller in his area was discharged. When the teller appealed his discharge, Dudley automatically came on to prepare the record for the review board. Dudley was already familiar with the case since he had prepared a written record of the teller's and bank manager's positions in earlier stages of their conflict. Briefly, the teller was prone to making errors in his daily tallies of money taken in versus money paid out. Investigations by the auditor showed no reason to suspect fraud. The trouble seemed to be mostly that the teller was too anxious to keep the customer line moving fast, sacrificing accuracy to speed. His supervisors had warned him repeatedly about the discrepancies, urged him to slow down, and made suggestions about how he could improve his accuracy, but the teller kept right on making mistakes. He wanted to please customers. He wanted also to get promoted to some such position as customer representative. Others in the branch found him likable. The errors, however, could not be tolerated, and so the bank decided to let him go.

Believing the bank's action to be unfair, the teller contested his discharge. His arguments were turned down both by the branch manager and the division manager. At this point he appealed to the Problem Review Procedure, and Don Dudley started work on the book.

Dudley drew up written statements of the teller's views as well as his supervisors'. He presented each side as factually and objectively as he could, and when he was done, he showed them to the parties for their approval and any corrections. Every contention or issue raised by the teller, such as that the errors in his tallies were not as serious as management claimed, or that his goal was simply speedy customer service, Dudley answered as best he and management could. Under the rules of the Problem Review Procedure, he was required to show a response to every issue raised by the grievant whether or not the point seemed to be relevant. For instance, the teller alleged that the branch manager sometimes brought beer to his office. Though the point seemed irrelevant to the reasons for discharge, Dudley had to answer it factually.

In addition, Dudley included all appropriate exhibits, such as copies of performance appraisals, written warnings, and memos. All told, the book ran to about eight single-spaced typewritten pages.

Shortly before the review board was scheduled to meet, Dudley sent copies of the book to each member. The members included three peers of the teller, chosen by him from a random computer listing, a vice president, also chosen from a random listing, and a vice president from staff relations, who ran the meeting. Dudley also attended, but as a resource person, not as a voting member. The teller knew of the date and time of the review board meeting and stood by to come in if requested, but the board did not think it needed to see him.

At the session, the chair began by asking if there were questions about the record. Various matters were clarified, some by Dudley. Next the group turned to the merits of the discharge. One member felt that though the teller had made errors, he should be given a chance at the other job he sought since he was bright, likable, and well motivated. The others disagreed. The sessions continued for an hour and a half, after which time the chair called for a vote. The majority favored the discharge, and Dudley was instructed to notify the teller. The group executive for the northwest area followed with written confirmation to the teller that he was fired.

For the sake of uninhibited discussion, no minutes were taken at the meeting, and no tape recording was made. However, Citicorp attorneys would have had a good paper trail at their disposal if the teller had decided to sue the bank. This paper trail would have included a well-documented account of the teller's work history at the branch bank, the warnings he received, and descriptions of management's views of the case as well as his own.

Organizing the Book

A good example of the tight organization of the book on an employee grievant comes from the case of "Georgia Brown." Brown was fired. Appealing to the employee relations group, she failed to get the decision of her supervisor reversed. She then asked for a hearing by the Problem Review Procedure. The human resources generalist who wrote up the case, after a lengthy investigation, pitched the single-spaced write-up around five topics, each underscored as a heading:

The issue: Was Brown's discharge consistent with Citicorp's policies and practices?

Background facts: In this section, the generalist listed the undisputed facts of the case, such as Brown's length of service at the bank, her job, her performance reviews, and the date of her discharge.

Synopsis of Brown's appeal: In this section the generalist summarized Brown's claims, regardless of their relevance in the minds of management or the employee relations investigator. These claims ranged from the reasons Brown believed she had been unfairly sacked to her contention that her career path at the bank was being blocked by management.

Management's response to Brown's claims: In this section of about four single-spaced pages, the generalist summarized management's answers to each of Brown's allegations, whether or not it thought them relevant. For instance, to the relevant claim that she had been unfairly fired, management responded with the supervisors' explanation of the warnings, her failures and errors, and so forth; to the irrelevant claim that her career path was being blocked, the supervisors responded by noting that the bank held out no defined career paths, that this was only a colloquial expression.

Human resources investigation: In this section the generalist summarized the factual information learned on the issue of whether Brown was in fact discharged in violation of the bank's policies and practices. Though a reviewer of the case might conclude that the firing was or was not justified, the generalist did not offer such a conclusion.

To select board members, the staff relations department went to two areas of the bank with which Brown was not associated; that is, since she was employed in the individual bank, they went to random listings of employees in the so-called institutional and investment banks. The staff does this as a matter of policy in order to assure objectivity at the hearing.

After the board came to a decision, it sent its written recommendation to the sector head—the executive in charge of the various divisions of the individual bank. The group executive studied the recommendation, asked some questions of the Problem Review Procedure chairperson, and approved the decision.

A Grievant Stops Short of the Problem Review Procedure

An employee whom I shall call "Ed Evans" worked in a middle management position in one part of Citibank. At certain seasons, business was fairly heavy in the area where he worked, and during those seasons the only way the work could be done on time was for employees to continue past five, sometimes well into the evening. When this was necessary, management did everything it could to ease the inconvenience for them. It paid for their dinners. It saw them safely to their cars or public transportation. (It did not pay them overtime since they were classified as exempt employees.)

Evans was a fine worker—hard-working, capable, cooperative, well liked. However, he left the office on the dot at five, and it was important to him to leave promptly then because the custom in his home was to assemble at six o'clock and sit down together at the supper table. At six o'clock, the Evanses—Ed, his wife, and their four children—dropped whatever they were doing and ate as a family. It was as if a whistle blew then. On his $28,000-a-year salary they did not own a new car, own their house, or take fancy vacations. But they did have that precious thing called *family*.

During one busy period, Evans got called in by his manager. The manager asked why he had to leave at five. Evans answered, and the manager listened—rather enviously, it would seem—to his explanation. Who could fail to sympathize with this man? Nevertheless, the manager shook his head. "You cannot stay on this job and *never* work overtime," the manager said. "Even if you do super work between nine and five. One of the requirements of your job is that you work past five from time to time, otherwise we cannot get the work out. I can't have fifty people doing it one way and one person doing it another even if I do like your reason for getting home by six. It won't make sense to the others."

Evans wasn't convinced. Knowing that a strong human resources department existed to work out conflicts that couldn't be resolved by mutual agreement, he went to that department and presented his views. The people with whom he talked listened carefully, investigated his situation, and told him that reluctantly they had to agree with the supervisor. For a while Evans thought of taking his case to the review board but decided against it. The more he talked, the more apparent it became that it wasn't reasonable for him to march to the step of a different drummer—at least, at five o'clock during the heavy business seasons. He decided not to contest the supervisor's decision.

A Port in the Storm

The great majority of problems that subordinates cannot work out with their supervisors never go to the Problem Review Procedure. They are solved informally with the help of human resources generalists. In fact, one bank executive told me, most employees probably know little about the formal hearing procedure even though it is described in the handbooks and bulletins. But they do know about the staff relations division, and when they get in trouble they go to it. Then, if necessary, they learn about the existence of the procedure. This fact may have a greater influence on supervisors than any decision the board has made.

Hundreds of complaints and problems are handled informally each year. During the past six years, human resources generalists have processed the following numbers of cases:

1982	293
1983	320
1984	379
1985	473
1986	700[1]

Each of these cases might have progressed to a review board but for the consulting and counseling offered.

Not only is the human resources department known, but its members tend to have quite a bit of visibility. One human resources manager told me that he was sitting in a branch bank waiting for some help on a personal IRA account. During the short time that he waited, five Citicorp employees came up to him and said they would like to see him. "Maybe three-quarters of the employees don't understand the Problem Review Procedure," he said, "but they know whom to come to when they have a question."

Fernandez, who is jovially dubbed the "Chief Justice Rehnquist" of the bank because he oversees the Problem Review Procedure, picks employee relations specialists carefully, for temperament and aptitudes as well as special skills. For example, one of them is fluent in Spanish, an important advantage in an area where many employees are first- or second-generation Puerto Ricans, Mexicans, or others from South American countries. Another came to the job with experience in handling irate customers. All are good communicators.

A woman whom I shall call "Anita Aguillar" came to the bank and for seven months worked as a manager. She did not get a managerial title, however; she was given to understand that that would have to wait until budget approval came a little later on. Although she was paid as a manager, she wasn't eligible for certain benefits without the title.

After seven months, the business function she was in was moved away. She was left with nothing. Placed on "job search," she talked with a human resources manager and had her résumé circulated among different departments of the bank. Under

[1] As of November 1986.

the rule in force then, she could keep on this way for three months; then, if she had not been placed, she would have to leave.

After a month on job search, the human resources manager who had been helping her left the bank. She began to feel desperate about her prospects. "I needed the work, and nothing was happening," Aguillar said. So she went to an assistant vice president in the staff relations department and explained her problem. The assistant vice president went to a new human resources generalist who was being assigned to her group and recommended that she be treated as a full-fledged manager even though she didn't have that title. "They *intended* to give her a managerial title," the assistant vice president said. "In a few months, formal approval would have come."

The new personnel officer agreed, Aguillar was treated as a manager, and in a few weeks she was placed happily in a new managerial position. She never had to turn to the Problem Review Procedure. Referring to the staff relations department, she said, "It was nice to know that there was a port in the storm."

"The greatest benefit of the Problem Review Procedure," said one staff relations officer, "is the feeling it gives employees that there is another avenue than slugging it out with the boss. They don't have to duke it out with the boss to get a resolution. It's the hope of a fair resolution that they value most. Sometimes they will use the threat of going to the board as a cudgel over the boss, like a person saying, 'I'm going to sue you,' but most of the time it's simply the fact that there's an alternative that makes the difference." This official also believes that employees are impressed by top management's involvement, especially the fact that the board decision is reviewed by a group executive reporting to Citicorp chairman John S. Reed.

Support and Evolution

What kinds of problems go to the Problem Review Procedure? "Decisions concerning performance appraisals, salary, promotions, and discipline are typical of the types of decisions challenged when employees turn to the Problem Review Procedure," says Fernandez. "However, the staff is not limited to these issues. The procedure is meant to be a recourse of appeal for any work-related issue."

Also, it is available to employees in any Citicorp office in the country. For example, recently a review board met in Buffalo. When a board is convened in other cities, it is picked as in New York from random listings of employees in areas other than the complainant's place of work.

What programs complement the Problem Review Procedure? Perhaps the most important one is supervisory training. Courses are offered to the different departments, divisions, and groups—no one has to take them—and they cover such problems as managing problem employees, performance appraisal, and discipline. Cases, role playing, and other devices for dramatizing problems and answers are used. The managers and supervisors who attend may be toughest on people at their own level. For example, when a case is discussed from the bank's files, the class may say, "Why wasn't the *manager* put on documentation? He handled this terribly." One may leave the classes thinking that if there were some way to make training one hundred percent effective, there would be no need for a Problem Review Procedure!

Another important set of programs is attitude surveys. They are administered on a decentralized basis and sent out about once a year. The response rate is very high—close to 90 percent—and some of the same questions are used year after year in order to discern trends in morale, attitudes, and feelings about work at the bank. Of the one hundred fifty items on the questionnaire, between thirty and forty deal with supervision. For instance, respondents are asked to comment on such statements as "My supervisor needs more training in communication" and "When I have too much to do, I can go to my supervisor and ask what my priorities are." It is likely to take an employee three-quarters of an hour to answer the questionnaire. The results are compiled, statistically analyzed, and fed back to individual managers as well as to top management. In the case of bank managers, a representative from human re-sources sits down with the executive and goes over key issues in the findings for the bank in question. What does the manager think about this finding or that? What action does he or she plan to take to deal with the issue? In this way, many problems are dealt with before they erupt into appeals to the Problem Review Procedure.

Another complementary measure is the Committee on Good Corporate Practice, established in 1980. Comprised of five high-level Citibank officers with broad experi-ence, this committee, says Fernandez, serves as the "last court of internal appeals" and "the last line of defense against the sad consequences of a public dispute."

Two Citicorp publications are important. *Working Together* is a very readable, lively booklet that tells employees what the bank expects of them and what they can expect from the bank. *Seven Ways to Solve a Problem* is a neatly laid out and illustrated booklet that explains to employees the different options they have when they have problems; they can resort to counseling, the medical department, and other pro-grams as well as the Problem Review Procedure.

The procedure did not land full-blown on the doorstep of Citicorp. From the middle 1960s to 1976, the bank limped along with a system that was intended to resolve employee disputes in a fair and objective manner, and that succeeded some-times but not nearly often enough. One of its troubles was lack of clarity: it was not clear to employees who made the decisions or what the steps to a final decision were. Another trouble was that complaints and cases often took much too long to resolve. It is not known why Citicorp chose this particular approach in the 1960s instead of, say, the ombudsperson approach or the open door approach.

When Fernandez and his associates looked freshly at the system in 1976, they decided first on some criteria for a satisfactory procedure. For instance, they wanted a system that employees could understand how to use and feel comfortable using. Again, they wanted one that wouldn't take an interminable amount of time to process a complaint. They wanted to bring in line managers—they didn't want the procedure to be known as a "personnel process," or to be thought of as a way of wresting power from line managers. In a paper he wrote in 1983 for the Educational Fund for Individual Rights in New York, Fernandez also stated that an objective was "to establish a structure encompassing the principles of due process." This was one of the first times that a corporate executive used the term *due process* to describe an internal complaint procedure.

With these criteria and standards in mind, Fernandez's group revised and rewrote the Problem Review Procedure in its present form. In a relatively short time, both the visibility and use of the system improved dramatically. In 1977, two cases came before the board; in 1978, eight; in 1979, nine; and in 1980, ten.

Streamlining the Procedure

Today, a decade after the overhaul just described, the staff relations group is pondering possible revisions in the Problem Review Procedure. "What we're trying to do," says Fernandez, "is to simplify the procedure without sacrificing quality. Can we make it less complex? Can we move complaints along faster? There is a tendency now for people to forget that what they're trying to do is resolve issues equitably." He and his associates worry that the very task of preparing a book may be seen as overwhelming, and that the number of pages and exhibits may obscure for board members what the central facts and issues are. It must be remembered that the "judges" are chosen from areas outside the complainant's. In the Georgia Brown case, for instance, they came from sectors other than Brown's—valuable for the sake of objectivity and a fair hearing but a problem in terms of the time required for them to separate the chaff from the wheat when presented in a long and complicated book.

As it operates now, the procedure is also open to criticism for the amount of time it takes. The average length of time from the date an employee appeals in writing to the board and the date when the board considers his or her case is about six months. This is not bad, especially when compared with the waiting period in court. However, if this six-month period could be reduced, a lot could be gained from the standpoint of both the fingernail-biting manager and the anxious employee (to say nothing of the burden on staff relations specialists and others in the human resources department).

What Fernandez's group is working on, therefore, is a procedure that would combine the benefits of the current one with fewer of its liabilities. They are working on a written form for appeals that would highlight the main issues and allow a limited space for explanation. This would keep the complainant from rambling unnecessarily or producing claims and exhibits that lack relevance. They are also playing with the idea of putting in a deadline for the supervisor's response; for instance, failure of the manager to respond in writing within forty-five days might automatically escalate the claim to the next step in the procedure, that is, consideration by the board. The deadlines in the current procedure, by contrast, are loose.

Two memoranda prepared by the staff relations department show the kind of thinking that is driving Fernandez's group. Exhibit 1 profiles a good procedure in terms of values and requirements. Exhibit 2 summarizes the staff's thinking about the purpose, prospective gains, and features of a good procedure.

EXHIBIT 1

Positive Aspects of an Effective Problem Review Procedure at Citicorp

- Employees believe the corporation cares.
- Written documentation in the event of a lawsuit.
- Facts committed to writing for future reference.
- Employees are aware of the process and believe they can escalate an issue to a higher level outside their department.
- Retaliation is prohibited.
- Provides a mechanism for internal versus external problem resolution.
- Allows for an impartial review of the facts.

EXHIBIT 2
Overview of a Grievance Procedure at Citicorp

Purpose

- Provides an internal system through which employees may express concerns and seek review of managerial decisions and practices with which they disagree

Benefits

- Reduces risk of third-party intervention
- Minimizes costly litigation
- Identifies problem areas within an organization requiring management's attention
- Fosters a positive climate
- Helps retain good employees

Characteristics of an Effective Grievance Procedure

- Timeliness
- No retaliation for use of procedure
- Objectivity
- Appeal to higher levels
- Management support
- Easy access
- Established procedure
- Confidentiality of advice and counseling
- Problem resolution removed to independent body
- Investigation, conciliation, mediation

Values in the Workplace

"Citicorp," said one executive, "is an MBO-driven company. It is driven by goals for people as well as for sales, costs, and profits. The people goals are harder to quantify but they are real."

Addressing the Third National Seminar on Individual Rights in the Corporation in 1980, William I. Spencer, then president and chief operating officer, offered these observations:

> Today's workers no longer view employment as an extended period of involuntary servitude, after which they hope—in retirement—to enjoy the fruits of their long labors and leave something to their children. The modern trend is to view employment as one of many life interests—all serving the common purpose of self-fulfillment, which usually includes a sense of social purpose. Thus, workers are more determined than ever to bring into the workplace the same values they cherish outside the workplace.
>
> This includes such intangible values as self-respect, dignity, and individuality. It also includes the particular values enumerated in the Constitution. Workers no longer consider the "Bill of Rights" something to be stashed out of sight, like a wet umbrella, when they arrive at work. They expect such guarantees as "due process," "privacy," and "free speech" to follow them to their desks and work stations. After all, a right that doesn't apply through much of your waking day and which you can be fired for exercising, isn't much of a right.

Although an idealist, Spencer was not naive about the prospective gains from fair hearing procedures, even the best. He said:

> We are under no illusion that any of our programs, or all of them combined, will eliminate employee dissent. An employee who has used all these available procedures to get a fair hearing, and a decision from the Committee on Good Corporate Practice, may still go public with a complaint. That is the real world. So long as the issue is disputed in good faith by all parties, we have no complaint.

Control Data's Review Board

In February 1983, Control Data launched its Review Board. Composed of two peers of the grievant plus one executive, the three selected at random for each case, the board appears to have been very successful. In the first four years of operation, the board heard thirty-one cases, with about one-third being decided in favor of the grievant and two-thirds in favor of management. (One of several unique features of the system is that one side or the other is sustained; the board can't "fudge" or opt for a middle way.) Allowing for the fact that today's employee population of thirty-four thousand is less than in prior years, that usage means that about one employee in four thousand goes to the board every year. Managers have brought 19 percent of the cases.

Like an appellate court, the board decides on the basis of a written record and does not hear oral testimony. Although its conclusions are not final—strictly speaking, they are recommendations to the vice president of human resources, not decisions—they have always been affirmed. There is a conviction in the company that,

Company: Control Data		Products/Services: Computer systems and services
Headquarters: Minneapolis, Minnesota		
		Date of Interview: February 18, 1987
Sales: $3.35 billion (1987)	Number of Employees: 34,400	

among many other benefits, the system encourages managers to manage individ-ualistically at the same time that they meet certain employee relations standards.

One of the interesting things about the Review Board is its genesis. It was not chosen in a hit-or-miss manner or by borrowing another company's approach, but by carefully analyzing the Control Data organization, its personnel history, and the values management sought in employee relations. In 1979, a "white paper" was written, and out of the information and ideas set forth in that document were born the principles that govern the Review Board process today.

From Research and Words to Action

In 1979, Control Data had had more than twenty-five years of experience with a nonunion grievance process for resolving work-related problems of employees. It was a good process. Nevertheless, there was a feeling in management that the company was now ready to take another step toward the goal of fairness and equity in the workplace. The existing process meant that an employee who felt that he or she had been dealt with unfairly could appeal up the line. The trouble, as some executives viewed it, was that soon the employee got lost in an upper haze, like someone climbing a mountain. Also, of course, line managers had a tendency to support each other when a subordinate challenged one of them.

So Norbert R. Berg, deputy chairman of the board, asked David G. Robinson, now in charge of the company's Employee Advisory Resource, to study the subject and make some proposals in writing. Although he didn't have much time, Robinson was able to pull together a good deal of data and, out of his experience at Control Data, outline the elements of a more advanced system than the company had in 1979.

Robinson's white paper was about nine thousand words long. He lost no time in establishing his desire to stake some new ground, for the title was "Towards En-hanced Employee Justice," words that are not common today and were even less common in the 1970s. He pointed out that in a totalitarian organization, employees are powerless in many ways. For example, a person who challenges the system is likely to be considered "guilty until proven innocent." If there is to be justice in the workplace, he asserted, there must be "some mechanism to challenge the power system," in particular, a grievance resolution program. Near the end of the introduc-tion he introduced the phrase *due process* and defined it as "the fair, reasonable, and expeditious treatment of employees who choose to challenge the system." Due process, he pointed out, must not be maintained at the expense of the decision-making authority of management. It should be kept in balance with authority, serving to reduce arbitrary and capricious management decisions but going no further.

Robinson then described five models of grievance procedures for nonunion em-ployees. These models included conventional systems of appealing up the line, a system of appealing to an outside arbitrator, and a peer review system "most fre-quently used in organizations with high proportions of professional and technical personnel such as universities and medical centers." He summarized statistics from a national study on the use of such systems. At the time there was no system like that Robinson proposed for Control Data.

He went on to describe the elements of a good grievance resolution system. For instance, he stated that access to the system must be considered a right, not a privilege, else management retaliation will ruin it. He stated that it should be made clear to employees what kinds of issues are grievable, and he emphasized the need in the process for some means of equalizing nonmanagerial employees with managers, who have superior experience and training and, often, communication skills.

Robinson then took a look at the Control Data organization, concluding "that we have much work to do." For instance, it was not as clear as it should be that filing a grievance was an employee right. Again, he observed that it was not unknown for managers to intimidate and retaliate against a person challenging a superior's decision.

Moving on to action steps, he proposed that a panel of employees be established to review cases, that the evidence considered be written evidence rather than in-person testimony, that the conclusions of such a panel be advisory and not final (with the possibility that management might want to consider making the group's decisions binding after several years of operation), and a variety of other steps and features. In addition, he urged the company to move from research and deliberation to the actual development and implementation of an "internal arbitration system." His schematic chart for these stages is reproduced in Exhibit 1.

As a result of the white paper, a series of task forces was formed. One included, in addition to Robinson, a corporate attorney, the vice president of personnel administration, and a vice president from operations. "We met and we met and we met," Robinson recalls. The end result was the peer review system that has been in operation for the company as a whole since early 1983.

Desirable Features

As they looked ahead to what features and characteristics a review board should have, the task force executives agreed on such matters as the following.

As little "legalese" as possible.   Robinson recalls that in beginning discussions he often used legal phrases like *plaintiff* and *defendant*. "We decided to get rid of words like that," he says. "We decided that we didn't want the new system to sound legal. We wanted to make it peculiar to an employee relations environment. We said, 'We're talking about basic concepts of justice, not legalese.' So we worked real hard to take that kind of language out."

Written record without oral testimony.   The task force members wanted a jury-type system because its verdicts would be more credible and fairer. They also agreed that the "juries" should consist of more peers of the grievant than of managers at a higher level. To keep matters simple and inexpensive, however, the executives believed that the hearings should be held as often as possible at company headquarters in Minneapolis or in nearby St. Paul. Moreover, they agreed that oral testimony should be eliminated. For one thing, this would help to reduce the adversarial quality of the proceedings. Also, the task force felt that the prospects of fairness were better if there were no personal appearances by the grievant, defending manager, or witnesses.

If only the written record were to be used, however, there had to be opportunities for both grievant and defending manager to correct statements made by the other that seemed misleading or incorrect. This conviction led to providing the grievant-manager interchanges, as will be described later.

Clean verdicts.   The task force also believed that the grievant should get all or nothing. The members didn't want the board to be able to placate both parties or create a gray area in which each got something. "We felt the boards would be

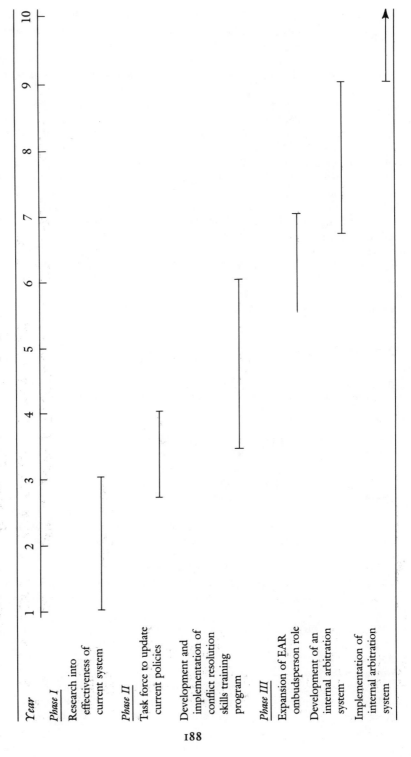

EXHIBIT 1. Time Frame Chart for Developing New Grievance System at Control Data (1979)

Year	1	2	3	4	5	6	7	8	9	10

Phase I

Research into
effectiveness of
current system

Phase II

Task force to update
current policies

Development and
implementation of
conflict resolution
skills training
program

Phase III

Expansion of EAR
ombudsperson role

Development of an
internal arbitration
system

Implementation of
internal arbitration
system

tempted this way," says Robinson, "but we didn't want them to try it. We wanted either for the grievant to get what he or she requested or to be denied. No fudging."

Unrestricted access. "In the beginning our biggest concern was frivolous cases," says Robinson. "Could we screen them out in some way? After a lot of discussion we decided that the answer was no. We shouldn't deny anyone access."

Advice and assistance. "We assumed," says Robinson, "that many individual grievants would need help if they were to have a chance to win at a hearing. They might not be as articulate, they might not know as much, they might not have the know-how that their superiors had. Somehow we needed to equalize them against the power of a large institution which thinks it is always right, but can't be." The Employee Advisory Resource, the company's employee assistance program, was seen as the means to this objective. Since 1974, EAR had been delivering personal and work-related problem counseling to employees. An ombudsperson concept had been incorporated in EAR since its inception.

Scope. The task force members decided that it would be best to restrict cases to those (1) involving work-related problems, and (2) where the application of company policy was questioned. If the problem was not work-related, the Employee Advisory Resource had a demonstrated capability to handle it. If the problem was work-related but did not involve policy application (e.g., length of workweek, places of work), then the employee should appeal to a different group. A new committee—the Human Resources Strategy Committee—was set up for that purpose.

As for who in the company was eligible to bring a case before the Review Board, the task force took a liberal view. It decided that "all domestic full-time and supplemental employees" could use the new procedure.

No outside arbitration. The task force members considered the possibility of outside arbitration as a final step but decided against it. They believed that the appeal process should end in the company and be kept under the control of managers and employees.

The foregoing list is not comprehensive but it will serve to convey the quality of the deliberations between 1979 and 1982. "We wanted a system," says Robinson, "that would be easy, quick to respond, not cumbersome, without a high potential to break down. By not having parties appear in person, we would lose some dynamic quality but reduce bias and keep the focus strictly on the facts of situations. We wanted the board to concentrate on one question: 'Was this a fair decision?' "

Thinking back to those formative years, James P. Stathopoulos, then vice president for employee relations, commented as follows in an address to the American Management Association:

> We had a grievance system at Control Data for more than twenty-five years, but it wasn't working because there wasn't a structured appeal process. If local managers decided to stop a grievance or ignore it, there was not justice. Unless the employee wrote a letter to the CEO or skipped around levels of management, there was no due process. The grieving employee had to risk retaliation.
>
> We wanted to remove risk for the employee, but we also wanted local management to deal directly and quickly with employee problems. We developed a structure that combined the best features of the old grievance structure with an appeal system that pushed justice down to the local level.[1]

---

[1] April 28, 1986 (unpublished).

Testing and Starting

When the task forces completed their studies and recommendations, top management bought the concept of a peer review system. The stage was now set for implementation. The following remarks by Fred C. Olson, the first ombudsperson in charge of the Review Board, tell part of the story:

> In the year preceding its institution nationwide, Control Data tried to test peer review at four sites. Although fewer than 1 percent of employees ever initiate a grievance, and only a fraction of those ever go beyond the first superior-subordinate stage, we still anticipated that a handful of cases would reach a peer review board.
>
> None did. This was partly because of our choice of sites, partly because of the reluctance of managers to acquaint employees with the process, and partly because of the reluctance of local personnel department people to be the first to "let one get away" from them.
>
> Ask any Control Data manager if he or she has work problems and the answer, of course, is no. (Not surprisingly, middle-level management held that peer review was unnecessary.) Without some signal from a person's immediate supervisor that says otherwise, the employee will find any system somewhat intimidating at best and, at worst, retaliatory. So in the test phase we concentrated on spreading the word at the level of first-line management and directly to employees.
>
> A question that came up during this period was, Why now? It was late 1982, a time of general recession and retrenchment, and some executives thought that any major employee-oriented program would undercut more pressing business at hand. Our response was that, first, it's a good and necessary policy and, second, if it's going to work it will have to be used in hard times too.
>
> Despite the lack of test cases, Control Data was sufficiently committed to announce peer review nationwide in February 1983. This brought nearly sixty thousand employees under its purview, which made it the largest such program in the country. Again we found a general reluctance to be the first to bring a case up, and managers and personnel people across the company went the extra mile to see that cases were resolved locally. While this was one of the desired eventual outcomes of peer review, it wasn't desired until the system at least had a chance to operate.
>
> In May the first case finally came to a board. Arising in a small manufacturing facility, it was essentially a personality clash between a strong-willed plant manager and a lower-level department manager. Officially, it involved the application of a performance improvement policy. Although division executives had reviewed the department manager and found the work of his department satisfactory, the plant manager blamed him for cost overruns and a host of other problems, and put him on a two-month performance improvement plan.
>
> At the end of that period the plant manager extended the performance plan without any comment on the original one. The department manager, convinced by now that his superior was trying to get rid of him, wouldn't sign the plan or respond to it. More evidence of uncooperative behavior, the plant manager said, and fired him.
>
> Because the plant manager was both his boss and the effective power in the plant, the aggrieved manager went quickly through peer review's first two steps. A grievance meeting was held locally, but no progress was made. The issue went to an executive at the next level, who upheld the plant manager. The department manager went to EAR requesting a peer review board. EAR attempted to mediate, but to no avail.
>
> We then assembled the materials and called together a board. The board found for the aggrieved manager. Accordingly, he was reinstated and given additional training, since he acknowledged that there were areas where his performance could be improved.
>
> The significance of this action was not so much who won as what happened: the process worked. A case came up, was handled, was decided, was noted in the manage-

ment newsletter—and suddenly peer review sprang full-blown into people's consciousness.

When the next case also went in favor of the complainant, some executive eyebrows went up. Fortunately, the careful deliberations of the first two boards indicated that, whatever the outcome, panel members were serious about getting at the facts and making the right decision. They were not about to rubber-stamp employee complaints. Styles differed and some clashes occurred, but the prevailing attitude was neither adversarial nor political. Still, the system seemed to be vindicated when the third case went in favor of management's position.[2]

Getting to the Board

Before a grievance gets heard and decided by the Review Board, it goes through several previous steps and receives the attention of many people. The great majority of grievances are dropped or resolved before seeing the light of a board.

Basically, the system launched in 1983 calls for the same initial steps as the old system did. If you are an employee with a work-related grievance, you talk first with your manager, and if that doesn't satisfy you, you go to the personnel department. The personnel manager determines if your grievance involves an application of policy; if it does, he or she tries to work it out with you.

If you still can't get satisfaction, personnel takes your dispute directly to the decision maker who seems the most appropriate, such as the plant manager if you are a machine operator or a controller if you are a cost analyst. You can talk with this executive by phone, if you choose, or meet privately person-to-person, or meet person-to-person with your personnel manager present. It's up to you.

In the first two steps just mentioned, you may express your grievance orally. However, if you go to the upper-level executive—what Control Data calls Step 3—you must put your problem in writing before you have your talk. The company offers several written guides to help you do this—one is shown in Exhibit 2—but if you want help, personnel or EAR will assist you.

Up through Step 3, the personnel department is your primary resource. Beth A. Lewis, who is with the Employee Advisory Resource as manager of work problems counseling and chairperson of the Review Boards, says that her group *can* get involved in these stages but sticks almost completely to the sidelines. "We say, in effect, 'Line organization, it's your ball. It's your responsibility to meet with the employee and provide any guidance or assistance. If investigations or meetings are necessary, it's your job to arrange them.' We in the Employee Advisory Resource are careful not to intrude on personnel's role. We do no direct investigation of a complaint during the first three steps."

By the time Step 3 is completed, most grievances go no further. In fact, 82 percent of them are either resolved or dropped during the first three steps. Of those that do progress to a Review Board, about five in six involve terminations.

Now let's suppose you are one of the 18 percent who are not satisfied with the upper-level management review of your complaint. What happens next? You contact the Employee Advisory Resource, talk with one of its representatives, and, if no satisfactory solution can be found yet, request a Review Board. Now the personnel department takes a lesser role and the Employee Advisory Resource takes over. As

[2] "How Peer Review Works at Control Data," *Harvard Business Review,* November–December 1984, pp. 59, 62.

EXHIBIT 2
How To Write a Grievance (Sample Format)

Employee Grievance

Provide a brief description of what you are requesting upper management or a Review Board to consider. Address what policy you believe was not appropriately applied to you.

> *Example:* "I am requesting an upper management review of my involuntary termination because I believe the nonexempt attendance control policy was not fairly applied to me."

Background

State the relevant events and facts that support your position. Provide a chronological account of events. Be as specific as possible, using dates, action taken, and names (for the Review Board statement use titles or generic identifiers instead of proper names, e.g., unit manager, co-worker, personnel manager).

> *Example:* "On March 12 I had car problems. I called my manager and was able to get to work by 11:00. However, my manager gave me an Appendix A, first warning . . ."

Summary of Issues

Summarize the main reasons for your grievance, and especially, the policy issues.

> *Example:* "I feel that my termination was unfair because . . ."

Request

Indicate what you are requesting as a satisfactory resolution of your problem.

> *Example:* "I am requesting that I be reinstated to my job with back pay."

Employee name
Grade and job title
Date

---

we shall see, it does a lot of work. One thing it does not do, however, is determine whether you should be going to the board. Lewis emphasizes, "The employee decides whether to request a Review Board. Often personnel and management ask me why a case is going to a Review Board when they believe policy has been followed. I explain that I'm not the judge. That's what the Review Board is for." The adviser may say that it looks as if policy is being followed, but he or she leaves the option for action to the employee.

The main task of the Employee Advisory Resource is to prepare what company people call a "casebook." This is a black notebook that describes your case as fairly and accurately as possible in writing so that the board members can reach an objective decision. It contains your description of your complaint, management's statement about why it acted as it did, a statement of the case as personnel sees it, your responses to management's statement and management's to yours, and any supporting documentation that seems relevant and useful. (Examples of these sections will be given later.) The casebook may be a dozen pages long or more than a hundred, depending on the case.

One thing that Lewis's group tries to make sure of is that you see all of the evidence and allegations against you. For instance, if your supervisor produces the testimony of a co-worker that supports management's action, the Employee Advisory Resource sees to it that you get that testimony in advance of the board meeting. In one case, such testimony was held back from the grievant through the first three steps in order to protect the employee who made it. When the case went to the Review Board and the testimony was put in the casebook, however, the grievant saw it. The name of the employee was carefully deleted, but every word that the board would hear and consider was revealed to the grievant.

Lewis says:

> My staff spends a lot of time in preparing the casebook. We want to make sure that the positions are presented as well and completely as possible. We also want to make sure that all parties share that information. Management may leave something out that would help its case—that's its decision, wise or not. But when the case goes to the board, there are no surprises for either side. All the cards are on the table. We make sure that the two sides communicate with each other. The cases that get messy are those where one side or the other tries to hold back on information, or doesn't clarify its position. Although we're on the sidelines in Step 3, we try to see at that stage that each side gets its evidence out, that all the relevant facts are described, that each side provides a rationale for what it did. If they do a good job at Step 3, the main thing we have to do for the Review Board is package the information. If the positions aren't presented well at Step 3, then we spend a lot more time getting the information and putting it together.

Often, she explains, writing the casebook means pushing the manager or grievant for details and specifics. What exactly did the manager tell the grievant on Thursday? How bad was the Friday snowstorm that made the grievant late, and what was said in the call from a toll booth?

If, as the grievant, you have trouble writing up your case, a member of the Employee Advisory Resource will help you. For example, you may "talk it" to the person; then he or she will write it out and let you see the result. The object is to equalize you with management as far as formal presentation and ability to articulate are concerned. The adviser may spend a lot of time with you at this stage.

"We are preparing one case," says Lewis, "where the grievant gave us nearly ninety pages of material to start with. We told him that won't work—it's too much for the Review Board to handle. We told him to cut the material down and focus it better. He wanted to write it himself so we let him. But we guided him. We told him that this point is critical to his case while that one isn't. We told him what parts seem to be too emotional rather than factual. We must provide a statement that management can respond to and that the Review Board can understand. Ideally, he should try to put his statement in ten pages or less."

One of the questions EAR counselors wrestle with is how much to "sanitize" a statement. Lewis likes to let something of the person's personality come through, whether positive or negative. She believes, however, that the emphasis of a statement should be on facts and issues. She believes that a person's race or age usually are not germane, therefore should be deleted from material in the casebook. As indicated, names, too, are deleted. Where they appear in documents from the files, names are whited out, and in statements by managers, grievants, and personnel people, generic words such as "the employee" or "the manager" are used instead of names.

"We try not to place ourselves in between managers and employees," says Robinson. "I think this is one reason for our success. We try to break down barriers and give information, we try to empower employees to ask the right questions of management, and we don't interpret corporate policy for anybody."

Inside the Boardroom

The power to make or break the review system at Control Data ultimately rests with the three members of the Review Boards. Will they act objectively on the basis of the facts? Or will they approach a case thinking, "Let's win this one for the little fellow"? Will they try to decide cases on the basis of some quota system—say, 60 percent for management and 40 percent for grieving employees, or vice versa— or purely on merit? Will they be dominated by management?

The "law" that the boards seek to uphold is the set of corporate policies and procedures published by the company. All employees are entitled to the benefit of this law, from the highest-ranking to the lowest-ranking. Most grievants whose cases are heard are nonmanagers, but managers, including one who was a division controller, have used it, too. (One manager's case will be described later.) In its first four years of operation, as mentioned earlier, the board decided thirty-one cases. Close to one hundred seventy cases went to Step 3 of the four-step system; about half of these were resolved through mediation, or dropped before completing Step 4, and about 30 percent of the balance were resolved during Step 3. The company does not try to track the number of complaints handled by management and personnel at Steps 1 and 2.

This number of cases was only a fraction of the number brought to the Employee Advisory Resource by employees. The total number of all cases handled from February 1983 to February 1987 was about sixteen thousand.

Exhibit 3 summarizes the cases heard by the Review Boards during a recent year.

Selecting Members

The Employee Advisory Resource ombudsperson—as of this writing, Lewis— directs the selection of a board. The procedure is simple. Depending on the job family, she may try to get the two peers of the grievant from the Twin Cities area. She specifies job family, position code, and grade levels (grievant's grade or higher) for a computerized retrieval. She excludes the grievant's division and facility. An executive member is selected from a separate listing. She may select alternates if she feels they may be needed. In selecting the peer members, she does screen to assure that the employee does not have a work history that might bias his or her opinion. For example, an employee with documented attendance problems would be excluded from reviewing a case involving attendance policy.

The identities of all members, like that of the grievant and defending manager, are

EXHIBIT 3

Cases Heard by the Review Boards, 1985

Job Family	Issue	Outcome	Vote
Production	Posting	For management	2–1
Management	Disciplinary action	For employee	3–0
Production	Termination for discipline	For management	3–0
Engineer	Termination for attendance	For management	2–1
Management consultant	Termination for performance	For employee	2–1
Computer operator	Termination for discipline	For management	3–0
Programmer	Termination for discipline	For management	2–1
Technical writer	Termination for performance	For management	3–0
Production supplemental	Termination for attendance	For management	3–0

confidential. Once the members serve and make a recommendation, they are through. When the next case comes, she starts the selection all over again.

The fact that two board members come from the grievant's job family is very important to the credibility of the system. As one Employee Advisory Resource person put it, "The grievant can say, 'This guy is my peer. He's out there in manufacturing, just like me. It's not someone sitting in an office somewhere. The people who are going to decide my future will understand what I'm going through.' "

How much of a board member's time is needed for a case? It may range from several hours to a dozen, depending on a number of factors. Robinson says:

> Several days before the hearing, the members get the black casebook. Some casebooks are thin, some are very thick. The members are expected to read the material, make notes on it, and come to the board meeting prepared. That includes any questions they may have about the situation described. The casebook alone is the basis of the discussion; nothing else. An hour and a half, two hours, maybe more may be required for this preparation. The meeting itself may last from half an hour to four hours. So it doesn't take an awful lot of a person's time. We designed it this way.

The persons selected are expected to serve. The peer members are notified by their personnel managers, and they are excused from serving only if the vice president of personnel and administration approves. In the case of the executive nominee, Robinson fights, if necessary, to keep him or her from getting out of serving. He demands a good excuse, and if not convinced, he will go to the manager's boss and argue that the person should serve. In the great majority of cases, however, this is not necessary; the nominees are glad to do their stint.

Although Lewis sends the members guidelines for serving on the board in advance of the hearing, she does not give them any formal training about, say, analyzing evidence or evaluating testimony. "We rely on the board members' judgment about things like that." She is responsible for scheduling board meetings and notifying grievants and defending managers of the dates set.

Deliberations

As the Employee Advisory Resource ombudsperson, Lewis chairs the meeting. She does not, however, have a vote; her role is to coordinate, expedite, guide, and serve as a resource to the members. She prescribes no rigid format for meetings, allowing each board instead to follow a different course depending on members' inclinations, but she does work from an agenda. For instance, she introduces the members to each other, reviews the objectives of the meeting, collects a pledge of confidentiality from each member, and after deliberations start, guides the discussion as necessary to keep it from going off the track. Also, she makes sure that each member participates and that all relevant issues are discussed.

Board meetings are always held at Control Data headquarters in Minneapolis, but if a member works in a distant facility, Lewis brings that member into the discussion by teleconferencing. "Ideally, we want all three members to sit down across from each other at a table. Where that is impossible, we use teleconferencing, with two members here on the line with the third member in another city. We don't fly that third member here to join us. Teleconferencing has worked successfully when we have tried it."

The board has only the materials in the black casebook available. As mentioned, the grievant and defending manager do not appear before the board, nor are outside parties—advocates, representatives, or negotiators—allowed to argue for one party or the other. Experience seems to confirm that, with the casebook alone as a basis, objectivity is improved. "I believe," says Robinson, "that you lose a lot of fairness in a corporate hearing system by having the 'plaintiff' and 'defendant' come face to face with the board. We want all board members to deal with the same facts, the same deck of cards."

What is a case like for the defending supervisor, especially if he or she loses? Olson comments:

> Managers on the losing side of peer review cases sometimes complain, understandably, because outsiders decide local personnel issues. They also claim that their position comes across much weaker on paper than it actually is in the plant or around the office. How is it, they want to know, that a guy everyone knows is a jerk ends up a hero, with management as the villains?
>
> Our answer is based on the notion of objective policies. It's not enough to convince yourselves and your local headquarters that a personnel action is right. You have to take it out of the local context and have it be right as measured against a companywide policy. Wherever management is vulnerable in its treatment of an individual, under peer review the employee will get the benefit of the doubt.[3]

For the executive who serves on the board, termination cases are not likely to be unsettling. For the peers of the grievant, however, it may be very difficult to sustain

[3] Ibid., pp. 62, 64.

a firing. They do that often, as the record amply shows, but in the words of one executive, "They may look all over for reasons to overturn the discharge."

Why are so many Review Board cases termination cases? In 1985, for instance, seven of nine grievants were fired employees. One reason is that other kinds of cases are easier to resolve before a Review Board becomes necessary. A supervisor and subordinate have room to negotiate—a challenged work assignment can be changed, the arguable pay cut can be renegotiated. Assuming that the manager takes the board seriously and wishes to avoid a hearing, if possible, he or she can often work out a compromise or agree to add a condition that will make the subordinate happy. In the case of discharge, however, such options do not exist.

Voting

In beginning, Lewis asks the board members to decide whether to vote by secret ballot or by voice. "Sometimes," says Lewis, "a secret ballot makes the peers feel more comfortable, but usually the board agrees to a voice vote." Decisions do not have to be unanimous; a 2–1 vote will suffice.

When the peer review process started, some skeptics felt that the two peers would habitually vote for the grievant. The record does not bear out this fear. Turning back to Exhibit 3, for instance, we see that only two of the nine votes—those denoted in the second and fifth rows down—could conceivably have resulted from the peers teaming up on the grievant's side, and in the first of the two cases, that apparently was the way the evidence pointed because the manager, too, voted with the peers.

Time to Reach Decisions

An employee has six months to introduce a grievance from the time of the incident complained of. Policy states that complaints should be handled "in a timely manner," but time limits like ten or twenty days are not set because cases vary so greatly in content and complexity. For a Review Board case, the average amount of time consumed between complaint and final resolution is under six months. This includes about two months for the case to go through Step 3, and another three or four months for preparation and exchange of statements, conducting the board, and the final review by the vice president.

The Employee Advisory Resource rides herd on cases that do not get resolved at Step 3. "I'd like to see shorter time spans between Step 3 and a board recommendation," says Lewis. "We are working on that. Often, the biggest delays occur in waiting for information requested from the employee grievants. They promise us something by Friday, and then we don't hear from them until long after. In the meantime we can do some processing and legwork, but there is a lot we can't do until they give us the information to work from. Delay also may come if the case involves alleged discrimination. If so, it has to go through the corporate equal employment opportunity office first before the case goes to either Step 3 or 4—in other words, the discrimination part of the case always gets priority. This may add a month or two of waiting. If the grievant goes first to the equal opportunity office and gets no satisfaction, he or she can continue to the board. If the grievant continues to include the discrimination complaint as part of the case, management and personnel can respond that the equal opportunity office investigated the complaint of discrimination and found no violation of policy." In all cases to date, the grievant has dropped the discrimination complaint after such investigation and pursued the case on other policy issues.

Review by Vice President

After the board votes, its recommendation goes to the senior vice president of human resources for a final determination. Lewis summarizes the board's decision, including its rationale, and forwards that information to the vice president. "He can, if he wants, reconvene the board and ask it to reconsider the case. Or, in my recommendation it is conceivable that I might urge him to reconvene the board because I am convinced that part of the process didn't appear fair. Neither of these two things has happened, however. When *might* the vice president reconvene the board? He might believe that important information did not come before the board in time, saying, 'I think you should take this into consideration.' He might feel that the board went off the track or didn't offer a suitable rationale. If, however, he simply disagrees with the board's judgment but feels that it reviewed all the facts carefully and reached a decision thoughtfully, he won't reconvene it."

Communication and Administration

From time to time cases heard by the board are written up for *Current,* a company publication for managers. An example is shown in Exhibit 4. In the write-up, names are removed and the situation is disguised, with the emphasis being placed on the basic elements of the case and its implications for managers. The aim of the write-up is to show why the Review Board acted as it did.

Information about a case does not, however, go into the grievant's or defending manager's personnel folder. In fact, the personnel manager is explicitly made responsible for seeing that no records or documentation of the board meeting appear in the files.

The responsibility for notifying the parties of the board's recommendation and the vice president's decision lies with Lewis as ombudsperson.

Glimpses into the Black Casebooks

The black casebooks that board members study and discuss are crucial to the success of the process. If they do not give the board a fair, objective, factual view of the case, the peer review system fails.

I was permitted to look through a number of black casebooks. I found them quite interesting. They are easier to read and assimilate than a trial transcript from the legal system since they are succinct and well organized. However, they are like a good trial transcript in that they are suspenseful. As I read them, my sentiments swung from one position to the opposite and back again. For a while at least, I often found it difficult to make up my mind on the merits. In one case I felt something of a "Roshomon effect"; the reality of what happened seemed different with each person's account.

If there are secrets to the success of the black casebooks, they are three. First, the Employee Advisory Resource counselors strive hard to avoid biasing the reader; they give equal play to both sides at the same time that they try to let something of the personalities of the main players shine through. Second, they organize the material into discrete sections. This helps enormously in understanding the case. Third, they try to bear in mind that the readers are busy people and want to get to the heart of the matter as soon as possible. So they try to boil the material down to essentials, yet include as much as is necessary to convey an accurate picture of what went on.

EXHIBIT 4
Company Write-up of Review Board Decision

Case Study No. 1-A Performance-Related Termination

A manager was terminated because, according to his management, he was unwilling to cooperate on a performance improvement plan. The employee acknowledged having performance difficulties and agreed to improve. However, when a second improvement plan was presented to him, without any feedback on the results of the first plan, he refused to sign it, or even to state his objections to it. Management felt it had no alternative but to terminate him.

The employee felt trapped—he didn't agree with the plan but believed that the object would cause him further problems with his management. There were conflicting reports about how effective the work-related communications were between the people involved. The manager said the subordinate received ample feedback, the subordinate said that he received mostly threats, intimidations and verbal abuse.

The Board found substantial disagreement between the line manager's negative assessment of the individual and functional management's satisfaction with his performance. Presented with these conflicting viewpoints, the Board decided in favor of the employee. The Board recommended that his request for reinstatement with back pay be granted, and that recommendation was supported by executive management. The Board believed his manager had used the policies and procedures as a weapon against the employee and not as a constructive means for improving performance. Their review of the records convinced them that management had made a premature decision to terminate and was using the performance improvement policy to carry it out.

Key Points to Remember:

- There was no record that the most critical performance-related communications took place.
- The nature of the working relationship between the individuals was an important part of the Board's consideration.
- Conflicting assessments by management suggested that the interpersonal problems may have been greater than the performance problems.
- When considering this issue within the context of specific policy application, the Board had to determine whether basic standards of fairness had been met.

The casebooks are not identified by the principals' names, which are never given, but by a serial number. In the descriptions that follow, I shall disguise the situations still further in order to add protection for the principals.

Case of the expedient executive.   The first section in this black casebook is called "Employee Position." It is about six pages long. A division manager in Memphis tells how he was investigated in 1986 for a potential conflict of interest. In March he received a memo stating that he was being downgraded and that his incentive compensation plan was being revised because, it was alleged, he had misappropriated corporate resources and violated company policy.

The division manager disputes his superiors not as much on the facts of their allegations as the appropriateness of their actions. What he did, he insists, was what any able, results-oriented manager would have done to cut red tape and get the work out; in fact, he maintains that many other managers like himself were shortcutting the rules in similar ways. Also, he criticizes the approach of the investigating team from headquarters, maintaining that their methods were biased and inflammatory. Moreover, he says, he is being disciplined seven years after the event; during that period, he got several pay raises and fine performance appraisals. He maintains that he has never—not even as of the date of his statement—been told clearly what rules he violated, that his character has been unfairly maligned, and that he has never had an opportunity to confront his accusers. He requests that the Review Board restore him to his former grade, make up his lost salary, and remove any documentation about the case from his personnel file.

The next section in the casebook is entitled "Management Position." (The sections are clearly marked by colored tabs so that it is easy to thumb back and forth.) In this section of about six pages the grievant's superiors state why they did what they did. He was a good manager and was promoted regularly after coming to Control Data in 1971, they note, but in 1985 they discovered evidence that he had misused corporate assets. They ordered an investigation by an audit group. The audit group found that while he did not act illegally, he acted outside the corporate policies and procedures clearly laid down. For instance, he used travel advance funds for more than travel, put income from the sale of some company equipment in a fund for his employees without reporting it to the company, and put subordinates to work on remodeling his garage at home. The disciplinary action, says management, was fair and just.

Included in the management position is a memorandum detailing the investigation. For instance, the memo states that the manager admitted to using false travel advance requests on about twelve occasions in order to obtain funds to cover other business expenses. In no case, however, does it appear that the grievant gained personally from his corner-cutting.

The next section is entitled "Personnel Statement." In this short section the personnel department states its own position on the case—its understanding of the division manager's position and senior management's, its belief that the latter was justified in disciplining the grievant, and other matters. The personnel group points out that it consulted with the grievant's seniors early on and encouraged them to set a positive example by downgrading him rather than condone what he did because other managers were doing it.

The next section consists of the grievant's responses to the statements by management, the attorney, and the personnel group. For example, he corrects several facts in the statements, such as the date when he was named branch manager in Memphis. He points out that no senior manager ever directed him to stop using subordinates' credit cards in the way he did. He says that the company equipment he sold was scrapped equipment for which there was no market or use. He insists that the employees who helped make improvements on his garage worked only in the lulls between service calls from customers, and that none of the work interfered with their sales efforts or with customer service.

In the next section, management responds to the grievant's rebuttals. It maintains that the proceeds from selling scrapped equipment should have been called revenue and turned over to the controller, not put in a "morale fund" for employees. This deviation from policy, writes the grievant's seniors, is a serious violation.

The next section is entitled "Supporting Documentation." Here the Employee

Advisory Resource collects for board members copies of letters and other documents that are relevant to the case. All names and positions mentioned in the documents are whited out so that the board can review the case objectively.

The final section of the casebook is a succinct memorandum addressed to the vice president for human resources from the ombudsperson. It draws on the deliberations at the board meeting. A kind of postmortem on the case, the memo informs the vice president of some crucial facts on which the board's opinion hinged, such as its conviction that the grievant gained nothing personally from his shortcuts. The memo also notes that there is a gap between the norms at headquarters in Minneapolis and norms in the field, with field personnel believing that certain practices are "expedient" that strike headquarters executives as "amoral."

The last section includes a memo from the vice president indicating that he had reviewed the case and concurred with the board's recommendation.

The ombudsperson concludes the memorandum by describing the "Dynamics of the Board." One member was a controller from the research department, the writer states; another was a professional services marketer; the third was a field manager from the computer systems group. In addition to other positions of the board members, a few other facts about each of them is given. The writer notes that all had opinions about the case as a result of their reading the casebook before the meeting; however, each seemed anxious to check his or her views with the opinions of other members.

The memorandum contains an account of the Review Board's meeting. The board voted unanimously to rescind the disciplinary action against the division manager, the ombudsperson reports. It thought the discipline was neither merited nor appropriate in view of the circumstances. The grievant didn't know what he was being disciplined for. Too much time had elapsed between the infractions and the disciplinary action. And so on. On one issue the board was divided about the conflicting arguments, but on others it was of one mind. In view of the grievant's fifteen years of good performance, the board believed, it would have been more appropriate to give him a written warning than demote him.

Of course, the last two sections described were not in the casebook when the board members got it but were added after the meeting to complete the account of the case. The earlier sections giving the arguments on both sides, rebuttals, the investigators' findings, personnel's observations and opinions, and supporting documents were in the casebooks that were delivered to the board members in advance of the meeting. In a thorough and objective manner these sections provide the board with the facts needed to reach a decision.

Two other cases.   A second case that I looked at concerns a technician in California who was discharged for poor attendance. The tabbed sections of the black casebook follow a similar pattern to that for the division manager's case, except that the postmortem by the ombudsperson is quite short. Two things are of special interest about this casebook:

First, in the employee's statement a little more of her personality comes through the verbiage. In the grievant's arguments and rebuttals, one gets a sense of the technician's attitude, and it is telling. For instance, in one place she states:

> I ask you—how many people are you willing to lose to protect such narrow-minded, unprofessional behavior [as that of the grievant's supervisor]? You won't find any current employees in his department to confirm my statement as they fear for their continued employment.

Again, at the end of her position statement the grievant says to the board, "You can choose to believe their story [i.e., management's] or you can choose the TRUTH."

I suspect that all three members of the board, while not knowing the grievant, got a feel for her personality from such statements as the foregoing. While advising her to make her final statement factual and objective, the ombudsperson nevertheless let her editorialize and color her statements just a little so that the board members could sense her attitudes. The board upheld the termination.

Second, in the summary in "Dynamics of the Board" where the members and their deliberations are briefly described, the ombudsperson offers some suggestions for improving the handling of such cases in the future. For instance, suggestions for proceeding to a better factual investigation are given.

A third notebook I looked at documents the case of a writer who was fired from her job in Houston for failures in performance. Although the facts of the case seem fairly straightforward, the notebook is a fat one—a good deal fatter than the two previously described. It includes more than one hundred pages, most of them single-spaced, most of them letters, memoranda, and other documents included, I suspect, at the grievant's insistence. I mention this because it underlines the company's desire to avoid a prescribed format as much as possible. Some grievants want to "throw everything" at the board; some do not. Some managers want to defend their actions in minute detail; others do not. The company lets the casebooks vary widely depending on preferences such as these. What it *does* insist on is succinct statements of each side's position, opportunities for rebuttal statements, and such supporting documents and other materials as it believes necessary for a fair and thorough understanding of the case.

Ends and Means

"When the review system was designed," says Robinson, "we wanted to force an improvement in the quality of basic employee relations decisions at all levels. The Review Board was to be the lever to bring about this change. It was to give us the thrust needed. Judging from the indications we have, it has been successful in that respect."

Robinson emphasizes, however, that the system has not forced managers to change their styles. In fact, he feels that it has opened the door to more individuality of managerial style. "For instance, some managers feel liberated to be tough and autocratic because the process is in place. What the process says is, 'You must be fair.' The manager can be autocratic, if that is his style, but he or she cannot be unfair. There is a big difference. In effect, the process empowers managers."

An article based on a Control Data presentation at the 1986 American Management Association Human Resource Conference quotes Gwen Lerner, an attorney in the corporate legal department:

> The review board system encourages management to think twice about arbitrary actions. Review boards help to ensure proper use of management discretion and fair treatment of employees. And they allow problems in policies and practices to be found and fixed quietly, without the cost and negative publicity of a prolonged legal battle.[4]

[4] Lucinda Lamont, "Control Data's Review Process," *Personnel*, February 1987, pp. 9–10.

How might the system deter lawsuits? Lerner cites this example:

> An attorney for an engineer sent us a demand letter threatening a lawsuit for Control Data's failure to issue a written warning to his client prior to termination. The company's legal services department investigated the charge, utilizing the review board's record.
>
> The review board had upheld the engineer's termination. Evidence showed that the engineer had received many verbal warnings following a written performance improvement plan for unexcused absences without notice. Control Data strongly defended termination in response to the engineer's attorney, and the claim was dropped.[5]

The inexpensiveness and speed of the Review Board make it far superior, in the minds of many employees, to one possible alternative, outside arbitration. The AMA article quotes Stathopoulos as follows:

> Many individuals involved in formalized arbitration are spending $300 to $600 a day for arbitrators. Also, although there are many arbitrators available, only the top 20 percent are considered objective, fair, and articulate. Because everyone is trying to do business with the best arbitrators, there are long delays and expensive charges. We feel the review board system is far superior to the arbitration system.
>
> And because of the review system, we don't have a lot of things simmering within the organizations: those dysfunctional kinds of unresolved problems and unresolved grievances that can cause growing animosity between employees and management. These, of course, affect performance of individuals and the entire organization.[6]

Even when grievants don't get what they want from the board, says Lewis, "they feel they have been heard by someone other than their own management. It makes the outcome easier to accept." Robinson cites the example of an employee who was fired for poor performance during a period of layoffs. Believing that the work force reduction was a ruse to get him fired, the employee took his case to the Review Board. He lost the decision. Though he didn't get what he wanted, says Robinson, the board's judgment enabled him to hear the rationale for termination "from a neutral corner, from people with no personal investment in the case. That's satisfying to many people."

The Review Board system has produced another effect that should be mentioned: it has strengthened the hand of the personnel department. By making that department a watchdog for employee rights, rather than a mere implementer of management policies, it has given it additional stature and power in the corporation.

[5] Ibid., p. 10.
[6] Ibid., p. 7.

Employee Equity and Commitment at Donnelly Corporation

Donnelly Corporation is one of the most remarkable companies in the United States—not so much for its products, quality control, or market share, although its achievements in production and marketing are great, as for the depth and breadth of employee commitment in the company. Since employee commitment is a difficult quality to measure, it is hard to compare the attitudes of Donnelly employees with the attitudes of employees elsewhere. It might be pointed out that the average absenteeism rate at Donnelly is 1.6 percent as compared to a national average of about 3 percent (excluding vacations), or that the turnover rate is 0.4 percent, far below the national average for manufacturing. However, such figures do not do justice to the company's work force. Perhaps the best way to characterize employee attitudes at Donnelly is to say that they came closer to the legendary qualities of

Author's Note: In April 1988, after this write-up was completed, Donnelly went public for the first time, raising $6.3 million to reduce long-term debt. The company, however, continued to be closely held by insiders.

Company: Donnelly Corporation		Products/Services: Auto mirrors, digital products, specialty coatings
Headquarters: Holland, Michigan		
		Dates of Interviews: May 21, 1986 (and July 1976)
Sales: $75 million (1987)	Number of Employees: 1,200	

commitment in leading Japanese concerns than do employee attitudes in any other U.S. organization that I know of.

For many years the main stimulus of this spirit was probably the chief executive, John Fenlon Donnelly, who died suddenly in June 1986. Some employees still remember, for instance, that when the firm was small, he made a point of remembering every employee's birthday. He toured the plant almost every day and talked to operators and supervisors. After the company grew, such personal gestures became impractical. However, John Donnelly found ways to *institutionalize* his concern for people. One of the most important of these ways is what company people call their "equity structure," referring not to a financial situation but to procedures and mechanisms for resolving individual complaints and concerns. Complaints are heard by informal work groups, a system of equity committees, and the Donnelly Committee. This process is the subject of this section.

It will become evident that the Donnelly approach is quite different from that of any other company described in this book. In part this stems from the fact that the company is smaller than the others. But there is another and more important reason. The concept and thinking behind Donnelly's approach are different. First, *representation* is a vital principle. The members of many of the groups that hear and resolve complaints are elected; those who are not elected owe their membership in the hearing group to job relationships or particular posts of responsibility. This representative feature of the system has characterized the company's approach since the beginning. Second, *authority* is delegated freely to these representatives even though the majority are nonmanagers. The groups that hear complaints have final authority to deal with the problems that come before them, subject to the complainant's right to appeal a decision. Their authority is not advisory; they do not make recommendations for top management approval. They have decision-making authority in every sense of the word, and their judgments are not subject to the review or approval of line management.

Robust Growth

First, where and how has Donnelly grown?

The company is privately owned, its stock is controlled by the Donnelly family, and a majority of the directors are family members. Since it began in 1905, the center of operations has been Holland, Michigan. A town of about fifty thousand people, Holland is located thirty miles west of Grand Rapids on Lake Michigan. Started by Dutch Calvinists in the mid-1800s, the town is dominated by people who believe in hard work and self-reliance. In recent decades the character of the town has changed somewhat as Chicano families from the Southwest and white families from the South have moved to Holland to get jobs.

For more than half a century, the dominant executive in the company was John F. Donnelly. He first became president in 1932 when his father died. He had intended to go into the Catholic priesthood, and he was in fact preparing to become a priest when the family and company called him. After helping the company to reorganize without his father, John Donnelly left to return to his first love, the seminary; his place was taken by a man from outside. However, the new president did not work out, so John Donnelly was called back. This time he stayed for good. (His interest in the church did not diminish, however; he stayed active in it and for several years held a leading post in the national Catholic lay organization.)

Under John Donnelly, the company prospered. Sales increased many times over. Production operations expanded from one plant to two, and from two to three. An extremely practical man in the sense that he knew financial and operating details backward and forward, he was also a scholar in that he read prodigiously, conversed readily about different philosophies of management, and had a probing, inquiring mind. Although idealistic, he was relentlessly thorough in decision making. A close observer once remarked: "He projects a very tough and demanding attitude in one-to-one situations. On technical issues he insists on detail and all the supporting data. Often, say around a major capital expenditure request, he gets highly involved in all the nitty-gritty of methods and processes. And he always follows up. Meetings usually start with John pulling out a file full of detailed comments from the last meeting."[1]

From the time he became president, John Donnelly felt dissatisfied with traditional approaches to organization. It was not until shortly after World War II, however, that he heard about the Scanlon Plan and began a conceptual as well as practical breakaway from industrial convention. According to one local legend, he learned about the Scanlon Plan by accident: a truck driver reported that he had made a delivery to the Herman Miller Company, furniture manufacturers in nearby Zeeland, and found officials there "handing out money" to employees. Following up on the report, John Donnelly learned that the other company had adopted the Scanlon Plan and was paying out bonuses to employees, their share in a profit increase.

It was in 1952, Donnelly said, that "an associate of Joseph Scanlon from the Massachusetts Institute of Technology—Carl Frost—introduced us to the principles of the Scanlon Plan. Scanlon believed that everybody in a company not only *could* be more productive but *wanted* to be."[2] Under Donnelly's leadership, the company began to develop relationships between work teams, suggestions, sales, and profits. As he saw the system begin to work, he became interested in ways to extend it and make it work more fully. For instance, he found it useful to involve equipment operators in the selection and design of equipment. Again, he devised a system of human "linking pins" to improve communication and coordination between work teams: each team had one influential member who was also a member of a team at the next higher production level. And when an operator came up with a suggestion that looked good to his or her work team, the team became empowered to put the idea into practice rather than leave the championing of the idea to a representative at a Scanlon Plan committee.

By the early 1960s, Donnelly was convinced that the principles of employee participation could be extended from shop and office operations to matters of discipline and equity. He began to think of the organization as having two sides—operations and governance. Operations consisted of the activities normally associated with a manufacturing company—procurement, production, research and development, marketing, and so forth. Governance consisted of personnel policy, grievances, pay, benefits, and so on. He felt that the same assumptions could be made about employee interest and competence on the governance side as had been made on the operations side.

The mechanism that he created for employee governance came to be called the

---

[1] L. E. Greiner and V. A. Faux, "Donnelly Mirrors, Inc.," Harvard Business School case no. 9-473-088 (1972).
[2] "Participative Management at Work," an interview with John F. Donnelly by David W. Ewing and Pamela M. Banks, *Harvard Business Review*, January–February 1977, p. 117.

Donnelly Committee. It still exists and is very important today. It no longer does the whole job by itself, however. It concerns itself mostly with plantwide issues, leaving the majority of formal grievances and many other matters to groups called "equity committees." Also important are informal ad hoc line groups. Before complaints become formal grievances for an equity committee, they are aired and often settled by these ad hoc groups.

This system of mechanisms and procedures for handling the day-to-day running of personnel matters is known at the company as the equity structure. The equity structure operates independently of line management. However, since it is managed by operators and supervisors, it is closely tied in with line operations, practically and philosophically. It is not a "staff" function, at least not in the sense that employee relations and human resources departments in most other companies are staff functions different from line operations.

The equity structure plays a strong and crucial role in the life of employees. It does not eliminate conflict and squabbles, nor does it try to. It does not have such saccharine aims as making the work force a "big happy family." But it comes as close to guaranteeing a fair resolution to disputes as any method that employees can think of, and it is a major factor—possibly *the* major factor—in creating a reputation for the company as a good place to work. According to William Lalley, head of personnel, the company doesn't need to advertise new job openings unless they are very specialized. "If we put a notice on Friday on the bulletin board that we'll be taking applications for a job, you will see a lot of cars sitting in the parking lot early Monday morning," he said. "When we ask applicants why they're interested in Donnelly, they often say because they know somebody who works here."

Today the company operates three nonunion plants in Holland and one union plant in Ireland. (Despite the fact that a half dozen unions represent workers in the plant near Dublin, that organization has an equity committee system somewhat like the home company's.) Donnelly makes a high percentage of the mirrors used on automobiles, modular molded assemblies for automobile windows, thin film coatings for glass, and several other products. Evidence of the company's fine track record in quality control is that it has a contract to make parts for Honda in Japan. Sales in the 1985–1986 fiscal year exceeded $100 million (as opposed to $15 million in 1972), and about twelve hundred people were employed in the United States along with about three hundred in Ireland (as opposed to total employment in 1972 of about four hundred).

Late in 1985, Dwane Baumgardner, president, described the company's business as follows:

> Donnelly is active in two major world markets. The first one is the world transportation market, for which we manufacture automotive mirrors, automotive windows, and heated windows for ships and trains. We have been producing automotive mirrors for over forty years. These include complete inside mirrors and flat and convex outside mirrors. Also, for about the last ten years, we have been producing modular rear quarter windows for the automotive market. About 80 percent of our world business is automotive oriented.
>
> The second major market we serve is the world information display market. Our products for that market all involve transparent conductive coatings on glass. We coat very thin glass that is used to fabricate flat panel displays, such as liquid crystal displays and electroluminescent displays in watches, calculators, computers, and automotive instrument panels.

About 20 percent of Donnelly's business involves customers outside the United States—in twenty-eight countries, both in Europe and Asia. Our goal is to increase this to about 40 percent over the next ten years.[3]

Informal Ad Hoc Hearings

If an employee has a grievance, his or her first step is, of course, to talk with the supervisor. If the grievant is dissatisfied with the supervisor's response, he or she must next contact the employee representative and see if the problem can be worked out. The employee representative is a person elected for two years by the work team that the employee belongs to. As we shall see later, the employee representative has several important jobs; this early role in handling grievances is but one of them.

If the problem still isn't resolved in a way that satisfies the grievant, he or she asks for an informal ad hoc hearing. (In the company this step is often referred to as "Step 3" or a "pre–equity committee" grievance.) Although this hearing is informal, there are a few musts. The grievant and the person whose action he or she is complaining about must be there, along with their equity representatives, and one or more other work associates for each. The person or persons who chair the equity committees of the grievant and grievee also must be there. If the grievant or grievee thinks still others will help, they can be asked to attend, too.

The purpose of the ad hoc hearing is to resolve disputes before they escalate and have to be handled more formally, and the procedure has succeeded in that purpose, reducing the number of formal grievances noticeably. If there is a secret to its success, it is probably the informality and spontaneity allowed. "Because it is un-structured," says Bernie Velthouse, a team leader of a production line in the convex bending group, "the grieving employee has a marvelous freedom. He can pound the table and shout. He can parade a few character witnesses. There aren't many rules."

No records are kept. The hearing can be scheduled for any time that is convenient for the people who must be there. If an official from personnel, the company president, or some other executive attends, he or she has no more rights than anyone else. The hearing can take place in any room that the conferees choose. Velthouse thinks it is easier to defuse a situation in this informal, spontaneous atmosphere than at later stages, when the lines become harder. He says, "A funny thing happens when I start writing up a complaint for an equity committee [the next stage]. I dig a trench for myself. A different mentality sets in. 'Here I am, buster,' I say, 'and I'm going to let you have it.' Step 3—the informal hearing—avoids this mentality."

An example of the kind of case that gets resolved at an ad hoc hearing occurred recently. Two plants were involved. A job opening occurred in the first plant, and an employee in the second plant whom I shall call "Pete" applied for it. Pete had worked for the company for twelve years and had a fine work record. He regarded the job as a step up. The foreman in the first plant, however, leaned to giving the job to a worker whom I shall called "Tim." Tim didn't have as much seniority as Pete had, but he was better acquainted with the kind of work that was involved, and the foreman liked him. Pete protested. "I've got more seniority than he does," he argued, "and company policy says that the job goes to the guy with the most seniority if he's qualified." Pete believed he was qualified. The foreman stood his ground. "That may be," he said, "but I'm under real pressure to get production out, I know Tim, and it'll take me less time to switch him into the new job."

[3]*Umtri Research Review,* September–December 1985, p. 46.

Neither could persuade the other, so Pete asked for an ad hoc hearing. He got his equity rep and a work associate to appear with him; so did the foreman. Each got the chairpersons of their equity committees to attend, too. Lalley, the personnel manager, joined the group. Behind closed doors, Pete and the foreman had it out, with an equity person chairing the meeting, focusing attention on the question and seeing that the discussion was orderly. The foreman argued that he had a tough production schedule to meet, and he felt his chances were better if he put Tim on the job. Pete kept reminding the group that he had more seniority than Tim, and he insisted that seniority was what counted under company policy. The policy manual said so. After some heavy discussion, the foreman capitulated. "Okay, I'll do that," he agreed. "I'll take the risk."

With the dispute over, the seven people returned to their work stations. It had been important to each of them to resolve the complaint then and there, if possible, without going to an equity committee for a formal hearing. They were glad they had succeeded.

The Equity Committee

If the complaining employee is dissatisfied with the decision of the ad hoc hearing, he or she can appeal to an equity committee. The procedure now becomes more formal. To begin with, the grievant must fill out a form (see Exhibit 1). In addition, the procedure is stricter, the hearing is usually longer, and except in a few cases, the decision is final.

There are five equity committees. They hear three or four cases a year, or one for every three to four hundred employees. Most of the cases come from the seven hundred fifty or so people who work in the plants; office workers and salespeople appeal occasionally to the equity committees, but not as often as plant people do.

As a rule, each work team in a business group (mirrors, modular systems, and diversified products) elects a representative to serve on the equity committee for the group. A team usually has between ten and thirty employees, and it is likely to elect a person who communicates well. The rep serves for two years and may be reelected, but for many employees one two-year term is enough. Half of every equity committee turns over every year.

A few top executives in the company have served on equity committees. More likely, however, they are seen at the meetings as a resource in case questions arise about the company or industry. "At first," said Kay Hubbard, a systems manager and author of several documents on Donnelly's equity structure, "we were a little worried that an executive sitting at the meeting would dominate the discussion. Fortunately, that hasn't happened. The members control it."

At a typical equity committee meeting, you will find twenty or thirty people. The majority of them will be the elected representatives. In addition you will see witnesses sitting along the sides of the conference room. If the question is the grievant's behavior during working hours, the witnesses may be people who saw her at a coffee break or in a car in the parking lot or who have worked close to her; if the question concerns stealing, they may be those who saw the grievant at a tool bin or heard him boasting or know his character well. Sometimes the witnesses will not be in the room but near it, asked to stay available on short notice if needed. The grievant and grievee are likely to appear only if asked to do so by the committee.

EXHIBIT 1
Complaint Form Used at Donnelly

Equity Procedure Complaint Form

Procedure (see policy book for complete procedure)

Goal—try to resolve the problem at earliest stage possible. If there is no resolution at that level, go on to the next.

1. Contact your supervisor. You may ask for a resource person to assist you.
2. Contact your equity committee representative to meet with you and the supervisor to resolve the problem. A third party resource may also be agreed upon.
3. A meeting of the pre–equity committee group (as defined in the equity procedure) should be arranged.
4. Fill out and submit a complaint form to your supervisor. Complaint may then be referred to the equity committee.
5. Equity committee decision may be appealed to the Donnelly committee under certain conditions.

Employee's Name _____ Date _____

Job/department/shift _____ Supervisor _____

Employee—What is your complaint? (Use additional sheet if necessary. Be specific, include dates and names.)

What, if anything, has been done so far about your complaint?

What do you think should be done?

_____   _____
Employee signature   Date

Supervisor—What are your comments about the complaint? (Use additional sheet if necessary. Be specific, include dates and names.)

What action do you recommend?

_____   _____
Supervisor signature   Date

It is up to the chairperson to run the meeting. That means seeing to it that the proceedings are fair and orderly, and that no one goes on a talking binge. Although records weren't kept at first, they are now because of the possibility that a dissatisfied grievant will go to the state labor board or the courts in hopes of getting a better decision. If that should happen—it has not so far—records of the testimony and decision in the equity committee hearing could become relevant.

"The reps receive training," said Lalley. He continued:

> They are trained for their role as equity representatives and in handling grievances. It is all done internally—no outside consultants. We use cases from our experience. We talk about the company's policies. The chairperson of the Donnelly Committee, some others, and myself put on the training sessions. Frequently we bring in former reps to help. A session may contain a discussion of a grievance that was brought up and how it was handled. There will be time to critique it. There may be some role playing in front of the group.
>
> The chairperson is given specific training. He or she may get training over a period of four or five weeks, such as getting the facts out on the table at the beginning of the meeting, using resources and witnesses, and what they should do when tempers start to get out of hand. Things like that.

A "Gray Area" Case

An equity committee may be able to decide a case in one session of a couple of hours. At other times, however, several sessions may be required, and each may last several hours. This was the case when an operator who had been fired protested his discharge to the equity committee for his business group.

The committee wanted to question the grievant in person, so he appeared one afternoon in March. About thirty people were in attendance in a conference room with a long table and chairs along the side. The grievant told the committee why he thought the firing was unfair and why he thought he could do a good job if reinstated. "We listened to a great deal of information," said John Duquette, a production superintendent who was on the equity committee.

> Not only was there a great deal of it, but it was conflicting. The fellow had three people testifying to the good quality of his work, and his supervisor had some people testifying that the quality was not so good. It was a very messy situation. The trouble was, different people had said different things to the grievant. They had given different signals along the way. The more we listened to what had been told to him, the more we wondered if he'd been treated fairly.
>
> The equity rep for the grievant was crucial. The rep remembered what was said at the different committee meetings, and that wasn't always consistent, either. Many times we asked the rep to identify the points in the testimony, what things were said to the grievant at different stages, and he did that for us. It had an important bearing on the outcome. We decided that the grievant should get his job back.

Duquette, who has served several times on equity committees and also has been a member of the Donnelly Committee at different times, remembers that the supervisor was angry about the decision. Duquette and others placated her. She wasn't wrong, they said, but neither was the grievant. It was a case of conflicting messages being sent to the grievant—not on purpose, but misleading him nonetheless.

Following Through

How do the equity committees implement their decisions? How do they make sure that their decisions are not paper decisions only, but translated into everyday operations?

If an equity committee makes a decision that changes policy or shifts the emphasis or direction of operations, it may decide to review what has happened in several months after the decision. The representatives themselves can report on developments from firsthand observation, for like the employees they represent, they spend most of their time in the plants, offices, and other buildings where the company operates.

If the decision of the equity committee involves personal relationships, as when someone is laid off or turned down on an application for promotion, following through depends on the supervisor in the case. In general, there appears to be almost unanimous opinion in the company that supervisors implement the decisions dutifully whether or not they like them. "The supervisor's peers have their eyes on him," said Velthouse, who in addition to running a production line has served several terms on equity committees and been a chairperson for one of those terms. "If a supervisor should take it in his head to try to disregard a decision of a committee, the peers tell him or her to watch out."

The test is whether employees who prevail against their supervisors are still around the company after a few years. For Donnelly, this test is no problem: one can walk through the facilities and see a number of employees who at one time or another in the past prevailed against their supervisors. One such employee is the grievant earlier described who was reinstated after receiving conflicting signals about his performance.

In an interview published in the *Harvard Business Review,* Paul Lubbers, then a tool and die maker and now manager of the tool room, commented on the aftermath of decisions favoring grievants. When we asked him if retaliation from supervisors was much of a problem, he explained: "I don't know of any cases of that. The supervisors know how the system works, and I don't think they are looking for retaliation. Besides, any employee is free to talk to the president when he comes through the plant, and they often do. If I've got a complaint, I could go out and mention it to him, even if I'm the lowest on the line. He'll sit down and talk with me or my team."[4]

Duquette believes that retaliation is insignificant because of the atmosphere and "culture" of the company. "When a supervisor loses," said Duquette, "the attitude of other people to him or her is usually, 'Nobody's right all the time.' The equity structure is a way of life here. There are no shortcuts, no ways around it, and everybody accepts that. In a sense, supervisors stand in awe of the equity system because it has been so fair and carries so much clout."

The Crucial Role of Reps

The representatives to the equity committees play a crucial role. For one thing, they account for the visibility of the committees more than any other single group; the chances are that more employees know about the system because of the actions of their reps than because of any other reason. For another, the reps try to take the

---

[4]"Participative Management at Work," p. 119.

viewpoint not alone of their constituents and not alone of top management or the owners but of the *company* as an ongoing enterprise. That is a tall order, but they work hard at it. "This company," said Hubbard, "is competing with companies it never dreamed of competing with in the old days. It is competing in more areas and wider areas. The reps try to come to grips with these realities in their meetings. They don't deal exclusively with complaints and problems." This may be one of the reasons why the committees are often considered to be rough on many grievants. "They can be a lot rougher about, say, absenteeism than their superiors would be, in my experience," said one close observer. "In fact, they sometimes apply too *much* peer pressure on some grievants."

During much of their service, reps find themselves having to burn the candle at both ends. The people I talked with estimate that serving on an equity committee takes an hour per day, on the average. There are no awards or extra pay for these employees' time. The reps are as accountable to their managers for getting the work out as anyone is. On top of that, they often find themselves in emotionally difficult situations, caught between conflicting factions or defending controversial situations. Many reps have, after serving their two-year terms, been only too glad to return to a normal employee status.

What is the appeal of this job? The reps find it challenging. It gives them looks at problems, people, and parts of the company they might otherwise have no knowledge of. Again and again the word *interesting* was used in the interviews. "It makes my job more interesting"; "it makes life more interesting for me."

However, the potential conflict with operations cannot be swept under the rug. There is always the danger that a rep's committee work (including not just the meetings but talking with constituents) will conflict with the needs of his or her boss who is under pressure to meet a production, clerical, or sales schedule. To minimize this conflict, reps and their committees take several steps. First, they make the meetings as regular as possible so that operating heads can anticipate them and plan around them. Second, a meeting will usually be scheduled at the beginning or end of a shift, not during it. Finally, a rep makes a point of going to his or her supervisor and requesting leave to attend the meeting; the rep does not say, "Oh, by the way, boss, I'll be at a meeting of the equity committee tomorrow at three-thirty."

Some years ago I talked with an employee in the molded products group named Jo Ann Czerkies. She described what it was like to represent a group of employees. She was talking then about the Donnelly Committee, because the equity committees had not come into existence yet, but if she were talking today she would be referring to the life of a representative to an equity committee. Czerkies said:

> I'll go around and inform my people about the issues that are on the agenda for a meeting. Sometimes I'll take a vote so I know exactly how they stand. But at the meeting, I may hear some new facts we didn't know beforehand. So I'll have to decide with that information how to vote. What I vote is not always agreeable to the people I represent, as I'll have to go back to them and explain the reasons why I voted as I did.[5]

Over the years, employees at Donnelly have put their thoughts about the rep's job and the responsibility of his or her constituents on the work team into informally prepared documents that are circulated in the plants and offices. These documents convey the spirit of the equity committee system better than anything in this chapter can, and so excerpts from them are reproduced in Exhibits 2 and 3.

[5] Ibid.

EXHIBIT 2
Excerpts from "The Perfect '10' Rep," July 1981

On a scale of 1 to 10, how would the perfect "10" Equity System representative act? This document is an attempt to capture most of these characteristics. . . .

II. *During the Meeting*

The individual rep can do much to assist during a meeting. The rep should look for ways to help the chairperson achieve meeting objectives, support other reps' self-images through attentiveness and acknowledgement of quality contribution and to work at understanding and being understood.

  A. Support meeting objectives, chairperson and other reps.
   1. Get quiet immediately when starting time arrives.
   2. Respond when questions are asked. Think through your answer/comment (engage mind before mouth) but do not wait to see what others will say. "I need more information" or "I'm not ready to vote yet" are useful responses.
   3. Listen attentively, carefully and openly to all discussion.
   4. Do not hold side conversations or create other distractions.
   5. Ask for classification on unclear issues. Stick to the subject.
   6. Be constructive and positive by signalling support for others. If a problem is noted, say, "I like that idea because . . . my concern is . . ." rather than "That won't work because. . . ."
   7. Signal approval or state your position pro or con when asked.
   8. As issues come to a head or near completion, the "10" rep proposes action as necessary.
  B. Taking notes: The prime responsibility is to listen and hear the discussion as it progresses. Note taking should not interfere with listening but should help the rep listen and retain information.
   1. Take notes on:
      a. Ideas the rep has if s/he must wait before expressing that idea.
      b. Important points made during discussion.
      c. Issue and rationale to share with the work team.
      d. Action the rep will take.
  C. Meeting minutes: Ask the committee secretary for wording to be used on key issues when needed. In this way, the rep can check his/her own information as well as a check on items to be put in the minutes.
  D. Make clear what assignments have been given to which rep.
  E. Give appropriate expressions of appreciation. . . .

III. *In communicating Equity decisions the rep:*

   1. Insures that the decision is communicated immediately and directly to the person with the complaint (include rationale).
   2. Rep carries decision and rationale back to the work team as a "hot" item, and supports the decision that was made.
   3. In the following weeks the rep works toward a comfortable "reentry" into work team for the person who filed the complaint.

EXHIBIT 3

Excerpt from "The Donnelly Equity Structure," July 1985[a]

VI. Employee Responsibility

. . . In order for the equity structure to function well, all employees must support it in a number of ways.

A. Make sure you understand the equity system at Donnelly; what it is, how it differs from and complements the work structure, what it means to you.

B. Elect someone as your representative who wants to represent you, who understands what is expected of a representative, and who will work hard for the good of your work team and the good of the company.

C. See that equity issues are brought up in your work team meetings and, if not resolved there, encourage your representatives to take them to the Equity Committee.

D. Help your representative communicate with your work team. Don't wait for him or her to come to you. Copies of all Committee meeting minutes are posted after each meeting on all bulletin boards. Check the bulletin board periodically, ask what happened at a Committee meeting, or tell your representative how you feel about an issue that the Committee is or will be processing.

E. Trust your representative—even when things may not go your way. Make it your responsibility to understand how and why decisions were made.

F. Accept the fact that your representative and his/her fellow Committee members are human and, from time to time, will make mistakes. Instead of undermining the system when this happens, help to shore it up with your support and commitment to correct inequities and, therefore, to grow as individuals and as an organization.

G. Finally, if you haven't already been one, tell your team you would like to be their representative. There is no quicker way to gain an understanding of and respect for the equity structure than to be a part of it.

---

[a]This document was written by Kay Hubbard.

At the Top, the Donnelly Committee

"The Donnelly Committee," explained Hubbard, chairperson of the committee, "deals with the same kinds of issues as the equity committees, but on a different scale. The equity committees decide issues affecting employees in the business and corporate groups they represent. The Donnelly Committee is different in that it makes equity decisions that affect everyone in the company." One exception to this general rule occurs when an equity committee cannot reach a decision and asks the Donnelly Committee to look at the problem. The kinds of issues that come before the Donnelly Committee include decisions on pay policies, issues involving holidays and fringe benefits, seniority policies, disciplinary rules, and possible exceptions to established personnel policies.

The committee has fifteen members. All but one of them are members of the equity committees; that one is the company president, who represents management. One member is elected by the supervisors, others are members ex officio because they are chairpeople of the equity committees, and eight are elected by the equity committees. Dwane Baumgardner, the president, goes to most of the meetings, which are held once a month during working hours. If he is out of town and cannot attend personally, he appoints vice president James Knister or another to take his place. Lalley, the personnel manager, also attends meetings regularly, though he is not a voting member.

Most Donnelly Committee members have been at the company longer than the average employee. There are some exceptions to this, however. For instance, one current member came to the company only three years ago.

An interesting feature of the committee is that unanimous agreement is required for a decision. If just one of the fifteen members refuses to go along with the proposed decision, it is blocked. This rule was adopted in 1975, and it is reviewed annually.

Immediately questions arise. Does the rule encourage "group think"? Does it put pressure on dissenters to knuckle under and go with the will of the majority? The committee has worried about such questions for a long time. Its feeling is that dissenters are not forced to go along. For one thing, committee members simply have seen no evidence of group think operating. For another, the unanimity rule does not mean that every committee member is in complete agreement with a proposal that passes, and will do everything possible to implement it. Rather, it means that every member feels able to live with the decision and defend it before other employees. It means that no member will try to undermine or defeat the decision when it goes into effect. For these reasons—one pragmatic and the other substantive—the unanimity rule stays in force.

The rule has some important things going for it. One is that no simple majority can "ram something down the throats" of the minority. This can be a very important value in a manufacturing enterprise like Donnelly Corporation. The reasons that majority rule makes sense in politics often do not apply to industry. Another reason was stated by John Donnelly. The unanimity rule means, he explained, that a committee member cannot pass the buck when he or she is questioned about the decision by other employees. If the committee passed the proposal, and the representative was at the meeting, he or she cannot avoid taking responsibility for it.

Hubbard, who was elected in May 1986 to her third two-year term as chairperson, says that one value of unanimous agreement is that "you don't tend to polarize." However, she adds, "the discussions can be lengthy. Sometimes we come back the next day to resume the talks. Sometimes we break into smaller groups to discuss the issue, or we do role playing to make certain we understand what the real issues are. After all that, we take a vote by a show of hands. If we don't have agreement, we continue to try for a compromise."

She finds the committee hard work, but exciting. "There are times when being chairperson of the Donnelly Committee is not fun," she was quoted as saying in the company news bulletin, "but overall it's probably the most meaningful thing that I've done at Donnelly." She began working in an entry-level position at the company in 1972.

Unordinary Actions

In my interviews, one Donnelly employee quoted a saying that many company people subscribe to: "The equity structure allows ordinary people to do quite unordinary things." The truth of that observation may be nowhere so much in evidence as on the Donnelly Committee. One day when I was interviewing, the committee adjourned and I saw some weary-looking members return to their workplaces. One of them explained to me that the group was trying to agree on a proposal for a pay raise for the forthcoming year, and having a hard time getting agreement. The person who had spoken most eloquently against the raise, I was told, was a machine operator who was worried about the difficulty it would create for company salespeople when they had to sell higher-priced products. The machine operator was not being altruistic but worrying about the future of the company. Another example given me was of a member who voted, in the depth of the Michigan recession in 1980, for a proposal that in effect would eliminate his job—because he found the logic from a company standpoint irrefutable.

However, no one in the company with whom I talked tried to paint an all-rosy picture of proceedings in the Donnelly Committee. It was emphasized to me over and over that some sessions get bogged down in acrimonious debate, others in trivia. One committee member described an agonizing case that came before the group and consumed a great deal of its time. The grievant was a man who had suffered a leg injury. Procuring a medical statement about his disability, he had gotten a change in jobs. Now he felt he could go back to his old job and wanted the medical disability removed from his personnel file. He requested an ad hoc hearing and got it, but was turned down; then he went to the equity committee and presented his case, and again got turned down. Now he was before the Donnelly Committee. One of the reasons he was eating up a lot of time was that he couldn't tell the committee clearly what he wanted. The same man had filed grievances before, again consuming a lot of people's time without seeming to have a good, clear cause.

And then there is always the problem of committee work peaking at the same time that there are hard deadlines to meet in the plant and offices. "Just when it seems that your plate is full—everything you can handle on your job—you get called by your committee chairperson," said one employee. "Can you attend a meeting on Thursday morning at eight-thirty? Things don't happen evenly, and you have to double up."

The following suggestions for committee members say something about the spirit with which meetings are approached:

> Try to be aware when discussion is reaching a point of diminishing returns. When it becomes clear that further processing will not resolve the issue, Committee members should feel free to request the opportunity for a "breather" to consult their teams or for a fresh start the next day when people may have better perspective on issues.
>
> Don't let the pressure in the meeting build to the breaking point. Especially if there is a small minority dissenting, a special effort should be made to separate and clarify the issues. The Committee should deal with one issue at a time. It might be helpful if the Committee could request that a few people speak for each side, using resources outside of the Committee, if necessary, in order to sharpen the issues and focus on the real concerns.
>
> Care should be taken not to allow win/lose situations to develop. Representatives should take the responsibility to provide help for their fellow members. It is perfectly legitimate to ask a silent representative what is going on inside his/her head.[6]

---

[6]"The Donnelly Equity Structure" (company document), pp. 14–15.

Making the System Work

Employees use a number of "tricks" to make the equity structure work effectively. For instance, committee leaders look for win-win solutions, if possible; that is, answers to a complaint or concern that will please both the grievant and the supervisor. Again, they try to keep the hearings from sounding adversarial, like a case in court. Also, they don't worry about ugly acts or practices coming to light. If a manager or supervisor somewhere is cutting corners or making unethical deals, the feeling is that it is better to know about it soon as a result of a complaint and hearing than to allow the practice to continue unchecked, as often happens in an authoritarian structure where devious managers can cover up and stonewall. As Hubbard put it, "You pay now or you pay later, and usually you are better off paying now."

However, the main reasons why the system works as well as it does are three:

First, the equity system has been in place at Donnelly for many years. Although the system is different today from what it was in the past because it keeps changing and evolving, the principle of fair hearings and the desire for equity are longstanding. The majority of employees in the company have known no other approach since joining the organization.

Second, the equity structure is compatible in philosophy with much of the work structure. Participative management is an element of many approaches used in production, and the kinds of attitudes it engenders are consistent with the philosophy of the committees. (Many of the work teams, for example, help select their own leaders.) They also set their production goals, plan how best to meet them, and set their own rates and standards. Many employees' pay is based on evaluations made by their peers.

Third, the most powerful man in Donnelly Corporation, John Donnelly, supported the equity structure enthusiastically. He supported not only the system as it evolved through the years but also participative management as a philosophy for manufacturing, product development, and leadership. Impatient with authoritarian, top-down approaches to management, he told a Harvard Business School casewriter in 1972: "As a businessman I can see that traditional management is just a damn inefficient way to operate. American industry is losing its trading position in the world because of its failure to allow people to be human or mature or adult in their work situations."[7]

He believed that respect and dignity could and should be everywhere in a company and were more important than any technique of operations:

> It's not the production line that's the evil, it's the thinking behind it. If the line makes it more convenient for someone to do his work, then it's not necessarily bad. But it's how he is treated that's important. If he wants to change the job—is there a way to do it? Or if he wants to do different work—can he? Every man should be master of his own destiny. I know that if I had to do a production job, I would sooner do a monotonous job in a place where I was respected than do a varied job where I was not respected. We've tried to provide a context for respect here.[8]

He believed that achievement should and can be democratized:

> A few people hog achievement. They say, in effect, "Look at the big success I am," and everyone else has to say, "Yes, you're a success, and I hope you can continue." But

[7]"Donnelly Mirrors, Inc.," p. 2.
[8]"Participative Management at Work," p. 127.

the others would like to be successes too. What we've got to do, I think, is make it possible for more people to share in the enjoyment of success, in the psychic increment of work. Like so many of the good things in life, this part of business success is divisible without being diminished. People can get satisfaction from a group effort as well as from individual effort. This is a good thing for business, because in an industrial organization it's group effort that counts. There's really no room for stars in an industrial organization. You need talented people, but they can't do it alone. They have to have help.[9]

He was convinced that the value of an idea had little to do with the rank or authority of its conceiver or promoter:

I don't see how a company can operate without levels of responsibility, because problems come in a variety of sizes, kinds, and complexities. But there has to be a free flow of information back and forth, and there has to be a consideration of ideas coming up from other areas. While there are levels of responsibility, it isn't compartmentalized. A manager would be doing a stupid thing to say, "Well, he's below me, so you can use my ideas instead of his." When you stress the very dogmatic type of position of authority, it's almost automatic for a man to say, "I'm above him, so my ideas are better than his." It's a matter of emphasis. When the chips are finally down, the top man has to see that a good decision is made. If the team can't do it, he has to make the decision. But if he relies on his position all the time for the quality of the decisions, the quality will suffer.[10]

These beliefs did not automatically create the equity structure, but they helped to provide a climate in which it could take root and flourish.

What About the Future?

In view of its past and present, one might think that the Donnelly Corporation's approach to justice and equity in the workplace has an excellent chance of survival. It probably has. However, there are some problems and possible stumbling blocks to deal with.

One problem is staffing. There are some tried-and-true veterans to keep the tradition going. For instance, Baumgardner is emotionally and intellectually committed to the equity structure. John Donnelly had prepared him for his role, and company operations have been able to continue without a hitch since the former CEO's unexpected death in June 1986. With Baumgardner in management are many other executives and supervisors who have been steeped in the equity system. Nevertheless, a number of company veterans have recently left or will leave soon, and while they will be replaced with care, it cannot be taken for granted that their successors will perpetuate the traditions and spirit of equity that have characterized the past four decades.

Consider a specific example. One Donnelly employee told me of an old-timer who got sick leave in order to have heart surgery performed. When he returned to his job, his boss, who happened to be a precocious young supervisor recently brought in from another company, told him that his pay would be reduced. The reason, explained the boss, was that the employee who had taken over the job temporarily

[9] Ibid., p. 124.
[10] Ibid., p. 127.

during the medical leave had showed that the old-timer hadn't been doing the job efficiently. When the supervisor sent the requisition for a reduced salary (all company employees are on salary) to the personnel office, an employee there questioned the change. "This doesn't seem right," she told the supervisor. "We don't do this sort of thing." The supervisor retorted, "This is the way I want to do it." When Lalley, the personnel director, returned from a trip and reviewed the controversy, he upheld the employee in personnel. "She's right," he told the supervisor. "We don't do it that way in this company."

In this case the issue was readily resolved, but it so happens that Lalley is one of the veterans who will soon retire. Will his successor support the company's traditions as surely and quickly as he did?

One team leader told me, "It's difficult to be a supervisor in this company." Supervisors can't order their subordinates around; they must be good listeners, good responders, good thinkers—in short, good leaders. As an illustration, the team leader told me about a supervisor hired from another company who had sent out a memo stating that trips to the bathroom would no longer be permissible except at certain times. When someone suggested that it would be better for him to tell the crew first that he was having such and such a problem and that he wanted their ideas on how to handle it, instead of sending out the order without consultation, he snapped, "I'm running this show." He was soon disillusioned of that notion, but the point is that this authoritarian concept of the manager's job is common in other companies, and often the concept comes in with a new manager, as it did in this case, despite the company's screening efforts.

When the new manager finds that a dictatorial style is not permissible in the organization, he may have a traumatic task trying to adjust. One experienced observer in the company estimates that the success rate for supervisors who come to Donnelly from other organizations, colleges, or business schools is only about 50 percent.

When talking to applicants for supervisory positions, the company conducts careful and thorough interviews. It investigates applicants' attitudes toward employees, authority, equity, and many other subjects. It tries to explain its philosophy clearly and carefully so that new supervisors will know that they are getting into. It feels uneasy about using tests because under Michigan law there has to be a proven correlation between test results and managerial performance, and such tests are hard to come by. For all its efforts, however, the company continues to find it difficult to recruit outsiders who are well matched to the style of supervision that is desired. This means that there will continue to be problems of consistency and quality control in supervision.

Finally, the future of the equity structure is tied to success in the work structure. Some observers feel that production and product development have not benefited from the bold innovativeness that has carried the equity structure to its current level. Be this as it may, there is no way the company's commitment to employees can keep evolving and developing unless the enterprise continues to flourish as a product developer, manufacturer, and marketer in one of the most competitive environments in the world. The prognosis looks good, but the task will be a demanding one.

The Guaranteed Fair Treatment Procedure at Federal Express

For the management and staff of Federal Express, the Guaranteed Fair Treatment Procedure (GFTP) is a lot of work. Rewarding, yes, but time-consuming and sometimes upsetting. For employees, however, the GFTP is a wonderful opportunity, and from the standpoint of employee relations philosophy, the GFTP is a marvelous tool. Just as the engineer says, "I want an alloy with such and such properties" or "I want a vehicle that can perform in such and such a way," the management of Federal Express has said, in effect, "We want a climate of mutual trust and respect between management and hourly employees. How can we get it?" The GFTP, in its opinion, is one of the most important means.

Management supports the procedure in every way it can—with money, with time, with communication, with constant monitoring. It feels that the company could not operate as it does without the GFTP. Perhaps the most striking show of top management support comes from the chief executive officer himself, Frederick W. Smith. He sits on the Appeals Board (one of two adjudicating groups in the GFTP) almost every Tuesday. The meetings may last for an hour or all day, depending on

Company: Federal Express		Products/Services: Small package air express
Headquarters: Memphis, Tennessee		
		Date of Interview: January 26–27, 1987
Sales: $2.61 billion (1987)	Number of Employees: 34,000	

the number and complexity of cases to consider. The board members say that Smith has the best attendance record of anyone in the group. He has sat regularly on the Appeals Board since the GFTP was started in 1981. (Two predecessor systems had been tried and discarded.)

Further evidence of the seriousness with which GFTP is managed is the reporting system. In a variety of ways management keeps informed about employee reactions to the procedure. In addition, it analyzes operations continually and keeps more numbers on what is going on than does any other company we know of with a similar procedure.

The return on such investments? Executives believe that the GFTP, used by 18.6 employees per thousand in 1986, is partly responsible for the absence of unions at Federal Express. They also believe that it has contributed to a higher and more uniform quality of management, and that it gives top executives a deep-down look at how policies are working and what changes in them, if any, might be useful.

Almost everyone has seen Federal Express trucks in the neighborhood, but the organization itself is not so well known. Here are a few facts relevant to the GFTP process:

- The company is by far the youngest company considered in this study. Smith started it in 1971 with a small band of people and a few secondhand planes. An ex–Vietnam War pilot, he flew a cargo plane himself now and then. (He conceived the notion of the company while a student at Yale in the 1960s. According to the legend, he described the concept in a paper for one course and got a C– on it.)
- Since 1971 it has been growing by leaps and bounds. The company is under the jurisdiction of the National Railway Labor Act, not the National Labor Relations Act, as many transportation companies are.
- The company owns about fourteen thousand five hundred trucks and other vehicles, about one hundred thirty planes, and sixteen satellite earth stations.
- To indicate the incredible volume of parcels that are flown in, sorted, and flown out again between the hours of 11:00 P.M. and 3:00 A.M. in the Memphis sorting center, one night in December 1986 about nine hundred seventeen thousand domestic parcels were processed along with more than ninety thousand packages for foreign countries.

Bird's-Eye View

The procedure has five components. The first three are not unusual. They consist of appeals to the supervisor, senior manager, and senior vice president of the division, in that order, with deadlines of seven days in each case for a decision to be given the complainant. Although undramatic, these steps are very important to the system, and about half of all complaints, in fact, are resolved at Step 2.

Components 4 and 5 are the unusual ones. Component 4 is a Board of Review. There are five members, selected in ways to be described later, and they generally include a couple of managers along with three peers of the complainant. The complainant, the defending manager, witnesses, and others also attend the hearings. Boards of Review are normally held within thirty days of the date when granted, and although, strictly speaking, their decisions can be overturned by the Appeals Board, this has never happened. The boards have great power and, for all practical purposes, decisive power.

The Appeals Board members are Smith; the chief operating officer, James L. Barksdale; and the senior vice president, personnel division, James A. Perkins. Charlie Hartness, who is managing director of human resources analysis/employee relations, usually sits in on these meetings, as do others from the employee relations department. The Appeals Board is the "supreme court" of the company; its decisions are final. Unlike the supreme courts in our legal system, however, it also has executive powers; that is, it can decide on policy changes, direct that they be carried out, and oversee the process.

For an outside observer, the numerology is somewhat confusing. When complainants are dissatisfied with the decisions they get at Step 3, they are more likely to go next to the Appeals Board than to a Board of Review. If the Appeals Board wants a "jury" to hear the case, it initiates a Board of Review. Sometimes a complaint goes directly to a Board of Review from the senior vice president's review, but in the majority of cases that happens only after the Appeals Board hearing.

The company makes no secret of the fact that often managers' decisions are reversed. This is considered normal and does not reflect badly on the managers concerned. In 1986, just over 61 percent of GFTP rulings upheld the managerial decisions that were contested.

In fiscal year 1986 ending on May 31, there were 37 Boards of Review cases and 209 Appeals Board cases. All in all, there were 726 GFTP cases that year. Close to half of them involved terminations, about one-fourth involved warning letters, and about one-seventh involved allegations of unfair treatment by a supervisor or manager. (The 340 termination cases, by the way, represented about two-fifths of the involuntary terminations recorded in 1986.)

Exhibit 1 summarizes usage of the GFTP from 1982 to 1986. Exhibits 2 and 3 categorize the usage and correlate it with employment.

Who are the most frequent users of the GFTP? Hourly paid employees and lower-level managers file the majority of complaints, but they are by no means the only users. From time to time a director will file a complaint (directors are at the third level of management at Federal Express), and once a vice president of the company filed one.

The GFTP does not stand alone as a voice for dissatisfied employees. For one thing, they have the "open door." An employee writes a question on a slip of paper and, normally within two weeks of sending it to the open door office, gets an answer. In regularly distributed surveys of employee opinion, the survey-feedback-action program, they can express their opinions about how good a job of managing the company is doing. An employee who believes that he or she has been discriminated against can turn to the EEO Department which is responsible for investigating such complaints and establishing and implementing the company's strong affirmative action efforts. In 1984, Professor Alan F. Westin of Columbia University reported, following a series of interviews, that Federal Express "is known for good affirmative action programs among the peer companies, EEO agency officials, and minority-rights leaders we interviewed."[1]

Perhaps most important of all, the company has a strong personnel division. As noted, the personnel head, Perkins, sits on the Appeals Board with the two top executives. The employee relations and other groups in personnel are very influential and enjoy a great deal of respect from the line.

Partly because it is ringed by strong support systems, the GFTP does not have to

[1] "The Guaranteed Fair Treatment Procedure at Federal Express Corporation: An In-Depth Profile" (New York: The Educational Fund for Individual Rights, February 1985; unpublished), p. 12.

EXHIBIT 1
Usage of GFTP

FY 82[a]

Step 1	8		Terminations	39
Step 2	24 (TR)		Warning Letters	9
Step 3	10 (1-OT; IR)		Selection Process	2
Step 4	1 (TR)		Unfair Treatment	6
Step 5	19 (2R; 18R)		Other	5
Totals	61 (1-OT; 4R; 18R)			

FY 83

Step 1	38 (3-OT; 2R)			Terminations	159
Step 2	160 (24-OT; 17R)	Total Employment	15,890	Warning Letters	73
Step 3	48 (3-OT; 8R)	GFTs per 100	2.08	Selection Process	39
Step 4	8 (3R)	employees		Unfair Treatment	36
Step 5	85 (2-OT; 7R; 88R)			Other	24
Totals	331 (32-OT; 34R; 88R)				

FY 84

Step 1	38 (7-OT)			Terminations	246
Step 2	295 (67-OT; 27R)	Total Employment	25,449	Warning Letters	164
Step 3	60 (5-OT; 3R; 38R)	GFTs per 100	2.05	Selection Process	66
Step 4	14 (2-OT; 5R)	employees		Unfair Treatment	31
Step 5	128 (6-OT; 12R; 118R)			Other	14
Totals	521 (85-OT; 41R; 148R)				

FY 85

Step 1	102 (11-OT; 1R)			Terminations	404
Step 2	417 (118-OT; 65R)	Total Employment	31,758	Warning Letters	285
Step 3	118 (15-OT; 2R; 18R)	GFTs per 100	2.78	Selection Process	95
Step 4	22 (2-OT; 11R)	employees		Unfair Treatment	43
Step 5	147 (9-OT; 18R; 218R)			Other	57
Totals	884 (153-OT; 86R; 228R)				

FY 86

Step 1	79 (20-OT; 1R)			Terminations	340
Step 2	339 (99-OT; 61R)	Total Employment	38,956	Warning Letters	181
Step 3	99 (6-OT; 10R; 88R)	GFTs per 100	1.86	Selection Process	60
Step 4	37 (3-OT; 22R)	employees		Unfair Treatment	107
Step 5	209 (6-OT; 12R; 298R)			Other	38
Totals	726 (134-OT; 106R; 378R)				

---

[a] Figures based on a partial year, March through May 1982.

Source: Federal Express.

EXHIBIT 2

Data on Rulings and Reasons for Filing

In fiscal year 1986, 61.6 percent of the GFTPs filed were upheld, and 38.4 percent were overturned. Most GFTPs filed that year were resolved at Step 2. Twenty-five percent reached the Appeals Board.

The Appeals Board rulings on the 181 cases it heard are shown below:

Upheld	109 (60.2%)
Overturned	43 (23.8%)
Boards of Review	29 (16.0%)

There were 37 Boards of Review in fiscal year 1986. Twenty-nine were initiated by the Appeals Board and eight were initiated at Step 3 by a senior vice president. The 37 Boards of Review resulted in the following:

Upheld	12 (32.4%)
Overturned	25 (67.5%)

In fiscal 1986, complainants' concerns were resolved as shown below:

Step 1	79 (10.9%)
Step 2	338 (46.8%)
Step 3	88 (12.2%)
Boards of Review	37 (5.1%)
Appeals Board	181 (25.0%)

The top ten GFTP reasons for which grievances were filed in fiscal year 1986 were

1. Three warning letters	89
2. Absenteeism/punctuality	55
3. Unfair selection process	54
4. Misconduct	46
5. Poor performance	36
6. Failure to report a vehicle accident	33
7. Miscellaneous	31
8. Unsatisfactory performance review	29
9. Unacceptable conduct	25
10. Alcohol abuse	22

Source: Gail Pinkney, "A Look at Fiscal Year 1986," Federal Express.

EXHIBIT 3
GFTPs versus Employment

GFTPs per thousand employees:	
1983	20.8
1984	20.5
1985	27.8
1986	18.6
Total number of GFTPs filed:	
1983	331
1984	521
1985	884
1986	726
Total employment at Federal Express:	
1983	16,000
1984	25,000
1985	32,000
1986	39,000

Source: Data presented by Gail Pinkney for Federal Express.

go begging for users. It has high visibility, and employees who feel that they have not been treated appropriately are usually quick to use it. In one sense, however, the system operates under a misnomer. Hartness explains as follows:

> We call it the "Guaranteed Fair Treatment Procedure," but fairness and justice are perceptual. If you get yours and I get mine, I call that fair. If you get yours and I don't get mine, I call it unfair. The only thing we can guarantee is that you get to go through the process consistent with the eligibility guidelines outlined in the policy.

Why This Approach?

In 1981, when GFTP was launched, Federal Express had several company models to use if it wanted to. For example, there was Bank of America's ombudsperson system, IBM's investigator system, and Polaroid's employees committee. Why did the company take the GFTP route instead?

Some executives feel that the GFTP appealed because it symbolized the desire for clear and open channels between hourly employees and top management. In Hartness's words, "It gives the CEO himself visibility. Employees like to know that they can go right up to Fred Smith if they need to."

Other executives feel that GFTP is a good fit with the kind of employee who works for the company. Barksdale puts it this way:

> Basically our system was designed for the courier, an hourly worker who hasn't been with us for a long time. Federal Express doesn't have a whole lot of culture and traditions—not yet. There hasn't been enough time. However, we have a clear situation. We're the largest nonunion transportation company in the country. Historically, the industry we're in has been unionized. Also, we know certain things about our

employees. Most of them are not motivated to go into management. They want to get paid well and treated fairly and then go home. They are suspicious of management bull. The GFTP is as good a process as we can have without inundating us with bureaucracy and words. It is believable in most cases, it is speedy and efficient, and it gives complainants their answers in writing.

Still other executives emphasize how GFTP fits the bill in a company of Federal Express's size and character. Perkins says:

> We studied IBM's Open Door and other grievance procedures at people-oriented companies. We wanted to institutionalize an employee's right of appeal without fear of retaliation. We had five to six hundred locations of Federal Express people in the United States, and we wanted to resolve as many cases as possible at lower levels of management, yet give complainants access to the upper levels at headquarters when they needed it. The GFTP seemed to meet those requirements. It might not always. If this company grows, say, to one hundred thousand employees, the Appeals Board might have many more cases, and that might put a great strain on the system. At the moment, however, it seems to meet the need. It is consistent with what we ask of employees. We're a service-oriented company, and we want the "discretionary effort" of employees—a helpful attitude, courtesy with customers, and so on. GFTP fits in with this need.

Procedures of Boards of Review

As far as I know, no other American company and no government unit in this country has an organization like Federal Express's Boards of Review, especially when the board is seen (as it should be) in relationship with the Appeals Board. I will describe it and the Appeals Board first as mechanisms. Since these descriptions may make a vibrant procedure seem dry, I will follow with a few examples and vignettes.

When?

Broadly speaking, if you are an employee with a complaint, you may be granted a Board of Review in two ways:

1. At Step 3 in the GFTP, the senior vice president may, at his or her discretion, initiate a Board of Review.
2. If the senior vice president does not grant the requested relief, you may go to the Appeals Board (Step 5), and that group may initiate a Board of Review. In 1986, as Exhibit 2 indicates, the majority of Boards of Review cases happened in this way.

Who?

Membership on the Boards of Review is not constant. It varies with each case. The procedure works in this way:

> As the complainant, you nominate six employees at the same job level as yours or higher. You send these names to the chairperson, and he or she chooses three persons from your list.
>
> From the current roster of company employees, the chairperson nominates four people. You select two from this list to serve.
>
> These five employees are the voting members of the Board of Review. The chairperson does not vote. The pro-employee tilt of the board does not concern top management; it feels that the record justified its approach.

From both lists of nominations, relatives, close friends, and others who may be biased for or against the complainant are excluded.

The chairperson is chosen by the senior vice president who initiated the Board of Review at Step 3 or by the Appeals Board. The chairperson is not in the complainant's chain of command.

In the beginning, management deliberately chose *not* to have a chairperson with voting power—especially tie-breaking voting power as in some tribunals set up by collective bargaining—because it felt that this would weigh the board too heavily toward management. The chair is responsible for guiding the proceedings, seeing that a decision is reached in good time, and writing the parties involved with the board's decision.

How?

The hearing is held in the city where you work. You appear with any witnesses you wish to bring, and so does the manager whose actions you object to. The hearings may last for a few hours or a full day. A write-up on the bare-bones facts of your case is made by someone on the employee relations staff, usually the person who has been following the case through previous steps. Board members get this write-up on the morning of the hearing.

During the session you will see no court reporter taking testimony and no tape recorder. Paola High, manager of employee relations, mentions several reasons for this absence. It makes employees nervous. It tends to give too much formality to a proceeding that management hopes will be informal and comfortable. And it is expensive. In many cases transcripts of a Board of Review proceedings could cost several thousand dollars.

If anyone present at the hearing wants notes, he or she is free to scribble. At the end of the session, however, all notes become the property of the employee relations division.

At the beginning of the hearing, you will hear the chairperson emphasize the importance of confidentiality. Board members will be asked to discuss the case only with each other and not with outsiders.

Scope of Decision

The board has great power. It may find for the complainant or for the manager. It may reduce a penalty or substitute one of its own choosing, for example, a warning for a dismissal. If it believes that the policy the manager acted on is unclear or that it has been carried out inconsistently, it may refuse to apply it. It may recommend to the Appeals Board or to some top executive that a policy be changed or rewritten, and this recommendation becomes binding on the company with the approval of the Appeals Board. As one example of the board's power, Westin mentions a case in which a senior manager was fired because she falsified the record of delivery for a Federal Express parcel. By a 5–0 vote the board overturned her dismissal but concluded that she was a poor senior manager and should be retrained for a first-level managerial job at another location.[2]

[2] Ibid., p. 45.

Training

Sometimes the employee relations staff will write up a case for training purposes. "Our objective," says High, "is to communicate a teaching experience, something that may help managers to manage." The staff also is developing some cases for chairpeople of future boards so that they can grasp some of the questions and problems that arise before actually serving. When such cases are written, they are disguised as necessary so that people involved will not be embarrassed.

Operation of the Appeals Board

The Appeals Board is different in many ways from the Boards of Review. It meets on Tuesday mornings, and on most Tuesdays in the year. Like the Boards of Review, it has both "judicial" and "legislative" powers, but its say is final in every sense. It may interview the complainant, defending manager, and witnesses if it wants to, but in the majority of cases it does not. It is unique in American industry because of the fact that the chief executive officer normally chairs the session. Even if the CEO did not attend the meetings, however, the board would be unusual.

I attended a meeting of the Appeals Board. Smith sat at the head of the table and Hartness at the opposite end, but the seating was informal and the atmosphere was friendly and relaxed. The conference room was between the offices of Smith and Barksdale. It was not large or imposing. The furnishings were pleasant, and there was a large window at one end. Barksdale and Perkins, the second and third voting members, were present; Linda Carter represented the employee relations group that had prepared write-ups of the cases to be considered, and she knew the backgrounds of the situations. Several times she filled members in on some aspect or question about the cases.

The meeting I attended took less than an hour. Many meetings run much longer—several hours or even all day. At the meeting I attended only two cases were discussed, but on many occasions a dozen or more cases are considered. In the words of Westin, it is a "source of wonder" that so much top executive time and attention go into Appeals Board hearings. I know of no other system that can match Federal Express's in this regard.

The board members came to the hearing prepared. The "Fact Sheet" on each case, prepared by the employee relations staff, had been given to them before the weekend, and so they had had time to mull over the situations. This proved to be an advantage, for Smith had simply to mention the case to be discussed, and the members were prepared to discuss it. The Fact Sheet for each case began with a page of hard data—the complainant's name, job title, station, employment history, reason for complaint, and so forth. The managers and staff people involved were listed along with their telephone numbers so that they could be called readily, if desired. Attached to this first page was a succinct write-up of the situation; in one case, this write-up consisted of two single-spaced typewritten pages; in the second, one such page. In each write-up the manager's position was given first—what management had done, why, and so forth. Then the employee's position was given. In one case there was a concluding paragraph of "Employee Relations Notes," which consisted of relevant information provided independently of the management and employee positions.

In the discussion of one case, which involved an accident to a Federal Express truck, the board members began wondering just how apparent the damage was—or should have been—to the driver. When Carter produced a Polaroid photograph of the truck, the question was answered. Later I asked Barksdale about this. He answered that it was an almost routine occurrence. "Employee relations have got so good at anticipating our questions," he said, "that we don't have to ask for more facts very often. We ask complainants to appear sometimes, but usually the reason is that we want a 'feel' for the person, not that we need more factual information."

In about 70–75 percent of the cases, on the average, the Appeals Board lands on the side of the manager or supervisor. "But when I tell this to managers," says Hartness, "they can't believe it. They think the reversal rate is much higher. Their *perception* is that the employee usually wins."

Many cases that go to the Appeals Board, however, do not get decided by it. As Exhibit 2 shows, it sends a fair number of cases (in 1986, about one in six) to the Boards of Review for a hearing on the facts. If an analogy to the legal system is desired, this is like an appellate court remanding a case to a trial court for a firsthand hearing of the evidence.

At the meeting I attended, both cases were decided in favor of the manager. In one, however, there was some lively discussion of whether the case should be sent to a Board of Review to hear the facts—the members decided against that—and of whether a company policy was understood well enough. "The policy seems clear enough," said Smith, "but I wonder if somehow we've failed to *communicate* it well enough." Although the consensus was that a good enough communication job had been done, each member took away the question, and it will doubtless be borne in mind if cases like this one come up again.

After an Appeals Board decision, the employee relations specialist who wrote the Fact Sheet generally writes the letter to the parties involved. The staff group is likely to discuss the points to be written before the specialist goes to the word processor, and I was interested in the attention the board itself gave to this matter. Barksdale offered Carter some opening words: "Dear ———: Because you failed to report an accident and falsified . . ." Smith asked her to be sure to attach a photocopy of a paragraph in the policy manual emphasizing the importance of reporting to company operations. Board members wanted to make sure, in other words, that the employee knew exactly why they decided as they did.

A Manager's First Board

A man whom I shall call "Tim" is a senior manager at Federal Express. His office is in Memphis. Also, he teaches in the Leadership Institute, where managers and supervisors are instructed in the arts of management. (The official title for such an instructor is "preceptor.") Not long ago Tim served on his first board of review. He remembers:

> I didn't know anything about the case until I got to the city where the board was to be held. They arranged for my plane ticket and told me where to go—a Marriott motel. I arrived there the night before the hearing, and at seven-thirty the next morning I was at the meeting room.
> It was an ordinary-size room. About fifteen by twenty, I'd say. Comfortable, pleasant. The hearing was in the city where the complainant worked, but they chose a Marriott rather than a conference room at the company station in order to get us away from the site and let us be objective. The complainants feel more at ease, you know, if they're on neutral ground.
> The chairman was there to meet me. There was also one employee relations rep [the

specialist who followed the case through the early steps], a personnel representative, and four other board members. I was one of two managers selected by the chairman. The other three were employees nominated by the complainant. They were couriers in the local station.

The chairman, who happened to be a managing director of ground operations, told us what our function was. Then he gave us packets containing facts and other documents concerning the case. He said he would give us time to mull the material over. We took half or three-quarters of an hour to do that. We kept mostly to ourselves. We didn't talk much. We just read and got a feeling for what the case was about.

It concerned a courier who had gotten three letters of warning and was terminated. It happened that the courier had been hurt one day at work. The doctor gave her a temporary leg brace and said she shouldn't stand for long periods. This was okay, but then she began not showing up for work, or failing to get to work on time. She missed a couple of days and was late several times. Her supervisor warned her once, then twice, all as required by policy. Finally, he gave her a third warning and then let her go. She contended that she was forced to work in a poor situation—that it wasn't her fault. The main question for us board members was whether management had done everything it could to make it possible for her to keep working in a service agent position.

After we had read through the information in our packets, the chairman asked the manager and complainant to come in. We sat at a rectangular table about fourteen feet long. The chairman sat at one end, we five board members sat along one side, the complainant sat at the end opposite the chair. The manager sat opposite us and to the left of the complainant, as did a personnel rep. A rep from employee relations also sat there.

The complainant stated her case, then called her witnesses. They waited outside the room until called. We on the board and the manager questioned her and the witnesses. Then the manager gave his side of the case and called his witnesses. We questioned them. Six witnesses in all. Then the manager and complainant gave their closing statements—several minutes for the complainant, a little longer for the manager. That done, they left.

By the time they left, it was mid-afternoon. We had had lunch served to us in another room. We deliberated for about three hours. We argued why the complainant should be allowed to stay on and why she shouldn't. Supper time came; we ate together. Finally we were ready to vote. We voted by secret ballot. The decision went for the manager. At seven-thirty we broke up and left.

I have thought about that day many times. For the three fellow couriers of the complainant it was a very emotional case. They had worked with her for several years. To vote that she was wrong was very hard, but at least one of them did that—maybe more than one. I remember one of them cried about having to decide the fate of a person he had worked with. They did what they felt was right. We all did. Nobody had to lecture us.

When we were deliberating we gave the chairman various recommendations. Management hadn't done everything right, we felt—it failed in several ways, not seriously, but enough to make us want to do something. We wanted to make sure, you see, that this situation wouldn't happen again. I believe those recommendations went into the letter that the chairman wrote.

Early the next morning I flew back to Memphis.[3]

A Chairperson's Story

A man whom I shall call "Jason" is managing director of a corporate department. His account of a Board of Review that he chaired follows:

---

[3] Various facts in this case are disguised to protect the identity of the employees involved.

As a managing director, I'm in a pool of managers who may be called on to chair Boards of Review. One day Linda Carter called me from employee relations to ask if I could chair a board. I said yes. I like the GFTP process. I think it's one of the best things Federal Express is doing. I felt honored to be asked to chair a Board and see the system work.

Linda sent me a training manual for chairpersons prepared by the employee relations group. It made my job a lot easier. It is in a three-ring binder. There is a section on every aspect of chairing a meeting, including sample letters to witnesses, the short rationales that board members are asked to supply when they vote by secret ballot [e.g., "the manager's action was too hasty," "the employee's honesty is beyond doubt"], and so on.

I called the complainant and got his list of six names of employees with equal or higher job classifications than he had. These were his nominations for the board. From that list I picked three to serve. At the same time I gave the complainant a list of four employees whom I was nominating and asked him to pick two. On my list were two managers and two nonmanagers. I felt that the complainant, being a nonmanager, would feel intimidated if all four of my nominations were managers. He picked one manager and one nonmanager. I don't know how much research he did on the four—how much checking around to find out about them. I did that on the list of nominations he gave me, however. I wanted to find out if any of them had been subjected to discipline in the past. I called the director for the area and asked if he knew anything about the six nominees. I also called the personnel rep there to ask if any of the six might be very biased, in his opinion.

When I called the complainant's nominees, two of them refused to serve because of bias—they said they couldn't be objective. But three others agreed readily to serve. I didn't need to convince any of these people about the importance of serving, but I did tell them I thought it was important to be able to render an unbiased opinion (for or against the complainant).

The five members we got for the hearing were, in my opinion, fair-minded. They may have had minor biases, of course, but I felt they were all open to the facts and sincerely wanted to discuss management's actions objectively.

Prior to going to Chicago, I reviewed all past disciplinary actions that employee relations gave me to review. I was encouraged not to make up my mind about who in this case was right and who was wrong. I had no vote, yet I could bias the proceedings by my attitude, so it was important to keep my mind open.

I notified all the witnesses about the date and place of the hearing. I helped them with their flight reservations. I made sure they notified their managers when they would be away. Under the rules, the complainant and manager had to give me a list of witnesses they wanted to call at least five days before the proceedings.

On the scheduled day we started at seven A.M. We met at a hotel in the area. The meeting room was big enough to hold fifteen or twenty people, if necessary. All through the day I did my best to keep things informal. I didn't want a courtroom atmosphere about the place. At lunch, for instance—it was served buffet-style near the conference room—the people mixed and chatted about sports and things. They didn't talk about the case.

I took the chair at the head of the table. The board members sat on the right-hand side as I faced them. The manager and the complainant sat on the left-hand side along with Linda Carter as personnel representative. The end of the table was where witnesses sat when they came in.

Both sides brought witnesses. The complainant brought more than the manager did. In my opinion, half of the complainant's witnesses gave testimony favoring management more than it favored the complainant. My impression was that the complainant hadn't briefed them very well. For instance, they seemed surprised by many of the questions that the board members asked. This was in contrast to a previous Board of

Review case where I had sat as a voting member. In that case, the witnesses seemed well prepared.

When the witnesses talked, I had to interrupt occasionally to get them back on the subject of our case. The complainant had been disciplined in a previous case, and they would talk about that situation. I had to remind them that we weren't talking about that case now.

I didn't worry a great deal about precedent, only about the merits of the case in front of us. I left it to the personnel rep to discuss previous cases when they were relevant. We also talked at some length about company policy and its implications.

After lunch and after the complainant, manager, and witnesses were gone, the board members argued about details in the testimony—what this witness had said, what that one meant, and so on. A statement by one of the complainant's peers, a witness called by the manager, was a key item. The board discussed it at length. There was also a long discussion about what was reasonable for the manager to ask the complainant. A state vehicle agency had notified the complainant about a certain action, but the complainant had been using several different addresses and had not received the notification. *Should* he have found it and read it?

It came time to vote. I instructed the board members about the mechanics of voting but no more. The ballots were secret. I counted them. Linda verified my count. The decision went for the complainant.

A Board of Review is allowed to recommend relief action. In this case, four months had gone by since the discharge. The board recommended that the complainant be awarded back pay from the date of termination and reinstatement in a different part of the company under a different boss.

I notified the complainant immediately, calling him in and giving him the result. I told the manager of the result, too. In telling them, I didn't talk about right and wrong, only that this was the outcome that in the view of the board seemed most reasonable.[4]

An Employee Goes to the Appeals Board

An employee whom I shall call "Jim," an hourly employee at the time, wanted a job in the ground support equipment group. When an opening was posted, he applied immediately. Unfortunately, his application was lost. He managed to get interviewed, however, but friends in the desired job area told him that already people were being hired off the street for the job.

He filed a GFTP complaint, stating that he thought he should get what he had applied for. He sent the complaint to his supervisor, as prescribed by Step 1 in the GFTP, and in a week he got his answer, which was no. Then he went to Step 2. Because of vacation schedules, it took about a month for him to get a reply (extensions of time were duly requested by the managers involved). Again he was rejected. He was short of the required credentials by one training course, he was told, and the job area couldn't take him, even though he promised to take the course, because he might fail the course. He went to Step 3, writing out his complaint by hand, telling management what he wanted and what he would promise to do, finding out from employee relations where to address the complaint. The company policy manual, which he was readily able to locate and read, told him what items of information his complaint should contain. After one week he got his answer, another no.

He decided to go to the Appeals Board. He asked an employee relations rep how to appeal. The rep wrote up his complaint and submitted it along with a file of information—reports on his appeals at Steps 1, 2 and 3, his performance reviews, a

[4] Ibid.

report on the investigation by employee relations, and so on. He did not appear personally before the board. In a short time the board replied by letter—a final no. If he would take the needed training course, said the board, he would qualify for the opening. Then the next time the job was posted in the desired area, he could apply again.

Naturally, he wasn't happy about this result. On the other hand, he felt he had had a useful experience. "I got the feeling it wasn't a win-or-lose matter or me-against-them. And whether you like the result or not, going through the process gets rid of your grudge."

Jim says that he checked around with other employees before filing a complaint in the GFTP procedure. He wondered if he had a fair chance to succeed. "I had written some nasty letters, including to Fred Smith, and I wondered if they would affect my case. Some people I consulted told me I shouldn't have worded the letters so strongly—not good for my future prospects here. As it turned out, the letters didn't seem to affect my case at all, and the case hasn't seemed to affect my prospects at the company. When I applied to become a manager, a packet of material about me was put together. No record of the GFTP was in that packet. I had several long individual interviews for the managerial job and a long interview by a panel of managers. The GFTP wasn't mentioned, nor were the letters."

Jim got the job and since late 1986 he has been a manager with more than twenty employees reporting to him.

The Sensitive Role of Employee Relations

One of several crucial gears in the working of the GFTP is the employee relations group. It reports to Hartness, and Hartness in turn reports to the personnel head Perkins. Employee relations not only keeps tabs on Boards of Review and Appeals Board proceedings but it also investigates cases, helps employees to present their appeals, and as we have seen, sits in on cases as a resource to the chairman and board members.

Employee relations, says High, learns of appeals to the Appeals Board or the Boards of Review by means of a report that all departments file weekly—the critical activities report, a confidential company document. Monitoring this stream of data, employee relations always knows in advance of cases that are coming up. "If an ER specialist has been working on the case, that person is assigned to go with it the rest of the way. If not, we assign a specialist to it. When we assign specialists, we do so on a rotating basis. We know which specialists are working on what because we have weekly meetings, and at these meetings everyone learns what everyone else is doing. We are not a large group." A weekly meeting in Memphis is likely to be attended by about nine people.

Usually one employee relations specialist stays with an appeal until it is finally resolved. The group discourages employees from shopping around among its members for advice because of the confusion caused. "John told me this, and Mary told me that—whom shall I believe?" Often an employee will seek the help of a certain specialist because of the latter's reputation in handling appeals.

Whether discussing a case with the complainant or the defending manager, employee relations specialists try to be very discreet. For instance, they avoid predictions. "When employee complainants come to us," says High, "we don't tell them what their chances of success in the GFTP are. The same with managers. If they come to us, we may offer suggestions on handling the problem but we don't tell them what the odds are." Even in a case of egregious behavior, the specialists will take this stance. "You never know," says High. "There may be some special circumstances that will influence the decision."

Although some managers may believe that employee relations specialists are advocates for complainants, the group itself does not see it that way. According to Carter, "We don't root for management *or* for the employee complainant in a case. One of our objectives, since we're a nonunion company, is to resolve personnel problems and continue to make a union unnecessary."

With stations all over the country and abroad, a great many of the complaints that employee relations gets involved in do not arise in Memphis. "When that happens, we may be able to get all the facts we need over the phone," explains High. "If necessary, though, we will go to the station and talk to people. When we investigate, we always contact the personnel rep at the station. (Every station has one.) That person knows about the complaint because one of his or her responsibilities is to help employees file GFTPs." The small staff in Memphis, in other words, is not on its own.

How do employee relations and top management evaluate the success of GFTP? Hartness explains that every year his department surveys its "customers" in the company, that is, employees who use or might use GFTP. These internal questionnaires show that employees have a good understanding of the system and that its credibility is very high.

Training

How are managers trained to regard and use the GFTP? The employee relations group has a good deal to say about this. After new managers go through the Leadership Institute, they can elect to take a one-day course on GFTP. This course contributes to the forty hours of course work they are required to take during the year. Attendance is never a problem because managers know that sooner or later they will have firsthand experience with a GFTP, and the course helps them on such practical questions as how to write a letter in response to a complaint as well as in understanding the basics of GFTP.

"We write cases for discussion drawn from past experience," says Carter. "The cases may be disguised to protect the people involved. In the class, managers try to decide the case as if they were on the Appeals Board. We discuss different ways of looking at the case as well as its lessons for managers. There usually are eighteen to twenty-three people in the class."

High adds, "The course helps managers accept GFTP and not to be afraid of it. They learn that it is not a disgrace to defend against a GFTP complaint. The course teaches them that employees have a right to use GFTP, in accordance with eligibility guidelines, whether management's decisions are right or wrong. Just because an employee questions your decision in a GFTP complaint doesn't mean that you're wrong, and if the decision goes against you, that doesn't mean you're a bad manager."

But while learning to recognize that GFTP is necessary and essential, many managers still see it as a pain in the neck. "I can empathize with them," says Hartness. "A couple of years ago I remember going through my morning mail on the desk one day and seeing that a GFTP complaint was being brought against me because of a selection decision that I had made. I remember thinking, 'Oh God, do I have to go through this?' And it was my own process! That GFTP happened to go all the way to the Appeals Board. So that the employee relations department could be kept out, to avoid bias, someone from another department did the investigation."

Costs and Benefits

After six years of operation, the GFTP has elicited very strong support at Federal Express among both managers and nonmanagers. It has its costs, but these appear to be eclipsed by its advantages.

Taking the cost side of the ledger first, one expense surely would be the time of top management. The three top executives who sit nearly every Tuesday at an Appeals Board have a great many things to do besides consider cases of unhappy couriers, applicants for promotion, and other employees, some of whom have weak cases but figure they have nothing to lose by trying.

A second cost is a certain amount of unhappiness and anxiety in management, especially middle and lower management. For these people, too, coping with a GFTP case brought by a subordinate takes valuable time that might be devoted to something else. In addition, a GFTP causes fingernail biting; it means that the supervisor's decision may get reversed, and no matter what is said to the contrary in training and company literature, that can be unpleasant and sometimes embarrassing.

Then there are the financial costs. These may be small for cases in Steps 1, 2, and 3, and sometimes even for Appeals Board cases. They can be absorbed in the employee relations budget and may not alter it much at all. Boards of Review cases, however, produce a more noticeable cost. When a board meets at a station, the expenses are paid by that station. These expenses consist of travel to and from the hearing for the chairperson, employee relations specialists, and board members who must fly in from other cities; the motel or hotel rooms; and meals. Generally the complainant's selections are from the area, so their expenses are nominal. The defending manager's selections, however, may come from anywhere, and so their travel bills may be high. (As noted, there are no transcription costs; if the participants want notes, they write them themselves.) As a result, a case that winds up before a Board of Review is likely to be a good deal more expensive than other GFTP cases.

Taking time and all other costs into consideration, the average GFTP is likely to cost in the neighborhood of $3,000 to $5,000. Compared to many other costs of running a sizable organization, says one executive, this expense is "peanuts."

As for the benefits and advantages mentioned by Federal Express people, they might be listed as follows:

1. *Averting unionization.* Barksdale observes, "If we can give employees a good grievance process in the company, they won't have to go outside to get it. If they feel that management listens to them, they won't want a labor union. GFTP is a formalized way of making sure that we listen to them."

2. *Fewer legal actions.* Among executives there is a general feeling that Federal Express contends with fewer lawsuits than it would have to contend with without GFTP. If the litigious employee claiming wrongful termination, discrimination, or some other cause went through GFTP before leaving the company, there should be a good file or paper trail for the legal department to use. Even if the employee did not go through GFTP, the paper trail is likely to be better as a result of managers' having gotten into the habit of documenting their talks with and observations of problem employees.

Much the same goes for state agencies enforcing equal employee opportunity laws. Personnel groups in the company brief state agencies on GFTP. When a Federal Express employee goes to such an agency, the state official is likely to ask, "Have you been through the Guaranteed Fair Treatment Procedure?" If the employee says no, the official is likely to say, "Why don't you do that?"

3. *Good employees.* Despite management's sincerest efforts to recruit, train, and coach good supervisors, supervision is not always perfect. Without the GFTP good employees may become the victims of supervisory oversight, whim, or some other fault. With GFTP, this is much less likely to happen.

4. *Pinpointing problem supervisors.* Cases filed in GFTP are a good way of detecting weaknesses in management. Barksdale says, "GFTP bubbles poor managers to the top just like a cork pops up in water. That wasn't our intention in creating the process, but it is a happy result of it."

5. *Good managers.* "At the same time," says Barksdale, "the process shows the strength of many managers. We probably see more cases of good managers in GFTP than of poor managers. I've been amazed again and again at the care and thoroughness of many managers' work."

6. *Reducing chronic grumbling.* At Federal Express, as almost everywhere, chronic malcontents create headaches for managers—but the problem appears to be less, not greater, because of GFTP. "GFTP stops them," says one executive. He thinks there may be three reasons. For one thing, an Appeals Board or a Board of Review is a *group* decision. No longer can the grumbler blame his or her troubles on one supervisor. Second, chronic grousers may be stymied by the effort required to write out a statement with specifics of how they were mistreated, what kind of relief they want, and so on. Third, the very existence of the GFTP tends to throttle malcontents. A supervisor or co-worker can say, "If you don't want to use the process, then please shut up."

In any case, there appear to be few cases of more than one GFTP brought by the same employee. "It's when you *don't* have a process like this," says Barksdale, "that the sorehead gets to be the team leader."

7. *Identifying policy problems.* Many executives feel that the GFTP has put the spotlight on occasional instances of poor policy implementation. Sometimes this is the fault of the organization, sometimes of the policy. "I would say," says Barksdale, "that many of the serious changes in policy we have made in the past three years have been the result of the GFTP process. It helps us to keep policies evergreen. In a procedure-oriented business like this one, that is important."

Hartness gives an example. "A change we made in the vehicle accident policy came about because of Appeals Board and Boards of Review cases. A pattern appeared. An accident would not be reported because it seemed minor and the driver of the other car seemed unconcerned, but the next day the other driver would come to us with a tale of woe. So we changed the policy to what it is now: if *any* contact or collision with another car happens, it should be reported by our driver. We call it not an 'accident' but an 'occurrence.'"

8. *Executive time.* Earlier it was noted that GFTP takes the time of executives. It also may be a great time-saver. Barksdale reports: "A fellow walked in here once. He wanted an appointment to talk for an hour about a complaint he had. He was very upset. I told him, 'We've got a process for complaints. If you file your complaint in GFTP, you'll get a hearing. But if you sit here and take an hour talking to me, I don't know how fair and impartial I can be.' He said, 'You're right.' He filed a GFTP, and it turned out that he was right. Now, that was a lot better way than taking an hour of my time complaining that he was a victim of unfairness."

9. *Morale.* "Lots of the advantages of GFTP that you hear mentioned are bonuses, by-products," says Hartness. "Its principal value is that it maintains a perception among our employees that there is a way of dealing with a perceived injustice. The

employee thinks, 'I know exactly what to do when I think I've been treated unfairly. I don't even need to ask anybody, if I don't want to. I can read what to do on a plaque.' " (In all buildings there are wall plaques describing how to use the GFTP.)

Looking Ahead

GFTP is not the first grievance procedure created for Federal Express employees, and the GFTP we know today is not the last word. Management is toying with several ideas for improvement. For one thing, there is the possibility that some day the Appeals Board will be broadened to include two senior vice presidents on a rotating basis. This would make it a five-member board, and the advantage would be that more executives could get a firsthand feel of the problems and complaints brought up and of their possible implications for policy and administration.

Another modification being considered is compression of the time spans allowed for handling complaints. "If everything is done according to the book," says Hartness, "it will take seven or eight weeks to go completely through the process, excluding a Board of Review, which may take another four weeks. We think this is too long, especially for someone who has been terminated. However, I don't think we should speed up the process at the expense of quality, especially, adequate investigations. If we're going to compress the time allowances, we've got to find a way to do so without affecting quality, and if we can't, I think we should leave the process the way it is. In a sense, we're driven by our own standards. If we can deliver a package from Boston to San Francisco by ten-thirty A.M. the following day, why can't we process complaints faster?"

The company doesn't look the other way when a manager sits overly long on a GFTP complaint. The division director or vice president is likely to call him if he or she procrastinates. The control making this possible is a weekly report showing every GFTP case in the system. It tells the division head what complaints come from people in his or her organization and whether they are ahead of or behind schedule.

In the meantime, the GFTP continues to serve a vital purpose of the company. Just as, say, an architect designs spaciousness into a building by using windows and skylights, so the architects of Federal Express have designed an employee attitude into the organization by creating the GFTP. Perkins put it this way:

> We once had a management consultant, Charles Hughes—a dynamite person—who convinced us of the control we had over our organization and its attitudes. He said that people are going to adopt some form of behavior that will ensure that their basic needs are met. For instance, suppose we didn't have the GFTP. Then there would be no way to have complaints reviewed. Your boss could walk into your office and say, "You're fired." The need for a means to have your complaint reviewed is a basic need because no one wants to be subjected to capricious action. So employees are going to do something about that. For example, they might bring in a third party to help them—a union.
>
> We control the kind and type of employee relations that we have at Federal Express. If we have a poor environment, that's our fault as managers, not the fault of employees. It's our fault because we haven't put up the proper safeguards and procedures. We're not treating them with respect, or we're not training them properly, or something else. When you look at the situations where people are dissatisfied or discontented or unproductive, you always find that is the case. Here we try to tell people what to expect. We try to treat them fairly and with dignity and respect. The GFTP is one of the ways we do that.

How the Grievance Review Panel Works at a General Electric Plant

The grievance review procedure at General Electric's range plant in Columbia, Maryland, may have the distinction of being the most-cloned procedure for resolving complaints in U.S. manufacturing—and possibly in all industry. The heart of the procedure is the grievance review panel, consisting of two salaried employees and three hourly paid employees. The panel operates with relatively simple rules, it has high visibility in the plant, and, in the opinion of the plant's nine hundred to one thousand employees, it works fairly. Generally considered to be the brainchild of the plant's savvy and soft-spoken manager, Joe Carando, the panel decided its first case in October 1982 and has decided about seventy-five cases since then. The usage ratio is about one case per year per fifty employees. The membership rotates as far as the hourly employees are concerned, but the two managerial employees do not rotate. The waiting period for grievants may be less than for any other formal hearing system in industry.

The range plant is in an enormous one-story building in Appliance Park, which is a huge space on the east side of a city that was planned on drawing boards and rose

Company: General Electric Company	Products/Services: Electric ranges
Headquarters: Columbia, Maryland, plant	
	Date of Interview: October 9, 1986
Sales: N/A	Number of Employees: 950	

from open fields in the late 1960s. When originally conceived, the plant manufactured microwave ovens as well as electric ranges; also, it employed twice as many people as it does today. But the production of microwave ovens was sourced out, leaving ranges as the sole product. With the exception of maintenance and tooling, few operators work at so-called skilled jobs. However, because of imaginative efforts to reduce costs and improve efficiency by involving operators in the running of operations, the plant may be on the verge of using employees' *minds* more than numerous U.S. manufacturing plants do. The grievance review panel, as we shall see, is part of a bold employee relations philosophy that manifests itself in a variety of ways.

Birth of a New Attitude

For years after starting operations in 1971, the Columbia plant used a fairly conventional approach to complaint handling; that is, employees could take their complaints up the line, beginning with their supervisors, then to the supervisors' bosses, then to the bosses' bosses, and so forth. Apparently most employees didn't regard the procedure highly, and that opinion appears to have been shared by at least some managers. There was employee discontent in the plant, according to John D. Coombe, an outside attorney who wrote about the plant's hearing system.[1] He says there were nine attempts by unions to organize the work force during the first eight years, and six of these led to elections conducted by the National Labor Relations Board.

"People stopped using the grievance procedure," says Mike Plienis, a supervisor in assembly operations for seven years and now a supervisor in the fabrication shop (he began in August 1971 as an hourly employee). "Lots of attitude problems developed. People would start a grievance and just give it up as a waste of effort. The attitude problems were fairly general and showed up in different ways. Molehills got turned into mountains, things went wrong that shouldn't have, quality wasn't as good as it could be, management and the work force didn't get along, the 'them-uns' and 'we-uns' attitude grew, absenteeism was too high. It was too easy for somebody to wake up in the morning and say, 'Gee, I don't feel like putting up with that today, I think I'll take off.' People didn't intentionally hurt you—but they didn't do anything intentionally to help you, either."

"We asked for a new procedure," says Carando.

> We wanted to get wider involvement. The original procedure had no hourly people involved at all, only salaried people, and I suggested that we get hourly people into it. Harvey Caras, then manager of relations with hourly paid employees, came up with a plan that basically is what we have now. One of the questions was the makeup of the panel. How many should be on it? Who? It took us a long time to decide that. If we had only one hourly employee, we figured that person would be seen as a token member by the work force. If we had two hourly people, we faced the frightening prospect of 2–2 splits. So we decided on three hourly employees plus two managers.
>
> Of course, many managers who heard about this were skeptical. "How can you let yourselves be outnumbered and keep your right to run the business?" they asked. We answered, "If we can't convince at least one hourly employee, maybe we're wrong." In other words, if the two managers see a case clearly in such and such a light, they should be able to persuade at least one other panelist and make it a 3–2 majority.

[1] "Peer Review: The Emerging Successful Application," *Employee Relations Law Journal*, Spring 1984, p. 663.

According to Caras, questions about how the panel would work were discussed for many months at training classes. When he, Carando, and other managers thought they had a good plan for the procedure worked out, they scheduled a review of it in the plant auditorium. Many people attended on their own time. Carando asked for volunteers for a program to train panelists; thirty-nine employees said they would like to attend. Each took, on his or her own time, an eight-hour series of classes. Over the years the training has been lengthened and improved, and today, according to G. R. Richardson, manager of employee and community relations, there also are many more employees available to serve on the panel—close to forty.

Management at the plant is pleased with the results of the grievance procedure. It believes it contributes to a good industrial relations climate. Management also feels that the procedure has helped to reduce the threat of unionization. Executives' strong feelings about the union danger were captured several years ago in an article by Caras and Robert T. Boisseau, Richardson's predecessor as manager of employee and community relations:

> As the second largest nonunion plant in GE, located in the highly unionized Baltimore area, we had been a constant target of union organizers throughout the 1970s.
> The production and quality of electric ranges and microwave ovens, as well as good human relations programs, were severely hampered by extensive time devoted to union campaigns. . . . Our winning majorities were constantly under 60 percent.
> More importantly, each election divided our people into pro- and anti-union camps, causing major morale problems from which it took months to recover.[2]

Boisseau and Caras wrote that they both were personally familiar with the ineffectiveness of the grievance procedure as sponsored by many unions. They added:

> It was hard at first to believe that it could be attractive to our people. But we also knew that in the hands of a skillful union salesman, the union's grievance procedure could certainly be made to sound like something far greater than it truly is, with its representation, documentation and arbitration.[3]

Yet they saw the grievance procedure as a strong selling point for union organizers:

> With much-publicized give-backs and wage freezes, it is very difficult for union organizers today to promise nonunion employees a big pay raise if they join the union. Likewise, with union companies closing down and laying off, it is not likely that nonunion people will accept promises of job security as something a union could honestly deliver.
> So what then can the union really guarantee nonunion people? What can they do differently? Formal grievance procedures are one of their few remaining lures.[4]

If there was one secret in the plant's approach to a new and better grievance procedure, it was put in seven words by Coombe. The plant manager, he said, was "willing to share final decision-making authority." This important concession runs

[2] "A Radical Experiment Cuts Deep into the Attractiveness of Unions," *Personnel Administrator,* October 1983, p. 76.
[3] Ibid., p. 77.
[4] Ibid., p. 76.

against the grain of many executives' thinking in the United States, but with Carando willing to make it—and not only willing to make it but able to live with it and ensure that the rest of management complied—the new procedure was off to a good start.

Before a Complaint Becomes a Grievance

The success of the grievance review panel is due partly to several steps and forces that are not, strictly speaking, part of the panel procedure itself but elements of the *system*.

Steps 1 and 2

As explained by Richardson, employees with complaints do not begin with a formal grievance to the panel. They begin by writing out a grievance—with the help of an employee relations specialist, if the employee desires—and depositing it in grievance boxes located throughout the plant. Exhibit 1 shows the one-page form; yellow and pink copies are attached to the white copy on top. Copies of the form are easily available in boxes about the plant and in the employee relations specialist's office.

Within three working days complainants are promised a meeting with the unit manager, and within two working days after that, they are promised the unit manager's answer. If these deadlines are insufficient because of complexities or other problems, they can be extended by mutual agreement.

If grievants are dissatisfied with the unit manager's answer, Richardson explains, they can go to Step 2, that is, submission of the complaint form to the subsection manager. That manager is given five working days to meet with a complainant, and five working days after that to give the complainant an answer.

If employees are still dissatisfied, they can go to Step 3, that is, they can either submit the grievance form to the operations manager or to the grievance review panel. In either case, ten working days are allowed for a meeting, ten more for an answer.

These terms are spelled out on the back of the grievance form where no one can miss them. That is one distinctive aspect of the grievance procedure. The other is the short deadlines for meetings and answers. An important assumption is that complainants should not have to hang by their thumbs for long waiting for their day in court and "judgment." The company feels that it owes them speedy replies.

Training

"The training program is perhaps the most creative and important aspect of the GE system," wrote Coombe. Employees who have taken the eight-hour course (on their own time) say that they are trained in the nature of factual evidence and interpreting it (especially oral testimony); they are versed in the legal and ethical aspects of handling grievances; they are given practice in careful listening skills; and they engage in role playing, for example, reacting to a person describing a grievance.

In counseling employees who have taken the course and become available to serve as panelists, Carando says that he makes no bones about the fact that some cases will be very tough. Discharge cases are the leading example. "I tell them some of these will test them," Carando states. "I remind them of the job they have pledged to do, which is, first, answer the question, Did the employee break the rules? and second, answer the question, Did the supervisor's punishment 'fit the crime'?"

EXHIBIT 1
Grievance Form

GENERAL ⟨GE⟩ ELECTRIC

Grievance No. _____

Appliance Park–East
Columbia, Maryland

NAME _____	BUILDING _____
SUPERVISOR _____	SHIFT _____ PAY NO. _____

THE PROBLEM IS:

THIS IS WHAT SHOULD BE DONE:

_____   _____
Grievant Signature   Date

I am not satisfied with the decision and wish to appeal to:

☐ STEP 2

_____   _____
Grievant Signature   Date

☐ STEP 3 (Choose one)

    ☐ Operations Manager

_____   _____
Grievant Signature   Date

    ☐ Grievance Review Panel

_____   _____
Grievant Signature   Date

White - Employee Relations
Yellow - Employee
Pink - Reference File

The Employee Relations Specialist

The employee relations specialist plays a crucial role in the success of the grievance procedure and in employee relations in general. The current employee relations specialist, LeRoy Brown, describes himself as "a salaried guy with two hats." He is a part of the management team; at the same time, he represents all employees in the plant on grievances and is an employee advocate for whoever wants his help. He handles nine or ten complaints a month that are resolved without going to the grievance review panel. In the case of grievances that do reach the panel, he may help the employee in framing the complaint; if the employee desires, he will also help present the complaint to the five panelists.

Brown also counsels supervisors. Supervisors who are thinking of taking action against subordinates may run their ideas past him first. "What do you think?" the supervisor asks after presenting the problem. As a result, says Brown, his job can be tough and tricky. "I have to have the confidence of supervisors. I also have to have the trust of hourly people, their faith that I'm really going to represent them fairly."

Brown succeeds in this difficult role by combining candor, tact, and a strong emphasis on the facts of a situation.

> When employees come to me with complaints, I coach them on how to present them. I may get them to practice what they're going to say and how they're going to say it. Sometimes I suggest that the problem be resolved without going further. I'll go to the foreman and say, "Hey, if we're going to take this to the grievance panel, they're going to beat your socks off. You didn't give this guy a proper warning, or follow the procedure." The foreman may see things differently then and agree to change his or her decision. Sitting on that grievance panel are three employees, the plant manager, and the employee relations manager. He or she wants to make sure that the action taken is proper and will stand the test of the panel.

Brown may advise complainants about weaknesses in their position, too. "Occasionally I'll see a lot of errors in a person's case and tell him, 'They'll tear this apart.' We had a case once where a setup man didn't set a die properly and was removed from the job. He had made the same error on previous occasions. In contesting his removal he couldn't remember setting up that particular die. I asked him, 'You're going to walk into that panel and tell them that you don't remember that setup? How's that going to look?' But if the employee doesn't agree with me, I don't force him. The setup operator didn't, and so I let him do it his way."

Brown emphasizes that he never plays the role of judge. For instance, he doesn't tell the panel that a complainant is in his opinion lying. He makes the opening statement to the panel and then turns the rest over to the complainant. "The five panelists take total control then," he says. "Whom they want to talk to, what they want to investigate—that's their decision. I'm completely out of it and don't get involved again unless the panel requests more information."

The Life of a Panelist

Because of Steps 1 and 2, the cases that go to the panel tend to be those best decided by a jury system; that is, they involve applications or interpretations of policy on which reasonable people may differ.

The composition of the panel, as noted, is three hourly paid employees and two salaried employees. The latter are Carando and Richardson; the former are drawn at random by the complainant. Brown explains the drawing as follows:

> The names of all people who have qualified for the panel are in a big box in my office. When the complainant comes in, we shake the box up, and I let him or her reach in and pull out four names. We spread them out on a table and look at them. The complainant puts back in the box one of the names—the person he or she feels least comfortable with. The three names left are those who will sit at the hearing.

At present, all panelists have served six or more years at the plant. This length of service is not, however, a formal requirement. The hearings take place during working hours.

Is Carando's presence on the panel intimidating to the hourly employees? None of the five panelists with whom I talked feel they were ever under pressure because the plant manager sat at the table with them. Nor does there appear to be any evidence that his presence has ever influenced voting. No voting records are kept, but the panelists' impression, at least, is that one or more of them probably have voted differently from Carando on many occasions. Whether this is a tribute to his particular style or whether it would happen with most plant managers, we don't know; thus far, Carando has been the only head of the operation since the grievance review panel started.

What is it like to be on a panel? One operator who has served on three panels during the past six years says that the atmosphere is fairly relaxed. "Everyone in the room is on a first-name basis with the others," he says. "You feel free to ask any question, you don't feel 'unequal' with anyone. If you want a record or a witness, you ask. The employee relations manager chairs the meeting, and the person with the grievance has always appeared to present his or her case. The panel tries to be consistent with the past, so the chairman tells us about any previous cases we should know about."

In presenting the complaint, the grievant may offer as much written documentation as desired. Next, the supervisor against whom the complaint is made defends his or her position. The supervisor suggests calling another supervisor, manager, or peer of the employee if that seems useful. The panel decides whether to call the witnesses. Any employee who is requested to attend as a witness has the right to refuse. Also, ex-employees may be called as witnesses. In some cases the panel interviews a long series of witnesses. According to Richardson, in one recent case a half dozen witnesses were interviewed by the panel.

No minutes are kept. No tape recordings are made.

Hourly and salaried members alike emphasize that the tone of the meetings is almost always factual. "Theatrics don't help much," says Plienis. "The panel wants to know what happened, why, how, what was done about it." Plienis has had one decision as a supervisor overturned by the panel. He also says that he has the "dubious distinction" of being the first supervisor ever to go before the panel.

Rules and Guidelines

The published guidelines for the panel are simple:

- Panelists shall be fair and impartial in all decisions.
- Panel members shall fully investigate each grievance before making a decision.
- All decisions shall be made by a majority vote of the panel.

- Panels may uphold, deny, or modify a grievance.
- All decisions made by the panel shall be binding and final.
- Any information presented to panelists by anyone involved in the case shall be kept in strictest confidence.
- All statements and votes made by panel members shall be held in strictest confidence.
- Final decision reached by a panel shall be a group decision and not that of any one individual or group of members.
- Panel decisions shall be limited to interpretation of company rules and policies. No panel shall have the authority to change company policy, pay rates, or job evaluations.

In addition, the employee handbook—about seventy pages long—is often referred to. The company updates it every few years.

Subject to the last rule mentioned—that the panel must limit itself to interpreting and applying company policy—almost anything is grievable. Brown states, "If an employee is unhappy about any incident, we tell him to grieve it. He can grieve practically anything he wants."

Decisions

An important feature of the decision making is that all voting is done by secret ballot. This is vital not only to the tone of the meetings, as described, but also, as we shall see presently, to preserving confidentiality. No one knows for sure how any other member votes. After the votes are cast and tallied, the decision goes to whichever side has three or more votes.

The panel can affirm the complainant's case or the supervisor's in the exact manner requested. It may also change the supervisor's decision, if it wants. If, say, a foreman demotes an operator from a job permanently because of an egregious error, the panel is free to affirm his demotion but limit it to a certain period of time.

Regardless of the closeness of the vote, all five panel members sign a letter telling the supervisor and complainant how the panel decided. Any member can volunteer to write this letter. Sometimes it is instructive. For example, it may tell the supervisor or complainant that he or she has such and such a weakness or shortcoming and should correct it in the future.

Confidentiality

The GE plant in Columbia has many visitors inquiring how its procedure works, and one of the questions they almost always ask has to do with confidentiality for the panel members. For instance, is it awkward for them to face their co-workers after deciding a controversial case?

The five panelists I saw did not feel this was a problem. One explained: "They really don't know unless you choose to tell them. The complainant doesn't know either. There's no way they can tell who voted for and against the complainant. All anybody knows is that a majority voted in such and such a way. Shop talk isn't a concern." Another panel member said, "Actually, nobody even knows who's on the panel in the cases I know about. The members keep it confidential what they're doing, and I suppose that sometimes somebody tells others in the plant, but not that I know of."

Difficulties and Rewards

The toughest part of a panel member's job is having to affirm an employee's discharge. "You feel bad," one panelist said. "Nobody likes to vote a person out of a job. But then I say to myself, 'Well, it would have happened if there wasn't a panel procedure, wouldn't it?' The panel doesn't do anything new to the employee."

Also, the panelists are aware that some employees know that their cases are at best a long shot. One panelist explained: "What have you got to lose by going to the panel? Nothing. It doesn't cost you anything. You do it on company time. A guy may be in trouble because of an attendance problem. The absences may be clearly marked on a log, and that will be put in evidence at the meeting, but the person tries us anyway. 'What have I got to lose by trying?' "

The reward that is appreciated most seems to be the broadening effect of serving on a panel. One panelist mentioned that she has gotten insights into operations at grievance review meetings that she wouldn't have been able to get if the plant were unionized and had an arbitration procedure, for there is no employee participation under the union procedure. Words like "instructive" and "educational" were used often in describing the experience. No panelists have withdrawn their names from the pool since the procedure went into operation.

Logging Cases

Note that the grievance form in Exhibit 1 is very short. Its purpose is not to make a case but simply to log the information necessary to categorize the complaint and assign it a case number. In the words of one manager, the form enables an employee to say something as simple as "I've been unfairly discharged, and I would like to have my job back."

Reversals and Ratifications

Here is a brief sampling of some cases that have come before the grievance review panel. The names of the employees and some minor details are fictionalized.

1. "Sam" had worked for two years as a setup man on dies. It was considered a very good job, and the pay was good. For reasons that never became clear—probably just carelessness—he left some clamps loose one afternoon on a setup job. This was a serious mistake; conceivably a loose bolt could fly up and kill an operator. Fortunately, the mistake was discovered before an accident could happen. A year earlier, however, Sam had violated another safety procedure, and the foreman had documented that error in Sam's file. Immediately he took Sam off the job, put him on a job with a lesser rating, and told him that he could never work on setup again. Sam went to the panel. In his testimony he insisted that he hadn't left the clamps loose. When questioned, however, he couldn't remember setting up the die where the incident occurred. Partly because of this weakness in his case, the panel sustained the foreman's decision.

2. When he was manager of employee and community relations, Caras reported a case involving "Tim," who wanted a job change and was denied it by the supervisor. The supervisor's grounds were that the change was for less than six months and the job sought was a lower-rated position; a personnel rule prohibited downgrading and returning to the original classification within six months. Taking his case to the panel, Tim cited extenuating circumstances and argued that he should be excepted from the six-month rule. The panel ruled against him. One of the hourly members said, "We sympathize with the guy, but a rule is a rule and it's the same for everyone."[5]

[5] Ibid., p. 78.

3. In a case reported by Coombe, "Alice" and "Betsy" both bid for a setup job for a welding machine. The foreman knew and liked Alice; he didn't know Betsy, but Betsy had more setup experience and a good work record. The foreman chose Alice for the job. Angry, Betsy went to the panel. She had higher seniority, she argued, as well as more experience on setup work. After a lot of questioning and deliberation, the panel overruled the foreman and gave the job to Betsy.[6]

4. "Cory" was discharged for insubordination. Her work record showed previous incidents of insubordination and also of using profane language with her supervisor. She went to the grievance review panel. The supervisor who had fired her was now working in another company, but the panel members wanted to talk to him. He agreed to sit down with them after work one day. After satisfying themselves that he had done the right thing, they let the discharge stand.

One panelist with whom I talked had himself once been fired (before becoming a panel member). Fortunately, he appealed to the review group and was reinstated.

Do some cases defy solution? The panelists with whom I talked agreed that some cases appear to have no good answer; that is, every solution the panel can think of seems to fall short of what the majority finds satisfying. One panelist commented, "When you do run into cases like this, it sure helps to have four other people to talk it over with."

Perspectives

The Columbia plant's grievance procedure reportedly has been adopted in eight other General Electric facilities. In addition, it is one of the few that I heard managers mention during my field trips. It has been written up in several professional journals, including those cited in this chapter. It is the subject of regularly occurring visits from businesspeople in other companies and parts of the country. One such contingent—a team of managers and operators from a Michigan corporation—was on the premises when I visited.

One of the most observable effects of the panel, in the minds of managers at the GE plant, is on the quality of supervision. All agree that supervisors simply don't operate in quite the same manner now that they did before 1982. Plienis was perhaps the frankest of the supervisors with whom I talked. "How does the panel affect me? It makes me a better manager. It makes me do my homework. If I want my decisions to stand up, I have to go in there knowing that I did the right thing and can prove it."

If a supervisor makes a decision that appears, when the employee challenges it, to be dubious—perhaps on the merits, perhaps because of lack of documentation—managers believe that he or she has a strong incentive to correct the decision before it can go to the panel.

When supervisors find that they will have to appear before a panel, they take it seriously enough to talk it over with colleagues. Plienis explains: "They'll get together at lunch or some other time, and the supervisor who's going to the panel will state his or her case. They'll say, 'Fine. State your case to us like you plan to tell the panel.' If the case is weak, they'll say so."

Can operators use the threat of going to the panel as a kind of club to make the supervisor do what they want—the "I'm going to get you if you don't do what I

[6]"Peer Review," p. 663.

want" approach? The supervisors with whom I talked think the answer is no. They feel that if they have done their homework and tried to be fair and consistent, no bluff will alter their decisions.

One of the strengths of the grievance review panel is that it is part of an employee relations approach that encompasses a variety of other activities all designed to stimulate cooperation and teamwork. For instance, several years ago Carando encouraged the organization to create "sounding boards." These are groups composed of hourly employees from different areas who mull over pressing problems and propose solutions to management. The concept appears to have paid its way many times over. Also, the plant has created quality circles and a fifteen-month self-development course to foster more employee involvement in the business.

Finally, the plant is experimenting with the "self-directed work force." Carando explains the philosophy as follows:

> It's our attempt to get employees to "take ownership of their jobs." We want to get them to do more running of operations themselves, to make more of the decisions that we normally have a salaried person make. We have to do everything we can to get unit costs down. We have nine hundred to one thousand people working in a building that used to house two thousand, and so we have more capacity than we need. We've got to get as efficient as possible to offset that. We are looking very hard at the amount of salaried overhead we have. If we can get the hourly employees to take on more, we can reduce that cost. Our aim is to become very efficient.
>
> The efforts we make are very simple. There's nothing complex about them. I told the hourly people recently, "When you came here to work, you came with two arms and two legs, and we've used all four of them pretty much. But there's something that we haven't used, and that's your brain. We're going to start making more use of it." I recognize, of course, that not all hourly employees here want to think—some actually just want to do their job and nothing more. But that's a small proportion of the people. Most want more out of life than that. You're in the factory about nine hours a day, counting your lunch hour, and that's a large percentage of your day. You want to be more than a robot during that time.

The Management Appeals Committee at Honeywell

Since 1981, two divisions at Honeywell have been served by the Management Appeals Committee, popularly known as "MAC." The two divisions are the Defense Systems Division and the Underseas Systems Division, both located in metropolitan Minneapolis. Until recently, the two divisions were one. When they split and became separate entities, they chose to keep MAC as it was and share the responsibilities and benefits of operating it. The seven members of MAC, all managers or supervisors, are drawn from the two divisions, and salaried employees of both divisions are entitled to use it if they can't get their disputes with their supervisors resolved at lower levels. (Nonsalaried employees at the two divisions are represented by unions and have a separate grievance procedure.) MAC's decisions are final. Since 1981 it has heard fifteen cases, resolving more than half of them in favor of the complaining employee. Since the two divisions employ about four thousand salaried employees between them, this means that about one employee in 1,865 uses it annually.

The appeal procedure culminating in MAC was originally drafted by Thomas J.

Company: Honeywell Defense Systems and Underseas Systems Division		Products/Services: Military systems, products, and components
Headquarters: Minnetonka, Minnesota		
		Date of Interview: February 19, 1987
Sales: $875 million	Number of Employees: 4,000	

Radziej, now group director of human resources for the Defense Systems group. Radziej convinced others in management that such a procedure was a valuable means of coping with the problems of retaining a diverse work force at Honeywell, and that it supported an environment of trust for all employees.

Not long ago, MAC decided a case that, more than any other case described in this volume, demonstrates the ability and willingness of some corporate due process agencies to stay independent of the will of line management. As we have seen, these agencies are very young in this country, and certainly they wrestle with many problems. Yet the MAC case demonstrates what a bright and significant future due process may have if its main commitment is to principles of equity and justice. Let us turn to that case next.

The Committee That Wouldn't Feel Intimidated

Not long ago MAC heard the appeal of an engineering manager whom I shall call "Ben." He had worked for Honeywell for thirteen years and, at the time his case was heard, supervised about ten people. The story is told by a member of MAC who is a line executive:

> Ben had been told by his boss that he wasn't cutting it. As a result he was going to get downgraded and suffer a severe pay cut. The reason given him was poor performance. Up to this time, however, he had always had good appraisals and compensation.
>
> On the face of it, Ben probably wasn't going to go any farther up in the company. He was about eleven years from retirement.
>
> However, he had no reason to believe he wasn't hacking it. He was doing his job as he always had. He wasn't a case of the Peter Principle or anything like that. He was getting the work out and getting along with the people he worked with. All of a sudden, however, he was told that his work was unsatisfactory and that he would be downgraded. He was mystified as to the reasons. So were we. What part of his work was unsatisfactory? When did it change? When did he go downhill? When we began digging into questions like these, the answers didn't look good.
>
> It *looked* to us as though Ben's supervisor was just carrying the mail for his boss, a high executive in the company. Now, I know that guy well and I respect him a lot. He is well regarded in management. I couldn't believe what we found. It *appeared* very much that this guy, this "superchief," was just doing a number on Ben because he didn't like him. The reasons weren't clear. I'm still not sure of them. But the superchief was saying, "Ben has got to go," and I don't think he was going to be satisfied with a demotion and pay cut. Although this is pure speculation on my part, I think he believed these measures would drive Ben out of the organization. He may have thought that Ben would opt for retirement, or find a job somewhere else in the company—take anything just as long as it got him out. Because this demotion didn't mean only a pay cut, it also meant a loss of face.
>
> To us on MAC the decision to demote Ben looked as capricious as could be. There was no documentation, there was no paper trail whatsoever that showed specifically where Ben was falling down. Instead, the criticisms of Ben's performance were generalities—"You're not aggressive enough," "You're not proactive enough," "You're not developing your people sufficiently," "You don't understand the new ways that we're operating in today's environment," and that sort of thing. All fuzzy, vague statements that left us uneasy.
>
> At the hearing we saw two people, Ben and his immediate supervisor. We met in a conference room of the Underseas Systems Division. We sat at a long table, the members of MAC plus the human resources representative. The chairman sat at one end of the table, and the chair at the opposite end was the "hot seat" where the people

testifying sat. It's nearest the door. When the person came in, we would say, "Have a seat" and try to keep things informal and relaxed. We have coffee. Humor gets injected. Still, it's hard for the people testifying to relax because it's a stressful situation.

Ben impressed us all. When he came in, I said to myself, "This has got to be an embarrassment for him even though he think's he's right." We told him he had the floor. The chairman said, "You can take ten, fifteen, twenty minutes, whatever you want, to tell us why you're here, what you see as the problem, and what you think is the remedy, what the outcome ought to be. We'll hold off asking questions until you're done."

When Ben began talking, he didn't try to butter anybody up. He was very professional, very calm. He had his notes organized. He wasn't like some we see, who are their own worst enemies. They have all this tacky-tacky paper, and they can't find their references, and they ramble around—no wonder it takes forever to get the story of what happened. But not this man. He gave it to us bing, bing, bing. That's why he's in management. It's a delight to deal with this sort of employee.

While he was talking, his supervisor was out there in the corridor cooling his heels. We all knew this. When we took a coffee break and streamed out, we came face to face with the supervisor. Ben greeted him and said to us, "This guy is a great boss. He's going to tell you that everything I said is true. Aren't you?" There was good rapport between those two. Yet here they were, appearing before us and one saying, "You're not cutting it, and I'm going to downgrade you and reduce your pay," while the other says, "The hell you are, I'm going to MAC. What do you think about those apples?" But here in front of us the two were meeting each other at coffee break, and they're congenial. This was a little unusual.

As I said, I think the supervisor was a middleman. He liked Ben and respected him, but he had a dirty job laid on him by his boss, and he had to do it. There were no hard feelings between those two. Ben said, "He's going to tell you there's nothing wrong with me," and that's what happened.

When it came the supervisor's turn to talk, we saw what a tough situation he was in. We told him, "It sounds as if you were a passive middleman in this. It sounds as if your boss was saying, 'I want you to get rid of Ben, and maybe step one is to downgrade him and take a bunch of money away. Then he'll do what he ought to do.' " We could see that the supervisor was in a very uncomfortable position. Basically what he told us was, "Ben is a good man, but he really can't be effective any longer in that job." But when we asked him, "Do you think he should be downgraded, that he's no longer capable of doing the work?" he answered, "No, I think he can do it. But I think he could do it somewhere else." In effect he was telling us, "Don't put me to the wall any more, because I've got a job to do, too, I've got a boss to please—and this is just the way it is."

But in our decision we said, in effect, "That ain't the way it is. You don't can a guy like that in this division or force him out or take money away from him. If he can't work anymore in your environment, what you must do is place him somewhere else in the company in an equivalent job at an equivalent level. Work the problem out on a lateral basis so that he doesn't lose pay and doesn't lose grade. *You* take the responsibility for doing that, placing him somewhere else without hurting him."

What made our decision extra "squirmy" is another circumstance. The manager over Ben's boss reports to the general manager for our entire division. This man is an absolute dream of a general manager—fair-minded, straight, honest, competent, and all the rest. Before the manager over Ben's boss decided what to do, he reviewed it with this general manager, and the general manager had concurred with it. Well, hell, MAC is a creature of the general manager! It was the general manager who established this thing for the sake of due process, and here we are, overturning a decision that he concurred with! We're saying, "This isn't right, you're not going to do it in that way, you're going to work out some other way," when the general manager supposedly had heard the decision when described to him and had said, "Fine. Go do it."

This is a test of our board. If we on MAC all say, "Well, if the general manager has said it's fair, it's got to be fair," how much are we worth? But we don't know how much the general manager was told. We don't know how much the picture was laid out for him. We just heard that there was a meeting and that he had nodded. All we can do is tell ourselves, "If he saw what we've seen, he wouldn't buy it either."

We met at about one in the afternoon. The meeting was scheduled from one to four-thirty, which is typical. That leaves us free to schedule a second afternoon to finish hearing testimony. Often it takes us all afternoon just to hear the person with the complaint, and another afternoon to hear the complainant's boss and other individuals whom we want to hear from. There may, finally, be a third or fourth session where we try to put it all together and come to some conclusion. The series of meetings may cover several weeks because we're all busy, and you don't say to seven busy people, "We're going to have the second meeting tomorrow afternoon and the third meeting the next afternoon." At the same time, we can't drag things out forever because sometimes we're dealing with a person whose pay has been suspended. In a typical case, therefore, it may take in the neighborhood of three to five weeks to conclude our work and produce a written decision.

In this case, however, we heard all the arguments and arrived at a recommendation in one afternoon. We concluded that day at about five-thirty. This case wasn't subtle. We didn't have to keep working to find out what had been going on, thinking to ourselves, "The truth must be in here somewhere." Not this time. This appeared to us to be an open-and-shut case, no two ways about it. We reached a decision and issued our memo the very next day.

All of us took notes at the meeting. There was no tape recorder, no secretary. The human resources rep served as the recording secretary. The notes I took were all for me—memory joggers. Afterward they entered my personnel file.

When we were done with Ben and the supervisor and said goodbye to them, we went around the table. Each person told us where he or she stood on the case. The chairman doesn't say, "How many think the employee is right? How many think the manager is right? Raise your hands." We just start in no particular way around the table and say what we think and what we would recommend. From one person to the next. One says, "I agree with Dave on this, but I don't buy that, and so I think the guy shouldn't get a pay cut." Another says, "I agree on that, but I don't agree on this, and so it seems to me . . ." Everybody speaks, the chairman coming last. Next we try to reach some sort of consensus. One asks, "Dave, why do you think this fellow shouldn't get a pay cut?" or "How come you think Nick isn't smart enough to know that such and such makes sense?"

This sort of discussion went on, but it didn't take long to reach a consensus. Then we sat back and said, "Now we'll find out if MAC is for real or not." We knew it was going to be tough. We knew that the manager over Ben's boss was going to be madder than hell, and the general manager might be, too. Who were we to intervene in something where he had said, "This is the way it's going to be"? The general manager had approved a decision, and now we were coming in at the eleventh hour and saying, "That ain't right, and you can't do that." The general manager could overrule us. Our recommendations are final, but in the end MAC is a creature of the general manager, and if he says, "I don't buy that," he's going to get his way. Let's not kid ourselves. That has never happened, but it *could*. He can say, "I think you blew that one. We're not going to do it that way." He has that power.

Of course, if he does that, I think some of us would have had serious thoughts about continuing on MAC. I know I would have. I don't want to serve if I think that as long as we have no hard cases, we'll get upheld, but when the general manager's ox is gored, we'll be told to go away.

The general manager didn't overrule us. Our decision stood. It is being implemented now.

As Ben Remembers

The members of MAC were surprised to have Ben use the procedure. He was an accomplished manager, whereas most users of MAC tend to be technicians and operators. He was a white Caucasian male, whereas most users of MAC tend to be minority group members and/or women. The corporate memoranda on MAC open the procedure to "any salaried employee," but there seemed to be a general expectation that managers, especially managers above the lowest levels, would not use it often if at all.

What prompted Ben to go to MAC? "I thought," he told me, "that it was the only way I could get a fair shake. If I didn't use it, disaster was certain." When he was told that he was to be downgraded and take a large pay cut, he believed the action to be terribly unjust—due more to a personality conflict than performance. Although he was aware of MAC, he knew no one who had used it. When he asked a supervisor if it was available to him, the supervisor checked with the human resources department and answered that it was.

Ben's analysis of why he was being demoted is as follows:

> It started last spring. My supervisor was told by his boss to put me on probation for not doing things that the boss believed important. Four allegations were made against me. My supervisor emphasized, in passing them on to me, that the allegations were his boss's opinions, not his, and the boss wanted him to tell me this. I took the allegations seriously and worked on them.
>
> In November, I was called in to my supervisor's office and told that the boss had decided I was to be downgraded by two grades and given a substantial salary cut. I said, "For what?" The supervisor answered, "For not correcting the deficiencies." I said, "But I did correct them!" The supervisor said, "Don't shoot the messenger. This is the boss's decision, and nobody is going to change his mind." It was then that I decided to fight.

Why did the senior manager dislike Ben? What lay behind his determination to get Ben out of the organization? Ben reflects as follows:

> I think the problem occurred in 1979. I worked then for the guy—he was a Honeywell veteran—and we had a disagreement. The disagreement was partly philosophical. In my files I found his documentation of a meeting we both attended in 1979. Apparently, that was the basis for his unhappiness. He felt that our management styles were too diverse. He thought I should be more actively involved in subordinates' problems. He wrote, "Ben doesn't seem to realize that I am the boss." The incident he referred to, I believe, was an effort he had made to get me to change a trip I had planned. Just before I was to leave, he had wanted me to go somewhere else. I had said no, my appointments with customers were too important, and that I would go to the other place but after the trip already planned. Later he sent me a memo. I included a copy of that memo in my presentation to MAC. It said, "You don't seem to think I'm the boss. You don't seem to listen." Things like that.
>
> Six months later he transferred to another part of the division, and I no longer worked for him. It looked as if the problem might blow over. But then he came back into the picture here last spring, and I wound up in his organization. It took him thirty days to decide it was time to get me out. Apparently he remembered that incident in 1979. Now he was going to get me.
>
> He listed in writing four changes he wanted me to make. We didn't discuss them; he just sent me the memo. I had six months in which to make them. As the months went by, he didn't ask me how I was coming along. He didn't talk to me at all. At the end of

the six months he told my supervisor to downgrade me because I hadn't responded to the memo. My supervisor told me, "I don't have a problem with you, but he sure has. I tried to argue for you but was told, 'Don't bother.' "

Ben now sat down to prepare his case before MAC. It was not easy. He recalls:

It took me about two weeks to prepare my presentation. I responded to the four allegations in a summary of about two typewritten pages. This summary was followed by a four-and-a-half-page typewritten backup plus four exhibits. I sent this written material to MAC two weeks in advance of the hearing. I tried to assess the problem objectively and put it in a time frame so that everyone could follow it.

At the hearing, I appeared first. I told them my story. They asked questions for a couple of hours. I said that two supervisors had volunteered to testify for me, and gave the committee their names, but the committee never contacted them. When I left I met my supervisor, who was waiting to appear. He went next.

Before I left, the committee told me that they might not have a decision for me until after Christmas. Actually I only had to wait two days. I got a letter stating that there was a "lack of evidence" to justify downgrading me and reducing my salary. The committee recommended that I be transferred to another part of the company, staying at the same grade and pay level. The transfer was to be accomplished in sixty days. The letter was signed by all members of the committee.

I feel that MAC's refusal to be intimidated adds a lot to its credibility in the company.

What Makes MAC Tick?

In February 1987, when I interviewed at Honeywell, Lawrence M. Schriver was chairman of MAC. Schriver was director of materials management in the Underseas Systems Division. He explained that the seven members are appointed for three-year terms, and that their terms are staggered so that the committee always has a majority who are familiar with its practices. MAC strives for diversity of background among its members, so that one consideration, when new faces must be added, is that they must add balance to the committee. "What we do is go to the manager of an organization and ask for suggestions," he said. "After he produces some suggestions, we look at what the people have done." Two qualities that he regards as invaluable for a committee member are sensitivity and consciousness of individuals' rights.

Roy Henderson, who acted as recording secretary for the committee in early 1987, emphasizes that it is considered an honor to be asked to serve on MAC. The new member gets a letter from the general manager confirming his or her appointment, and that letter goes into the person's personnel file. The letter from the general manager, says Henderson, makes it clear to the person that top management wants him to serve.

MAC decides by majority vote, and at least five members must be present at a hearing to make a quorum. Much of the time the chairman takes his turn asking questions like any other member, but if necessary he will step in and keep the discussion from going off the track. When the letter goes out conveying the committee's decision, all members who heard the case sign the letter. While those who dissent from the majority can indicate their disagreement, they must sign the letter. Says Schriver:

We announce our ruling on the case and we may comment on the problem. For instance, if the employee is in trouble because of a tendency to create discord, we may mention that, or we may concede that the person has seniority but does not seem to be performing well on the job. We may tell the person what he or she must do to change the situation.

If, as in the case of the demoted engineer, the decision goes against management and management is instructed to arrange a change or transfer, specific deadlines may be given for the action to be taken, such as thirty days or ninety days.

It is up to the recording secretary, who is assigned by the Human Resources Department, to see that MAC's instructions are carried out. The secretary also sees to it that the people involved understand the decision. Describing the case of a computer operator who went to MAC after being refused a promotion, Henderson comments:

> I wrote up what I heard the committee decide, then reviewed the draft with all seven members present at the hearing. They would tell me, "I also said this," or "What I really said was that," so I would revise the draft and show it to them again. It might take a while to get all their signatures because of travel, but after I had them, the letter would go out. In this case I went to the supervisor and told her about the outcome, then the employee who had brought the complaint. I went also to the supervisor's manager. Do you understand MAC's decision? Do you see why they went that way? In this case management was happy, but sometimes they are not. If not, they may go to the president or general manager and protest the decision. That isn't likely to do any good since the committee's decisions are final.

As for the paper trail, the written summary of the case is entered in the complaining employee's file if he or she wishes that; otherwise it is not. Always, however, the Human Resources Department keeps the record of the proceedings.

MAC cannot change company policy but it can recommend changes in policy. Recommendations go to the Human Resources Department for evaluation and, if found valid, implementation.

The time required to hear evidence and reach a decision varies widely. In one case, notes Schriver, something like four days of committee members' time was required over an extended period, but in another case, only a small fraction of that much time was needed.

The defending supervisor or manager does not know in advance how the complaining employee will defend himself or herself. "But the manager knows what action was taken and why," says Schriver. "If the complaining employee makes a special charge, the manager learns soon enough from the questions we ask."

The division's memorandum on MAC makes clear that the complaining employee can ask someone else to present his or her case. "If you feel more comfortable in having a third party of your choice accompany you *at any step in this process,*" says the memo, "you are encouraged to do so. The only limitation is that the person be a current employee of this division." Usually, says Schriver, that third party is the employee relations representative. He recalls:

> One complainant didn't appear personally at all. The employee relations rep spoke in her behalf. It's a little like having your lawyer represent you in court. This complainant had gone to her doctor, and he advised against her appearing before the MAC. She was too nervous, too excitable. So the employee rep spoke for her. She had been fired, and we rehired her.

As with other company procedures described in this volume, management hopes that most disputes between managers and subordinates will be resolved at earlier stages, making a committee hearing unnecessary. In Honeywell's Defense and Underseas Systems Divisions there are three earlier steps. The corporate description of them and Step 4 is shown in Exhibit 1.

Finality of Decisions

"In theory," one manager told me "MAC's decisions are final." Why the qualification? Henderson describes a case that happened:

> An employee was terminated and appealed to MAC. She won a reinstatement. MAC directed the employees in her unit to apologize to her, and she to them, for their past behavior. She apologized as directed but her fellow employees refused to apologize to her. "No way," they said. "She was disrespectful to us. We tried to support her but were treated poorly by her. We were maligned and abused. If she comes back, we resign." Close to a half dozen good employees took this position, and they were adamant.
>
> The director of the unit said he needed the employees and couldn't get along well without them. He went to the vice president and general manager. "I tried to carry out the committee's instruction but they won't have it," he said. "Give it another try," the general manager said. So the director went back and tried again to placate the unyielding employees. He had no luck at all. So he returned to the general manager and told him what had happened. Satisfied that the director had done everything possible, the general manager talked to MAC, and MAC reversed its decision. It did this even though it had already written the complaining employee that she had her job back.
>
> I had to tell her that MAC had reversed its decision because of the employees' reaction. Since we couldn't find another home for her in the company, she had to leave.

Recollections and Reactions

In the following paragraphs, several people who have been involved in MAC hearings for different reasons recall their impressions.

Corporate attorney who presented employee's case:

> The employee, who had been fired for performance failures, including absenteeism, knew me and asked me to present his arguments. We went into the conference room first. About six people were there at a long table. It was very informal—not at all like a legal hearing. The chairman started the questions, then the other members came in with questions. The chair kept it moving. We had a lot of exhibits to substantiate the employee's position. The exhibits showed that he had done better than management thought. We also put forward that the employee had been going through treatment for chemical dependence, in this case, alcoholism.
>
> After our presentation, the manager came in and made his. He brought his own manager as a witness.
>
> Shortly after, MAC's decision came in a letter. MAC reinstated the employee but said a position should be found for him elsewhere in the company. It mentioned the extenuating circumstance of his chemical dependency and the treatment he was getting.
>
> The last I knew, the employee was doing fine in another division. But for MAC he would have been fired.

Defending supervisor:

> The complaining employee, who reported to me, went first. He thought he should have gotten a promotion that he didn't get. We had his performance failures docu-

EXHIBIT 1
Excerpt from "Employee Due Process Procedure,"
Honeywell Defense and Underseas Systems Divisions

Step 1. First, take your concern to your immediate supervisor. The concern should be fully discussed with your supervisor to get a mutual understanding of the issue(s). You are encouraged to discuss the issues fully and frankly.

Your supervisor has the responsibility to listen, investigate, evaluate, and respond to you with a complete and equitable answer.

Step 2. If there is a personality conflict between you and your supervisor, or a concern exists that you feel your supervisor is unable or unwilling to resolve, you can take your concern directly to your Employee Relations Representative who will assist you in resolving the problem.

In this step you and your supervisor will be interviewed by the Employee Relations Representative. Copies of these interviews will be available upon request to the parties reviewing the concern. The Human Resources Department will listen, investigate, and help find a solution to the problem.

Step 3. If you feel that your concern has not been successfully resolved after discussions with your Employee Relations Representative and your supervisor, your next step should be a formal review of the concern with your Department Manager and Director. This meeting can be arranged by your supervisor or your Employee Relations Representative. Your manager will examine all the facts presented, conduct further interviews as required, evaluate the solutions available and provide you with a prompt answer.

If for any reason you are not satisfied with the solution presented, proceed to Step 4.

Step 4. In Step 4, you have the opportunity to discuss your concern with the Employee Relations Representative's Manager. If, after this discussion, no equitable solution has been reached, the Employee Relations Manager will make an appointment for you to present your concern to the Management Appeals Committee (MAC). This presentation can take place in any of the following ways:

- You can present your concern to the committee.
- You can select the Employee Relations Representative to present your concern.
- You and your Employee Relations Representative can jointly present your concern.
- You and the third party of your choice can present your concern. You may also include your Employee Relations Representative at your option.

mented well, especially his absenteeism—the days he was gone, the reasons given, the length of time away, and so on. We had no witnesses, just the documentation. I thought I was well prepared, but still it was an unnerving experience. Facing those seven managers sitting around the table! Not knowing what they were going to ask me! And I didn't know what defenses the employee had made, what he had told them.

All seven MAC members asked questions. One would ask a question, then another would follow up with a related question. They asked about his car problems. For each one he had given an excuse—but it happened too many times, and the times were too long. They asked about his unexplained disappearance from work, and about the phone calls where he talked too long. It went on for thirty or forty-five minutes. It was very unsettling—I couldn't go back to my job that afternoon.

Then came the letter sustaining our action, and Roy Henderson talked to me about the decision. I was very relieved!

Employee who brought a complaint:

Management had promised me a promotion but I wasn't getting it. I found out about MAC from Roy Henderson, the employee rep, and he told me what to do. I wrote out my complaint in longhand, documenting it as well as I could. It took me a week or two to finish it, mostly because of delays in getting the facts I needed. It was three or four pages long. I didn't show it to anyone before going to MAC.

I waited in a chair outside the door. When they were ready, Roy signaled me to come in. It was an ordinary-size conference room, and the committee members sat around a table. I told them who I was, and they told me who they were. They went around the table introducing themselves. I read my statement to them—it took about fifteen minutes. They then asked lots of questions, but I didn't feel as if I were under cross-examination. After about an hour I left. They asked me if I wanted a record of the case in my personnel folder, and I said yes.

When the letter came, I was informed that I wouldn't get the promotion. I was given to understand that the findings were final, there was no appeal—the case was closed. Naturally I was disappointed. However, the letter said that if I worked hard from January to May and did certain things, I would then get promoted as I desired. I did that and got the promotion.

Would I recommend MAC to a friend with a problem? Yes.

The Visibility Question

Some managers don't worry about the extent of employee familiarity with MAC. A computer operations manager, for instance, told me that all employees in her unit seemed to know about the procedure. Once a year or so, she said, a flier telling about MAC comes to each of her employees with his or her paycheck.

However, some managers and executives are concerned about this question. One of them is William J. Conroy, head of a department in Defense Systems that employs about 220 people. He told me:

How many employees in the division know about MAC? This is the question that worries me most. This division of Honeywell has done a lot of pioneering in the people area, and I'm very proud of it for that. What bothers me is that I suspect that if you were to take a poll and ask employees about MAC—ask them, "What does due process mean to you?"—you would get a very mixed result. Some would know about our due process procedure, but many others would not. I would guess that maybe half of our people know that we have something different here and that it is available to anyone who wants it. Periodically we pass out a memo to all employees reminding them that we have a due process procedure, but I wonder if that is enough. You won't find MAC described in the employee handbook because that is written for all Minneapolis operations, and the other divisions here don't have a procedure like MAC.

The question is how much should we promote it. How proactive should we be in telling everybody about MAC? I don't know. We don't want to promote it so much that we get employees to take all disputes with their supervisors to MAC for you want those two to work out their problems if they can. Only the real hard cases should go to MAC. We don't want to fan the flames, in other words. We don't want to go around asking, "When's the last time you used MAC? What's the matter? You're not very aggressive. . . ." At the other extreme, we don't want to keep our light totally under a bushel.

In Defense Systems, our personnel people encourage employees to use MAC when the situation seems appropriate. In Underseas Systems they tend to leave it to employees to decide that. There they suggest MAC only if the employee asks for another channel. Maybe that is one reason that MAC gets more cases from Defense Systems than from Underseas. What I'm saying is, we can change the level of awareness of MAC by what and how we tell people about it.

Conclusion

Like any group of human beings, MAC can make a decision on an employee, on the basis of one afternoon's testimony, that may jar with the perception that colleagues and other departmental employees may have. One supervisor told me about a case of an employee in her work group who went to MAC claiming harassment and unfair treatment. Virtually every person in the group disliked the grievant, agreeing that she might have made a good first impression on them but that on a day-in, day-out basis they found her insufferable. She was undependable, deceitful, and abusive. Yet when she went to MAC she was able, because of her articulateness and dramatic talents, to make a good impression, and she got the decision she wanted. Her colleagues felt hurt and resentful. The grievant was getting paid for being a troublemaker! Fortunately, the grievant soon left the company and the problem disappeared, but the example illustrates a problem that every company tribunal has—and, for that matter, any judge or jury. With only oral testimony and summary documentation to go on, it is possible for the "judges" to get a different impression of reality from that of the people who work side by side with the petitioner. Even if the "judges" happen to be right, the result is not good from an employee relations standpoint.

"However," the supervisor hastened to add, "MAC certainly beats going to court."

In its six years of operation, MAC has produced important advantages for the Defense and Underseas. Systems divisions. "Without question," says Beverly A. Bryant, contracts counsel for Honeywell and a member of MAC, "managers are taking more pains to document poor performance carefully and follow corporate procedure when warning or discharging a poor worker. Before MAC they might not have been so careful about doing this. One result is a great advantage if the employee takes us to court."

The word gets around among supervisors that failure to document may cost in more ways than one. "Some of the management reversals that have happened since I have been on MAC," says Schriver, "probably wouldn't have happened if the managers had documented better." Schriver adds:

> We tell supervisors that the case has got to sell itself. We can't take your word that your action was justified. Maybe in truth you have a strong case, but if you didn't do your homework, it won't sound good to us.

Schriver also feels that MAC encourages managers and subordinates to step up their efforts to work out their problems. He says: "Word gets around pretty fast that such and such a department has a case pending. The department will try very hard not to appear before a MAC a second time."

Finally, there is a conviction among supervisors that MAC has helped to develop employees. One supervisor gave me this example:

> One disappointed person in my department went to MAC. It turned out to be one of the best things he could have ever done. At the hearing he heard the reasons why he had not got the advancement he wanted. He grew up a lot from that experience, from hearing it from *them*. We had told him what things he needed to do to get advanced, and he thought he had done them, but his managers didn't. He just wasn't willing to listen to us. When he heard it from MAC, he took it in. He's a terrific employee now, and he has got the advancement he wanted.

The Employee Relations Committee
at John Hancock

At John Hancock Mutual Life Insurance Company, one of Boston's most visible corporations because of a spectacular sixty-two-story, glass-walled building that serves as corporate headquarters, employee due process comes to a head in the employee relations committee. Five people serve on this committee, and they are permanent members. This is not to say that the committee experiences no turnover, for it does; but none of the members sits only for one case or for a limited term such as two or three years. The committee reports to John Hancock's management committee, it is likely to handle fifteen to twenty cases a year, and strictly speaking, its decisions are advisory. Because of the way it works, however, its advisory role may make it more powerful in the company, not less.

Although the employee relations committee is not as old as its counterparts at IBM, SmithKline Beckman, Donnelly, Northrop, and several other companies, John Hancock enjoys an unusually long heritage of strong employee relations. For instance, it has operated employee counseling programs for some thirty-five years, whereas most such programs in industry are ten years old or less. Also, it has long

Company: John Hancock Mutual Life Insurance Company		Products/Services: Insurance, financial services, investment management
Headquarters: Boston, Massachusetts		Date of Interview: June 23, 1986
Sales: $5.3 billion (premiums)	Number of Employees: 10,000	

made special efforts to enable handicapped people to work in its offices. This solid infrastructure in employee relations underlies part of the success of the employee relations committee and explains why some of its jobs look easy when they would be anything but easy in many other companies.

Complaints and Complainants

The employee relations committee handles written complaints from about six thousand employees in the Boston area and about four thousand in field offices around the country. The great majority come from the Boston-area people. According to Chairman Michael B. O'Toole and Vice Chairman David L. Murphy, Jr., many complaints are due simply to supervisors failing to follow company procedure. A subordinate is fired without the required warning, a performance appraisal misleads a subordinate into thinking the wrong thing, and so on. A good many other complaints are due to pitfalls in communications. "Often employees don't hear what their supervisors tell them," says O'Toole. "And sometimes their supervisors *think* they made something clear to them—say, a warning about poor performance—but didn't really."

Underlying reasons like these are two more basic causes of complaints. First, John Hancock is anything but a staid Boston insurance firm; it has been changing rapidly since 1980. A traditional mutual life insurer until the late 1970s, the company added a mutual fund and a property and casualty insurance firm and then, in rapid succession after 1980, a brokerage network, a real estate investment organization, a home mortgage financing operation, a consumer bank, an investment counseling firm, and other operations. In 1985, total income was close to $5 billion. Although such changes have added excitement and growth potential to the company, they have also caused strain and displacement in many offices.

Second, the company's promotion-from-within policy tends to put some people in the managerial ranks who have trouble making the transition from an operating specialty to administration. "They didn't have the chance," says Murphy, "to profit from managerial mistakes early in their careers. They become executives before learning how to put someone on probation, or to give a warning in the right way to a poor performer, or to talk to a subordinate candidly about his or her work. Also, it is hard to discuss their mistakes with them if they are still thinking in technical terms."

For one reason or another, therefore, fifteen to twenty complaints a year are filed with the employee relations committee. However, it is the belief of O'Toole, who brings to the committee experience in a variety of line management positions, that the fifteen or twenty don't represent all the complaints that could—and sometimes should—be made. "Some problems are not brought to us for a good reason," he says. "A subordinate has to be pretty desperate to sit down and write a complaint against a boss that he or she has been working for—maybe for five or ten years. They know that the committee will do its best to prevent the boss from retaliating, but there are subtle methods of retaliation that are almost impossible to prevent. This may not be so important for many secretarial and clerical people, because there is almost always an opening somewhere else that they can transfer to. But this can be very important at the sales executive level or the account executive level. Here there are people who aren't so portable."

What about people at the other extreme—the chronic complainers? Murphy and

O'Toole believe that candor with such people, when they come to the committee, usually discourages them. O'Toole says:

> If we don't think a person has a substantial complaint, we tell him so. In the early stages of the committee, we got quite a few complainants from what I call the "lunatic fringe." We spoke frankly to them, and they didn't bother us again. For example, a woman came to the committee with a written complaint that appeared to have no merit, and we gave her our candid reactions. We also talked to her about *her* responsibilities. It's one thing to talk about what the company is responsible for, another to talk about employees' responsibilities to the company. They are important. She didn't come back to us, not with an unsubstantial complaint. Another employee came to us with what we thought was an imagined complaint. He claimed his supervisor was too harsh on him. We pointed out to him that his error rate was far above anyone else's in his department. We told him that in our opinion his low rating was justified, that his probation was warranted because of his many errors. He had a poor attendance record, too. He tried to use that as an excuse. We told him that we didn't doubt the legitimacy of his illnesses, but we said that the company has a right to expect attendance unless the employee is incapacitated. "This often means coming to work when you don't feel well," we told him. We reminded him that December is a heavy month for the company, and his poor attendance in December added a burden for other members of his group.

Caryn Harding, the senior counselor in the Employee Assistance Program, says that she and her two colleagues also discourage chronic complainers. Confronting them with the facts of their performance—"reality confrontation," as she calls it—the counselors try to head them off at the pass. "They come to see us in the counseling unit," she says. "We're the gatekeepers, you see. We may find that for them to write a complaint would be a colossal waste of the committee's time. After we get their side of the story, we investigate. If we find that their record is poor, we level with them. 'You were absent thirty days in the past year, and we can't have that in this company,' or 'You had five trainers and complained about each one, and you still can't do the job.' We tell them, 'Let's think about how you can do better. . . .'

"Of course, if the complainant insists on going before the committee, I can't stop him or her," adds Harding. "I think that some of these people who want to file ridiculous complaints merely want attention. They also want to feel that they went to the limit before being turned down. They want their 'day in court.' They may want to make their managers sweat. They know that no manager wants to go before the committee if he or she can help it. They know the manager doesn't want to be bothered with getting a lot of documentation together."

In 1985, the employee relations committee considered twenty cases. The counseling unit probably handled one hundred more that might have gone to the committee if the complainants had had no counselor to talk with.

From Complaint to Recommendation

Before the employee relations committee can go into action, it must receive a written complaint. "We tell the complainant that we will try to get back to him or her in thirty days, " says O'Toole. "We may not be able to, depending on vacations, a high number of people to talk to, and so on. If our recommendation after the investigation and hearings supports management, we send a memo to the complainant, with a copy to the manager, and that's the end of it. David prepares the memo, I sign it."

In many cases, however, the committee recommends against management or urges a change in management's original decision. "If our recommendation favors the employee and requires management to do something," says Murphy, "we talk to management first, get it to agree and 'buy into the recommendation,' then turn to the employee and tell him or her what we have got management to agree to. We send a copy of our memo to management as well as to the employee. It will be pretty specific about what needs to be done. If we are uncertain about management's willingness or ability to follow through, we may do a little monitoring. This isn't a big deal—maybe just a few phone calls. Mike knows a lot of people in the company, so he can move around and find out what's happening. That's another way. We try to do it simply. We're not heavy on memoranda and formality and all that kind of thing."

Despite the committee's effort to wind up a case in thirty days, a couple of months may go by between the time that a written complaint is filed and the time that a recommendation is reached. This is because several stages must be gone through. At the outset, the complainant is likely to wait a week or two before appearing before the committee. Then a couple of weeks may elapse before the committee can hear management's side from the supervisor or others whose acts were challenged. Next, some time may be required for committee members to interview colleagues of the complainant and others whose testimony may shed light on the case. If the complainant works in a field office some distance from Boston, more time may be used up in traveling. These extra delays may not be typical, but they do happen sometimes.

Exhibit 1 shows the complaint report that the employee fills out for the committee (one of the counselors may assist him or her in this task, as we will see later). Exhibit 2 shows the form for the counselor's summary of the case. When completed, both forms go to the committee, if the employee seeks a formal hearing, to give the members a brief factual overview of the case.

In 1981, the first full year of operation for the employee relations committee, five complaints were heard, considered, and decided; in 1982, no cases were heard; in 1983, two cases came before the committee; in 1984, eighteen cases were heard; and in 1985, twenty cases were processed. Every six months the committee reports on its activities to the corporate management committee.

Why did the company choose this particular form of due process? "The employee relations committee was chosen because of our experience with the employee counseling program," explains Murphy. "For years that program was the focus of job complaints, and people liked the way it worked. Only a new stage had to be added. One thing we did *not* want was an investigator from one department poking into another department's operations."

O'Toole remembers that a couple of top executives came to him after the company fought off a union attempt to organize employees in 1981.

> They said they wanted to set up an employee relations committee, and I became one of the first members. We were asked to propose an approach. We wrote some rules for filing a written complaint, the time to be allowed to reach a decision, and so on. We kept the rules fairly loose, and the first few complaints we got were handled loosely. The resolution was not terribly satisfying—to me, anyway. We would go up the line and tell management that we had such and such a problem here. I didn't look on it as a great assignment. Then came a top management change, and Bill [William L.] Boyan, the executive vice president, asked me to take on the chairmanship of the committee. With

EXHIBIT 1
Complaint Report

TO: EMPLOYEE COUNSELING UNIT: _____

FROM: DEPARTMENT: _____

          DIVISION: _____

          DATE: _____

NATURE OF PROBLEM OR COMPLAINT:

SUGGESTED REMEDIAL ACTION:

SUBMITTED BY: _____

                    _____

                    _____

---

more support, we were able to evolve to the stage we are in today. We asked employees if they would like to appear before the committee when they had a complaint, and they started coming. We became very serious about wanting to do the right thing. We weren't trying to salve the political conscience of the company. We weren't trying to make the numbers look good.

The change came in 1983. In that year the employee relations committee got the green light to talk about itself in company publications and employee manuals. The results began showing a year later.

Powers and Scope

The employee relations committee is a standing committee appointed by the president and management committee. It is not part of the personnel department. It is not a subcommittee of another committee. Also, its members are fully engaged in other activities. For instance, O'Toole heads up a program in which senior execu-

EXHIBIT 2

Case Summary Form

(1) Case Number _____
(2) Name _____
(3) Supervisor _____
(4) Manager _____
(5) Director _____
(6) Job Grade _____
(7) Job Title _____
(8) Date of Intake _____
(9) Date of Entry _____
(10) Unit _____
(11) Department _____
(12) E.A. _____
(13) Visits _____
(13a) Revisits _____
(13b) Phone _____

(14) Sex
   1 = Male
   2 = Female

(15) Race
   1 = White
   2 = Black
   3 = Hispanic
   4 = Native American
   5 = Asian
   6 = Other

(16) Marital Status
   0 = Unknown
   1 = Single
   2 = Married
   3 = Divorced
   4 = Widowed
   5 = Separated

(17) Children
   1 = Yes
   2 = No
   3 = Unknown

(18) Living Status
   0 = Unknown
   1 = Living Alone
   2 = Living w/Peers
   3 = Living w/Parents
   4 = Living w/Spouse
   5 = Single Head of Household

(19) Insurance
   1 = N/A
   2 = H.M.O.
   3 = John Hancock
   4 = John Hancock P.P.O.
   5 = Unknown
   6 = None

(20) Job Classification
   0 = Unknown
   1 = Skilled
   2 = Professional
   3 = Clerical
   4 = Technical
   5 = Unskilled

(21) Source of Referral
   1 = Supervisor/Manager
   2 = Coworker
   3 = Workshop
   4 = Advertising
   5 = Self

(22) Job Problem Counseling
   1 = N/A
   2 = Performance
   3 = Attendance
   4 = Tardiness
   5 = Performance appraisal
   6 = R. Discrimination
   7 = S. Discrimination
   8 = A. Discrimination
   9 = Management
   10 = Coworker
   11 = Probation

(continued)

EXHIBIT 2 *(continued)*
Case Summary Form

---

12 = Salary
13 = Harassment
14 = Co. Policy
15 = Job Posting
16 = Termination
17 = Job re-write

(23) Personal Problem Counseling
  1 = N/A
  2 = Alcohol
  3 = Drug
  4 = Polydrug
  5 = Psychiatric/emotional
  6 = Family–Marital
  7 = Medical
  8 = Financial
  9 = Child Care
  10 = Career Development
  11 = Legal
  12 = Stress
  13 = Physical Disability
  14 = Housing

(24) Action Taken
  1 = N/A
  2 = Informational Contact
  3 = Assessment and Referral
  4 = Short-term Counseling

(25) Management Consultation
  1 = N/A
  2 = Yes
  3 = No

(26) Nature of Complaint
  1 = N/A
  2 = Job Performance
  3 = Progressive Discipline
  4 = Discrimination
  5 = Advancement
  6 = Management Style
  7 = Company Policy
  8 = Salary

(27) Complaint Action Taken
1 = N/A

2 = Step I   Counselor contacted management at employee's request and relayed results of management contact to employee.

3 = Step II   Counselor continues to intervene with management and employee to resolve complaint.

4 = Step III Employee returns completed complaint report form to Employee Counselor.

5 = Step IV Counselor notifies management of receipt of complaint report form which precipitates complaint resolution.

6 = Step V   Complaint is heard by Employee Relations Committee.

---

(28) Number of charge-back hours _____

tives coordinate multiple product lines in an effort to improve service to clients; Murphy is vice president of corporate personnel and spends long hours on employee benefits, performance appraisal systems, and other personnel activities. The other three members are similarly engaged in many tasks besides resolving employee complaints.

As mentioned, the committee does not make decisions, but recommendations. Its recommendations always appear in writing. However, the line between recommendations and decisions can be a wavery one. "We agree on what we think should be done and how," says Murphy. "We don't stop at mediation, as ombudspeople do. We don't just facilitate. We go to the manager and get him or her to agree with our recommendation. We may have to negotiate, we may end up agreeing to a course of action that is a little different from what we first planned. We don't say, 'Here is our decision, implement it.' On the other hand, we don't back down on what we think is right."

O'Toole stresses the fact that each member of the committee himself or herself reports to someone else in the company and therefore must be aware of the social and political environment. If necessary, he says, the committee would go to the executive vice president or president in order to overcome management resistance to a recommendation. It hasn't had to do that yet, but it stands ready to if it ever sees the need.

Ironically, the fact that the committee plays an advisory role appears to add, not detract, from its powers. This is because managers who might be tempted to refuse to cooperate know that they will have to explain themselves to a senior, and that can be awkward and—at least, if the committee's judgment is right—compromising. In effect, the committee tells a manager who tries to balk, "Either you work it out with us or, though we won't want to, we'll have to go up the line."

In its recommendations, O'Toole stresses, the committee tries to be practical and realistic. "We have got to be sympathetic with supervisors and managers. We don't want to be seen as second-guessing them. That's one reason we have managers on the committee, because we want to be seen as people who know what it's like to be out there. Management is not an exact science. Credibility is crucial for us, and if we get into a tough situation sometimes with a senior manager, it's even more crucial."

To broaden its credibility with the rank and file, the committee includes one member from a minority group and three women. At one time it debated whether to broaden its membership by adding several employees at clerical or other nonmanagerial levels, but decided against such a move on the grounds that it would make proceedings unwieldy. Even with only five members, sometimes a meeting cannot be scheduled at a time that everyone can attend.

What about supervisors who are tempted to retaliate against subordinates who go to the committee? The possibility is always on committee members' minds, and they often frame recommendations in such a way that they can cope with it. "If our recommendation favors the subordinate," says O'Toole, "we outline what management has agreed it will do and invite him or her to let us know if it doesn't seem to be complying. So the employee can always come back to us if that happens. The employee can always say, 'They're not doing what they said they would do' and open up the complaint again. Of course, there are also some very subtle ways of retaliating against a subordinate, and I don't know if we're ever going to be able to handle that. It occurs at all levels in a large organization."

Although most of the complaints heard by the committee come from the Boston area, its powers extend to the field offices. Not long ago, for instance, O'Toole and Murphy went to an office in California to investigate and resolve several complaints. In such cases, two or three members may represent the committee in order to save time and expense.

In his semiannual report to the executive vice president, O'Toole reports on the cases considered and sometimes offers impressions gained from the hearings and investigations. What do the cases say about the way the company is run and any changes that might need to be made? One of these reports so impressed one member of the management committee that he sent copies of it to everyone in his organization, from vice presidents to supervisors.

Hearing Both Sides

By virtue of its more or less permanent membership, the employee relations committee gains a singular advantage: it develops an instinct for sensing the merits of complaints and defenses, acquires an ear for truth and fiction in claims and counterclaims, and becomes wise in the art of asking discerning questions. Such skills, in turn, enable the members to save a great deal of time in investigating complaints and reaching decisions.

Committee members may spend many hours investigating complaints. "We're pretty thorough," says Murphy. "We may spend an hour and a half interviewing one individual. We may talk to the complainant's co-workers, to witnesses, to immediate supervisors, to managers up the line." In discussions, Murphy and O'Toole sometimes take contrasting roles, with one taking an aggressive, critical, "prove it to me" stance, while the other adopts a more conciliatory tone.

When a complainant or other employee appears before the committee, the members do their best to put the person at ease. "They are good at that," says Harding. "Nevertheless, if you're a complainant, coming into the conference room and seeing five people sitting there can be intimidating. You're a little guy, they're big shots. Even though they don't cross-examine you as at a trial and ask questions in an accusing way, they may scare you. If you're nervous, your reaction may be, 'They don't believe me. They don't trust me.' This can be hard. So we tell complainants that they can bring someone with them if they want to. It can't be a lawyer, it must be someone in the company. However, it is often hard to get your co-workers to appear with you. They don't want to be part of an unpleasant scene. So they may ask me to accompany them, and often I do that. If they're scared, they may even ask me to prepare their case for them, and I'll do that, too."

In the beginning, the committee made it optional for the complainant to appear in person before it. For several years, however, that option has been dropped, and the committee now expects all complainants to come, talk to it, and answer questions. However, Murphy emphasizes, the complainant and defending manager don't appear at the same time. "There would be advantages if they did," he says. "For example, we wouldn't have to hear one side and then go to the other side later with questions. But the pluses of not appearing together—especially avoiding adversarial tones—outweigh the advantages."

One of the things that committee members try to clarify is exactly what the complainant wants done. Does he or she want some protected status or guarantee for the future or simply an apology from the boss? Is the aim simply to get the warning canceled or to win some advance or promotion as restitution?

The committee follows no rules of evidence, as in a law court. Also, generally the committee does not vote on a proposed recommendation, but arrives at its conclusion by consensus. "I can remember only one real split in the committee," says Murphy. "Our continuity of membership is a big help in this respect, for we know how everyone thinks. I don't think we could operate by majority rule. The differences are more in the qualities of issue before us—what are the most important determining factors?—than right or wrong. Usually, after we have talked for a while, we agree on a general viewpoint and attitude toward the case."

Perhaps there is no more penetrating glimpse of the committee's approach, philosophy, and power than some comments made by O'Toole on a West Coast case. Following several written complaints by employees in a field office there, he and Murphy packed their bags and flew out. They spent several intensive days hearing the complainants and their supervisors and interviewing others who knew the situation. The problem and possible recommendations became so complicated, in fact, that they taped sheets of paper to the walls of one hotel room to outline the different facts, assumptions, and alternatives. "When we reached our conclusions," O'Toole said, "we sat down with the department head and discussed our analysis with him. We want the committee to have credibility with management, you see. We don't want management to thumb its nose at us. Well, we convinced the department head about our position on the case and what seemed to us to be wrong in the department's operations. When we wrote our recommendation, therefore—and we did it with that conversation in mind, his views and our own—we knew that it would be backed by management."

The Counseling Connection

As noted, the employee counseling program at John Hancock plays a vital role in the success of the employee relations committee. Conceivably, the committee might be inundated with complaints but for the success of the counselors in resolving problems at an earlier stage. However, the relationship is valuable both ways. That is, the committee has become quite valuable to the counseling program. Harding explains: "When I started in counseling here in 1978, I didn't have much clout. When I called managers to ask about complaining employees, I got rebuffed a lot. The employee relations committee was not in existence then. I didn't have anything behind me. If a horrendous wrong was done to an employee, there wasn't an awful lot I could do to correct the wrong. Employees were likely to go next to a state commission—much more likely than they are apt to do now. Some would call the president's office in disgust. 'You really can't do much for me, can you?' That isn't true now. With the committee there, and everyone knowing it, a manager has a good incentive to work something out so that the complaint won't go further."

Here is an example of the new clout of the counseling group: a woman from a racial minority group complained to her boss about racist slurs by a co-worker. The manager asked the colleague to apologize, and that was done. However, the woman felt that the apology was cosmetic, and she resented having the offender get off so easily. She wanted him out of the work area. When she approached the manager with that demand, he balked. She went next to Harding. After listening to the woman's story, Harding went to the manager, heard his side of the story, and told him she thought the two should be separated. He was upset at that. "Listen," he said, "she's nothing but a troublemaker. She invited the abuse by calling the co-worker a fat slob. He's not really a racist, believe me." Harding was not persuaded.

"I know, " she said, "but look, we have to do it this way." She explained that she had consulted with the equal employment opportunity director and that official had agreed with her. If the woman went to the employee relations committee, her case would be loaded, Harding said. Reluctantly, the manager backed down and transferred the offending worker to another area.

To give me a sample of the counselors' workload and its relationship to the committee, Harding leafed through her records for the previous four months. During that period, she and her two colleagues considered forty "real" complaints; that is, complaints that appeared to have some substance. Of these, four went to the employee relations committee. The complaints involved the usual range of problems—unfair supervision, questionable applications of company policy, poor job performance evaluations, denials of promotion, and so on. When a complaint appears to merit investigation, the first thing the counselors do is ask the complainant for permission to talk with the supervisor and/or others immediately concerned. Absolutely no futher steps are taken unless the employee agrees.

"Often," says Harding, "they want to find out first if they really have a substantive complaint. They ask me, 'What do you think? Have I been treated fairly?' I may answer, 'It doesn't look that way,' or 'Yes, in view of the circumstances, it seems to me that you were treated fairly.' If the latter, most of the time that ends it. We have a fair amount of credibility, you know."

In addition to the forty complaints just mentioned, Harding and her colleagues considered, during the four-month period, thirty cases involving personal problems and obstacles that employees felt in doing their jobs. The subjects might range from noise or smoke to family worries, and the employees wanted the advice of a neutral person.

As mentioned earlier, the counselors try to confront a complaining employee with reality. If the person's record is spotty, if he or she appears to be a chronic complainer, or if something else is awry, the counselors point that out. If the complainer comes in determined to take the case to the employee relations committee, the counselor describes what that step is likely to involve. "I can't tell you how many times," says Harding, "I've given the complaint report [see Exhibit 1] to the complainant and never gotten it back for action. They lose their nerve, or decide it's not worth the trouble. The 'Suggested Remedial Action' section is very important. What does the complainant want to happen?

"When the complaint form is filled out and returned to me, I notify Dave Murphy that a formal complaint probably is on its way. I summarize everything I know about the case: what the employee told me, what management told me, and so on. I also attach copies of records that I feel may be important. I have the complaint and my memo photocopied for each of the five committee members and sent to them."

On a number of occasions, as explained, Harding helps complainants prepare their presentations and goes with them to the committee meeting. Once the presentation is finished, however, she leaves the room.

The counseling group reports to Murphy as vice president for corporate personnel.

Committee Members in Action

Here are the highlights of two cases considered by the employee relations committee.

Case of the upset security officer. An employee whom I shall call "Dylan

O'Brien" had been a security officer at John Hancock for five years. A rather secretive man who kept his private life to himself, he lived with his mother and felt responsible for her welfare. When she got sick and had to go to the hospital, he became very distraught. Unfortunately, during this period of great emotional strain, his name came to the top of the watch commander's list for extra duty, and one day he was called. The assistant watch commander informed him that the officer assigned was incapacitated and that since O'Brien's name was at the top of the list, it was his turn to go on extra duty. When O'Brien said he couldn't because his mother was in the hospital, the watch commander reminded him that this extra service was mandatory and everyone understood that; no officer on duty could leave until a replacement came, and so it was a requirement that others be available in rotation to take the place of anyone who couldn't appear on schedule.

Angrily repeating that there was no way he could be made to come, O'Brien hung up on the commander. The commander called him back and told him he was putting him on probation for unprofessional conduct.

In due course, a very unhappy O'Brien appeared before Harding to tell his story. Soon after that, he filled out a written complaint. Harding made a report on her talk with O'Brien and sent that with his complaint and explanation—a long and involved one—to the committee.

On Tuesday afternoon at the scheduled time, O'Brien walked into the conference room and met the five members. He took one of the empty chairs—it didn't seem to make any difference to anyone which one—and sat down. "Now," said O'Toole, when the door was closed, "tell us in your own words what your complaint is. From time to time we'll ask you questions. Take all the time you want. There are no rules about this—we're informal—so tell it in any way you want."

From time to time during his explanation, O'Brien's voice broke; he was obviously under tremendous strain at home and greatly disturbed about his rebuke from the watch commander. From time to time he lashed out or was incoherent. Gently the members asked questions, learning that the security operation was fairly militaristic (perhaps it had to be in order to work), that O'Brien, like the other officers, carried a weapon, and that once before, O'Brien had been placed on probation after being found dozing on the job. O'Brien also revealed that he had not told the watch commander or others about his mother's illness, but had assumed that they knew. "They *should*'ve known," he insisted. "The commander too—how could he *not* have known?"

Next, the committee asked the assistant watch commander to appear. "We almost always do this separately," explained Murphy. "We don't want to bring the complainant and supervisor together unless forced to. It may take extra time to do it this way, but it avoids emotional confrontation. We generally begin with the complainant, and when we're through, we may ask the person whom he or she thinks we should talk to next. Normally we work our way up the line, going from the immediate manager to his or her boss, and when we do, we try to avoid bringing the managers together, too, because the senior person may intimidate the junior if there's a difference of opinion."

From the assistant watch commander, the commander himself, and others in the system, the committee members learned that O'Brien was a loner and appeared to have no friends. Bosses, peers, and juniors agreed that he was a difficult man to get along with. They had a healthy respect for his ability, though. He knew his work; also, he was good at training newcomers to the force.

"What we tried to learn," said O'Toole, "was whether the commander was consistent and fair in managing the operation. Was he discriminating at all? Was he playing favorites? Was he allowing O'Brien, or anyone else, to be picked on or victimized?"

After completing their talks with the managers and witnesses, the members met to agree on a recommendation. They decided that management had been within its rights to tell O'Brien that he had to report and, when he didn't, in putting him on ninety-day probation. The commander and assistant commander ran a tough operation, but they ran it fairly, in the committee's opinion. Murphy then wrote the recommendation of the committee, O'Toole signed it, and copies went to O'Brien and the department heads. "This letter had to be negative," explained Murphy, "but we try for a positive outcome if we can. For instance, we mention the things that are important, such as attendance. We try to make it a learning experience. We also pointed out that the probation was for ninety days only, and that then it would be considered over and forgotten by the department."

The case consumed four meetings of about one hour each. Since five members attended each meeting, the overall time taken was about twenty hours, not counting the writing of the letter and miscellaneous telephone calls.

Case of the surprised secretary.   A general secretary whom I shall call "Elaine Kozmetsky" came to the committee to contest her discharge. She said that the first inkling she had had of her superior's disapproval was when she told her that Friday, March 22, would be her last day at John Hancock. She alleged she was given no reason for being fired, no warning in advance of the notice, and that she had believed that the people she worked for (she performed secretarial duties for seven or eight managers in market analysis) were all pleased with her work. Shortly after she was notified about being fired, she saw her job posted in the weekly company news sheet.

When it was the boss's turn to testify, however, the manager told the committee that she had indeed warned Kozmetsky—not once, but several times. "She is a nice person," the boss admitted, "and she's willing and eager. But, one, she's a chatterbox. Two, she makes errors—lots of her work has to be retyped. Three, she's not good at setting priorities."

"Why didn't you put her on probation?" asked one of the committee members. "I thought of that," the boss replied, "but I decided not to so she could hunt for other jobs in the company with a clear record."

Beginning their investigations, the committee members learned that Kozmetsky was regarded as a "good kid" by others in the market analysis department where she worked. They agreed that, yes, she talked a little too much, but they thought that her work on the whole was okay. A mistake now and then, but nothing really bad. It also came out that her boss was regarded as a bright, competent woman, but demanding to the point of sometimes being picky.

After a short while, the committee members agreed on a picture of what had happened: Kozmetsky's boss had talked to her, as claimed, but hadn't made it clear to her that her job was on the line. The boss may have thought she made it clear, but either she didn't say what she thought she had said, or she didn't say it in such a way that Kozmetsky understood. In either case, communication had failed. The committee decided the boss should have known better than to leave it at that. Kozmetsky was entitled to know clearly and unambiguously where she stood and that she was really (if not technically) on probation.

In its memo to the boss, it did not fault her for her judgment, only for not giving the secretary a clear enough indication of disapproval so that the young woman could correct her ways. "We understand your rationale for not placing her on probation," the memo said, "but we believe it should have been done." It said that Kozmetsky should be allowed to stay in the company, but on probationary status for two months and in another department. Her performance during those two months was to be evaluated in five ways, including excessive talkativeness, errors in letters, and inability to follow instructions. If she didn't measure up by the end of the probationary period, she was to be terminated from the company.

"I had her read this letter and sign that she understood it," said O'Toole. As for the boss, though her knuckles were rapped by the recommendation, she agreed to it.

After improving steadily during the two-month period, Kozmetsky was offered a permanent position in the new department. Her supervisors are pleased with her work, and she is happy. "Without our process," says O'Toole, "she would have been fired and, going to another place, probably would have had the same experience as in the market analysis department. It wasn't until we told her *clearly* about her problems that she understood and began correcting herself."

Problems and Values

Early in the 1980s, the employee relations committee might have been viewed as a threat by some managers and supervisors at John Hancock. However, there is practically no evidence that it is so viewed now. In fact, the committee may be winning a reputation as a valuable resource and sounding board. Not long ago, for instance, management asked the committee to study the problems facing a group of highly technical people in the company and advise it on how best to handle those problems.

Possibly the greatest value of the committee has been its influence on managers. Its very presence is a cogent reminder that the company's personnel policy is to be followed both in letter and spirit. One executive told me:

> I have been amazed most by the deterrent effect of the committee. Managers think twice now when they are tempted to shortcut a policy or be arbitrary in some damaging way. I find managers awfully willing to compromise when they see that the facts aren't on their side. Before 1983, this wasn't true. Managers didn't have to back down, and they didn't. They stuck together like glue even when they realized that maybe they weren't doing something right. Not so now. With the committee a force, they're likely to say, "Maybe we better take another look at this." If you're on weak ground, it's not a pleasant prospect to think of being grilled by five committee members.

O'Toole and Murphy believe that there may be something like one hundred fifty serious complaints a year that never get written up for the committee because they are resolved by informal action and give-and-take. How many of these one hundred fifty are due to the chastening effect of the committee? It is almost impossible to tell. But even if one said that only half are resolved because of the committee's presence, that is a tremendous gain.

The committee has had another type of deterrent effect. In the judgment of observers, it seems to have discouraged lawsuits and actions by state agencies. Says Harding, "The state employment agencies are not contacting us as frequently as they did before late 1982. The committee is definitely a deterrent to employees tempted to go to the courts. I don't think that in the past four years anyone who has gone to the committee has later sued the company."

If the committee has a problem, it is probably visibility. Since 1983, it has had the green light from top management to make itself known to employees, but there continues to be a feeling around that not enough employees know about it. "We keep running into people who don't know anything about us and should," says O'Toole. Neither he nor Murphy wants to go all out in an "advertising" program for the committee, for that might attract a type of employee whom no one wants to encourage. On the other hand, they would like to get the word out to more employees who might have a sound reason someday for turning to the procedure. "There's a limit to how much you should keep talking about yourself," cautions Murphy, "but we have some channels that we might use more often—the *News Weekly* [a company publication for employees], training courses, a better location in the employee handbook." In addition, Harding has designed a three-hour workshop on the complaint procedure and related issues, and she devotes about a half hour to the procedure in another workshop on managing problem employees.

In the meantime, word of mouth is working in favor of the committee and, given more time, this will surely exert a strong positive influence.

More than Four Decades of Due Process at Northrop

Northrop Corporation, one of the nation's top aerospace concerns, has a grievance system for nonunion employees that has been in operation since 1946. It is unusual in several respects. First, only one other company, Polaroid, has a procedure dating back to 1946. Second, Northrop's is one of the few systems offering outside arbitration as a final step, and the step is frequently used. Third, Northrop's own people may represent employees in arbitration, sometimes winning against management.

About 1 percent of eligible Northrop employees use the grievance procedure. Eligibility is limited to nonsupervisory employees who have completed their probationary period and work twenty or more hours per week. The Management Appeal Committee, the company's "supreme court," hears and decides about thirty cases per year (about one per one thousand five hundred eligible employees), hearing the grievant, the defending supervisor, and witnesses while carefully maintaining an informal, nonadversarial atmosphere.

The company is the only large aerospace firm in southern California that is not unionized. Close to a quarter of the employees have been with the company for twenty

Company: Northrop Corporation		Products/Services: Military aircraft, weaponry, space products
Headquarters: Los Angeles, California		
		Date of Interview: June 4, 1987
Sales: $5.6 billion (1987)	Number of Employees: 47,000	

years or more, and it is the only aerospace company listed in *The 100 Best Companies to Work For in America*. At the end of 1986 Northrop had forty-six thousand eight hundred employees, its sales had doubled in the past five years, and most industry analysts, according to *The Wall Street Journal*, regarded it as the best-positioned defense contractor for the next decade. Although a great many factors and people are responsible for this success, the company's grievance procedure, along with those who make it work, must be counted as an important contributor.

Let us begin with a brief look at how the company's due process approach developed and at the powerful infrastructure that makes it work. We can then turn to the main features of the approach, some case examples, and a new grievance procedure designed for managers.

A "Mad" Move That Worked

From a fairly small shop prior to World War II, Northrop grew by leaps and bounds during the war years. One of the things the company did to manage this growth was add a personnel department. The chief executive officer and founder, John K. Northrop, did not lose his zeal for handling the day-to-day problems and complaints of employees, however, and more and more people went to his office for help. Observes Lawrence R. Littrell, corporate director of industrial relations:

> Many times the problems Jack handled dealt with employee discipline, and most often he would see to it that nothing really bad happened to anyone—he was that kind of guy. However, some people who got favorable decisions from Mr. Northrop really didn't deserve his help, and others who did wouldn't go or couldn't get to him in time. Inconsistencies grew, along with demands on his time, and it became apparent that a better way of handling personnel complaints and problems was needed.[1]

Out of this recognition came the idea for a nonunion grievance procedure with arbitration as the final step. The idea was unprecedented and, to a great many people in and out of the company, appalling. What? Let a neutral group in the company and then, if necessary, an outsider judge whether a line manager's personal decision should stand? Sheer madness! Nevertheless, top management went along with the revolutionary proposal, and in 1946, a grievance procedure for all nonsupervisory employees, hourly and salaried alike, went into being. For at least a decade Northrop would be the only nonunion company west of Polaroid in Boston that operated a grievance procedure, and for several decades it and Polaroid were the only ones with grievance procedures culminating in arbitration.

Management's motives were not purely idealistic or altruistic. In 1945, unions had tried to organize Northrop employees and, despite wages, hours, and working conditions comparable to the best in the industry, had come close to succeeding. Management was dismayed. If it was to succeed in keeping a union-free environment, it must close the gap between what a unionized company could promise and what a nonunion company could offer. The nonunion grievance procedure appeared to be the obvious answer. But in the aviation industry, Northrop was alone in its

[1] "The Grievance and Arbitration System for Nonunion Employees at Northrop Corporation," in Alan Westin, *Resolving Employment Disputes Without Litigation* (Washington, D.C.: Bureau of National Affairs, 1988), p. 115.

thinking. Such well-known competitors as Douglas and Boeing did not share its convictions.

The grievance procedure instituted in 1946 was much like the one in use today. Why did the company choose this particular form instead of some other approach? Littrell believes the answer is that executives didn't know about any procedures other than those created under collective bargaining:

> [They were] the only model there was. We were trying to put something in place that would give our people what was being offered to them by the union. The unions kept hitting us for not having a procedure that would permit our people an impartial view of their problems. So Roger McGuire [Industrial Relations head] said, "Let's do it."

For more than forty years now unions have not come close to organizing more than a small fraction of company employees. Where a union presence can be detected, it is likely to be as a result of historical accident or an acquisition, such as plants Northrop has acquired that happened to have a union shop, or a small group of welders that had been organized as far back as 1941. Somewhere around three thousand employees of a total in excess of forty-six thousand belong to an independent union, the UAW, the Machinists, or some other group. The employees of one organization that Northrop bought in 1971 in Kansas City were organized when the company acquired them, but in 1985, in an election between two competing unions and a no-union alternative, they voted to decertify their existing union and give the Northrop system a try.

Northrop's competitors in the aerospace industry all have unions—in the case of one competitor, around a dozen unions—and management feels that it is blessed to be spared that problem. One expert I talked to calculates that Northrop's production costs are about 25 percent below those of one leading competitor, mostly due to the fact that Northrop doesn't have a union. It does not have to cope with such union-ordered moves as the slowdown (McDonnell-Douglas in Long Beach was in the throes of such problems during the time of my interviews in Hawthorne), nor does it have to contend with the adversarial attitudes that unions are seen to encourage. Says Littrell:

> We don't have people whose job it is to create an "us versus them" mentality. If employees feel they have problems, we sure as hell want to hear about them and get the problems resolved right away. Also, we don't have to contend with a lot of frivolous grievances filed by a union for political or bargaining purposes.

A Thin Line on a Hard Road

While the most visible part of Northrop's grievance procedure is the administrative officer hearing, the Management Appeals Committee, and arbitration, the foundation is informal hearings and mediation by the employee relations staff. Employees with complaints are expected to go to the staff within five working days after the event in question. A member of the staff tries to resolve the problem in ten working days; only if the employee relations representative cannot achieve a resolution— usually he or she can—does the grieving employee go up the line with a written grievance.

In Littrell's view, employee relations plays a crucial role. Its effectiveness is due not alone to its own efforts, however, but in part to the existence of the system. He says:

> The employee relations staff serves as the counselor, shop steward, and business agent for the aggrieved employee. They are also the counselor and sometimes the conscience of management. They walk a thin line on a hard road, and they do it very well.

How do employee relations representatives work? David Woodward, employee relations administrator, comments as follows: "When an employee complains of unfair treatment, we usually have a meeting in my office with the supervisor. We get a lot of complaints resolved this way, because many times the problem is a misunderstanding."

Occasionally, Woodward says, the supervisor may resist a logical resolution, in which case the employee relations representative tells him or her, "Fine, I understand you, but there may be another side to the story, and the employee has a right to use the formal grievance procedure to resolve this complaint." Most supervisors and managers know that the rep refers to the prospect of a hearing at the management level. If that happens, the supervisor may be reversed if he or she lacks a strong case for taking the action decided on.

All members of the employee relations staff are degreed specialists, but the qualities that makes them good rarely show on a résumé. Says Littrell:

> Basically, we look for native talent rather than try to train it into people. Their talent shows in their daily work, their interfaces with their peers in employee relations, ways they suggest to supervisors for handling problems—it's an almost continuous performance. We look for people who want careers in the human resource field. It doesn't hurt to have a specific education in human resource management, but it isn't the be-all and end-all. Maybe they have taken specialized courses at community colleges, but at most universities these days the undergraduate degrees are in economics—you can't get a degree in industrial relations at any university I know of. We look also for the types of educational efforts the individual has made since graduation. Specialized courses are available through UCLA, the Industrial Relations Institute here in LA, and there are some private institutions concentrating now on training industrial relations people. We look for experience in industrial relations and employee relations.
>
> It may take a while to orient the person to the way we do business, but we do that with training. Most of our first-level management training courses are given by our own people, not outsiders. We look for the ability to deal successfully with different kinds of employees—the guy that comes off the floor into the employee relations specialist's office, his or her manager or supervisor, the manager's manager, and the vice president. We look particularly for honesty and forthrightness and the ability to sell the Northrop philosophy to managers and grievants. Hopefully, if the disgruntled employee is flat out wrong, the employee relations rep will be able to "gruntle" him; and if the manager is taking a line that is inappropriate, hopefully the rep can convince him that he should back off. Some managers can make life for a rep hard, so it's important that reps be pretty tough and able to withstand pressure.
>
> Reps should be good at writing up complaints for employees when grievances can't be resolved informally by mediation. We look at how well they prepare the cases, how well they present their cases to the administrative officer and to the Management Appeals Committee, how many mistakes they make, how many times they "blow it," how often if at all it appears that they gave the wrong information to grievants or managers—those sorts of things. At the hearings we listen to their answers to questions

asked, and we get a pretty good feel for who knows what they're doing and who doesn't.

You have to have a lot of sensitivity to be a successful rep. You have to be pretty quick on your feet, able to recognize quickly what you're dealing with and to change your tactics to fit the situation. You have to know when to come down and start pounding the table and when you can get there with gentle persuasion. You have to know when to call in the boss, and you have to know what the boss is going to say. It's an art.

Littrell feels that another important skill that distinguishes a good employee relations rep is writing up cases persuasively:

> When I was working as a rep, I would almost always write the grievance for the applicant because he or she didn't know what to ask for. He would say, for instance, "I want my job back." Quite often he would forget to add, "And I want back pay," so I'd have to add that in. I felt that it was my responsibility to see that in the written grievance he or she asked for everything they were entitled to, and that the case was presented in the most persuasive way possible, and that if I could help him or her do it better because of whatever limitations they were working under, I should do that.

Woodward believes that it is very important for reps not to be afraid of line management. If the employee has a valid complaint, it's important that it be pursued as far up the chain of command as necessary to get proper resolution. He says:

> The minute they get afraid of supervisors and managers, the system will collapse. ER reps know what's right and what's wrong, and if they say to themselves, "If I go this way, management will beat on me, so I better not do it," you might as well forget the system.

Working with a grievant on a formal written grievance may take quite a bit of time, especially if the grievance goes all the way up to the Management Appeals Committee. Over a period of four to ten weeks, the rep may see the employee several times a week for an hour or two at a time. All together, says Littrell, the rep may spend forty to fifty hours on the complaint.

At the Aircraft Division in Hawthorne, where I conducted most of my interviews, there is one employee relations rep for about every one thousand employees. The ratio is not a constant throughout the corporation; it fluctuates depending on a variety of circumstances and conditions, and in one division it may fluctuate over the years depending on various conditions.

Going Before the Administrative Officer

If dissatisfied with the results obtained with his or her management, the grievant sends a written grievance to the administrative officer. Administrative officers serve throughout the company. As a general rule, they are program managers. For instance, the F-5 fighter program has for its administrative officer the head of production in that program. The F-18 program has a similarly situated department head for its administrative officer. Some programs may have several administrative officers if their size justifies that. The administrative officers report to vice presidents.

In the opinion of the employee relations reps I talked with, the administrative officer step has a sobering effect on both the grievant and his or her supervisor. Woodward explains:

> An employee goes to employee relations to file a grievance. His complaint is reviewed by the employee relations representative and discussed with the supervisor involved. It is possible that the issue may be reviewed by three levels of management. If the grievance is not resolved, management is informed that the grievance will be appealed to the program manager who is the administrative officer.
>
> The meeting with the administrative officer must be within five working days of the date of the original grievance. In some cases, the employee relations representative may discuss the grievance with the administrative officer so he can have a feel for the problem. In the conference the employee explains his reason for filing the grievance. Both the employee relations representative and the administrative officer take notes. After the grievant leaves, the notes are reviewed, and his or her side of the story is discussed. In most cases, the supervisor is not present during this part of the procedure.
>
> Usually both the administrative officer and the employee relations representative will have questions that need to be investigated. Since the administrative officer must issue a decision within ten working days after the date of the hearing, a time is scheduled for another meeting. At that meeting, the administrative officer and employee relations will review the grievance with the additional information obtained from their investigation.
>
> If the manager who is involved in the grievance has not clearly proven his or her case, or if the issue falls in a gray area, generally the administrative officer will decide for the grievant. It is important that the employees know that the company does listen to their complaints and the grievance procedure works. Also, the administrative officer knows that if he does not resolve the grievance, it will probably be appealed to the next level in the grievance procedure, the Management Appeals Committee (MAC). One of the members of this committee is the vice president to whom he reports.
>
> In other words, the administrative officer is under pressure because of the system just as the supervisor was. There was pressure on the supervisor to make sure he or she was right, and now there's pressure on the administrative officer to make a good decision. He knows if the grievance is not settled it will be heard by his vice president and the other members of the Management Appeals Committee.

An example of a case heard by an administrative officer involves an employee named "Martin F." Management gave him a final warning notice for threatening and intimidating his lead man. Because Martin F. had been given oral warnings for previous confrontations with co-workers, and also because he had a first warning notice for absenteeism in his file, management felt that strong discipline was in order. After hearing the case, however, the administrative officer felt that the discipline was too harsh. He reviewed Martin F.'s three years working for Northrop, three years of mostly good performance. He reduced the final notice to a second notice, and Martin F. accepted this compromise.[2]

In the Aircraft Division, attendance, substandard work, job classification, and discrimination are the four most common issues of written grievances; they account for well over half of the cases. Of all written grievances filed, a third or more are typically solved at the administrative officer level. This may be twice the number of resolutions at the supervisor level, and four or five times the number resolved at the next higher level, the Management Appeals Committee.

At all levels, the procedure is very important. The manager may correctly decide, let us say, that a certain employee doesn't have the abilities and aptitudes the depart-

[2] Ibid., p. 125.

ment wants, but if he or she fails to follow the rules in dismissing the person, at some step of the grievance procedure the manager is going to get reversed. "We're going to have to put this person back to work until you discipline him in the right way," he or she will be told. This emphasis on procedure helps to develop a strong consciousness of personnel policy among managers and supervisors.

Management Appeals Committee Hearings

If grievants are not satisfied with the decisions of the administrative officer, they may appeal within five working days after receiving that executive's decision to the Management Appeals Committee. This is the highest tribunal in the company, and four decades of operation have made it a very effective body.

Three vice presidents sit on the committee—the division vice president of the organization in which the grievant works, the division vice president of human resources, and the corporate senior vice president of human resources or his designee. The committee's hearings are likely to consume most of the day, and there may be twenty-five or thirty hearings per year.

The employee relations administrator for the area in which the grievant works puts the facts of the case in writing, prepares a folder for the committee members, schedules a convenient date for a hearing, and attends the session. In the summary for committee members he or she outlines the grievant's position, management's position, and what company rule is in question, what the issue or issues are, and what the committee must decide.

Woodward describes a typical Management Appeals Committee meeting as follows:

> The grievant enters the room, the committee members introduce themselves and tell the employee why they're there. Then they say, "Go ahead and tell us what happened." There is coffee, the atmosphere is relaxed and informal. The grievant tells his or her story, the committee members ask questions. They may ask questions as the grievant goes along, or they may save their questions until the end, whatever seems more comfortable. When they and the grievant are through, the grievant leaves, going back to work or (if terminated), departing from the premises.
>
> Grievants usually appear by themselves. Neither at this stage nor previous stages are they allowed to bring attorneys. Only at an arbitration can they do that. However, if they have difficulty presenting themselves—say, because of language—they may have a spokesperson from the company.
>
> The grievants usually appear cool. It is sometimes the supervisor who may not appear cool. It was they who took the actions, and they must justify what they did. If they can't they may not look too good in front of the vice presidents of their organizations.
>
> The administrator has witnesses ready to appear when the committee wants to see them. They appear one at a time after the grievant leaves. If I'm the administrator, I will have explained the procedure to them. I will have told them to make sure they tell the truth, and I'll tell them to say "I don't know" if that is an appropriate answer. Getting, instructing, and scheduling witnesses takes a lot of time, and it is important that they be ready when called.
>
> The order in which witnesses are called depends on several things. The committee members may ask me about the witnesses in advance and ask for my advice on the order of appearance. Sometimes after interviewing one person, the committee members will ask who's the next witness and what can he add, and after I tell them, they may decide not to call the person.

After all the witnesses have gone, the committee sits back and discusses the case with the doors closed. In many instances they will reach a decision then and there.

The employee relations administrator must know the case well because the committee members ask him or her all sorts of questions. If the administrator doesn't have the answer, he or she is asked to investigate the question and report back to the committee, sometimes to the individual members, and sometimes to the full committee if it reconvenes to discuss the additional information.

Once a decision is reached, it is the responsibility of the ER rep to put it in writing, with the emphasis on accuracy and succinctness.

Littrell, who has served on many committees over the years, adds these thoughts and observations:

This afternoon we have a meeting scheduled at one o'clock. First we'll sit down with the employee relations rep—this is before the grievant comes in—and we'll ask him or her about the case. Usually the first question is why are we here. Usually by the time the hearing is finished, two or three hours later, we know darn well why we're there, and the reason may be different from what we at first thought. It's amazing how much new data comes out in one of those meetings that isn't on the statement. For example, quite often the witnesses that the grievant calls will do him in—they won't support his story. You wonder why in the world he ever called those guys as witnesses because they contradict his statements. He says he was there on the job at seven forty-five, they say they didn't see him come in until ten—that sort of thing.

The committee hears the witnesses serially. The witnesses do not hear each other's testimony. We always try to see all of the witnesses that the grievant wants called.

There are surprises. One time we found out that one of the organizations had installed a no-fault attendance system. Under this system it didn't matter why you were absent, but if you were absent too much, you were going to get canned. That system was different from any other organization's under the authority of the vice president, and as it turned out, it wasn't fair. So we reversed the manager's decision. It so happens that the Ventura Division [in another part of Northrop] has a no-fault attendance policy, but it was installed with everybody's concurrence. Not so with this organization just mentioned. The no-fault policy wasn't studied and adopted after discussion and after everyone was told about it. That's why it wasn't fair.

After the witnesses have left, each of us has a pretty good sense of what the others are feeling. Usually someone takes the lead and says, "Well, I think it ought to go this way." There may or may not be disagreement. If there's disagreement, we argue among ourselves about the proper position to take. I sat on a committee not too long ago where an individual was laid off because of his job classification. (Under our company policy, we lay off by job classification in the salaried ranks.) He happened to be the only guy in his classification. But it turned out that while there were three or four different job classifications in the organization, the people in them were all doing exactly the same thing, and so the question really didn't revolve around the layoff, it revolved around the propriety of the classifications. We saw they were not proper. You shouldn't have four people in four different classifications all doing the same kind of work. So we said, "Look, go back and get your compensation people to run a study and properly classify these people, and then we'll take a look and see whether or not the guy was properly laid off." As it turned out, he wasn't, and so he was reinstated with back pay.

A file is kept of Management Appeals Committee documents and decisions. If the grievant is dissatisfied with the committee's decision and goes on to arbitration, the arbitrator's decision is added to the file.

What about the possibility that a supervisor rebuked by the committee will retaliate against the employee? Northrop executives do not discount this danger. Littrell observes:

> It's human nature for a manager not to feel good about the guy that beat him or her before the person's bosses on the committee. The decision may reflect badly on the manager. I think you've got to worry about retaliation, however subtle, when the employee returns to work. Fortunately, we have a management climate here that says that you shouldn't retaliate. And if retaliation is suspected, employee relations has a face-to-face talk with the manager and says, "Look, this is not right. You got reversed, but we all make mistakes. It's not going to affect your career, so you shouldn't really be letting it affect the career of the guy who filed the grievance, either."

What types of cases come before the Management Appeals Committee? In 1986, the issues ranged from alcohol and waste of material to discordant behavior and poor performance. Nearly a quarter of the cases involved complaints over poor performance reviews.

How much time is consumed in getting to the Management Appeals Committee? The recorded times vary enormously, from a few weeks in one case in 1986 to a couple of months in another case that year. Vacation schedules, witnesses, delays in investigations by employee relations reps—these and other circumstances create a large variance. Typically, however, four or five weeks may elapse between the time that a written appeal is filed to the time that a hearing is held and a decision rendered. The committee works under a rule whereby it must render a decision within fifteen working days of the hearing.

How many decisions go against managers and supervisors? In 1984, not an atypical year, nine of fifteen committee decisions went against the manager; four decisions were compromises; two went for management. This compares with thirty-one of forty-seven cases decided against management by the administrative officers, with six compromises and ten affirmations of management's action; and with eighteen of twenty-four agreements that went against management in informal mediation between manager and subordinate by employee relations reps, four compromises in such negotiations, and two agreements by subordinates to accept the managers' decisions. Although these proportions are by no means standards or averages, for the ratios fluctuate a great deal from year to year depending on layoffs, reorganizations, and other matters, they make it clear that the Management Appeals Committee, like the administrative officers and employee reps, approaches cases with independent judgment and is beholden to no one except the corporation.

The number of hearings conducted annually by the committee has increased noticeably over the years as the work force has grown and employees' perceptions of the committee have grown more positive. I talked to one person who has been active in the due process procedure since the early 1950s. He recalls that when he started, very few cases came before the committee during the course of a year.

Later we will look at some examples of committee decisions when we consider arbitration cases.

Where the Company Never Loses—Arbitration

Grievants who don't like the decision of the Management Appeals Committee have five working days to appeal to arbitration. The procedure is simple, and employees of all sorts have used it. Also, says Littrell, Northrop has never lost a case.

Literally, this is not true; he means that while arbitrators' *decisions* may go against the company, the company always wins by demonstrating its good faith to employees and—often—by learning something.

Northrop pays the arbitrator's fee, which is likely to range between $300 and $500 a day. The hearing itself is likely to take a day (though some have gone much longer than that), and the arbitrator is likely to charge for one or two days for preparation of the decision. Grievants can choose attorneys to represent them (in which case the grievants pay) or employee relations reps (in which case the company pays). The latter have a fine track record in arbitration cases, and employees often choose them instead of attorneys. Management sees no inconsistency between having a person on the company payroll taking an employee's case to arbitration because its goal in having arbitration as a final step is fairness and justice in workaday relationships.

The hearings are held in conference rooms on the premises. Grievants who are still employed are paid for time spent in arbitration during their work hours, as are witnesses. Under the rules, arbitrators must render their decisions within thirty days of completion of the hearings. Woodward (who has represented employees several times in arbitration and "won" several cases for clients) explains as follows:

> When a grievant asks for arbitration, employee relations writes the California State Mediation and Conciliation Service and asks for a list of five arbitrators. A copy of the list is mailed by the service to the grievant and another copy to the company. If I happen to be the employee relations rep who is involved, I get on the phone with the grievant or we get together in my office. I ask him to strike a name from the list. I then strike a name, and I ask him to strike another. Then I strike one of the last two names for the company. The arbitrator who is left is the one we ask to handle the case.
>
> The employee relations representative then contacts the CSMCS and tells them which arbitrator was selected. The state contacts the arbitrator, and the arbitrator gets in touch with us. We set a date, time, and place for the hearing.
>
> The hearing is usually in a room in the area where the grievant and the witnesses work, so that they can get there easily. Management sits on one side of the table, the employee on the other. The arbitrator begins by explaining the arbitration process and why he's there. The company representative and the grievant's representative read opening statements explaining what they will prove. The moving party's case is presented first. The company brings its witnesses in. They're sworn in just as in court. The company gets them to tell their story by asking questions. It may bring in some exhibits to back its arguments, always doing so through its questions of the witnesses. The exhibits are agreed to and numbered; they are called "company exhibits." Next, the grievant's representative cross-examines the company's witnesses. Then the arbitrator asks the grievant if he or she is ready, and that side of the case is told. Witnesses are sworn in, testify, are cross-examined, and re-cross-examined. At any time during the proceedings the arbitrator can stop the testimony and ask questions for clarification.
>
> The arbitrator may not be familiar with the aircraft business, and so the company takes pains to have questions and answers that will help him or her understand the industry. The arbitrator may, in fact, be escorted to the shop or office area where the employee works to actually see the work and how it is performed.
>
> The proceedings generally are conducted by the company and employee representatives. One time a grievant I was representing asked the arbitrator, "Can I make a speech?" The arbitrator said, "You can, but I should warn you that what you say may go against you." I told the grievant, "If you have to say something, keep it short." He talked, and didn't keep it short. He hurt his own chances for a favorable award.
>
> Most arbitrators' decisions go for the company. This is not too surprising, considering the totality of the grievance procedure. If the company's position is not a strong

one, the grievance has, in all likelihood, been settled before reaching the arbitration step.

Northrop's policy of paying the arbitrator's fee and expenses has caused some knowledgeable observers to raise their eyebrows. Won't this bias the arbitrator in favor of management? Littrell comments as follows:

> This result [biasing the arbitrator by the company's picking up the tab] has not been our experience and perhaps reflects a lack of faith on the part of critics in the professionalism of the community of arbitrators. Be that as it may, we bear the cost of the arbitration for the very practical reason that most of the employees who seek arbitration of their grievances simply couldn't afford it if we did not. We really find that when we deserve to win, we usually do, and when we don't, we lose. But win or lose, the very existence of the final arbitration by an independent professional arbitrator demonstrates our intention to be fair to our employees and to provide a system of due process which we believe validates that decision.[3]

Littrell believes that the possibility of arbitration strengthens the hand of employee relations when dealing with a grievance:

> Managers know that somewhere up the line they may get an arbitrator saying, "Boy, you really blew this one, Mr. Manager," and so they have to think. That is one of the benefits of having the arbitrator at the end of the line—it gives employee relations people some clout. They can say to the manager, "Look, in all the history of arbitration, no arbitrator ever supported the position you're taking, Mr. Manager, and if this case goes to arbitration, as it very well may, you're going to get reversed. We don't think it's a good idea to get egg on your face."

Littrell feels that arbitration also has a good effect on the Management Appeals Committee and tends to counteract any tendency to get too concerned with the effect on supervisory authority of a decision in favor of the grievant.

How does the company ensure that the arbitrator understands its approach to employee relations? An eighty-two-page booklet entitled *Working with Northrop* goes to the arbitrator; the same booklet is given to every new employee. In these pages management spells out as concisely as it can its policies regarding employee pay, benefits, seniority, attendance, security, standards of conduct, due process, and other matters. Exhibit 1 contains an excerpt from the section specifying offenses for which an employee can be disciplined.

Littrell feels that the company communicates to the arbitrator in another way:

> The way we conduct the hearings says a good deal to the arbitrator about our desire that he make a proper and fair decision. We don't pound the table a lot. We don't conduct ourselves in as adversarial way as we might, and I've been in hearings where the arbitrator says that this is much too friendly to be an arbitration. "I can see from the way you're conducting this hearing that the maintenance of the relationship with the grievant is extremely important to you," he'll say.

The number of annual arbitration cases fluctuates widely, depending on layoffs, reorganization, and other matters. In 1986, there were thirteen applications for arbitration; in 1984, there was only one.

[3] Ibid., pp. 120–121.

EXHIBIT 1
Excerpt from *Working with Northrop*

---

4. Major Offenses

The following offenses are subject to the disciplinary action indicated:

1. Insubordination—Willful disobedience of any reasonable and legitimate instructions issued by any member of supervision or anyone authorized to act in such capacity.
2. Negligence in performing duties.
3. Failure to report any errors, damage, or poor workmanship to supervision.
4. Quitting work, sleeping, or loafing during work hours.
5. Theft, unauthorized removal, or willful damage of any property belonging to another employee, to Northrop, or to a Northrop customer.
6. Sale or solicitation for the sale of stolen property on company premises.
7. Falsifying, altering, or omitting pertinent information on any company records, or giving false replies or testimony to official company representatives in any matter relating to company activities, business affairs, and like matters.
8. Deliberately clocking another employee's card in a time clock or badge in a badge reader or allowing another employee to do the same for you.
9. Unauthorized acquisition, use, release, duplication, or removal of company records, employee lists, or any other form of company information without the prior, explicit permission of the supervisor in charge of the activity concerned.
10. Using company owned or controlled material, time, equipment, or personnel for any unauthorized purpose. This includes using company data processing resources for any purpose except authorized company business.
11. Counterfeiting or utilizing counterfeit or spurious company product acceptance or work completion stamp, identification badge, gate pass, parking permit, record, identifying insignia, or other such item.
12. Using another employee's product acceptance or work completion stamp, or permitting another employee to use your stamp, or failure to properly safeguard your stamp.
13. Using another person's badge or pass to gain admission to company premises, or to a controlled area within such premises, or permitting another person to use an employee badge, gate pass, vehicle pass, or parking permit for such purposes.
14. Unauthorized duplication or use of keys or any device used for locking or securing company premises or property.
15. Using another person's data processing identification code and password, or permitting another person to use your code and password.
16. Unauthorized entry to, or exit from, company premises at any location at any time.
17. Horseplay, wrestling, dangerous practical joking, or throwing of objects.
18. Creating, encouraging, or participating in disorders, violence, or any other activity in which the intent or result is the disruption or interference with the conduct of company business or the performance or working duties of others.
19. Creating discord or lack of harmony by actions such as ridicule, disrespect, defamatory statements toward or concerning others in such a way as to interfere with company business.
20. Threatening, intimidating, coercing, harassing, or interfering with any employees in the performance of their duties both on and off company premises.

(*continued*)

EXHIBIT 1 (*continued*)

21. Committing any act of violence against another employee, including fighting on company premises.
22. Introduction or possession of firearms, explosives, knives, or any other instrument which can be used as an injurious or deadly weapon on company property.
23. Immoral or indecent conduct on company premises.
24. Introduction, possession, sale, purchase, solicitation for sale, or use of intoxicating beverages or illegal or illicit drugs or substances on company premises, or reporting to work under the influence of same. Northrop reserves the right to chemically analyze or test beverages, medicines, drugs, etc., brought on company premises. If you appear to be under the influence of intoxicating beverages or narcotics, the company may require a blood test or other drug/alcohol screening. An employee's consent to submit to such a test is required as a condition of employment and the employee's refusal to consent may result in disciplinary action, including discharge.
25. Gambling, conducting a lottery, or engaging in any other game of chance on company property at any time. With prior management approval, there may be occasions where lotteries and raffles may be authorized for company-sponsored activities.

Source: Working with Northrop (Northrop Corporation, 1985), pp. 66–68.

Suppose an employee loses in arbitration and goes to the courts. Will the courts defer to the arbitrator's decision? While it is likely that the courts will continue to review arbitrations when they see some special principle involved,[4] Littrell hopes that the day is not far off when exceptions will be few and far between:

> Some time ago an employee was discharged and went through our complete grievance procedure. He was represented by an attorney in arbitration, and the arbitrator's decision went against him. He then went to the courts and is now suing the company for wrongful discharge, intentional infliction of emotional distress, and all the rest of the things that go with such a case. We are about to file our motion for summary judgment arguing that the case was settled in arbitration. We are saying that with the courts' traditional deference to arbitration, this case ought not be heard in the legal system. If our argument stands up, I think we will have established something very important for a lot of people who are interested in grievance systems.

Case of the peripatetic pugilists. A case that recently went to arbitration involves a Northrop employee whom I shall call "Rick Gerard." In the washroom prior to lunch break, Gerard and another employee whom I shall called "Tim Jonas" got into a nasty argument in the course of which Gerard may have accidentally spit on the other man (missing front teeth would have caused this). Later, as Gerard sat in his car eating lunch, Jonas came up to him, they exchanged words, Jonas swung at Gerard through the open window, and Gerard may have swung back. Both men were fired for fighting on the corporate premises (see Rule 21 in Exhibit 1).

---

[4] In *Holodnak* v. *Avco Corporation*, 514 F. 2d 285 (U.S. District Court, Connecticut, 1975), for example, the court overturned the arbitrator's decision on the grounds that the plaintiff's constitutional rights to free speech were violated.

Gerard, who had been with Northrop for ten years, wanted his job back. First he went to employee relations, then to the administrative officer for a hearing. The administrative officer denied his request on the grounds that while he may have been less at fault than Jonas, he was nevertheless engaged in violence. Then he went to the Management Appeals Committee with a four-page statement and such exhibits as his attendance record, performance record, and the injury report of the company nurse who treated him following the fight. At the committee hearings, he produced seven witnesses. His principal contention was that he did not start the fight and was only defending himself when he struck back at Jonas.

In a letter to Gerard signed by all three members, the committee told him that the discharge stood because, in its opinion, he was a participant in the fighting.

Gerard then went to arbitration. He chose Woodward to represent him; the company was represented by another employee relations administrator, Robert M. Sochacki. The arbitrator was Philip Tamoush, a well-known arbitrator from southern California. Two weeks after the one-day hearing in Hawthorne, Tamoush rendered his decision, a nine-page double-spaced opinion that started with the issue, proceeded to the rule prohibiting fighting in *Working with Northrop,* and went on to summarize the facts of the case, the contentions of the parties, the arbitrator's findings, and his conclusion. Tamoush decided in favor of Gerard on the basis that he was victimized by the attack and, if he bruised Jonas, did it in self-defense. He ordered Northrop to reinstate Gerard with full back pay and benefits. However, he stated that his award "should also be considered to be a written, final warning notice for a first offense" to Gerard, and directed Gerard to get his front teeth fixed so as to avoid unintentionally inflaming other employees in the future when he argued with them.

Case of the misplaced pin.   In a second case that ended up in arbitration, an employee whom I shall call "Dan Stone" was fired for poor workmanship. He had placed a pin in an assembly incorrectly, and it had fallen out. Stone had three written notices for poor workmanship in his record; at the same time, he had a workmen's compensation claim against the company.

Going to employee relations, the administrative officer, the Management Appeals Committee, and finally to arbitration, Stone claimed that the pin fell out by accident and that the error was not his fault; he also claimed that Northrop was conspiring against him because of his workmen's compensation claim. Management defended that the error was unjustifiable, with carelessness the apparent cause, and that Stone's compensation claim had nothing to do with its action in firing him.

Agreeing with management, the arbitrator upheld Stone's discharge.

Keeping Tabs

Management keeps a close watch on various indicators of how its grievance program is doing—number of appeals to administrative officers, the Management Appeals Committee, and arbitration, the subjects of such appeals, outcomes, and others. Littrell pays special attention to the number of times first-level management decisions are changed at higher levels and by the committee. He worries if there are too few reversals, for he knows that mistakes in judgment are bound to be made by supervisors, but he also worries if there are too many reversals. He says:

> If we found that no reversals were happening, I would have to wonder whether employee relations is doing the job it should. Are we being tough enough on manage-

ment? Are we seeing in depth the problems that exist on the floor? On the other hand, if management lost too many, I would begin to worry about the possible breakdown of our philosophy of management and whether we are really living up to the principles we espouse of being a good place to work and treating people fairly.

At a meeting of employee relations representatives that I was invited to sit in on, the chairperson went around the table, asking each person in turn where his or her cases stood, noting on the weekly grievance activity report (a computerized print-out) changes in the status of cases pending, and asking for thoughts and reactions based on the past week's contacts. Discussion was open and candid, there was a great deal of give and take, and I considered this to be an excellent way of discussing firsthand information and funneling it up in management. Meetings like this take place regularly in all parts of the company.

Woodward thinks ex-employees are a good source of information:

> All terminating employees are personally interviewed. Then about three months after the person leaves, he or she is sent a questionnaire. It includes questions about how the person felt about the grievance procedure—whether he or she knew about it, perceptions of how it worked, and so on. This information is a useful check for us.

"We are not a big company for making surveys of current employees," says Littrell. Instead, he and other managers do a lot of talking to people, and they use that information to check the corporate pulse.

A Grievance Procedure for Managers?

At the time of my interviews in June 1987, management was considering a proposal for a new feature: a formal grievance procedure for managers. As *Working with Northrop* spells out in the first line describing the grievance procedure it has operated since 1946, that procedure is for *non*supervisory employees. A manufacturing superintendent or a financial supervisor would not be able to appeal to the administrative officer and the Management Appeals Committee. In practice, managers' complaints of unfair treatment have been deliberated carefully by senior administrators—there has been no unilateral firing or demotion—but no procedure has been spelled out in print.

What precipitated the proposal was the dismissal of a vice president several years ago. Although he was a popular executive, senior executives felt that they had strong and clear reasons for letting him go. The word went around, however, that he had been summarily fired—the careful deliberations of division managers and the corporate office were not broadcast. The result, says Littrell, is that managers here and there began wondering about their own futures in the company. "If this could happen to good old Sam, the same thing could happen to me." The managers took their concerns to the division vice president of human resources, and in due time the human resources committee sought to resolve the problem.

Littrell, who is on that committee, says that it ruled out the idea of arbitration as a final step in the new procedure. There were too many reasons why arbitration wasn't suitable for a manager, the group felt. As the last step in the new process, the proposal calls for a Senior Management Review Board comprised of the vice president of human resources in the division in which the grievant works, the senior vice president of human resources or his or her designee, and the division vice president and general manager or his or her designee. Only members of management are eligible to use the new procedure, and they can appeal to the employee relations manager and then the Review Board only if their complaints involve discharge, discrimination, or discipline. Such matters as eligibility for participation in bonus plans, performance reviews, and selections for promotions are specifically ruled out.

In October 1987, the rules for the new procedure, culminating in a Senior Management Review Board, were sent to division heads and divisional vice presidents of human resources in southern California.

Observations

Northrop's grievance procedure works, says Littrell, "because we want it to work and take pains to see that it works. And it works because we have good people working hard to make it work." [5]

It is hard to state the reason for Northrop's success more succinctly. There is no secret to it, no magic formula—only desire plus talent plus elbow grease. Although the desire may have rested mainly with top management in the late 1940s, today it seems to pervade the organization. "I don't know," says Littrell, "that you are ever going to get immediate support from first-line supervision for a system that is going to challenge their authority." So it is crucial that top management commit itself at the outset (and stay committed). After a while, however, middle and lower-level management learn that the procedure doesn't turn their world upside down, and then they, too, begin to support it.

In passing, several features of Northrop's system deserve comment:

1. *Time requirements*. Management makes a strong effort to keep grievance appeals moving so that they are resolved without long delays. The employee relations staff is given ten working days after receipt of a grievance to resolve it; the administrative officer is given ten working days to render a decision after the conference with the grievant and the employee relations rep; the Management Appeals Committee is given fifteen working days after the hearing to issue a decision; the arbitrator is asked to render his or her decision within thirty days after the hearing.

Nevertheless, a grievance may be in the pipeline longer than these numbers indicate, and that is due not to lack of attention to the deadlines, but to delays in obtaining a hearing date at the next higher step. For instance, reviewing the grievance activity report for 1986, I see a grievance over a layoff that took nearly three months to go from the initial contact with employee relations to a committee decision; a grievance over a first-warning notice for creating discord that took a little over eight months to reach a committee decision; a grievance over a performance review that took about seven months to reach a committee decision. In a large company where due process may require the involvement of senior executives, there is no easy way to schedule hearings quickly; the pressures of work and travel may lead to delays of weeks and possibly months. It may be only in the smaller organization that a grievant can hope to get to the top in a few weeks.

2. *Arbitration*. Management's perception of the value of the arbitration step will surely surprise many outsiders. The experience with arbitrators seems to have been generally good, in management's opinion. Reading a number of arbitrators' opin-

[5] "The Grievance and Arbitration System for Nonunion Employees at Northrop Corporation," p. 127.

ions, I got a good impression of their neutrality, objectivity, and professionalism. In talks with Northrop people I heard no complaint that arbitrators work on a quota system, giving, say, 60 percent of their decisions to grievants and 40 percent to the company (a rule of thumb often quoted in unionized companies). Northrop's relationship with arbitrators is good, its selection process gives it a measure of control over the choice of arbitrator, and the fact that its personnel policies are carefully spelled out gives the arbitrator a clear "law" to apply.

For the many business executives in this country who hold arbitration in great suspicion, perhaps the most surprising fact is that Northrop's own employee relations representatives may argue a grievant's case instead of an outside attorney. They have done that and won, and management holds no grudge. I heard no rumor that the rule (put in during 1983) will change.

Littrell believes that the arbitration step has been quite valuable. "The thing that makes managers listen and employees believe," he says, "is the existence of the grievance procedure and, most important, the potential that in any given case management's decision may be judged by an arbitrator outside the influence of management."

3. *Control.* Although in 1946 Northrop may have looked to union grievance procedures as a model for parts of the new nonunion procedure it instituted, there is little resemblance with union procedures today. The employee at Northrop is always in control of his or her grievance; no one else ever decides whether to continue the grievance or to use it as a bargaining point to gain certain concessions from management. If the grievance is settled informally, only the grievant has the power to make that possible.

What is more, Northrop's system appears to engender an employee relations climate where grievances don't mushroom into unmanageable numbers. At the time of my interviews in Hawthorne, one of the company's major competitors had about three thousand grievances outstanding. The impression was widespread that a large number of these grievances had been "manufactured" for purposes of union-management negotiations. At Northrop, by contrast, the largest *annual* number of grievances ever recorded was less than two hundred. This difference gives the company an important advantage in cost control.

The Employees Committee
at Polaroid

At Polaroid Corporation, employee complaints are handled by the Employees Committee. Established in 1946, the approach is one of the two oldest systems of employee due process in American industry (the other is Northrop's, started in the same year). Polaroid's chief executive at the time was Edwin H. Land, the legendary scientific genius who invented the instant photographic process in the 1940s. (Now seventy-seven, he devotes all of his time to research at the Rowland Institute for Science in Cambridge, Massachusetts.) In Land's words: "It was my invention. It was a very natural outgrowth of my relationship with Polaroid employees at the time. It meant that the employees' elected officials could meet with me and pass on employees' concerns to me."

The approach is as different from other corporate hearing procedures as Polaroid cameras are different from competitors' products. Both in concept and execution, it

Author's note: Early in 1989, Polaroid made headlines for its success in defeating a takeover attempt by Shamrock Holdings, Inc. A key factor in Polaroid's success was its employee stock ownership plan, which controlled 14 percent of the company's stock and refused to sell shares to Shamrock.

Company: Polaroid Corporation		Products/Services: Cameras, film, accessories
Headquarters: Cambridge, Massachusetts		Dates of Interviews: September 15, 16, 23, October 22, 1986
Sales: $1.6 billion (1987)	Number of Employees: 13,400	

is unique. Land's successors at Polaroid, William J. McCune, Jr., and now I. M. Booth, have been deeply committed to the Employees Committee. They value its contribution to labor peace—the company is nonunion and has escaped much of the turmoil that has plagued industrial relations in other manufacturers. They also believe it has helped management create a climate that encourages employees at all levels to participate in the making of decisions that affect them.

The members of the committee are elected by all employees. It represents all hourly and nonsupervisory exempt employees to management; it always takes the viewpoint of the employee and never judges the merits of a case on its own. With one exception, the final decision on a complaint is always made by one or more executives. That exception occurs when the employee, dissatisfied with management's final decision, elects to take the grievance to arbitration. When this is done, which is rarely, the company abides by the decision of the arbitrator.

Grievances are not the only job of the Employees Committee, and the Employees Committee is not the only way management supports a healthy, creative work climate for its ten thousand employees in Massachusetts and thirteen thousand four hundred employees worldwide. The company is known for its openness, good pay scales, generous fringe benefits, and employee education programs. Also, Polaroid is notable for freedom of speech; at all levels, employees seem to feel free to speak their minds on company policy without fear of recrimination.

Reps and Steps

"If you are an employee and you have a problem, you should talk it over with your supervisor before you approach your rep," says Nick Pasquarosa, chairperson of the Employees Committee. Pasquarosa is one of thirty-two members of the committee; he has been a committee officer since 1976, and was elected chairperson in 1983. "In fact, when you talk to your rep, that's the first question he'll ask you—'Did you talk about this to your supervisor?' If you didn't, he'll ask you to go back and do that before he'll talk with you. When you do talk with him, he wants to understand your problem. He doesn't judge whether you're right or wrong; he just wants to be able to represent your point of view."

"Of course," says Bill Graney, vice chairperson of the committee, "he may guide you a little. He might cite some past cases that are similar to yours so that you can decide better whether to press on. But whatever you decide, he represents you. It doesn't matter if he personally thinks you're way off base. If you say, 'I want to grieve,' then we grieve." Graney was elected to the committee in 1969.

After that first talk, the rep may go to the supervisor himself—with or without the grievant. If the grievant isn't satisfied with the supervisor's answer, the next stop is the general supervisor's office; the next step after that is the division manager.

"If after these informal talks, you're still not satisfied," says Pasquarosa, "then you file a formal grievance in writing. Step 1 is to the department manager with copies to others who are involved in the case. That manager responds in writing. If you're not satisfied with the answer, you can elect to go to Step 2, the division officer. Again, you write up your grievance. Step 3 is to the Personnel Policy Committee or 'PPC,' as it is called. A panel of three corporate officers hears your case; your rep also attends the hearing along with local management and Employees Committee officers. You present your side to the panel, the managers present their side. The panel officers ask questions. Afterward they give you their decision in writing. If you're not satisfied with their response, you can go to the president. If you're still not satisfied, you can request arbitration. The company decides whether it will go to arbitration; if it does, it pays the arbitrator. If you want an attorney to represent you at the arbitration, however, you must pay that fee yourself. The company and the Employees Committee jointly pick the arbitrator."

"At Step 3," Graney points out, "Nick or I always get involved. Before that, the grievant's rep is the only one on the committee who is involved, even though the grievance may come through this office. But from Step 3 on, Nick or I will be present at the hearings."

The rep—sometimes more than one rep—becomes involved as necessary in helping the employee write his or her grievance.

"There's not really a form for writing up grievances," says Francis Kearns, a former chairperson of the Employees Committee. He left the committee in 1978 to become a production supervisor in the Waltham plant of Polaroid. "Rather, there's a *format*. You describe the incident and the facts, why you're grieving, and what kind of action or remedy you want. You can use up to ten pieces of paper, if you want." Kearns emphasizes the importance of stating what kind of remedy the grievant desires. "If the case ever gets to arbitration, the arbitrator wants to know specifically what the grievant is requesting. If he rules in the grievant's favor, he'll give only what is requested. For example, if the grievant doesn't request back pay for such and such, the arbitrator won't give any. He'll just reinstate the employee (or whatever else is requested)."

As a formal grievance goes up from Step 1, a package of written materials tends to develop. At each stage, the complaint is restated and answered; also, other comments and notes may be added. By the time the PPC, the president, or the arbitrator gets the grievance, the package will show the history of the preceding complaints and answers.

How long grievants must wait for decisions depends a great deal on what stage or step they are in. When grievances are informal, the waiting period from incident to decision may be very short; much of the time, in fact, the answer is forthcoming at the meeting with the supervisor or manager. In Steps 1 and 2 of a formal grievance, waiting periods are very short, too. When a formal grievance goes to the PPC, president, or arbitration, however, the period may stretch out to twelve months, in some cases.

Most grievances come from nonexempt employees. However, now and then a nonsupervisory exempt member will grieve. Although many nonexempt employees have issues during the course of a typical year, the overwhelming majority of these complaints never become formal grievances. In fact, the number of formal grievances is likely to be less than one hundred per year (about one per one hundred employees in Massachusetts). Of these, the PPC may hear about twenty, and a fair number of these may go on up to the company president. The number of cases ending up in arbitration is surprisingly small. Kearns estimates that the number must be less than twenty during the past twenty years.

Leo LeClaire, who is a director of personnel, emphasizes the crucial role played by the informal system. "We are strongly in favor of it," he says. "If you emphasize it like we do, it should reduce greatly the number of formal grievances you have. When you find that a long time goes by between the date of the incident and the final resolution of the complaint in the formal system, usually that's because folks spent so much time trying to work it out informally." LeClaire believes that the reps do a great deal to ease the strain and time pressures of formal and informal grievances. "They try to screen out nonsense and baseless complaints. They try to dissuade employees who don't have legitimate concerns."

Conceivably a "baseless complaint" could go up through all steps in the informal system and then through all five steps of the formal system. This has not happened yet, however—probably because of the behind-the-scenes efforts of adroit reps.

As for the subjects of grievances, they cover the same ground as in many other companies—discharges, failures to get jobs applied for, performance evaluations, merit increases, disciplinary warnings, denials of requests for shift or job changes, and so on. Of these, disciplinary warnings may be the subject most often grieved.

The role of the Employees Committee in representing employees may lead to curious situations. As suggested, the committee does not state independent positions on issues under grievance. In forty years, it hasn't deviated from this policy. (In this respect, as in many other respects, it is unlike unions.) Always it represents the viewpoint of grievants, most of whom are hourly employees but some of whom are nonsupervisory salaried people. As a result, different members of the committee have occasionally represented employees whose interests are adverse to one another. This has not affected the committee's credibility with management, however, and it has never been an issue in employee relations.

At the PPC Level

As noted, about twenty formal grievance cases are appealed from division managers to the panel of three corporate officers—the PPC. Many of these grievances concern rejections of applications for posted job openings; others concern discharges and alleged inequities in pay.

According to John Harlor, vice president for corporate personnel, about twenty-five corporate officers are available to sit on a PPC panel. Many of these officers are likely to serve one or more times per year. Harlor used to sit on the panels but hasn't since becoming head of personnel.

The PPC's only function today is to hear grievances. Until a few years ago it was a permanent group appointed by the president and was entrusted with policy-making.

Extremely Capable Members

The Employees Committee has thirty-two members. They are elected by ballot by defined groups of employees in buildings and sections of buildings. Since the late 1960s, they serve for two-year terms and can be reelected. "At election time," says Jim Murphy, a machinist who has been with Polaroid for sixteen years, "the candidates for the committee come around and talk to you at your work. They tell you what they want to do if elected—for example, what programs they want to push."

Generally speaking, members are extroverts, good mixers, popular people. Vice president for corporate materials and systems management Christopher C. Ingraham, who has watched many committees come and go, states, "The individuals who get elected are by and large extremely capable people. Personally, I have found them very helpful. Years ago when I was a supervisor, for instance, several came to me confidentially and gave me some very good advice on how to be a better supervisor. It was the kind of advice you are lucky to get from a good boss."

Most members are hourly employees, but a few are salaried people who are not supervisors. (Anyone who supervises people is ineligible for membership.) In addition to machine operators, machinists, maintenance workers, and others from the plant floors, therefore, the committee includes such people as technical specialists, financial analysts, research and development technicians, and model-makers. In short, the committee is a pretty good cross-section of nonsupervisory employees at Polaroid, at least as far as jobs are concerned. Critics point to the absence of women reps and the scarcity of black reps. Since the membership is elected, however, this is something that only the rank and file can do something about; neither committee officials nor corporate management are in a position to decree more representation from these groups.

The life of a committee member has both drawbacks and rewards. The drawbacks have to do mostly with the time demands. Speaking from experience, Kearns puts it this way: "If you do your job as a rep effectively, you can't do it all in working hours. The consequences of what you're doing or not doing weigh heavily on you. You're dealing with people's welfare and morale. They depend on what you do. So it becomes a pressure-packed job, and you don't leave it behind you when you leave the shift." Probably no day goes by at Polaroid when at least one rep somewhere is not representing an employee with an issue.

On the rewards side, committee members find the work exciting. "Without it," says Kearns, "I couldn't have seen the broad scope of the company, I couldn't have met with a lot of different people at different levels of management and from different disciplines. I had been with the company for several years before going to the committee, but I had done nothing like that before. I couldn't have if I hadn't been on the committee. It was a great experience, an education. It was a tremendous confidence-builder, too."

How are new reps trained? They are coached by veteran reps known as "coordinators." Also, they learn a lot simply from rubbing elbows with older reps at meetings and in discussion groups. In addition, Pasquarosa and Graney have developed a training program for reps. The teachers are brought in from outside the company, but the subject matter has been carefully worked out by the two officials. It covers such topics as the nature of power and influence, negotiation skills, and effective presentation of facts and arguments.

Scope and Power

In at least four respects, the Employees Committee is unusual. As far as I know, only one or two other companies have a system with any of these features.

First, the committee has no visibility problems. Everyone at Polaroid appears to know about it. This is due in part to its broad role in personnel policy (to be described shortly), but even if it were not for that, it is likely that every employee would know about the group. One reason is the election process. It is a superb publicity device, though that is not its purpose. As noted, candidates go around speaking to constituents, and almost everyone votes for a candidate in the "primaries." In addition, the committee has developed a two-hour slide presentation about its origins and functions, and this is shown from time to time in the different plants. The plant manager arranges the time for the presentation to be shown.

Second, the committee is autonomous. It governs itself, without controls from management, and it does not report to a top executive or department. If it were to be shown on an organization chart, it would be shown without accountability lines to any office on the chart. Its only accountability is to the employees who elect the members. No senior executive attends its meetings.

Third, grievances are but one part of a rep's job. Pasquarosa explains as follows: "When an employee is elected to the committee from a building, he or she is concerned with a lot of functions and activities in that building. *One* of them is conflict resolution. Another is local issues and problems, that is, questions about the operations in that particular building. When reps get good at this second part of their job, we expand their scope so that they work on corporate issues—revisions of policies, new practices proposed, and so on. This third activity means that they are dealing with large groups companywide. How do we effect a planned layoff better? Why does management want to change such and such a policy? Is the trouble in the policy or in the administration? And so on. In short, the rep's job is multilayered."

Graney adds: "The personnel department does a lot of the same things that we do. However, it tends to be management's representatives, whereas we on the committee are the *employees'* representatives—hourly and salaried both. What we bring to a meeting with personnel managers is a knowledge of what employees think and what their priorities are. The personnel department may have the same issues on its list as we do, but it will have a different view of what employees want."

Proof that the committee's special talents are recognized is top management's use of it as a sounding board for ideas it is considering. From time to time management asks it how a certain personnel problem shapes up in its eyes, or whether a personnel proposal should be changed in some way.

How did this unusual power and scope develop? In 1946, as noted, Land started the committee as a way of funnelling employee reactions and ideas to him. In March 1955, Land advanced the concept another step; he sent a memorandum to division, department, and section heads stating that thereafter the Employees Committee would have a strong voice in planning and formulating personnel policy. By 1969, the committee's participation in the early stages of policy design seemed to be firmly established. In 1975, the committee expressed its expectation that it would be involved in every stage of personnel policy matters. With the exception of emergencies, this expectation appears to have been met; the committee seems to have been involved in practically every major personnel policy formulation since then. To illustrate the range of this involvement, in a recent year it met with top personnel officials on such matters as grievances, vacation policy, outside hiring, the voluntary severance program, workers' compensation, company store profits, corporate ethics policy, storm pay, benefits, deferred compensation, and the planned Christmas shutdown, among many others.

Fourth, the committee concerns itself with both the informal and formal grievance systems. Unlike the systems set up by other companies, it does not leave the handling of informal grievances to the personnel department, the human resources group, or some other agency of the company.

Consistent with this, reps are not concerned solely with grievances defined in some particular way but more broadly with employees' *concerns*. Pasquarosa comments: "A little old lady who has worked here for thirty-five years is upset that her supervisor doesn't say good morning to her. It is not a violation of policy for a supervisor to omit that greeting, so it may not be a grievance, but it is a concern to her, perhaps a big concern. So we'll speak to the supervisor. 'It might make her feel better if you said hello when you see her.' Something like that."

What is more, the committee does not try to develop a logical consistency in its approach, as courts of law do, but to make fairness its goal. Graney observes: "We try to take individual circumstances into account. This means that the same offenses may be treated differently. If, say, an employee violates a written policy on stealing, we don't look at how the last employee who committed a similar offense was disciplined, but at any unique circumstances that make this crime a little different. As a result, two employees committing exactly the same offense may deserve different measures of discipline, in our view. We don't try so hard to be consistent as to be fair. Fair means not necessarily equal penalties."

"In the informal system," says LeClaire, "almost anything is grievable. But when the employee moves into the formal system, it must be shown what company policy or practice was violated." In the view of at least one executive in the company, the Employees Committee is rarely short of ideas on how to link a complaint with corporate policy. The committee can almost always find a way, says the executive, to present the complaint so that it appears that policy may have been violated.

Case of the agitated applicant.   An employee whom I shall call "John Mortimer" was a film crew chief. (The job sounds supervisory, but it is not.) He had been at Polaroid for about ten years, had a fine work record, and aimed to advance to more interesting and higher-paying jobs, such as machinist. On his own he had taken a number of courses that were required preparation for a machinist. He was not, in other words, sitting back waiting for something nice to happen.

When Polaroid posted four job openings for machinists, he was one of the first to apply. He thought he had one of those jobs hands down. He would have to go to evening school a little bit more, but he had completed much of the preparation already, and he had a nearly flawless record in his favor. However, when he was called about the results of his application, he was told that, despite his qualifications, management had chosen four other applicants for the openings.

During working hours he got in touch with his rep. This was easy, since he usually saw the rep once or twice a day. He described the situation to the rep and told him he couldn't understand what was going on. "I had everything they wanted!" The rep promised to investigate. He found that Mortimer had scored the highest of about forty applicants on the test that had been given. The rep also got the names of the four employees chosen for the openings.

Mortimer said he would like to file a formal grievance. The rep did the paperwork, and a short time later, the two of them went during working hours to a grievance meeting at the 750 Main Street plant of Polaroid in Cambridge. "Going to the meeting," says Mortimer, "I was a nervous wreck. I still couldn't figure out any reason for being turned down, but I have never done anything like this before, and I wasn't comfortable." Outside the room where the grievances were being heard, he sat for a while with several others who had filed complaints. Close to twenty employees, he learned, were grieving the same rejection he had gotten. Talk wasn't easy.

When his turn came, he and the rep went in and found about ten people sitting around a large table. The group included a couple of men who had interviewed him for the machinist's job, a couple of supervisors, and several from the personnel department and the Employees Committee. The rep gave them the package for his case, that is, about a dozen documents dealing with his grievance. The panel members studied the package, then asked Mortimer several questions, such as "What kind of machinery have you run?" His rep spoke briefly about the strength of his application. Then the panel members asked him to leave the room, and while he sat outside, they discussed his case.

He did not have to wait long. In a few minutes he was asked to return to the room. There he was told that the panel was sorry about what had happened and believed he was right, that he should have gotten one of the jobs. The chairman said there was an opening for a machinist in the Waltham plant that they could give him. Would he like that? Elated, he said he certainly would.

After the personnel department processed his papers, he received a new work classification. He went to the additional classes required, and in a short time was working in the new job in the Waltham plant.

"If I hadn't gone to the Employees Committee," says Mortimer, "I'd still be a film crew chief." Later on he hopes to advance again, perhaps to some such job as model-maker.

Problems and Criticisms

So far as I can tell, there appears to be no party line among Polaroid managers. While there is a great deal of support for the Employees Committee, there are almost as many opinions about it as there are managers. Among these opinions is a sprinkling of criticism. Let us begin with that.

One executive with whom I talked believes that the committee is something of a drag. "It tends to resist change, to feel uncomfortable with the changes management wants to make," he says. "Also, it tends to develop an agenda of its own, quite different from that of the rest of the company. The reps slow down the decision-making process. They resist actions that a department wants to take. When a job opening is posted, they grieve the selection of an employee for it, slowing down the startup of work. Whether they win the cases or not, they slow operations to a crawl."

Another way that the committee stalls change, critics say, is its use of the so-called right of status quo. If the committee decides that it doesn't like a management proposal for change, it can request a "status quo," meaning that the change will not be acted on until the division heads review it. Since it takes a while for that to be done (the proposal is reviewed by lower levels first), everything is put on hold.

Another executive feels that too many reps work against improvements in the caliber of management. "Some will work with a supervisor to help him or her shore up weaknesses, but others will go after a supervisor with faults and try to destroy the person rather than help him. I sense a kind of antimanagement prejudice among some reps."

One executive feels that the committee makes it too hard for supervisors to let incompetent employees go.

> Supervisors tell me that they can't get rid of certain incompetents because the committee stands in the way. I think they are right. I don't like that. When employees perform poorly or have bad attitudes toward the company and work, I think we should be able to tell them to leave. I'm not talking about employees who suddenly develop problems, I'm talking about tail-end performers who are never going to help us much.

One manager believes that the many grievances over rejected applications for posted job openings are a waste of time.

Over half of the grievances that come to the PPC have to do with job selection. Now, when there's a job opening, many qualified people apply for it, yet only one can be chosen. The grievers say that the selection wasn't done fairly, that their seniority or other qualifications weren't taken adequately into account. The result is a judgmental harangue. My impression is that ninety-nine times out of a hundred, the grievance is resolved in favor of the candidate whom management wanted. It seems to me that this process is terribly wasteful, terribly unproductive. There must be a better way.

Another criticism is that the Employees Committee tends to become a crutch for management. Instead of communicating directly with employees, critics allege, management goes to the committee and asks it to do the communicating. "Maybe that's management's mistake, but with the committee there, and so visible, it's not an easy mistake to avoid."

Finally, LeClaire, a strong supporter of the committee, sees two problems looming in the near future. Although they affect the committee's role in policy-making more than its role in dispute resolution, the latter is affected. First, LeClaire believes that with so much change taking place in the company, it is critically important for the reps to stay in close touch with their constituents. "I'm not sure they are in close enough touch now," he says. Second, he sees Polaroid moving to more decentralized operations, and for a group like the Employees Committee, which is quite centralized, this movement can be very stressful. "I think they are going to have to make some changes," he says. "The area reps will have to work on the big issues more with local management than with the top management at headquarters. Their attitudes are going to have to change, and the committee will have to undergo some reconfiguration."

Support for the Committee

Despite the criticisms and reservations, the Employees Committee appears to be a strong fixture in the company. Here are some of the advantages cited by managers and hourly employees:

1. The committee has saved lots of good employees' jobs. These people might well have left the company but for the vigorous efforts of able reps. Not only is this beneficial to productivity but it is consistent with some of the values top executives believe in. "This management," says Harlor, "practically has an obsession for fairness. It always has, so far as I know. We bend over backwards to be fair—even to the short-term cost sometimes of the enterprise."

2. The turnover among hourly paid employees is very low—2.4 percent for 1986. In fact, say some managers, if employees who leave because of changes in family status, life style, and so forth are excluded, turnover is practically nonexistent. Surely the Employees Committee cannot take all the credit for this, or even most of it. Without question, however, its role in grievances contributes to a climate of loyalty, commitment, and the discouragement of turnover.

3. I. M. Booth, Polaroid's chief executive officer, is said to feel strongly that the Employees Committee provides insights that it would be difficult for management to gain otherwise. It brings a different perspective to management, enabling it to make better decisions. Even the committee's critics appear to agree that it has been a good sounding board for executives with new ideas.

4. "The higher you go in this company," says Harlor, "the stronger the commitment

to the Employees Committee as a way of life here." Since first-line supervisors probably have more contact with committee reps than with anyone else, top management's commitment tends to fortify supervision. (Ironically, many first-line supervisors, having formerly been hourly employees, feel that they are in a kind of no-man's-land between hourly people and top management. It may indeed be hard for some of their immediate supervisors to think of them as management, but the committee gives them a strong link with top management.)

5. In its role in dispute resolution as well as in its other functions, the committee seems to many Polaroid people to bring a fresh perspective, a new dimension to operations. It is as if the organization's thought processes were expanded, its collective brain enlarged. Since we began this write-up with a quotation from Land, the "inventor" of the committee, it may be appropriate to end with an excerpt from one of his papers:

> We let these humans minds [company employees, especially hourly and nonsupervisory people] walk in through the personnel door and we keep them separate by using our promotion systems and using all the lip service to democracy, which in this situation is a misleading and dangerous thing, because we substitute a political consideration, a warm and human consideration, a decent behavior situation, for something else. The "something else" should be the realization that these people coming in at random are carrying in them the greatest marvel of all times—the human mind that took hundreds of millions of years to make.
>
> We as technologists in industry do not use these minds at all. Instead of regarding them as minds, we substitute other criteria for usefulness. Whom do we use? We use the people who compete with us in college. We use the people who went to the same clubs. We use the people who talk the same language. We try to find people brighter than the people our competitors have, naturally, to play them off against each other as if they were a hockey game—but that's not enough, and now I am not talking about compassion and now I am not talking of a movement towards democracy. I am pointing out that because of some curious habit of mind we have, it is our custom not to use these mental mechanisms as they come to us in our industrial society. I would like to urge that what we need is a new art and a new science, and that new art and that new science is the one which, without involving emotion, examines the question of "how do you use human minds?" [1]

[1] Edwin H. Land, "The Second Great Product of Industry: The Rewarding Working Life," paper presented at fiftieth anniversary of the Mellon Institute, Pittsburgh, May 22, 1963, pp. 14–15.

SmithKline Beckman's Grievance Procedure

SmithKline Beckman's approach to employee due process is interesting for several reasons. For one thing, the approach combines flexibility with firmness. The company requires each division to have a grievance procedure—and the procedure must be effective—yet allows the divisions to tailor the procedure to fit their own situations. For another, the company's approach is both formal and informal. For instance, the grievance procedure for its Philadelphia operation, which is the one I will focus on in this section, has set rules for organizing the three-person committee and communicating its conclusions to the persons concerned, yet gives the committee considerable freedom in investigating the case and reaching a conclusion.

In addition, the company's approach is interesting because it is designed for a highly educated work force. A significant percentage of the thirty-two thousand employees have not only college degrees, but also masters and doctorates. Their jobs require considerable training as well as mastery of intricate processes. However, while this high intellectual quotient may influence the form of the grievance process, it does not (as some might too readily assume) eliminate misunderstandings, dis-

Company: SmithKline Beckman Corporation		Products/Services: Pharmaceuticals and health care products
Headquarters: Philadelphia, Pennsylvania		Date of Interview: July 22, 1986
Sales: $37 billion (1987)	Number of Employees: 32,000	

satisfactions, and petty friction in the workplace. Nor does it eliminate the threat of unionization. While SmithKline Beckman contends with no union presences, some of its competitors do.

In Philadelphia, the system is known simply as "the grievance procedure." It has been in place for about fifteen years and enjoys extraordinarily high visibility among the six thousand employees there. It processes around eight complaints per year, on the average, or one for every seven hundred fifty employees. It is supported by strong personnel and human resources departments, which work with management to solve the great majority of employee complaints long before they might become formal grievances.

Case of the reprimanded manager.   To see how the grievance procedure works, let us begin with an actual case from the files. With this as a reference point, we can then turn to some general questions and issues surrounding its use in the company's Philadelphia operations.

A manager whom I shall call "Paul" worked in the manufacturing end of the division. He was a capable and energetic manager. One day his boss phoned to ask him to attend a management meeting. Paul said he was too busy to attend. He was experiencing one or two personal problems, and he explained that he was "too strung out." "I would really like you to be there," the boss said. Paul repeated that he couldn't make the meeting. He offered to send an assistant as his surrogate, but the boss said that wouldn't do.

After Paul failed to show up at the meeting, the senior executive sent him a formal reprimand in writing for insubordination. The request was a reasonable one, the boss maintained; he warned that another episode like this one could be grounds for more serious disciplinary action.

Paul was unhappy. The reprimand, being a formal one, would remain in his file for three years. He felt that the boss's action showed lack of sensitivity.

Deciding to use the grievance procedure to overturn the reprimand, he went to George Partridge, vice president for personnel for Philadelphia operations. Partridge talked with his assistant, Mitchell Abramson, director of personnel administration. "Paul and his boss agree on the facts," said Partridge. "Do you think it's a grievable issue?" Both agreed that the case fell into a gray area; that is, it was neither a clear policy violation nor obviously out of bounds for the grievance procedure. In such instances, Partridge and Abramson tend to give the grievant the benefit of a doubt. Partridge said, "Let's put a committee together." He asked Abramson to think about prospective members.

A grievance committee always has three members. A personnel director always serves as chairperson; he or she must come from a part of the division outside that in which the grievant works. The second member must be at the director level or above from the business the grievant is in, but not in the same organization or group (e.g., sales, manufacturing, research). The third member must come from another business and understand the area or function in which the grievant serves (e.g., finance, office management). The collective purpose of these aims is to ensure objectivity and understanding on the part of the committee.

Abramson discussed his list briefly with Partridge, then began his calls. For chairperson, he got an experienced personnel officer who hadn't chaired a grievance committee for a couple of years. One of the prospects for the two other positions begged off because a couple of key people in her office were sick and she was having to double up, but he got a yes from the next person he called. In a short time he was able to call the chairperson and inform her that she had a committee.

With that job done, Abramson and Partridge retired and let the committee take over. As we will see later, they kept in touch with its progress, and at the end they looked at the committee's report, but they played no role in the investigation, discussions, or decision.

The chairperson got together with the two other members and they agreed on how to proceed. They spoke first with Paul, then with his boss, then with the personnel director who had been involved and heard both sides of the case. They spent several hours on these interviews. Next they reviewed their notes together and discussed their opinions. This took a couple of hours more. When questions about the company's personnel policy arose, the chairperson was able to answer them; if she had questions, she gave Abramson, Partridge, or another executive a call.

The committee concluded that the boss's reprimand was reasonable. It agreed with him that Paul's action was insubordination and that the reprimand should stay on Paul's record. This decision was unanimous—under the rules, it had to be. The committee than drafted a report for Partridge, incorporating the main facts it had found, its reasoning, and its conclusion. Although its conclusion was final, Abramson went over the draft quickly to be sure that it stayed focused on the issues under investigation. (There is always the possibility that a complaining employee, if dissatisfied with the grievance committee's conclusion, can seek redress with an agency or in court.)

After Abramson okayed the report, the chairperson sent it to the division vice president for personnel. Partridge then sent a letter to Paul summarizing the committee's decision, with copies going to Paul's boss and the personnel director who had been involved.

The grievance committee disbanded. It had accomplished its mission in less time than most committees do, partly because there was agreement from the beginning on the facts of the case. While it came down on the supervisor's side, many committees preceding and following it have decided in favor of the subordinate—there is no presumption that either side is right. As with all other grievance committees, its decision was final; no one, not even the chief executive officer, could overturn it.

Choosing the Approach

Why does the pharmaceuticals division have a grievance procedure? Why did it choose this particular form rather than one of the others that companies have tried?

SmithKline Beckman is more than a hundred fifty years old. (For more than eighty years of its history it was known as Smith, Kline, and French. The present name dates back to 1982.) During that century and a half it has been known to employees and customers alike as a very "caring" company. Evidence of this can be seen in the corporate archives—the handwritten letters of founders John K. Smith and John Gilbert, George K. Smith, Mahlon N. Kline, and many others. The pharmaceuticals division is the original business, and so it has been the flagship in employee relations policy.

The division established its grievance procedure about fifteen years ago. It was seen at that time as a good way to apply and implement an enlightened personnel policy, especially in a corporation that was growing by leaps and bounds. (The merger in 1982 with Beckman Instruments alone added about eleven thousand employees to the corporate payroll.) Moreover, the concept was flexible enough so that the corporation could require all divisions to have it. It does not require other divisions to follow the precise form that the pharmaceuticals division employs, nor does it require them to use the same lexicon for the committee and human resources officials; but it does require them to have an effective procedure. Thus, the divisions handle their employees' complaints, and the employee relations staff at the corporate level consults with the divisions when necessary. Depending on its own customs, traditions, preferences, and situation, a division management can vary the composition of the grievance committee, set different rules from any other division for the investigation, require different deadlines, and so on.

What benefits does the company find in grievance procedures?

First, they are evidence of top management's continuing commitment to equity in the workplace. As one executive put it, the message to employees is, "You have the right to disagree with your boss." While grievance procedures are but one of many ways that sensitivity to employee concerns is expressed, they probably contribute to the company's unusually low turnover rate.

Second, they are increasingly valuable as the industry becomes more turbulent. Competition is increasing, margins are decreasing. Although sales are growing overall, here and there layoffs have become necessary for the first time in the corporation's history. In such an atmosphere, conflicts are inevitable.

Third, an effective grievance procedure is probably a deterrent to lawsuits and claims before the Equal Employment Opportunity Commission and state agencies. While there is no hard data on this relationship, company executives feel that employees are less likely to go outside the company for help if they believe the company itself offers a speedy, effective process for complaint resolution. Daniel J. Phelan, corporate vice president for employee relations, told me:

> Sometimes the Equal Employment Opportunity Commission will be contacted by an employee or ex-employee who believes he or she has been discriminated against. The commission will tell them to use the company's internal grievance procedure first, before going to it. Also, the Pennsylvania Human Rights Commission has relied on our grievance procedure proceedings. In a couple of instances it has come down on the company side after reviewing the case with company management.

Fourth, an effective grievance procedure reduces the need for a union. Said Robert Turnbull, director of personnel administration in Philadelphia:

> Our reputation in employee relations is the important thing. Yet in this spot or that, employees may be brought to the brink if they don't have an alternative to going outside and hiring a lawyer. The presence of a grievance procedure goes a long way to meeting the need.

In the past decade, Phelan pointed out, only one organizing attempt in a company facility outside Philadelphia has gone to election, and it was unsuccessful. As mentioned earlier, however, other companies in the industry have unions.

Fifth, a grievance procedure may illuminate bad practices. In the words of Abramson, "If something bad is going on, it's better to find it out early so that we can correct it, rather than let it snowball and get out of control before detection." While not a major reason for having a grievance procedure, this benefit is a useful dividend.

Influence and Clout

The grievance committees at SmithKline Beckman are powerful. Their decisions are binding. As pointed out, even the chief executive officer cannot overturn them. A manager who interferes with or blocks the filing of a grievance is liable to discipline, including possible discharge. A manager who retaliates against an employee winning a concession from the committee also faces discipline, and it may be significant that no employee yet has filed a grievance alleging retaliation from a boss who was peeved by a decision (a case that would be accepted quickly if it should ever happen). Phelan says:

> A line manager who doesn't accept the grievance procedure would not be able to stay here very long. The chief executive officer is adamant about this. Some division presidents have accepted the findings of grievance committees even though they disagreed with their decisions. In one of our divisions, for instance, a client service representative told a customer to go jump in the lake. When her superiors heard about this, she was fired. However, when she filed a grievance, the committee reinstated her because of mitigating circumstances. The head of the division was beside himself, yet he went along with the decision.

In the pharmaceuticals division, the context and milieu in which the grievance procedure operates have a lot to do with its effectiveness. They are as valuable to the procedure as a strong offensive line is to a quarterback or a capable infield to a pitcher. Of many possible circumstances that might be mentioned, I will single out three.

First, the grievance procedure enjoys high visibility. This is the result of articles in company publications, its inclusion in the employee handbook, television programs, references in executives' talks, and other efforts. It seems safe to estimate that most of the employees—probably a good deal more than half—know about the procedure. This makes it hard for anyone to buck it. Presumably, there are employees who don't use it though they could and should, but if so, the reason is not likely to be ignorance.

Second, as we saw in the case of Paul, the grievance procedure is tied in with the office of the vice president for personnel. Both at the beginning and end, this executive plays a role, telling everyone, in effect, "This mechanism has the support of top management." For instance, in Paul's case, as in every case, the vice president and his assistant (1) decide that there is a grievance, (2) select the grievance committee, and (3) write the letters to concerned parties summarizing the findings and decision of the committee. Thus, their imprimatur is unmistakable.

In addition, they keep an eye on the proceedings. Abramson said:

> Before the report goes out, we like to eyeball it for possible legal ramifications or anything else out of the ordinary. We may ask a few questions of the committee. In addition, we want to be sure that the committee hasn't overstepped its boundaries by venturing into subject areas that aren't relevant to the case. While the committee is working, we stay out of the process, with one possible exception: if the committee is

taking too long to reach a decision, I may call the chairperson and remind him or her of the time that has gone by. Especially in termination cases, it is in everyone's best interest to wrap up the decision as soon as possible. In any case we hope to have the decision in sixty days or less.

In short, while the personnel heads may stay back, they are watchful and concerned.

Third, the human resources staff plays an important educational role for the line managers, reminding them of the company's commitment to equity and good working conditions. Jackie Vice, director of human resources for corporate staffs, makes the rounds constantly to counsel managers on personnel problems. Managers seek her out often when they see disputes looming, anxious to get her guidance and support in case the unhappy subordinates go to her with a complaint. When she sees managers digging holes for themselves, she tells them and, if possible, helps them out. In one case, a manager was about to promote an employee who had a poorer performance appraisal than a second applicant who wanted the promotion. It happened that the manager had given the second applicant "excellents" in his appraisal but didn't really mean them; he didn't want to confront the employee with evidence of mediocre performance. Going to Vice, the second applicant said, "Hey, what's going on here? I got this 'excellent,' yet he's giving the job to the other guy." When Vice learned the true story, she went to the manager and told him he couldn't do what he was doing. If the second applicant filed a grievance, she said, he would almost surely win. Seeing that she was right, the manager asked her for suggestions, and they worked out a solution to the problem.

Vice meets with every new employee in her area of operations. "When they associate my position with a face," she says, "they aren't so reluctant to come in." She urges them to come in early when they have problems rather than let the problems fester and possibly get out of control.

The effect of such meetings and exchanges is to bolster the grievance procedure. Human resources staff people are likely to know a lot more about the procedure than line managers do, and whether they refer to it as a carrot or a stick, it takes on added reality and importance in supervisors' thinking because of the conversations.

How the Procedure Works

The path of an employee grievance is clearly marked out, and it also is clear who can take that path and with what kinds of complaints.

What is a grievable issue? To begin, what kinds of things can an employee grieve? The complaint must be that the company's personnel policy or practice has been violated. Thus, employees cannot use the grievance procedure to complain, say, of a corporate strategy or growth policy; however, they can use the procedure if they show, for instance, that a supervisor may not have followed the rules in giving a discharge. Performance appraisals are a good case in point. A supervisor's *judgment* in rating an employee low or high is not grievable; the supervisor alone is considered able to make that call. However, if the supervisor promised to give the operator six months to improve and fired him or her after only three months, then the action could be grievable since it violates a commitment made, and the company's policy is to honor commitments.

Who can grieve? In theory, any employee can use the grievance procedure in the pharmaceuticals division. In practice, however, the procedure attracts some managers at the director level and below, and many nonmanagers, but not vice presidents and others in top management positions.

What help can a grievant get? An employee with a grievable complaint can turn to the human resources staff for help in writing up the complaint. The nearest group personnel representative—GPRs, they are called—is the best bet, but Vice or her assistant may help too. They may clarify what the employee wants—a job back, an opportunity, a disciplinary status removed, or whatever—or shorten the explanation, streamline the organization of the facts, or improve some other part of the complaint. In one case, an employee used up thirty typewritten pages to describe her grievance. A human resources assistant told her that such a long document would confuse the grievance committee, not persuade it, and helped her prune the document drastically.

However, grievants *cannot* bring attorneys or advocates with them to the committee. The company feels that this is likely to create an adversarial relationship and that a one-to-one relationship between the committee and the grievant is more productive. One executive recalled one exception to this rule, and that was the case of an employee with a serious speech handicap. The employee was allowed to bring a spokesman with him to the hearing.

How are committee members chosen? As suggested in Paul's case, the committee is chaired by a personnel official. The second and third members are chosen by the vice president of Philadelphia personnel with a preference for line managers who know something about the grievant's business or line of work but are unbiased by personal association with the grievant or supervisor concerned. However, if the grievant objects to this nominee or that, personnel will defer and choose someone who is acceptable.

The personnel heads cannot "command" a person to serve on a committee. If a desired manager is struggling with a heavy workload or feels that he or she cannot be objective in the case, personnel asks someone else to serve.

Where? When the committee meets to discuss an issue or hear the story of someone involved in the case at hand, it usually assembles in a conference room. There are no designated hearing rooms in the buildings and, indeed, the session is not run like a formal hearing, at least not like hearings as we think of them in collective bargaining and legislation. The people sit around the table in any way that is comfortable, and the chairperson tells the grievant, supervisor, or witness, "Tell us your side of the story." Grievants are assured that no reprisals from supervisors will be tolerated and that the act of grieving will not affect their careers negatively. These assurances are stated in the employee guidebook, but the chair likes to voice them anyway to clear the air.

The committee members investigate as widely as they feel the facts justify, and they talk to whomever they feel should be talked to. Usually this means, in addition to the grievant and his or her supervisor, the personnel representative who was involved in the dispute and any key witnesses whom the grievant wants involved. However, the facts of the situation may lead the committee to hear other people too. In one case, a woman complained that she was the victim of discrimination. She was being paid less than she deserved, she claimed; also, she had had to take abuse. Part of her allegation was that employees like her in her department had also been discriminated against. The grievance committee members therefore took a lot of extra time—several months, all in all—to talk to others in the department in order to investigate her claims.

How much time? Phelan said, "The committee tries to get its answer to the employees in thirty days, but often it takes longer. It may not be easy to get the committee members together because of travel schedules or other commitments. The average time required to investigate and reach a decision may be closer to sixty days than thirty."

Vice believes that a typical grievance takes about three full days of interviewing and discussion. Those days generally are spread out over several weeks or a couple of months—a few hours here, several hours there.

Turnbull, who has chaired two grievance committees, recalls one case where the members met ten times for about two hours each; also, since the grievant had moved to a western state, they had to make many phone calls. However, in another case in which Turnbull was involved, he and the other two members went to Boston for most of their investigation and completed it, as well as their decision, in two days. He believes that it is likely to take a week to pick the committee, a nominal amount of time for the members to schedule meetings, and several weeks to conduct investigations and reach a decision. In his experience, the longest cases have taken several months to complete.

Unanimity or majority vote? The first grievance committee on a case cannot make a decision without unanimity. If the members cannot agree, then, like a hung jury, it disbands and the personnel department appoints a second committee. That three-member group follows the same rules as the first one did, but only two must agree on the decision. In the pharmaceuticals division so far there has been only one "hung" grievance committee.

Coping with Chronic Complainers

The Philadelphia operation's grievance procedure is known widely among employees, and it has a reputation for fairness and efficiency. Is it not likely, therefore, to attract chronic complainers—or even worse, produce chronic complainers?

We need to to get one problem out of the way before setting forth an answer. To say that there is a chronic complainer problem in a company *may* simply be another way of saying that there is a department or departments that are so managed that they create discontent and dissidence. To the extent this is the case, the answer obviously is not to deal with the malcontents, but with their bosses.

This said, it can be agreed that in most organizations of any size, a certain number of people can be found who do more than their share of complaining, and that if they are an annoyance (which they generally are) the only way to do something about the problem is to deal with *them*. The question is, What effect does a good grievance procedure have? According to Vice:

> When I took my present job, my predecessor gave me a list of such people. Sure enough, they came with a litany of complaints—about the operation, about management, about this person or that, about all sorts of things. Let me tell you what I have found. They don't monopolize the grievance procedure. In fact, the grievance procedure is a way of discouraging them. When chronic complainers come in, I encourage them to file formal grievances. I find that this is a good way to deal with them—they won't stop complaining until an objective group looks at their situation. Unless and until that happens, they go on complaining endlessly to me and other, but when I do that, they are likely to stop. I think there are two reasons. First, the process of writing up a complaint is a kind of cathartic experience. It makes them stop and think. Maybe for

the first time they are forced to take responsibility for their complaints, and that alone may make them quit. Second, the decision of an impartial committee that they do or don't have a grievable issue with a remedy usually makes quite an impression. The message is, "This case is done." They can get over it then.

Solving Problems Before They Become Grievances

As pointed out earlier, part of the secret of the grievance procedure's success is the setting and environment in which it works. Just as it supports, it is supported. One of the most valuable allies of the procedure is the group personnel representative.

Speaking for the company as a whole, Phelan said: "The GPRs are mid-level managers who are personnel professionals. There is one of them for every two hundred or two hundred fifty employees. There is always one in the building where the employee works. The GPR is well known; also, he or she is trained in dispute resolution."

Phelan believes that the great majority of problems never go to the grievance procedure because they are resolved informally by the GPR, the complaining employee, and the supervisor. The solution may come quickly or over a period of time. But in one way or another the presence and ability of the GPR help to bring out a solution before further steps are needed. One of the executives I talked to had been a GPR earlier in his career at SmithKline Beckman. He thought that the experience gave him a taste of the work situation that he could not have gotten in any other way. "Being a GPR," he said, "puts you on the firing line day in and day out."

As for organizational status, a group personnel chief reports to two people. The first is the head of the business—animal health products, eye and skin care products, consumer products, or whatever. The group personnel chiefs also have a dotted-line relationship to the vice president of corporate personnel.

Conclusion

In SmithKline Beckman's Philadelphia operations, the grievance procedure has these important features:

The decision of the grievance committee is final and binding.

The chairperson of the committee is chosen from the personnel department. (One of the advantages of this is that questions about corporate personnel policy can be readily answered.)

To have standing as a grievant, an employee must have plausible grounds for complaining that a supervisor or manager has violated a written personnel policy.

Strict rules govern the selection of the grievance committee, which is handled by executives in personnel. Once it is chosen, however, the committee can proceed pretty much as it chooses (except that a personnel officer may prod it a little if it seems to be taking too much time to reach a decision).

To reduce the possibilities of an adversarial climate developing, the company does not allow grievants to bring along an attorney or spokesperson except in unusual circumstances.

The personnel department works hard and effectively to solve superior-subordinate problems before they become formal grievances. The department is strong and well entrenched in the company.

If there is any magic in the success of the grievance procedure, it is probably the strength of the personnel department. It lends its influence to the procedure. Not only is it represented on the grievance committee, but its presence surrounds the grievance process. In almost all cases, it is involved in the early stages of a grievance. When an employee wants to file a grievance, it decides whether the complaint is grievable. If its answer is yes, it appoints the committee members. And after they render their decision, it communicates the judgment to the employee, supervisor, and any other employees intimately involved in the case.

TWA's Novel and Successful Hearing Procedure

Trans World Airlines operates a grievance procedure for about seven thousand nonunion employees which employs, for termination cases, a professional outside arbitrator. This outsider chairs the System Board of Adjustment, a three-person board that hears cases that cannot be settled by supervision or middle management. For nontermination cases, the board is chaired by an executive from the personnel department. As for the other two members of the board, they are a nonunion employee chosen by the complaining employee, and a manager, usually at the manager or director level.

Subject to minor changes, the procedure has operated continuously since the early 1970s, appears to have a good deal of employee support, and is used frequently. Some fifty to seventy-five cases per year are heard by the board; a substantial number are resolved in favor of the complaining employee.

Most of the information used in this write-up comes from a paper delivered in 1986 by Mary Jean Wolf, a New York consultant who was formerly staff vice presi-

Company: TWA	Products/Services: Air transportation	
Headquarters: Kansas City, Missouri		
		Date of Interview: July 22, 1988 (by telephone and letter) to update 1986 article
Sales: $3.14 billion (1987)	Number of Employees: 27,400	

dent for personnel at TWA.[1] The material has been updated for me by TWA's manager for staff labor relations, Henry R. Cox.

The Operation in Brief

As in most employee complaint resolution procedures, you start with your supervisor, if you are an employee with a grievance. The supervisor responds in writing. If you are dissatisfied with this answer, you can take the second step which involves appealing to a middle manager who is outside your chain of command. Originally TWA did not have a second step like this; the step was inserted to build in more objectivity and also to solve more grievances before a full-dress board hearing is necessary.

If the middle manager doesn't give you an answer that satisfies you, you can take the third step and appeal to the System Board of Adjustment. If your boss wants to fire you, the chairperson is a member of the National Academy of Arbitrators; you pick the arbitrator from a list of ten names or so provided by the company. If your grievance involves some matter other than firing, the board is chaired by an executive from the personnel department. In this case, the company assigns the executive.

In either case, you pick the third member of the board. That person must be another nonunion employee. In the board hearing but not in Steps 1 and 2, you can hire an attorney to represent you if you want. If you pick an attorney to present your side, the company will have an attorney present its side. If you present your side yourself, your supervisor will handle the company's side.

You and the company can offer witnesses if desired. Before the hearing, you provide an advance list of them; management also lists its witnesses in advance. You and all witnesses travel to the site of the hearing at the company's expense, and in most cases the hearings are held on paid company time. (The exception occurs when the only time that the hearing can be scheduled is on your day off or at a time in the day when you are not working. In such a case you don't get paid extra for showing up.)

If you have a good case, your chances are good of winning. In 1985, for instance, half of twenty-four employees who would have been fired got reinstated instead. Of the thirty-seven grievances involving other than termination that year, the appealing employees won more often than management did, and a hefty majority were won all or in part by the grievants. In other years, the pattern has favored supervisors more. For instance, from September 1987 through July 20, 1988, the System Board of Adjustment heard fifty-one cases; in thirty-nine of them (76 percent) it denied the grievants, in two it upheld the grievants, in eight cases the grievants were reinstated without back pay, and in two cases management settled with the complaining employees.

The three-step appeal process is managed by the personnel department. It tries to administer the procedure as fairly and carefully as possible, making sure that you can obtain grievance forms easily, that deadlines are met, and so on. Personnel tries to schedule the hearing at your facility so that board members can see the workplace for themselves and so that expenses can be held down. The senior vice president of personnel does not get involved unless a grievance goes to Step 3, in which case he is the one who schedules the hearing.

[1] Mary Jean Wolf, "Trans World Airlines' Noncontract Grievance Procedure," *Arbitration 1986: Current and Expanding Roles* (Philadelphia: National Academy of Arbitrators, 1986), p. 27.

In some respects, this system is the same as it has been for many years at TWA, in some respects different. TWA first established a nonunion grievance procedure in the early 1950s. Then, the first two steps were heard by managers in the grievant's own chain of command while a panel of three company executives heard the case if it went to the third step. A written record was made of the third step. Grievants could, if they wished, go to a fourth step, in which a professional outside arbitrator made a judgment based on the record. Until 1970, managers and nonmanagers alike could use the procedure.

About 1970, some features in the procedure were changed. Managers were ruled out as potential users; the reason was that in one case, a manager had been fired and some embarrassment had been caused to TWA. Another change involved the board. Employees had made relatively little use of the procedure during the 1960s. To change this, the company revised the third step to bring in an outside arbitrator. (At first, this was done for all cases; later, in a cost-cutting effort, arbitrators were engaged only in cases of termination.) The arbitrator was brought in to make the procedure more appealing to employees in the face of a union organizing drive.

Then in the early 1970s, management, feeling bothered by reports that employees wondered if the system was biased, decided to change that perception by allowing the grievant to name a co-worker as a member of the board.

The two moves accomplished what they were designed to do. Employee use of the procedure, which had set no records in the past, began increasing. "The peer involvement feature has been extremely successful," Mary Jean Wolf states in her paper, "and has generally enjoyed very responsible support from the employee board members and representatives."[2]

Since the early 1970s, management has made only minor changes in the procedure.

Administration and Operation

Wolf says that personnel has found it nearly a full-time job to handle all the arrangements necessary to please everyone. The effort is probably more time-consuming for it than for the union in arbitration under a collective bargaining contract because union officers often exercise more control over matters.

What about the behavior of the employee member of the board? Wolf observes:

> The involvement of employees' peers has paid real dividends to the company since the co-worker often has insights on an issue that would not be available otherwise. And, while there may be a tendency on the part of the co-worker to support the grievant in spite of the evidence, there have been many instances where the co-worker has supported the denial of a grievance based on the facts brought out during the hearing, some of which may not have been obvious or available earlier. And in a number of cases where a grievant has been reinstated provisionally, the co-worker has been extremely helpful in counseling the grievant so that the problem does not recur. Finally, there is often background information that the co-worker provides that is helpful to the personnel department in terms of correcting inappropriate management practices or working conditions, and which may lie at the heart of the issue.
>
> When I surveyed the participants several years ago, this feature received the highest positive rating from the employees; 68 percent of the employees surveyed gave unqualified affirmative answers when questioned as to whether they felt that the co-worker on the System Board helped their cases.[3]

[2] Ibid., p. 28.
[3] Ibid., p. 31.

What has been TWA's experience with the arbitrators who are called in to chair the System Adjustment Board when employees appeal against getting fired? Both pluses and negatives can be cited. TWA often has found itself giving grievants the names of people with whom the company has had no experience. Since employees have a good network, it doesn't take them long to learn who on the list tends to reinstate grievants and who doesn't. Wolf says:

> Where we have had problems is where employees have consistently been reinstated by an arbitrator who simply appeared not to believe in termination, or who felt he was doing his share to prevent these employees from wanting to join a union, or who did not agree with our rather strict attendance control procedures. While this was the exception rather than the rule, such practices create some rather acute problems for those administering the procedure. Unlike a grievance process contained in a collective bargaining agreement, company executives know that this process can be unilaterally changed. It will come as no surprise to anyone in this room that managers often do not take kindly to seeing a terminated employee reinstated. What may be less obvious is that the backlash in this case can be rather severe, and has led to some high-level pressure to eliminate the procedure or at least the use of arbitrators.
>
> I have emphasized the importance of maintaining credibility with respect to the noncontract employee group. It is important to recognize, however, that it is equally important to operate so that senior management will continue to support the process. In the survey I mentioned earlier, the supervisors were far less sanguine about the benefits of the process than were the employee-grievants. What I am saying is that a tendency to reinstate employees not covered by a labor agreement may not work in the long-range interest of expanding the use of arbitration for such employees.[4]

Wolf adds:

> You should be aware . . . that we did have a rather unfortunate incident where, upon upholding a discharge for theft, an arbitrator was sued by the employee. What is more, a formal complaint was lodged with the National Academy claiming unprofessional conduct. While both issues were ultimately resolved and the arbitrator was completely exonerated, it left a negative impression on others and caused several arbitrators to remove themselves from our list. The assumption was that a union would have prevented this from happening.[5]

TWA believes that the benefits of the procedure for nonunion employees have far outweighed the administrative difficulties and the occasional problems caused superiors. For one thing, seven thousand employees remain nonunion. For another, lawsuits have been reduced. Wolf says: "TWA has avoided litigation through having terminations reviewed by an arbitrator, and where an employee *has* sued following arbitration, the company's position in court has been strengthened by the award."[6]

---

[4] Ibid., p. 32.
[5] Ibid., p. 33.
[6] Ibid.

Glossary

The definitions that follow are for readers desiring a quick working idea of the meaning of special terms used in this book. The definitions are not prepared legally or technically, nor are they always comprehensive. For elaboration of a term, see the text. Where a function denotes a person, process, and procedure, only one is defined (e.g., the term *adjudicator* is defined but *adjudicate* and *adjudication* are not).

adjudicator A person who decides on a dispute between two or more employees, with the power to enforce the decision and/or require management to enforce it.

appeal An employee's right, after receiving a decision regarded as unsatisfactory from a boss, personnel specialist, or other corporate officer, to go to a person or office with higher authority to seek a remedy.

arbitrator A person, usually not an employee of the company, who is chosen by the parties to a dispute and who hears the evidence submitted by the parties and renders an enforceable judgment. (*Note:* Sometimes the verb *arbitrate* is used loosely to refer to a manager's power to settle differences between subordinates.)

at-will employment As stated by a federal circuit court in *Payne* v. *Western & A.R.R.* in 1884, the common law doctrine that employers "can dismiss their employees at will . . . for good cause, for no cause, or even for cause morally wrong, without thereby being guilty of legal wrong"; this philosophy reigned undisputed in all states and jurisdictions until the middle of the twentieth century.

board Two or more duly appointed or selected employees, occasionally chaired by an outsider, who hear, analyze, and/or investigate the facts of an employee dispute and render an enforceable judgment; also called a *tribunal* (q.v.) or *company court*.

complaint resolution or **complaint-handling system** A combination of formal and informal procedures for receiving and registering employee complaints, offering counseling, investigating complaints, mediating and deciding disputes, recommending changes in corporate procedures, and so on.

confidentiality An employee's right to talk to a power mediator, investigator, or board without having the information circulated to others; the informant may give the officials permission to divulge necessary parts of the information to such others as they may need to talk with in order to determine the facts in dispute; the term also refers to an employee's right to withhold his or her personnel file from public scrutiny. See also *privacy*.

corporate "common law" The common principles seen in decisions of power mediators, investigators, and boards concerning the rights of employee complainants and defendants in corporate due process; the principles are emerging independently of corporate personnel policy and line management, and often without communication between the adjudicators in different companies.

corporate due process A fair hearing procedure by a power mediator, investigator, or board with the complaining employee having the right to be represented by another employee, to present evidence, to rebut the other side's charges, to have an objective and impartial hearing, to have the wrong corrected if proved, to be free from retaliation for using the procedure, to enjoy reasonable confidentiality, to be heard reasonably soon after lodging the complaint, to get a timely decision, and so forth.

dissident An employee who complains of unfair treatment or of an organizational practice or policy, or who takes other action to protest a practice, and who may or may not be loyal to the firm, willing to follow orders, and so on.

due process The legal concept of a fair and impartial trial in an appropriate law court, with such protections for a party as the right to be present, to offer evidence, to rebut the other side's claims, to be protected against hearsay evidence, and so forth.

employee A manager or nonmanager who works for and is paid by the organization.

employee objector A manager or nonmanager who objects to a company practice or complains of treatment received from a manager, supervisor, or other employees.

grievance procedure A communicated way for employees to register complaints of unfair treatment and have the complaints acted on; in this book, most grievance procedures referred to are nonunion, although the term springs from collective bargaining and still connotes, to much of the world, procedures stipulated in union contracts.

hot line A method for employees to communicate concerns immediately and often anonymously to a corporate office and get answers quickly.

investigator A person who looks into an employee's claims of unfair or abusive treatment, with power to get the facts on both sides from any person or department and to correct the wrong if necessary.

management reversal A decision by a senior manager or corporate due process agency to change a manager's decision after investigating a subordinate's complaint.

mediator A person who attempts to reconcile a dispute between two or more employees or persuade them to settle their differences, without power to decide the dispute and require the parties to abide by his or her decision.

neutral   An employee or outsider who has no personal interest in the outcome of an employee dispute and no initial bias or prejudice concerning the parties or merits of the dispute.

ombudsperson   An employee or outsider who hears an employee's claims or contentions, investigates the situation, and mediates the dispute.

open door   As used in most companies, a procedure for employees to complain up the management line when they can't resolve their complaints to their satisfaction with their immediate bosses; not to be confused with the Open Door due process procedure of IBM (see Part II).

peer review   A hearing of an employee's claim or dispute by other employees who serve at or near the same level of responsibility as the claimant, though not necessarily in the same department or area.

power mediator   An employee who ordinarily mediates disputes between employees but can, if necessary, get ready authorization to enforce his or her judgment about the dispute.

privacy   An employee's right to withhold his or her claims of unfair treatment and/ or actions in corporate due process from the scrutiny of other people not involved in the mediation or investigation; the term also refers to an employee's right to have his or her personnel file open only to those managers or personnel specialists who need access to the information in the file in order to perform their appointed functions.

redundant channels   Two or more procedures available to employees to register complaints or question company practices or situations.

representation   A procedure allowing an employee to have his or her case set forth or amplified by another person at a hearing.

tribunal   Two or more duly appointed or selected employees, occasionally chaired by an outsider, who hear, analyze, and/or investigate the facts of an employee dispute and render an enforceable judgment; also called a *board* (q.v.) or *company court*.

whistleblower   An employee or outsider who complains of or protests a corporate practice or policy using in-company or out-of-company channels to make the protest.

INDEX

327